The Frontline

Serhii Plokhy

THE FRONTLINE

Essays on Ukraine's Past and Present

Distributed by Harvard University Press
for the Ukrainian Research Institute
Harvard University

The Harvard Ukrainian Research Institute was established in 1973 as an integral part of Harvard University. It supports research associates and visiting scholars who are engaged in projects concerned with all aspects of Ukrainian studies. The Institute also works in close cooperation with the Committee on Ukrainian Studies, which supervises and coordinates the teaching of Ukrainian history, language, and literature at Harvard University.

Publication of this book has been made possible by the generous support of publications in Ukrainian studies at Harvard University by the following benefactors:

Vladimir Jurkowsky
Ilarion and Donna Kalynewych
Myroslav and Irene Koltunik
Peter and Emily Kulyk
Dr. Evhen Omelsky
Paul Sawka

You can support our work of publishing academic books and translations of Ukrainian literature and documents by making a tax-deductible donation in any amount, or by including HURI in your estate planning. To find out more, please visit https://huri.harvard.edu/give

Printed in India on acid-free paper

ISBN: 9780674268838 (paperback)
ISBN: 9780674268845 (epub)
ISBN: 9780674268852 (PDF)

Library of Congress Control Number: 2021939912

LC record available at https://lccn.loc.gov/2021939912

Cover and book design by Mykola Leonovych, https://smalta.pro

Table of Contents

Acknowledgments

I AM DEEPLY GRATEFUL to those who contributed most to the appearance of this collection. Oleh Kotsyuba convinced me to publish the book with my home institution, the Harvard Ukrainian Research Institute (HURI). My colleagues on the HURI Editorial Board, Michael S. Flier and George G. Grabowicz, supported the idea and provided valuable advice on how to improve the manuscript. Myroslav Yurkevich edited new chapters and standardized the editorial aspects of those chapters that were published previously. Kostyantyn Bondarenko prepared the maps used in this volume. Oleh Kotsyuba, with the assistance of Michelle Viise, guided the book through the editorial and production process from start to finish. Finally, I am grateful to the editors of the publications in which the texts included here first appeared for granting permission to publish them in this collection. I alone am responsible for any shortcomings, of which I hope there are not too many.

A Note on Transliteration

IN THE TEXT of this collection, a modified Library of Congress system is used to transliterate Ukrainian and other East Slavic personal names and toponyms. This system omits the soft sign (ь) and, in masculine surnames, the final "й" (thus, for example, Hrushevsky, not Hrushevs´kyi). The exception to this is the transliteration of the name of the medieval princedom of Rus´ and of personal names where the soft sign indicates the softness of a consonant before a vowel, for which "i" is used (thus Khvyliovy rather than Khvyl´ovy). Furthermore, well-known personal names such as Yeltsin, Yushchenko, and Yanukovych appear in spellings widely adopted in English-language texts, while the spelling of several other names of living authors follows their own preference. In bibliographic references, the full Library of Congress system (ligatures omitted) is used. Toponyms are usually transliterated from the language of the country in which the designated places are currently located. As a rule, personal names are given in forms characteristic of the cultural traditions to which the given person belonged. The Julian calendar used by the Eastern Slavs until 1918 lagged behind the Gregorian calendar used in the Polish-Lithuanian Commonwealth and Western Europe (by ten days in the sixteenth and seventeenth centuries and by eleven days in the eighteenth century).

Preface

ON FEBRUARY 24, 2022, the world woke up to a new reality. With an air attack on Kyiv and other Ukrainian cities in the early dawn, Russia started an all-out war on the sovereign state of Ukraine. Measured by its scope, the number of the troops involved, the magnitude of military and civilian deaths, as well as the number of refugees following the attacks, this new stage of war quickly became the largest and deadliest military conflict in Europe since the end of World War II.

The Russo-Ukrainian war began in 2014 with the Russian annexation of the Crimea; it remained largely ignored by the international community. Now, it became impossible to turn a blind eye to it anymore. The destruction of Mariupol, leveled by Russian bombs and missiles that have killed many civilians in the defiant port city, has also dismantled the type of magical thinking that many Western politicians and the public at large have resorted to for years: namely, that, if you disregard Russian aggression against Ukraine long enough, it will go away all by itself. The idea that appeasement works may be largely gone, but the question of what caused the war remains unanswered.

Most of the international attention has been focused so far on the narrative proposed by the aggressor himself, Russian president Vladimir Putin. That narrative falsely maintains that aggression against Ukraine was a response to NATO's enlargement with the addition of states of the former Soviet Union. But Putin's own pronouncements and writings prior to the new invasion suggest that the true reason and justification for his unprovoked aggression against Ukraine (whose attempts to join NATO had been placed in a holding pattern by the alliance long before the attack) were rooted in a particular version of the history of Russia and its relation to Ukraine that had been adopted by Vladimir Putin and certain members of the Russian political elite.

Putin has gone on record more than once declaring that Russians and Ukrainians are parts of one and the same people. He elaborated on this claim in his 2021 essay, "On the Historical Unity of Russians and Ukrainians," which became the first salvo in the coming war of narratives. Three days before the February 24 invasion, Putin returned to the history of Russo-Ukrainian relations in a speech in which he effectively withdrew Russia from the 2015 Minsk Accords. On that occasion, he portrayed the Ukrainian state as an artificial entity created by Vladimir Lenin and the Bolsheviks.[1]

Putin's abuse of history represented more than just another case of manipulating the past to provide the pretext for an act of aggression. It was also an expression of Putin's sincerely-held beliefs—beliefs that led him to misjudge profoundly the country he was about to attack. The expectation that the "military operation" would be over in a few days, with a victory parade in Kyiv and crowds of overjoyed "liberated" Ukrainians greeting his troops, grateful to be "reunified" at last with their Russian brethren in the historical womb of the one Russian nation, has not materialized.

The same Ukraine that Putin considered so hopelessly divided along historical fault lines and linguistic boundaries that it had no reason for existence and no defense against a Russian assault stood firm and fought back. The "nonexistent" Ukrainian nation of Putin's imagination mobilized quickly across linguistic, ethnic, and religious lines to stop Russian aggression.

Having bought into Putin's version of history, many citizens of Europe and the world have marveled at why and how Ukraine showed such unexpected strength and cohesion. At first, they watched with horror as Russia attacked peaceful Ukrainian cities and civilian populations; then they followed with amazement the heroic resistance of Ukraine's army and ordinary citizens to a full-scale offensive by the country's much more powerful neighbor. The present collection of essays provides answers to a number of key questions about Ukraine, its history, culture, identity and, notably, its long, tumultuous, and often tragic relations with Russia. Although conceived before the most recent escalation of the Russo-Ukrainian military conflict into an all-out war, it appears to be timelier today than ever before.

Ukraine made a dramatic entry into world politics and news media in 2013–14 with the events that became known as the Euromaidan Revolution, or the Revolution of Dignity. Hundreds of thousands of Ukrainians protested against the government's refusal to sign the long-promised association agreement with the European Union. The protests later turned against government corruption and the police brutality unleashed by the regime on the peaceful demonstrations. The resulting popular uprising in February 2014 saw the ouster of the authoritarian president Viktor Yanukovych, who fled to Russia.

Soon after, Ukraine found itself at the frontline of a series of even more dramatic developments: the illegal seizure of the Crimea by Russia and the Kremlin-provoked, -inspired, -funded, -armed, and often -manned war in the Donbas region of eastern Ukraine. On two occasions—in the summer of 2014 and in the winter of 2015—Russia sent its regular armed forces into battle in order to assure the survival of the two puppet regimes it established in the area. The war soon acquired the traits of a regional conflict with global ramifications and with no end in sight. At stake was the future of the global post-Cold War order and the fate of democracy in the post-Soviet space—factors that drew worldwide attention to the events in Ukraine.

Interest in Ukraine received a new boost in the summer of 2016 when Paul Manafort resigned from his position as the chairman of Donald J. Trump's presidential campaign. Later on, Manafort would be found guilty and sent to prison for a number of financial violations, including undisclosed payments received from the ousted Ukrainian president Viktor Yanukovych. In the summer of 2019, Ukraine reemerged in the news because of President Trump's attempts to coerce Ukraine's new president, Volodymyr Zelensky, into undermining Joe Biden—seen as the leading Democratic contender in the presidential race—by opening a criminal investigation into his son, Hunter Biden, and the latter's activities in Ukraine. In exchange, war-torn Ukraine would receive much-needed military assistance from the US—a temptation that the young democracy successfully resisted. In December 2019, the claim that President Trump had abused his power in dealing with Ukraine was confirmed and he was impeached by the US Congress. As a result, in the course of 2020, Ukraine remained at the center of a presidential campaign that propelled Joe Biden to victory.

Throughout these events, I found myself obliged to answer numerous questions about Ukraine from both journalists and the general public. Although those questions were informed by contemporaneous developments, a great many of them required probing into the country's history and culture to understand its present and future. My colleague Mary Sarotte and I sought to answer some questions about the recent history of American-Ukrainian and Russo-Ukrainian relations in an article for *Foreign Affairs* while the impeachment hearings were still going on.[2]

This collection of essays strives to answer the very same set of questions by looking at key moments in Ukraine's history and how the country relates to its own history today. As many of the essays show, history is central to Ukraine's current war with Russia and its relations with the West. As a genre, essay collections produce new knowledge and understanding by the collocation of individual texts, which places them in dialogue and reveals connections of which the reader—or even the author—were not previously aware. The heuristic potential of this collection became evident to me in the process of selecting, revising, and editing the studies that comprise this volume.

Most of the essays collected here were written and published in the last decade, which witnessed enormous change in Ukraine and Eastern Europe in general. During that period, Ukraine underwent the Euromaidan protests, a radical change of government, Russian aggression, the loss of the Crimea, and war in the Donbas—developments that I discuss above, that could hardly have been predicted a decade earlier, and that inevitably changed the self-understanding of Ukrainian society and its relation to its history. In the last ten years, history has taken center stage in Ukrainian politics and spilled over to the European and world scene. In fact, battles over history have launched and become part of a very real, not virtual, war.

In January 2010, a Ukrainian court ruled on the criminal responsibility of the Soviet leadership for the Holodomor—the Great Ukrainian Famine of 1932–33—and found Joseph Stalin and his associates guilty of causing the death of close to four million Ukrainian citizens. In the same month, before stepping down as president of Ukraine, Viktor Yushchenko bestowed the highest state award, the title of Hero of Ukraine, on Stepan Bandera, a radical nationalist leader of the first half of the twentieth century who was assassinated by a KGB agent in 1959. That decision aroused numerous protests in Ukraine and abroad, and the new president, Viktor Yanukovych, allowed a Donetsk regional court to rescind the award. Yanukovych did not stop there: bowing to Russian pressure, he refused to refer to the Holodomor as an act of genocide despite an earlier decision of the Ukrainian parliament on that issue. Ukraine was in turmoil about its history, and the political compass needle swung from pro-Russian to pro-Soviet to pronationalist, depending on the head of state.[3]

Before the end of the decade, Ukraine underwent a process of radical decommunization driven at least in part by the incompatibility of post-Soviet historical narrative, which presented the Soviet period in a predominantly positive light, and the Holodomor narrative, which portrayed the Soviet regime as a genocidal monstrosity. Another major factor contributing to that process was the drive to rehabilitate and fully integrate into the historical mainstream the story of the nationalist-led Ukrainian Insurgent Army, which fought for the independence of Ukraine during and after World War II. The decommunization campaign resulted not only in the demolition of monuments to Lenin and other leaders of the Soviet regime but also in the mass renaming of streets, squares, and even entire villages, towns, and cities, changing the map of Ukraine in a dramatic fashion.

Russian aggression turned not only Ukraine but also Ukrainian history into a battleground, demanding a response from Ukrainian society on a number of historical fronts. Russia's use of imperial history to justify its annexation of the Crimea and, in particular, its failed attempts to split Ukraine by creating a quasi-state of "Novorossiia" (New Russia) vaguely based on the area once claimed by an imperial province with the same name, rekindled long-standing Ukrainian interest in the history of the Cossacks, who settled the steppes of southern Ukraine prior to Russian expansion there in the eighteenth century. Moreover, Russia's use in its aggression against Ukraine of Soviet mythology, especially that of the "Great Patriotic War"—the Soviet component of World War II—provided additional fuel and rationale for the decommunization campaign.[4]

What I discovered while working on this collection but did not fully understand before was that, by writing these essays in the course of the last decade, I had become involved in a process of documenting new developments but also, more importantly, in an attempt to understand and explain them to myself and others in historical terms. I will explain below how the essays collected here contributed to both processes, by pointing out the relations between individual essays and the historical shifts that have been taking place during the last ten years in the self-perception of Ukrainian society and its attitude toward history.

The volume begins with a call to revisit Ukrainian historiography. The introduction argues for a new national history of Ukraine that would take account of the main historiographic trends and achievements of the past few decades and would explain the rise of the modern Ukrainian civic nation.

The title of the first section of the volume, "Cossack Stock," refers to the words of the Ukrainian anthem, a mid-nineteenth-century text that declares all Ukrainians to be of Cossack ancestry. Indeed, Cossackdom became the founding myth of the modern Ukrainian nation, yet Cossack history itself produced more than one mythology. The essays in this section deal with various aspects of Cossack history and the mythologies engendered by it.

The essay "Placing Ukraine on the Map of Europe" not only examines the first appearance of the term "Ukraine" on a European map but also discusses the synergic relationship between Cossacks and princes, who were represented as antagonists in traditional historiography. The next essay, "Russia and Ukraine:

Did They Reunite in 1654?" analyzes the pitfalls of the Pereiaslav mythology used in imperial and Soviet times to justify Russian domination of Ukraine and revived recently by neo-imperialist Russia to claim that Russians and Ukrainians are "one people." The essay "Hadiach 1658: The Origins of a Myth" considers the myth that served to counterbalance that of Pereiaslav by presenting the orientation of the Cossack state toward Poland as a preferable alternative. Finally, "The Return of Ivan Mazepa" looks at the ways in which Ukrainian society dealt with the imperial mythology of the Battle of Poltava(1709). I focus here on the Ukrainian reaction to Mazepa's depiction as a traitor to the tsar and the archenemy of Russia following his rebellion against the empire.

The second section of the volume, "The Red Century," includes articles and essays that discuss Europe's and Ukraine's bloodiest century—the twentieth. It begins with a reinterpretation of the Russian Revolution as a revolution of nations ("How Russian Was the Russian Revolution?") and discusses the reasons that led Lenin and the Bolsheviks to make concessions to the national aspirations of the Ukrainians. The section continues with two articles that discuss the Great Ukrainian Famine of 1932–33, recently recognized by the Ukrainian parliament and the parliaments of several other countries as a genocide. The first of those two articles, "Killing by Hunger," is a review of Anne Applebaum's award-winning book *Red Famine: Stalin's War on Ukraine*, while the second, "Mapping the Great Famine," presents the results of a GIS-based research project on the history of the tragedy that firmly categorizes it as a man-made famine.

The next two essays, "The Call of Blood" and "The Battle for Eastern Europe," discuss the importance of Ukraine for the international politics of World War II. In the first case, Stalin's decision to sign the Molotov-Ribbentrop Pact brought about a partial rehabilitation of the Ukrainian national project and rhetoric, since they were needed to justify the Soviet annexation of parts of Poland and Romania. In the second essay, I argue that Soviet-American relations deteriorated at the end of World War II as a result of the two countries' growing competition for Eastern Europe, which included Ukraine then and now. The impact of the start of the Cold War on the ordinary Ukrainian citizens is discussed in the essay entitled "The American Dream."

The third section of the volume, "Farewell to the Empire," includes essays on Ukraine's contribution to the collapse of the Soviet Union. The fall of the USSR, whose history is discussed in detail in my book *The Last Empire*, is here treated in a short piece entitled "The Soviet Collapse." The history and memory of the nuclear disaster at Chornobyl (widely known in English in its Russified form, Chernobyl), one of the factors in the collapse, is discussed in the essays "Chornobyl" and "Truth in Our Times." "The Empire Strikes Back" traces the evolution of Russian foreign policy toward Ukraine after the collapse of the Soviet Union and surveys the outbreak of the current conflict.

In this section, essays on the politics of memory provide a context for understanding the Russo-Ukrainian war and its contribution to major changes in Ukraine's memory politics. The essay "When Stalin Lost His Head" uses the story of the beheading of a Stalin monument in Ukraine to analyze the clash between Soviet and post-Soviet narratives of history and types of memory, both liberal and nationalist. This is also the subject of the essay "Goodbye Lenin!" which explains the changes in Ukrainian society's perception of history that became important contributing factors to the "Leninfall" (*Leninopad*), the grassroots campaign to demolish statues of Vladimir Lenin, and later to the parliament-driven process of decommunization.

Visions of Ukraine's European future and their relation to history are discussed in the four essays that constitute the fourth and final section of the volume, "European Horizons." The first of those essays, "The Russian Question," discusses the development of the Russian national idea and the nationalism that have shaped Vladimir Putin's thinking about history and have been used to justify the war. "The Quest for Europe" reconstructs the image of Europe as it appears in the writings of Ukrainian intellectuals from the nineteenth century on, arguing that the notion of Europe has been constructed as an antipode to Russia and continues to function in that capacity with regard to Ukrainian history and identity.

In "The New Eastern Europe," I discuss the post-Cold War shift in the application of the term "Eastern Europe" from the

Soviet satellite nations of the Cold War era to the former Soviet republics of Ukraine, Belarus, and Moldova. In the essay "Reimagining the Continent," I examine the consequences of that shift, as well as the rise of Ukraine as a new battleground between the collective West and Russia, for the new political and cultural map of Europe. I argue that the post-Cold War era has produced a new understanding of the limits and frontiers of Europe, which are now being contested in the war in and over Ukraine.

Although they cover a large swath of territory, both chronological and historiographic, the essays collected in this volume discuss only some of the key moments and themes in the history of Ukraine and Russo-Ukrainian relations. I believe, however, that, taken together, they offer a fairly comprehensive answer to the question of why Ukraine has been central to the East-West confrontation of the post-Cold War era and why it became the focal point of the current conflict—so far, Europe's largest and deadliest war of the twenty-first century.

I.

Quo Vadis Ukrainian History?

THE HISTORY OF UKRAINE as a territory, not unlike that of many other places, countries, and peoples, has its origins in the kind of historical writing that would probably be characterized today as global or transnational history. In the mid-fifth century BC Herodotus described what is now southern Ukraine and its multi-ethnic population, dominated by the Scythians but not limited to them, in his *Histories*. Comparing the Dnieper to the other rivers known to the ancient Greeks, he concluded that it was second only to the Nile. Thus the lands and peoples of Ukraine have been part of global history ever since the father of historiography wrote about them. Several centuries later, the first known inhabitants of the Ukrainian lands, the Cimmerians, made it into the Bible.

When the Rus´ chroniclers in the city of Kyiv began to write their own history in the mid-eleventh century AD, they already had a significant body of literature on the subject, written largely by learned Greeks, whose emperors and patriarchs had brought Christianity to the former Scythian lands a few decades earlier. The task of the chroniclers was anything but simple: they had to collect local lore and fit it into the Christian and imperial historical schema brought by the missionaries. They did their best to place themselves, their rulers, and their land in the narrative of the creation of the world, the myth of Slavic ethnogenesis, and the history of the Byzantine Empire. They insisted that they were in control of their own fate: allegedly, they had never been conquered and had invited the Vikings (Varangians) to rule over their land of their own free will, just as they had freely chosen

Christianity as their new religion. But the concept of world history and the chronological table they used to date the events of their past came directly from Byzantine writings.

The vision of Kyiv and Rus´ as parts of the Christian universe remained fundamental to the chroniclers' outlook despite the shock of the Mongol invasion in the mid-thirteenth century. But as the world of the Rus´ principalities became smaller, and the ambitions of their rulers local rather than regional or global, the chroniclers turned into guardians of local memory, which had little connection with universal history. Not until the sixteenth century did foreign writers again turn their attention to Kyiv and the Ukrainian lands, prompting local authors to relate their history to global developments. The onset of the Reformation, with its battles between Protestants and Catholics—in Ukraine, these mainly took the form of polemics over the Union of Brest (1596)—made the two camps think of Orthodox Ukrainians and Belarusians as participants in a broader religious struggle. Polemicists, both Orthodox and Uniate, conceived their history as part of an epic battle between Christianity and heresy. The Cossack wars that began in the mid-seventeenth century not only focused the attention of Western writers on the region but also led them to interpret the Cossack phenomenon as part of the general European wave of revolutions or of the Christian struggle against the Ottomans.

"Although Ukraine be one of the most remote regions of Europe, and the Cossackian name very modern; yet has that country been of late the stage of glorious actions, and the inhabitants have acquitted themselves with as great valor in martial arts as any nation whatsoever," wrote Edward Brown in 1672 on publishing Pierre Chevalier's history of the Cossacks in translation under the title *A Discourse of the Original, Country, Manners, Government and Religion of the Cossacks.*[1] In Brown's view, the Cossacks resembled his own countrymen in some measure, as they had won glorious victories at sea; the steppes settled by the Cossacks also resembled the sea and required a compass to navigate them. This initial attempt to explain Ukraine to the English reading public emphasized military and naval history, heroic deeds, and parallels with the English way of life.

The eighteenth century brought the ideas of the Enlightenment to Eastern Europe, where they found interpreters and promoters in enlightened despots such as Catherine II. The main task of local historians—first Cossack officers and then noblemen in the imperial service—became that of integrating their past into that of the empire even as they stressed the peculiarities of their region. That was a theme taken up by the Cossack chroniclers who wrote after the Battle of Poltava (1709). The genre was perfected by Oleksandr Bezborodko, a former Cossack officer who became one of the architects of Russian foreign policy at the end of the eighteenth century. His account of the post-Poltava history of his native Hetmanate described it as having benefited from the enlightened rule of Catherine II. The imperial authorities, for their part, were busy integrating the Ukrainian past into that of their respective empires. In Ukraine, a local governor general sponsored a *History of Little Russia* by Dmitrii Bantysh-Kamensky (1822). The Galician past was actively incorporated into the history of the Habsburg dynasty and empire.

The age of nationalism broke the link between local and imperial history, making the history of the nation and its territory the main object of study. Mykhailo Hrushevsky not only moved from one empire to another but also developed a nonimperial intellectual framework to create a historical narrative for the Ukrainian nation. National historians revolutionized historiography by abandoning the annals of dynasties and empires and studying the people. While they endowed their prospective nations with separate and unique pasts, their anti-imperial project also allowed for an element of universalism. Thus, most Ukrainian historians from Mykola Kostomarov to Mykhailo Drahomanov and Mykhailo Hrushevsky imagined their land as part of a future federation—Slavic in Kostomarov's case, European in Drahomanov's, and Russian in the case of the early Hrushevsky.

The twentieth century brought the idea of world revolution to Ukraine. Communist writers imagined Ukraine as part of a world community of socialist nations; some of them, such as Mykola Khvyliovy, called on the Ukrainian cultural elite to reorient itself toward Europe. Another, Matvii Iavorsky, saw Soviet Ukraine as a Piedmont for Ukrainians outside the USSR. The Stalin regime put a brutal end to such prospects, arresting and killing their exponents. The concept of the "history of the USSR" reduced the transnational aspect of Ukrainian history to an emphasis on Russo-Ukrainian relations—a restriction lifted only with the unexpected fall of the Soviet Union in 1991.

In the West, Ukraine and its history remained largely unnoticed throughout World War I and the interwar period, but the prelude to World War II, when Ukrainians found themselves involved in the Czechoslovak crisis and emerged as a factor in the German-Soviet partition of Poland, changed the situation. The Ukrainian émigré historian Dmytro Doroshenko published his survey of Ukrainian history in Canada, while the Russian émigré historian George Vernadsky gave his imprimatur to an English translation of Mykhailo Hrushevsky's survey in the United States. In the United Kingdom, W. E. D. Allen published his survey with Cambridge University Press. He defined the "Ukrainian problem" as "one of the chief reasons for the absence of balance in continental Europe."[2]

The European war soon became global, turning the attention of historians and the public at large away from Ukraine to Russia and the Soviet Union as a whole. But the war also contributed greatly to the internationalization of knowledge. In the Ukrainian case, it drove hundreds of thousands of Ukrainian refugees and quite a few professional historians to Central Europe and, eventually, to the United States and Canada. In the final analysis, wartime developments not only directed the attention of the English-speaking public to that part of the world but also produced English-language authors who were prepared to write about it.

The logic of the Cold War, which engulfed the world soon after World War II, promoted the spread of anticommunism and nationalism as a means of opposing the Russocentric Soviet historical narrative. But the origins of Ukrainian history as an academic discipline in North America also had distinctive transnational characteristics. When a chair of Ukrainian history was created at Harvard University in 1975, its first occupant was Omeljan Pritsak, a renowned expert on the languages and cultures of the Turkic world. His closest ally and cofounder of the Ukrainian Research Institute, Ihor Ševčenko, was an authority on Byzantine cultural history. Both wrote on Ukraine, placing its history and culture in the broad context of the Eurasian and Byzantine worlds. Pritsak's successor, Roman Szporluk, had made a name for himself as an expert on European intellectual history before coming to Harvard in the late 1980s. In terms of their academic background, interests, and expertise, the founders of Ukrainian historiography in the United States and Canada could not imagine Ukrainian history except as part of the Eurasian, Byzantine, or East-Central European worlds.

Rethinking Ukrainian History

The first North American academic debate on Ukrainian history took place on the pages of *Slavic Review* in 1963. It featured the Turcologist Omeljan Pritsak, the specialists on the Revolution of 1917–20 Arthur E. Adams and John S. Reshetar, Jr., and the intellectual historian of East-Central Europe Ivan L. Rudnytsky. Rudnytsky, who wrote the conceptual paper entitled "The Role of the Ukraine in Modern History," and Pritsak, who was one of the commentators, were post–World War II immigrants to the United States. Both had been influenced by Viacheslav Lypynsky, who initiated the multiethnic approach to Ukrainian history in the 1920s. The participants debated the issues of the historical or nonhistorical status of the Ukrainian nation, continuity in Ukrainian history, the nature of the revolution in Ukraine, and its historical position between East and West.[3]

Ivan Rudnytsky, who claimed in 1963 that Ukrainian historiography had not established itself in the North American academy and was at best an adjunct to Russian studies, organized a conference on Ukrainian history in Canada in 1978. It resulted in the publication of a collection entitled *Rethinking Ukrainian History*, including nine essays, as well as transcripts of a roundtable discussion on the major challenges facing Ukrainian historiography in North America. By the time of the conference, chairs of Ukrainian history and institutes of Ukrainian studies had been established at Harvard University in the United States and at the University of Alberta in Canada, and the training of graduate students in history had begun. Some of those students, including Orest Subtelny and Frank E. Sysyn, took part in the conference and published their papers in the collection. Also among the participants were Roman Szporluk, then of the University of Michigan, his former student John-Paul Himka, and Alfred Rieber's student at the University of Pennsylvania, Zenon E. Kohut, a member of the Harvard circle of graduate students.

The first question to be resolved by the conference organizers was whom they wanted to invite to the conference—Ukrainian historians or historians of Ukraine. They opted for the latter, inviting historians of Ukrainian and non-Ukrainian background. Among the latter was Patricia Herlihy, then of Wellesley College. The organizers still had to prove to themselves and others that "Ukrainian history" was a legitimate term for the history of the Ukrainian lands prior to the emergence of the name "Ukraine" as an ethnonym. Omeljan Pritsak resolved that issue during the roundtable discussion by pointing to Spanish history, which dealt with the history of Spanish regions long before the establishment of the Spanish state and its official name. Issues of periodizing Ukrainian history and establishing appropriate English-language terminology attracted most of the participants' attention during the roundtable debates. But the overriding concern, formulated by Rudnytsky in his introduction to the conference volume, was that under conditions preventing the free development of Ukrainian studies in the Soviet Union scholars of Ukrainian history in North America had to take on the task of representing Ukrainian historiography in the West.

"How should Western students of Ukrainian history respond to this distressing situation?" wrote Rudnytsky with reference to the sorry state of Soviet Ukrainian historiography. "Many in the Ukrainian diaspora community believe that Soviet ideological orthodoxy ought to be met with an equally rigid and militant 'patriotic' orthodoxy. In the conference organizers' view, such an approach would be self-defeating. What is needed is the application of free, critical thought, untrammeled by dogmas of any kind, whether Marxist or nationalist." Rudnytsky argued that historians of Ukraine in the West could remedy the "deformations" of Soviet historiography if "they themselves study Ukrainian history in a universal context." He wrote that, by treating Ukrainian history in the context of the country's relations with the Mediterranean world, Central Europe, and Eurasia, one could "bring to light

Ukraine's unique historical identity" and contribute to the "better understanding of the history of Eastern Europe as a whole."[4]

The two key decisions made by the conference organizers and participants—to broaden the field of Ukrainian historical studies by including non-Ukrainian scholars and make that newly constituted field an integral part of North American historical scholarship—were clear departures from the model of Ukrainian historiography practiced by Ukrainian émigré scholarly institutions, in particular the Free Academy of Sciences and the Shevchenko Scientific Society. Those decisions resulted in the training of a first generation of Ukrainian historians in history departments of North American universities and the subsequent publication of monographs, issued predominantly by the institutes of Ukrainian studies at Harvard and the University of Alberta.

Between 1982 and 1996, scholars associated with the new field published three surveys of Ukrainian history. Roman Szporluk's influential *Ukraine: A Brief History* (1982) placed the modern history of Ukraine into the context of nation-building processes in Central and Eastern Europe. From Harvard came the authors of two major syntheses of Ukrainian history: Orest Subtelny published his in 1988 under the title *Ukraine: A History*, while Paul Robert Magocsi joined the field eight years later with his *History of Ukraine* (1996). Subtelny's survey has often been regarded as representative of the national paradigm of Ukrainian history, while the second became an epitome of the multiethnic approach to the subject.[5]

The appearance of an independent Ukrainian state in 1991 had a major impact on Ukrainian historiography. Subtelny's survey, translated into Ukrainian, became a standard textbook in Ukraine for some time, replacing the Russocentric and class-based narrative of the Soviet period. It also competed there with outdated approaches and models rediscovered or "repatriated" to Ukraine through the works of Ukrainian émigrés belonging to the "statist" school of Ukrainian historiography. No less profound were the changes in the West, where the emergence of Ukraine on the political map provided much-needed political legitimacy for Ukrainian history as a distinct field of study.

But the validation took place in a very peculiar way, with a debate in the *Slavic Review* (1995) on an article by Mark von Hagen provocatively titled "Does Ukraine Have a History?" Von Hagen claimed that according to generally accepted Western political and academic standards, Ukraine did not yet have a history: in order to acquire that status, the subject would have to be fully incorporated into North American historiography. A number of scholars from the United States, Canada, Central Europe, and Ukraine were invited to respond to von Hagen's paper, indicating a major transformation of Ukrainian history as a subject of study. It was now attracting the interest of leading scholars of non-Ukrainian origin in the West, while those on the "ethnic" Ukrainian side included new arrivals from post-Soviet Ukraine, such as the present author.

Mark von Hagen's essay offered a critical but sympathetic review of the field and, more importantly, set an agenda for its future development. Returning to the question of the perceived lack of institutional, elite, and even cultural continuity in Ukrainian history, von Hagen proposed to turn Ukraine's "weaknesses" into strengths. "Precisely the fluidity of frontiers, the permeability of cultures, the historic multi-ethnic society is what could make Ukrainian history a very 'modern' field of inquiry," wrote von Hagen, who specialized in the history of the interwar USSR. He continued: "I want to make a case for the study of Ukrainian history and its re-emergence as an academic discipline both within and without Ukraine as a history intrinsically interesting precisely because it challenges so many of the clichés of the nation-state paradigm."[6]

The arrival of the transnational paradigm in the field of Ukrainian studies in general and Ukrainian history in particular was heralded by a collection of essays edited by Georgiy Kasianov and Philipp Ther in 2009 under the title *A Laboratory of Transnational History: Ukraine and Recent Ukrainian Historiography*. Andreas Kappeler, one of the contributors to that collection, has been particularly effective in revealing the limitations entailed not only in the national but also in the multiethnic paradigm. Ukraine, a country divided over the centuries by political and cultural boundaries, and probably more influenced by transnational trends than most other regions of Europe because of its statelessness, may well stand to benefit particularly from a transnational approach to the writing of its history.[7]

The Future of the Past

Historians from all over the world working on various topics in Ukrainian history gained an opportunity to evaluate the state of the field at three international conferences organized by the Institute of Ukrainian History, National Academy of Sciences of Ukraine, and the Harvard Ukrainian Research Institute in 2012 and 2013. The conference on Ukrainian historical writing of the interwar period was held in Munich in July 2012 and cosponsored by the Ukrainian Free University; the conference on the Soviet legacy, hosted by the Institute of History in Kyiv, took place in May 2013 with the support of a grant from the Renaissance Foundation; and the conference on the future of Ukrainian historical studies, cosponsored by the Ukrainian Studies Fund, was held at Harvard University in October 2013. Its theme, "Quo Vadis Ukrainian History? Assessing the State of the Field," provided the title and main theme of this essay.[8]

The conference took place and the first drafts of papers were written a few months before the Euromaidan protests and the Revolution of Dignity, followed by the Russian annexation of the Crimea and the Russo-Ukrainian conflict over eastern Ukraine. Some authors took those developments into account in revising their original contributions for the volume of conference proceedings published in 2016 under the title *The Future of the Past: New Perspectives on Ukrainian History*. I discuss their importance for the ongoing debate on the essence and future direction of Ukrainian historical studies below. National history, especially the national paradigm in the representation of the Ukrainian past, was an object of critical examination as well as a point of departure for most of the historians who accepted the invitation to take part in the conference.[9]

The most systematic attempt to take stock of the main characteristics, advantages, and disadvantages of the national paradigm was undertaken by Georgiy Kasianov and Oleksii Tolochko. They added their voices to the ongoing discussion on the multivolume history of Ukraine—the traditional "genre" produced by the Institute of History of the National Academy of Sciences[10]—and what it should look like if the "genre" is to continue. The authors pointed to the limitations not only of the national paradigm per se but also of traditional approaches to writing multivolume academic histories of Ukraine. They proposed to overcome those limitations by rejecting the "tyranny of territoriality" imposed by the concept of the modern nation-state and focusing instead on individual regions and/or territorial units larger than the nation-state.

These turned out to be the two main directions taken by the authors of *The Future of the Past* in their reexamination of Ukrainian history. What the study of Ukraine can tell us about Soviet, European, and global history was the question raised in Andrea Graziosi's discussion of his personal "discovery" of Ukrainian history. It was answered in the essays authored by George Liber, Hiroaki Kuromiya, and Mark von Hagen, who proposed to reinterpret Ukraine's twentieth-century history and political thought by considering them in the context of imperialism and anticolonial resistance. In von Hagen's view, Soviet policy in Ukraine had clear colonial underpinnings and produced anticolonial resistance manifested in such diverse expressions as the socialist writings of Pavlo Khrystiuk, the nationalism of Dmytro Dontsov, and the writings of Ukrainian national communists of the 1960s, such as Ivan Dziuba, who promoted Ukrainian-Jewish understanding.

Shifting from the transnational to the regional and back in an attempt to overcome the limitations of the national paradigm has become a prominent trend in Ukrainian historiography of the last few decades. Few regions of Ukraine have received as much attention from historians, both Ukrainian and non-Ukrainian, as Galicia. In the late eighteenth century, when the Habsburg historian Johann Christian von Engel produced the first Central European work on Ukrainian history, its two main parts dealt with the Ukrainian Cossacks and the Galician-Volhynian Principality.[11] The annexation of Galicia to the Habsburg Monarchy after the first partition of Poland launched a project of imagining and reimagining it in the context of Austria and Austria-Hungary, described with many important insights in Larry Wolff's *Idea of Galicia*.[12]

In his contribution to the conference volume, Wolff examined how Galician history was perceived by Habsburg elites in Vienna, Polish intellectuals in the region, and Ukrainian nation-builders such as Mykhailo Hrushevsky. Iryna Vushko added her voice to those who criticize the tendency of adherents of nationally focused historiography to absolve representatives of their own nations of wrongdoing or criminal acts committed against "others." She called on fellow historians to embrace the heterogeneity of Galician and Ukrainian history in order to "place Ukraine at the center of a European—not solely Ukrainian national—narrative."

Right-Bank Ukraine, which had received little attention in traditional Ukrainian historiography, was the focus of Faith Hillis's and Heather Coleman's contributions, which dealt with the second half of the nineteenth century. Both authors examined the formation of modern national identities in the region, while stressing its unique character and contribution to larger national and imperial identity-building projects. Hillis challenged the dominant "national awakening" paradigm in Ukrainian historiography and directed attention to proponents of Little Russian identity—an important factor in the history not only of Russian nationalism but also of Ukraine that was marginalized, if not completely overlooked, by historians working within the Ukrainian national paradigm. Heather Coleman stressed that in Right-Bank Ukraine no nation-building project could succeed without taking into account and accommodating the local identities of religious and cultural figures such as Petr Lebedintsev. This conclusion probably also applied to other regions of Ukraine.

While the transnational turn in the study of Ukrainian history came in the wake of disappointment with the national paradigm and growing criticism of the multiethnic approach, which replicated the shortcomings of the former on a smaller ethnocultural scale, a number of essays in the volume demonstrated the potential of the transnational paradigm to reinterpret themes that received considerable attention in the national and multiethnic narratives, offering new ways of understanding familiar phenomena. Yohanan Petrovsky-Shtern argued in favor of integrating ethnic histories into the history of Ukraine as a region and multiethnic community. The transnational, national, and multicultural converged in a new way in Mayhill Fowler's appeal to "go global" with the history of Ukrainian culture. Distinguishing "culture in Ukraine" from "Ukrainian culture," Fowler opted for the transnational approach to promote study of the former. She called for the "rediscovery" of imperial and Soviet layers of "culture in Ukraine."

Relations between history and society in Ukraine and abroad were featured in the essays by Marta Dyczok and Volodymyr Kravchenko. Dyczok discussed the clash of Soviet models of representing and interpreting the past with nationalist or nationally inspired visions of Ukrainian history. She pointed to the lack of consensus among politicians, historians, and society at large with regard to a historical narrative. Kravchenko explained the lack of consensus by taking a critical look at Ukrainian society's troubled relations with its Soviet legacy. He argued that the failure to "nationalize" the Ukrainian past had made elements of Ukrainian society receptive to the much more successful Russian project of reappropriating and recasting parts of Soviet historical mythology for purposes of Russian nation-building. Kravchenko suggested a way forward by integrating the Soviet historical experience into the Ukrainian national narrative and pointed to the "modernization" paradigm as the most effective tool for achieving that goal.

The essays collected in *The Future of the Past* give a good idea of the state of the study and, to some extent, also of the teaching of Ukrainian history outside Ukraine, particularly in North America, the center of non-Soviet research on the history of Ukraine prior to 1991. They also point toward new ways of examining the Ukrainian past.

Toward a New Narrative?

As in the late 1970s, when scholars of Ukrainian history in the United States and Canada gathered for their first conference to assess the state of the field, so today a new generation of historians is seeking to define the field in relation to dominant historiographic trends in Ukraine, where most research and writing on the subject is done, and to the historical profession outside Ukraine. Today, as in the 1970s, most of the "Westerners" reject the historiographic trend dominant in Ukraine. In the 1970s that trend was a variety of Soviet Marxist historiography; today it is the national narrative of the Ukrainian past. The task also remains largely the same as it was then—the integration of Ukrainian historical research and writing into world historiography, taking advantage of new trends emerging in the field.

Today, unlike in 1995, no one asks whether Ukraine has a history. As scholars of various backgrounds began contributing to the field, bringing in themes and approaches from other fields of historiography, the legitimacy of studying Ukrainian history ceased to be an issue. As noted above, the achievement of Ukrainian independence also served to legitimize the field. Recent research on Ukrainian history conducted outside the country has been profoundly influenced by the transnational and regional turns in historical studies. The same is true of the continuing interest in empires, borderlands, minorities, and national and cultural identities, as well as the growing interest in spatial elements of historical research. All these approaches help expand the boundaries of Ukrainian history and enhance its heuristic potential not only at home but also, as Andrea Graziosi has shown, with regard to European history as a whole.

Thus, Ukraine now has a history abroad. But does it have one at home in the sense defined by von Hagen—an accepted written record of past experience? The national narrative, now dominant in Ukrainian historiography at home, has encountered major problems in the last few years when it comes to its reception on the elite and popular levels. As Marta Dyczok and Volodymyr Kravchenko show in the above volume, the ethnonational narrative has exhausted its potential not only in purely scholarly and heuristic terms but also as an instrument for organizing the historical memory of Ukrainian society in such a way as to promote consensus. Should its practitioners be given another chance?

After all, Ukraine is still struggling with the process of nation-building, which most European countries completed in the nineteenth and early twentieth centuries with the help of the ethnonational historical narratives that most contributors to the above volume reject as not only outdated but also detrimental to a better understanding of the Ukrainian past and its significance. Is it fair to "impose" on Ukrainian society a historical understanding informed by the transnational processes currently taking place in the countries of the European Union at a time when Ukraine is surrounded by and obliged to compete, sometimes militarily, with states that have placed the national paradigm at the core of their historical identity?[13]

The events of the last few years—the Revolution of Dignity, the loss of the Crimea, and the insurgency and Russo-Ukrainian conflict in the Donbas region of eastern Ukraine—have helped mobilize Ukrainian society in defense of the country's integrity and sovereignty across ethnic, linguistic, religious, and regional lines. The tragic experience of war, resettlement, and lost territory has mobilized the Ukrainian civic nation. If one of the main tasks of historical writing is to explain a given society's origins to its citizens, there is no better way to do so than by writing a history of the land and its people, taking account of the country's regional and ethnic diversity while integrating its past into the history of the part of the world to which it belongs.

With historians of empires discussing ways of writing a "new imperial history," the time has come to put on the academic agenda the need for a "new national history," a genre of research and writing that would go beyond the ethnonational paradigm of the past and take advantage of opportunities presented by the global, transnational, multiethnic, and regional approaches to meet the growing demand of modern states, nations, and societies for common narratives and historical identities. Few countries are more in need of that kind of history than is Ukraine. The transformation of the Ukrainian historical narrative along the lines suggested by the new trends of historical research would make that narrative more inclusive and much more acceptable to various elements of Ukrainian society, which remains divided less by issues of language and culture than by the different historical experiences of Ukraine's diverse regions. That transformation would also make Ukraine more understandable to its European Union partners, whose history has often been the product of the same transnational processes.

I

COSSACK STOCK

2.

Placing Ukraine on the Map of Europe

THE WORD "UKRAINE," which is now the name of an independent country, has medieval origins and was first used by twelfth-century Kyivan chroniclers to define the areas of today's Ukraine bordering on the Pontic steppes. In the second half of the seventeenth century, the term "Ukraine" entered the international vocabulary as one of the names of the Cossack polity created in the course of the Khmelnytsky Uprising (1648–57). By that time, European geographers could already locate Ukraine on the maps produced by the French engineer and cartographer Guillaume Levasseur de Beauplan. But his was not the first depiction of Ukraine on a European map.[1]

The terms "Ukraine" and "Cossacks" appeared on European maps simultaneously in the first decades of the seventeenth century. Both terms were first introduced on a map of Eastern Europe produced by a group of cartographers and engravers assembled by Mikalojus Kristupas Radvila (Mikołaj Krzysztof Radziwiłł) the Orphan, one of the most prominent aristocrats in the Grand Duchy of Lithuania. The map, entitled "Detailed Description of the Grand Duchy of Lithuania and Other Adjacent Lands," captured not only major political and territorial developments but also social and cultural changes that had taken place in the region in the course of the sixteenth century.

The Radvila map covers the territories of the Grand Duchy of Lithuania as they existed before the Union of Lublin (1569) between the Kingdom of Poland and the Grand Duchy of Lithuania. It is supplemented by a separate map of the Dnieper River.

By far the most important development reflected on the Radvila map was the emergence of a border dividing the Grand Duchy almost in half. Some sections of the new boundary resemble the present-day Ukrainian-Belarusian border, following the Prypiat River and then diverging to the north. The word "Ukraine," used to describe part of the lands south of the new border, referred to the territory on the Right Bank of the Dnieper extending from Kyiv in the north to Kaniv in the south. Beyond Kaniv, if one trusted the cartographer, there were wild steppes, marked *Campi deserti citra Boristenem* (Desert plains on this side of the Borysthenes [Dnieper]). "Ukraine" thus covered a good part of the region's steppe frontier, which had become the homeland of the social group subsequently known as the Ukrainian Cossacks.[2]

The Radvila map provides unique insight into three inter-related processes that shaped the future of the Pontic steppes: the renegotiation of relations between the royal crown and the local aristocracy; the economic and cultural colonization of the Dnieper region; and, last but not least, the emergence of the Ukrainian Cossacks as a powerful military and, later, political and cultural force.

The Princes

The Radvila map is often attributed to Tomasz Makowski, its principal engraver, but was in fact produced by a group of cartographers that included Maciej Strubicz. Most of the work on the map was done between 1585 and 1603, while the first known edition was published only in 1613 by Hessel Gerritsz (Gerard) of Amsterdam.[3]

In many ways, the Radvila map was a continuation of work initiated by King Stefan Batory at the time of the Livonian War (1558–83) and may be regarded as sign of increased involvement of the aristocracy in the political, religious, and cultural realms previously dominated by the king. Radvila was assisted in his work by fellow aristocrats, and it has been argued that the information on the Dnieper settlements was supplied to him by his peer, the palatine of Kyiv and prominent Volhynian magnate Prince Kostiantyn Ostrozky. Not unlike the *Kronika polska, litewska, żmódzka i wszystkiéj Rusi* by Maciej Stryjkowski (1582), sponsored by a fellow Lithuanian aristocrat, Bishop Merkelis Giedraitis of Samogitia (Žemaitija), Radvila's map was not limited in scope to the Grand Duchy of Lithuania and included the lands of Rusʹ, which the Grand Duchy lost to Poland as a result of the Union of Lublin (1569). The elites of the Grand Duchy were clearly unhappy with the deal they got at Lublin in 1569 and were eager to renegotiate the political and cultural spaces created by the Union.[4]

All over Europe, the sixteenth century was marked by the strengthening of royal authority, centralization of the state, and regularization of political and social practices. The other side of the coin was increasing aristocratic opposition to this growth. Both tendencies were fully apparent in the preparation and conclusion of the Union of Lublin, which had as its goal not only the unification of the two parts of the Polish-Lithuanian state but also the strengthening of the crown. If King Sigismund Augustus wanted the Union, the aristocratic families of the Grand Duchy of Lithuania opposed it. But many of their concerns had to be put aside because of a growing external threat to the Grand Duchy that could be met only with the help of Poland.

In 1558, after taking control of the Volga trade route by defeating and forcing into submission the two successors of the Golden Horde, the Kazan and Astrakhan khanates, Ivan the Terrible moved his armies westward, trying to gain access to the Baltic Sea. The Livonian War, which Ivan started that year, would last for a quarter century and see Sweden, Denmark, Lithuania and, eventually, Poland involved in the struggle. In 1563, Muscovite troops crossed the borders of the Grand Duchy, taking the city of Polatsk (now in Belarus) and raiding Vitsebsk, Shkloŭ, and Orsha. This defeat mobilized support for the Union among the lesser Lithuanian nobility. Given Muscovite claims to the lands of Kyivan Rusʹ, which included not only Polatsk but also the rest of the Ukrainian-Belarusian territories of the Grand Duchy, the future looked bleak for the Duchy's ruling elite. Union with the Kingdom of Poland now seemed the only possible solution.

In December 1568, Sigismund Augustus convened two Diets in the city of Lublin—one for the Kingdom, the other for the Grand Duchy—in the hope that their representatives would hammer out conditions for the new union. The negotiations began on a positive note, as the two sides agreed to joint election of the king, a common Diet, or parliament, and broad autonomy for the Grand Duchy. Nonetheless, the magnates would not return the royal lands in their possession—the principal demand of the Executionists, a powerful group within the Polish nobility that demanded the recovery of public and royal lands illegally held by the magnates. Directed by Mikalojus Radvila (Mikołaj Radziwiłł) the Red, the leader of the Lithuanian Calvinists and the victorious commander of the Lithuanian army in its recent clashes with Muscovite troops, the Lithuanian delegates made no concessions. They packed their bags, assembled their retinues of noble clients, and left the Diet. This move backfired. Unexpectedly for the departing Lithuanians, the Diet of the Kingdom of Poland began, with the king's blessing, to issue decrees transferring one province of the Grand Duchy after another to the jurisdiction of the Kingdom of Poland.

The Lithuanian magnates who had feared losing their provinces to Muscovy were now losing them to Poland instead. To stop a hostile takeover by their powerful Polish partner, the Lithuanians returned to Lublin to sign an agreement dictated by the Polish delegates. They were too late. In March, the Podlachia palatinate on the Ukrainian-Belarusian-Polish ethnic border went to Poland. Volhynia followed in May, and on 6 June, one day before the resumption of the Polish-Lithuanian talks, the Kyivan and Podolian lands were transferred to Poland as well. The Ukrainian palatinates were incorporated into the Kingdom not as a group but one by one, with no guarantees but those pertaining to the use of the Ruthenian (Middle Ukrainian) language in the courts and administration and the protection of the rights of the Orthodox Church. The Lithuanian aristocrats could only accept the new reality—they stood to lose even more if they continued to resist the Union.[5]

Kostiantyn Ostrozky, by far the most influential of the Ukrainian princes, decided the fate of the Union and his land by throwing his support behind the king. The Lublin border, which cut the Grand Duchy in half and separated the future Ukrainian and Belarusian territories, reinforced differences long in the making. Historically, the Kyiv Land and Galicia-Volhynia differed significantly from the Belarusian lands to the north. From the tenth to the fourteenth century, they were core areas of independent or semi-independent principalities, and, if one judges by the Primary Chronicle and its continuations in Kyiv and Galicia-Volhynia, their identities differed from those of the other Rus´ lands. The location of the Ukrainian lands on the periphery of the Grand Duchy of Lithuania and the challenges they faced on the open steppe frontier set them apart from the rest of the Lithuanian world.

At the Lublin Diet, the Ukrainian elites saw little benefit in maintaining the de facto independence of the Grand Duchy, which was ill equipped to resist increasing pressure from the Crimean and Noghay Tatars. The Kingdom of Poland could help the Grand Duchy fight the war with Muscovy, but it was unlikely to assist the Ukrainians in their low-intensity war with the Tatars.

A different attitude might be expected if the frontier provinces were to be incorporated into the Kingdom. As things turned out, the Volhynian princely families not only kept their possessions but dramatically increased them under Polish tutelage. Kostiantyn Ostrozky, who played a key role in the Lublin Diet, kept his old posts as captain of the town of Volodymyr, head of the Volhynian nobility, and palatine of Kyiv.

The opposition between the Volhynian princes who helped Sigismund Augustus divide the Grand Duchy of Lithuania, among whom Ostrozky was the most prominent, and the Lithuanian aristocrats did not last very long, as both camps soon found common ground in developing political and cultural projects that strengthened their independence of royal authority. The cultural awakening took place on both sides of the new Polish-Lithuanian border, fueled by the political aspirations of the princes and directly linked to the religious conflicts of the time. In Lithuania, the Radvila family set an example of linking politics, religion, and culture. The main opponent of the Union of Lublin, Mikalojus Radvila the Red, was also the leader of Polish and Lithuanian Calvinism and the founder of a school for Calvinist youth. His cousin, Mikalojus Radvila the Black, funded the printing of the first complete Polish translation of the Bible, which was issued in the town of Brest on the Ukrainian-Belarusian ethnic border. John Calvin dedicated one of his works to him. Since the Polish kings remained Catholic, the dissident religion of their aristocratic opponents served to strengthen the latter's intransigence toward royal authority. This was true for both Protestantism and Orthodoxy. The initiative of the Radvila family in associating political opposition with religious dissent was picked up by their Orthodox counterparts.

The first to do so was an Orthodox magnate, Hryhorii Khodkevych (in Belarusian, Khadkevich), who, like the two Radvila cousins, had led the Lithuanian army as the Duchy's grand hetman—one of the supreme posts in the hierarchy. In 1566, two years after the appearance of the Polish Bible, Khodkevych invited two Moscow refugees, the printers Ivan Fedorov and Petr Mstislavets, to his town of Zabłudów (Zabludaŭ). At Khodkevych's request and with his sponsorship, they published a number of books in Church Slavonic there. Khodkevych died in 1572, causing the printers to stop their work, but his initiative would have consequences.

A few years after Khodkevych's death, Kostiantyn Ostrozky began his own publishing project in Volhynia. In 1574 he moved his residence from the Volhynian town of Dubno to nearby Ostrih. He hired an Italian architect then living in Lviv to build new fortifications, the remains of which can still be seen today in Ostrih. He also employed one of Khodkevych's printers, Ivan Fedorov, who was summoned to Ostrih to take part in the prince's most ambitious cultural undertaking—the publication of the full Church Slavonic text of the Bible. In his new capital, Ostrozky assembled a team of scholars who compared Greek and Church Slavonic texts of the Bible, emended the Church Slavonic translations, and published the most authoritative text of Scripture ever produced by Orthodox scholars. The project was truly international in scope, involving participants not only from Lithuania and Poland but also from Greece, while the copies of the Bible on which they worked originated in places as diverse as Rome and Moscow. The Ostrih Bible was issued in 1581 in a print run estimated at fifteen hundred copies.[6]

The close contacts between Kostiantyn Ostrozky and the Lithuanian aristocrats, as well as their shared interest in supporting cultural projects with broad political ramifications, support the assumption of those scholars who claim that it was indeed Kostiantyn Ostrozky who helped Prince Mikalojus Kristupas Radvila to produce the map of the Grand Duchy of Lithuania.

While Radvila harbored no political ambitions that might undermine his loyalty to the king and the Commonwealth—he converted from Calvinism to Catholicism and opposed the Zebrzydowski Rebellion of 1606—his map suggests that he had never given up the historical and cultural claims to the lands of the Grand Duchy lost as a result of the Union of Lublin. It was their interest in those territories, especially the ones located along the Dnieper River, that united Ostrozky and Radvila.[7]

Ukraine

The Radvila map of the Grand Duchy of Lithuania offers a look at Eastern Europe as seen from the palace window of a Lithuanian aristocrat, not a residence of the king or his servants. The mapmakers presented the old Grand Duchy of Lithuania as if it had never been cut in half by King Sigismund Augustus and his supporters at the Lublin Diet of 1569. Although the new borders of the greatly diminished Grand Duchy are marked on the map, they are hardly visible, and the map itself includes the old Lithuanian possessions all the way to the Dnieper estuary. The settlements most prominently marked on the map are not the administrative centers of royal rule but the seats of the princes, including Radvila's own Olyka, which ended up on the Polish side of the divide after the Union of Lublin, and the town of Ostrih, the seat of the Ostrozkys.

Both Olyka and Ostrih are located in Volhynia, the region that emerges on the map as the main stronghold of the princes. It extends all the way to the Dnieper, covering the region marked on the map as "Volynia ulterior, quae tum Vkraina tum Nis ab aliis vocitatur" (Outer Volhynia, known either as Ukraine or as the Lower [Dnieper]). According to the map, Ukraine, which is only one of three possible names of the region, extends from Kyiv, the seat of Ostrozky as palatine of the region, in the north, to the Ros River and the fortress of Korsun, built by King Stefan Batory in 1581, in the south. It borders on the steppes, called "Campi deserti" (Desert plains), which are depicted with numerous horsemen, suggesting a battleground more than an inhabited desert. It seems to be a fast-growing area, dotted with numerous castles and settlements that had not appeared on earlier maps. The Radvila map covers the territories of the Grand Duchy of Lithuania as they existed before the Union of Lublin (1569), which united the Kingdom of Poland and the Grand Duchy (Figure 1, pp. 206–7), and has a supplement consisting of a separate map of the Dnieper (Figure 2, pp. 208–13).

The reference to "Ukraine" as "Volynia Ulterior" speaks volumes about the views and ambitions of the Ostrozky and other Volhynian princes, the likely advisers to the makers of the Radvila map. This usage reflected the perception of "Ukraine" on the Right Bank of the Dnieper as the territories annexed to the Volhynian Land, while stressing the role that the Volhynian princes had played in the colonization of those territories. The lands marked on the Radvila map as "Ukraine," "Volynia Ulterior," and "Nis" had indeed become the playground of the Volhynian princes in the second half of the sixteenth century.

The Lublin Diet prohibited the princes from fielding their own armies in wartime. But because of the constant danger of Tatar attacks on the steppe frontier, the Commonwealth's standing army could not do without the military muscle of the princes. Ostrozky alone could muster an army of twenty thousand soldiers and cavalrymen—ten times the size of the king's army in the borderlands. At various times in his career, Ostrozky was a contender for both the Polish and the Muscovite thrones. The lesser nobles were in no position to defy the powerful magnate, on whom they depended economically and politically. Thus, Ostrozky continued to preside over an extensive network of noble clients who did his bidding in the local and Commonwealth Diets. Not only the local nobility but even the king and the Diet did not dare to challenge the authority of this uncrowned king of Rus´.

The Ostrozkys were the richest Ukrainian princes who maintained and increased their wealth and influence after the Union of Lublin, but they were not alone. Another highly influential Volhynian princely family was the Vyshnevetskys. Prince Mykhailo Vyshnevetsky branched out of his Volhynian possessions, which were quite insignificant in comparison with Ostrozky's, into the lands east of the Dnieper. Those lands were either uncolonized or had been abandoned by settlers in the times of Mongol rule and were now open to attack by the Noghay and Crimean Tatars. The Vyshnevetsky family expanded into the steppe lands, creating new settlements, establishing towns, and funding monasteries. The possessions of the Vyshnevetskys in Left-Bank (eastern) Ukraine soon began to rival those of the Ostrozkys in Volhynia. These two princely families were the largest landowners in Ukraine.

In the course of the fifteenth and sixteenth centuries, the Ukrainian steppes underwent a major political, economic, and cultural transformation. For the first time since the days of Kyivan Rus´, the line of frontier settlement stopped retreating toward the Prypiat marshes and the Carpathian Mountains and began advancing toward the east and south. Linguistic research indicates that two major groups of Ukrainian dialects, Polisian and Carpatho-Volhynian, began to converge from the north and west, respectively, shifting east and south to create a third group of steppe dialects that now cover Ukrainian territory from Zhytomyr and Kyiv in the northwest to Zaporizhzhia, Luhansk, and Donetsk in the east, extending as far southeast as Krasnodar and Stavropol in today's Russia. This movement and mixing of dialects reflected the movement of the population at large.

The major obstacle to the movement of the sedentary population in the Pontic steppes was presented by the slave-seeking expeditions of the Crimean Tatars and Noghays, subjects of the Ottomans. The Ottoman Empire, whose Islamic laws allowed the enslavement of non-Muslims only and encouraged the emancipation of slaves, was always in need of free labor. The Noghays and the Crimean Tatars responded to the demand, expanding their slave-seeking expeditions to the lands north of the Pontic steppes and often going much deeper into Ukraine and southern Muscovy than the frontier areas. The slave trade supplemented the earnings that the Noghays obtained from animal husbandry and the Crimeans from both husbandry and settled forms of agriculture. Bad harvests generally translated into more raids to the north and more slaves shipped back to the Crimea.

All five routes that the Tatars followed to the settled areas passed through Ukraine. The two routes east of the Dniester led to western Podilia and then to Galicia; the two on the other side of the Boh (Southern Buh) River led to western Podilia and Volhynia, and then again to Galicia; and the last passed through what would become the Sloboda Ukraine region around Kharkiv, going on to southern Muscovy. If the Ukrainian lands of the sixteenth century were incorporated into the Baltic trade because of the demand for cereals, their connection to the Mediterranean trade was due largely to Tatar raiding for slaves. Ukrainians became the main targets and victims of the Ottoman Empire's slave-dependent economy.

Michalon the Lithuanian, a mid-sixteenth-century Ruthenian author who visited the Crimea, described the scope of the slave trade by quoting from his conversation with a local Jew: "One Jew there in Tavria beside its only gate, which stands at the head of the customs office, seeing that our people were constantly being shipped there as captives in numbers too large to count, asked us whether our lands also teemed with people, and whence such innumerable mortals had come." Estimates of the numbers of Ukrainians and Russians brought to the Crimean slave markets in the sixteenth and seventeenth centuries vary from one and a half to three million. Children and adolescents brought the highest prices.[8]

The colonization of the steppe areas, marked by numerous settlements on Radvila's map, was spearheaded by the Volhynian princes and assisted by changes introduced in the region in the aftermath of the Union of Lublin. The Polish crown's creation of a small but mobile standing army, funded from the profits of the royal domains, helped repel Tatar raids and promote the continuing movement of population into the steppe. Another major incentive for the colonization of the steppe borderlands came from their inclusion in the Baltic trade. With increasing demand for grain on the European markets, Ukraine began to earn its future reputation as the breadbasket of Europe. This was the first time that Ukrainian grain had appeared in these markets since the days of Herodotus.

Unexpectedly, colonization was also aided by the introduction of Polish laws and regulations intended to prevent the influx of people into the borderlands, not to increase it. The European demand for grain turned cereal cultivation into a profitable business, leading to the revival of serfdom. A number of Polish laws introduced in Ukraine by the Third Lithuanian Statute of 1588 deprived peasants of the right to own land or move from one manorial estate to another. But the peasants—or, at least, significant numbers of them—refused to obey those laws. They simply fled to the steppe borderlands of Ukraine, where princes and nobles were establishing duty-free settlements that allowed the new arrivals not to perform corvée labor or pay duties for a substantial period of time. In exchange, they had to settle the land and develop it. As serfdom took stronger hold in the central provinces of the Kingdom and the Grand Duchy, more peasants fled to the east and south. Once their duty-free years expired, some stayed, while others moved deeper into the steppe, where they joined the Cossacks, the new borderland segment of the population that was growing in numbers and importance.[9]

The Cossacks are not shown as inhabitants of Ukraine and do not appear on the main Radvila map of the Grand Duchy of Lithuania. Ukraine seems to be reserved for the Volhynian princes alone. The Cossack settlements located along the Dnieper between Kyiv and Cherkasy, including the town of Trakhtemyriv, known to Polish chroniclers of the time as the Cossack headquarters, are not marked on the map as belonging to or settled by the Cossacks. The Cossacks do, however, receive considerable attention on the map of the Dnieper, which depicts the riverbed south of Cherkasy and is richer in specially inserted inscriptions than the main map.

The insert at the very bottom of the Dnieper map explains why the mapmakers decided to produce it. They allegedly did so for three reasons. The first was geographic: the Dnieper is presented as one of the two largest European rivers, the second being the Danube; the Volga is excluded as an Asian river. The second reason was historical: Grand Duke Vytautas, say the mapmakers, used to control the Dnieper estuary in days of old. The third reason was military and political: the Dnieper region, rich in natural resources, served as a point of origin for Tatar attacks on Volhynia and was home to the Cossacks, who disrupted Tatar slave-hunting expeditions. The Dnieper is shown on the map as the Borysthenes, and there are numerous other references to the ancient Greeks; the Tatars, for example, are called Scythians. But despite repeated allusions to ancient times, the mapmakers' attention to Cossacks and Tatars indicates their current rather than historical concerns.

The origins and activities of the Cossacks are described in a text box that appears on the Right Bank of the Dnieper. It reads as follows: "The Cossacks are a martial people, mixed with private [individuals], either deprived of nobility or avoiding corvée labor. . . . They live near the Rapids or cataracts on Dnieper islands fitted with roofs against storms of any kind. They are subject to the command of the chief of the Polish army. They choose their chief from among themselves and easily relieve him of his functions if he proves unsuccessful in subsequent affairs; sometimes they kill him. If they suffer from lack of pay, they customarily make sneak attacks on neighboring towns, and, having razed them, return weighed down with booty, as when, under [Ivan] Pidkova's command, they plundered and razed the Turkish sultan's town of Tighina in Moldavia. If one of their raids proves less than successful, they plunder their homelands so greedily that sometimes their fierce attacks are repelled, and they are defeated."[10]

Judging by the location of the text box with information on the origins and activities of the Cossacks, they occupied lands on the Right Bank of the Dnieper and settled islands along the river from the estuary of the Vorskla (on the Left Bank) to the rapids and the Tomakivka (Tomakówka) settlement beyond the rapids. But the Cossacks are not depicted as the first or only actors in the region. One of the text boxes tells of the construction of a castle on the island of Khortytsia by Prince Dmytro Vyshnevetsky in 1556. The only clearly defined Cossack settlement on the map is that of Tomakivka, which "was once a fortified town, as attested by its remains, and is now an island on the Dnieper rejoicing in the same name, on which the Lower [Dnieper] Cossacks live securely, as if in a well-reinforced fortress." Like other settlements on the Right Bank, it is marked with a cross, indicating that it is a Christian settlement. (With reference to the town of Cherkasy, the mapmakers explain that, despite unsubstantiated claims that its inhabitants were descendants of the Cimmerians of Homer's day, or professed Islam, it is in fact settled by Ruthenians of the Greek faith.) The map clearly puts the Cossacks on the Christian side of the divide, marking Tatar settlements on the Left Bank with crescents.

In general, this description of the Cossacks fits a much more detailed discussion of their history and way of life provided by the Polish historian Joachim Bielski in *Kronika Polska*, a history of the Kingdom of Poland written largely by his father, Marcin

Bielski, and first published in Cracow in 1597. There the Cossacks are represented as fishermen, trappers, and warriors who live on the Dnieper islands beyond the rapids. Bielski mentions Prince Vyshnevetsky and his settlement on Khortytsia Island, providing a detailed description of Cossack campaigns against the Ottomans and the Tatars, including the one led to Moldavia by Ivan Pidkova. Like the makers of the Radvila map, Bielski refers in his description of the Cossacks to Greek authors (he mentions the twelfth-century Byzantine chronicler Joannes Zonaras) but is silent on the ethnic origins of the Cossacks and their religious affiliation.[11]

How does the map's representation of the Cossacks relate to what we know today about their early history and way of life? The first Cossacks indeed lived on and off the rivers, relying not only on fishing but also on banditry, preying on merchants who traveled without sufficient guards. In 1492, the Ukrainian Cossacks made their first appearance in the international arena with such an attack on merchants. According to a complaint sent that year to the grand duke of Lithuania by the Crimean khan, subjects of the duke from the cities of Kyiv and Cherkasy had captured and pillaged a Tatar ship in what appear to have been the lower reaches of the Dnieper. The duke ordered his borderland (the term he used was "Ukrainian") officials to investigate the Cossacks who might have been involved in the raid. He also ordered that the perpetrators be executed and that their belongings, which apparently had to include the stolen merchandise, be given to a representative of the khan.

The khan's complaints to the grand duke were actually of little avail. The Lithuanian borderland officials, who happened to be members of Volhynian princely families, were trying to stop Cossack raids with one hand while using the Cossacks to defend the frontier from the Tatars with the other. In 1553, the grand duke sent the captain of Cherkasy and Kaniv, Prince Dmytro Vyshnevetsky, beyond the Dnieper rapids to build a fortress in order to stop Cossack expeditions from proceeding farther down the river. Vyshnevetsky employed his Cossack servants to accomplish the task. Not surprisingly, the Crimean khan saw the Cossack fortress as an encroachment on his realm, and four years later he sent an army to expel Vyshnevetsky from his redoubt. In folk tradition,

Prince Vyshnevetsky became a popular hero as the first Cossack hetman—the title that the Polish army reserved for its supreme commanders—and a fearless fighter against the Tatars and Ottomans. He also made it into the Radvila map, whose inscription provides information about the construction of the Vyshnevetsky castle on the island of Khortytsia.

By the mid-sixteenth century, the lands south of Kyiv were full of new or revived settlements, many of which were depicted on the Radvila map, including those of Cherkasy, Kaniv, Korsun, Trakhtemyriv, Moshny, and Olshanka. "And the Kyiv region, fortunate and thriving, is also rich in population, for on the Borysthenes and other rivers that flow into it there are plenty of populous towns and many villages," wrote Michalon the Lithuanian. He also explained the origins of the settlers: "Some are hiding from paternal authority, or from slavery, or from service, or from [punishment for] crimes, or from debts, or from something else; others are attracted to it, especially in the spring, by richer game and more plentiful places. And, having tried their luck in its fortresses, they never come back from there." Judging by Michalon's description, the Cossacks were supplementing their gains from hunting and fishing with robbery. He wrote that some poor and dirty Cossack huts were "full of expensive silks, precious stones, sables and other furs, and spices." There he found "silk cheaper than in Vilnius, and pepper cheaper than salt." These were delicacies and luxury items that merchants had been transporting from the Ottoman Empire to Muscovy or the Kingdom of Poland.[12]

The Cossacks became the direct responsibility of Kostiantyn Ostrozky, the most powerful Volhynian prince, in 1559, when he was appointed palatine of Kyiv. His jurisdiction expanded to Kaniv and Cherkasy, and his responsibilities included the Cossacks, who continued to cause problems at home and in the international arena. In 1577, a Cossack detachment led by a certain Ivan Pidkova captured the city of Iaşi, the capital of the Ottoman protectorate of Moldavia. Pidkova was later seized with the help of one of the royal borderland governors, Janusz Zbaraski (Zbarazky), and executed on the orders of King Stefan Batory. Under Batory, the first efforts to recruit the Cossacks into military service began, not so much to use them as a fighting force as to remove them from the lands beyond the rapids and establish some form of control over that unruly crowd. The Livonian War increased the demand for fighting men on the Lithuanian border with Muscovy, and a number of Cossack units were formed in the 1570s, one of them numbering as many as five hundred men.

The reorganization of the Cossacks from militias in the service of local border officials into military units under the command of army officers inaugurated a new era in the history of Cossackdom. For the first time, the term "registered Cossacks" came into use. Cossacks taken into military service and thus included in the "register" were exempted from paying taxes and not subject to the jurisdiction of local officials. They also received a salary. There was, of course, no shortage of those wanting to be registered, but the Polish crown recruited only limited numbers, and salary was paid and privileges recognized only during active service. But those not included in the register to begin with or excluded from it at the end of a given war or military campaign refused to give up their status, giving rise to endless disputes between Cossacks and border officials. The creation of the register solved one problem for the government, only to breed another.

In 1590 the Commonwealth Diet decreed the creation of a force of one thousand registered Cossacks to protect the Ukrainian borderlands from the Tatars and the Tatars from the unregistered Cossacks. Although the king issued the requisite ordinance, little came of it. By 1591, Ukraine was engulfed by the first Cossack uprising. The Cossacks, who until then had been harassing Ottoman possessions—the Crimean Khanate, the Principality of Moldavia (an Ottoman dependency), and the Black Sea coast—now turned their energies inward. They were rebelling not against the state but against their own "godfathers"—the Volhynian princes, in particular Prince Janusz Ostrogski (Ostrozky) and his father, Kostiantyn. Janusz was the captain of Bila Tserkva, a castle and a Cossack stronghold south of Kyiv, while Kostiantyn, the palatine of Kyiv, "supervised" his son's activities. The Ostrozkys, father and son, had full control of the region. No one from the local nobility dared to defy the powerful princes, who were busy extending their possessions by taking over the lands of the petty nobility.

One of the noble victims of the Ostrozkys, Kryshtof Kosynsky (Krzysztof Kosiński), turned out to be a Cossack chieftain as well. When Janusz Ostrogski seized his land, which he held on the basis of a royal grant, Kosynsky did not waste time on a futile complaint to the king but gathered his Cossacks and attacked the Bila Tserkva castle, the headquarters of the younger Ostrozky. An attack by one noble on the holdings of another to resolve a conflict over land was nothing unusual for the Commonwealth. It was unheard of, however, for a petty noble to assault a prince, and the Ostrozkys were caught by surprise. Soon the Cossacks were in control of another major fortress, this time on the Left Bank of the Dnieper—the city of Pereiaslav, whose princes had once ruled lands as far away as Moscow. Emboldened by these victories, Kosynsky marched westward to Volhynia, where he was finally defeated by a private army assembled by the Ostrozkys. Kosynsky suffered another defeat near Cherkasy, this time at the hands of another scion of Volhynia, Prince Oleksandr Vyshnevetsky.

The princes managed to put down the revolt without asking for help from the royal authorities. Ironically, the godfathers of the Cossacks punished their unruly children with the help of other Cossacks who were in their private service. By far the best known of Ostrozky's Cossack chieftains was Severyn Nalyvaiko. He came to Ostrih as a youth together with his brother, Demian, who became a member of Ostrozky's learned circle and a published author. Severyn, for his part, served the prince with his saber. He led the Ostrozky Cossacks into battle against Kosynsky's army and then gathered dispersed Cossacks in the steppes of Podilia to lead them as far away as possible from the Ostrozkys' possessions. The destination to which Nalyvaiko took them was the Ottoman vassal state of Moldavia. Once the Cossacks returned from their Moldavian expedition, Ostrozky tried to use them to pillage the estates of his opponents in the struggle over the church union. Nalyvaiko's Cossacks were spotted attacking the estates of the two Orthodox bishops who had traveled to Rome to petition for union with the Catholic Church. Attacks on other estates took the Cossacks to places as distant from the Ukrainian steppes as the lands of today's Belarus.

There was, however, a limit to what the Ostrozkys could control by manipulating the Cossack rebellion. The Cossacks elected their own commander, whom they followed into battle, but once the expedition was over, they were free to remove or even execute him if he acted against their interests. Then there were major divisions among the Cossacks themselves, which were not limited to registered versus unregistered men. The registered Cossacks were recruited from the landowning Cossack class, whose members resided in towns and settlements between Kyiv and Cherkasy. They had a chance to obtain special rights associated with royal service. But there was also another group, the Zaporozhian Cossacks, who had a fortified settlement called the Sich (after the wooden palisade that protected it) on the islands beyond the rapids. They were beyond the reach of royal officials, caused most of the trouble with the Crimean Tatars, and, in turbulent times, served as a magnet for the dissatisfied townsmen and peasants who fled to the steppes.

Nalyvaiko, charged by Ostrozky with managing the Cossack riffraff, soon found himself in an uneasy alliance with the unruly Zaporozhians. By 1596 he was no longer doing Ostrozky's bidding but acting on his own, leading a revolt greater than the one initiated by Kosynsky. The early 1590s saw a number of years of bad harvest, which caused famine. Starvation drove more peasants out of the noble estates and into Cossack ranks. This time the princely retinues were insufficient to suppress the uprising: the royal army was called in, headed by the commander of the Polish armed forces. In May 1596, the Polish army surrounded the Cossack encampment on the Left Bank of the Dnieper. The "old" or town Cossacks turned against the "new" ones and surrendered Nalyvaiko to the Poles in exchange for an amnesty. The princely servant turned Cossack rebel was executed in Warsaw, becoming a martyr for the Cossack and Orthodox causes in the eyes of the Cossack chroniclers.[13]

In the 1590s, the Cossacks entered into the foreign-policy calculations not only of the Commonwealth and the Ottoman Empire but also of Central and West European powers. In 1594, Erich von Lassota, an emissary of the Holy Roman emperor, Rudolf II, visited the Zaporozhian Cossacks with a proposal to join his master's war against the Ottomans. In the same year Aleksandar Komulović (Alessandro Comuleo) delivered letters to the Cossacks from Pope Clement VIII urging them to join the European powers in the war against the Ottomans. Little came of those missions, apart from Komulović's letters and Lassota's diary, which described the democratic order that prevailed in the Zaporozhian Host and enriched our knowledge of early Cossack history.[14]

Some scholars have suggested that Lassota or a member of his mission supplied Radvila and his cartographers with information on the Dnieper and the Cossacks. While this supposition seems far-fetched, there is little doubt that, with regard to the religious affiliation of the Cossacks, the makers of the Radvila map, Lassota, and Komulović shared the same position. They turned a blind eye to the division between Orthodox Cossacks and Catholic nobles, which was exacerbated by battles over the Union of Brest (1596). Instead, they treated the Cossacks as part of the common Christian bulwark against the Islamic threat presented by the Ottomans and their Crimean and Noghay subjects.

At the turn of the seventeenth century, Cossackdom was a relatively new political, cultural, and military phenomenon. Miraculously, it found its way onto a map that presented a princely view of Eastern Europe, oriented as much backward as forward. How did it happen? The answer lies in the political and economic interests of the Volhynian princes, who were busy expanding their possessions in the Dnieper region after the Union of Lublin. The princes and the Cossacks emerged as both partners and rivals in the colonization of the steppelands, defined on the Radvila map as "Volynia Ulterior," "Ukraine," or the "Lower Dnieper" area. The close relations between the two groups are reflected in the map references to Vyshnevetsky's expedition to Khortytsia, while their conflict finds reflection in the mention of Pidkova's campaign against Moldavia and occasional Cossack attacks on their own homeland, which may be understood as indirect references to the revolts of Kryshtof Kosynsky and Severyn Nalyvaiko against the Ostrozky princes.

The Cossacks are presented on the map as warriors protecting the borderlands of the Commonwealth and claimed as members of the Polish state and the Christian world. The latter claim reflects not so much the religious and ideological loyalties of the Cossacks as it does the hopes that the outside world invested in them in the face of growing confrontation with the Ottomans and their Crimean Tatar subjects. The Ottoman threat increased dramatically in the 1590s, as did the activities and revolts of the

Cossacks, making them attractive allies in the eyes of European rulers involved in military confrontations with the Ottomans during the rise of Ahmed I (r. 1590–1617). As Lassota and Komulović tried to recruit the Cossacks into the service of Catholic rulers, the Catholic bishop of Kyiv, Józef Wereszczyński, penned a treatise arguing for the formation of Cossack regiments in the lands south of Ukraine to protect the Kingdom of Poland from Tatar attacks (1596). The rapid transformation of the Cossacks from Cimmerian or Muslim Circassians into Christian warriors, which took place in the imagination of European rulers and diplomats of the 1590s, found its visual reflection on the Radvila map created at the turn of the seventeenth century.

3.

Russia and Ukraine: Did They Reunite in 1654?

In 1920, the prominent Ukrainian historian and political activist Viacheslav Lypynsky (Wacław Lipiński) published a book entitled *Ukraine at the Turning Point.* In it he discussed the dramatic changes brought about in mid-seventeenth century Ukraine by the Khmelnytsky Uprising, the rise of the Cossack state known in historiography as the Hetmanate, and the ensuing military confrontations, first with the Polish-Lithuanian Commonwealth and then with Muscovy. The book was later treated as a manifesto of the "statist" school of Ukrainian historiography.

Among Lypynsky's contributions to the study of the period was the introduction into historiographic discourse of the concept of the Pereiaslav Legend—a body of historical myths that developed in the eighteenth century around the Cossack-Muscovite agreement proclaimed in the town of Pereiaslav in January 1654. The agreement, formalized during the Cossack delegation's visit to Moscow in March of the same year, established the tsar's protectorate over the Cossack polity led by Hetman Bohdan Khmelnytsky. Lypynsky argued that by presenting the Pereiaslav Agreement as an act of voluntary union between the Little Russian (Ukrainian) nation and the Muscovite state, whose Orthodox religion it shared, the eighteenth-century Cossack elites eased the process of integration into the Russian Empire for themselves but compromised the interests of their state and opened the door to the creation of the concept of an all-Russian nation.[1]

What Lypynsky left out of his analysis were the ever-changing political circumstances under which the Pereiaslav Legend functioned in Ukraine after the defeat of Hetman Ivan Mazepa's revolt against Tsar Peter I. Twenty years after the Battle of Poltava (1709), the Pereiaslav myth provided historical ammunition for Cossack attempts to restore the "rights and privileges" guaranteed by the "Articles of Bohdan Khmelnytsky." That myth helped the Cossack elites restore not only some of their own rights and privileges but also the institution of the hetmancy, abolished by Peter I after the death of Mazepa's successor, Hetman Ivan Skoropadsky (1722).[2]

Another element of the Pereiaslav mythology that escaped Lypynsky's attention was the development of the "reunification of Ukraine with Russia" paradigm—the official formula that defined the purpose of the Pereiaslav Agreement in Russian imperial and Soviet historiography. The origins of the reunification paradigm, which dominated the Soviet historiography of Russo-Ukrainian relations for decades, can be traced back at least to the end of the eighteenth century. After the second partition of Poland in 1793, Empress Catherine II struck a medal welcoming Polish and Lithuanian Rus´ into the empire. The inscription read: "I have recovered what was torn away."[3] The same statist approach was reflected in the writings of the nineteenth-century Russian historian Mikhail Pogodin, a leader of the Pan-Slav movement. He claimed that the leitmotif of Russian history was the reclamation of those parts of the Russian land that had been lost to western neighbors since the times of Yaroslav the Wise. The first scholar to fully merge the statist and nation-based elements of the reunification paradigm in his historical survey of Russia was Nikolai Ustrialov, who maintained that all Eastern Slavs constituted one Russian nation and that the various parts of Rus´ professed a "desire for union."

Ustrialov's ideas shaped the interpretation of Russia's relations with its East Slavic neighbors for generations of Russian historians. At the turn of the twentieth century, a modified version of the Ustrialov thesis made up the core of Vasilii Kliuchevsky's argument.[4] Even some Ukrainian historians, such as Panteleimon Kulish, the author of the *History of the Reunification of Rus´*, bought into the idea. The same is true of nineteenth-century Russophile historiography in Galicia, but most Ukrainian historians, led by Mykhailo Hrushevsky, rejected the reunification paradigm.

They regarded Ukraine as a separate nation whose origins reached back to Kyivan Rus´: it had not been torn away from any other nation and thus had no need to be reunited with its other parts.[5]

Early Soviet historians concurred with Hrushevsky in regarding Russia, Ukraine, and Belarus as separate nations and kept their historical narratives apart in every period except that of Kyivan Rus´. But in the 1930s, as Russian nationalism (in its Great Russian form) returned to the political scene, that view was revised and elements of the old imperial approach reintroduced into the interpretation of the Pereiaslav Agreement. The view of the agreement as a continuation of Russian imperial policy was abandoned in favor of the "lesser evil" formula, whereby the annexation of Cossack Ukraine by Muscovy was viewed as a better alternative than its subordination to the Ottomans or to the Kingdom of Poland. After the Second World War, when class-based discourse declined and the Russocentric nation-based approach reemerged in Soviet historical works, the concept of "annexation" was dropped altogether and that of "reunification" reintroduced into historical discourse. A new formula was invented to describe the Pereiaslav Agreement, which was now to be called the "reunification of Ukraine and Russia."[6]

After the Second World War, there were two commemorations of the event in the Soviet period. The first, in 1954, was a large-scale event held with great fanfare and accompanied by the transfer of sovereignty over the Crimean Peninsula from Russia to Ukraine. The Central Committee of the Communist Party of the Soviet Union approved a collection of "Theses on the Three-Hundredth Anniversary of the Reunification of Ukraine with Russia" that shaped the interpretation of Russo-Ukrainian relations until the end of Soviet rule. In 1979, when the 325th anniversary of the Pereiaslav Council rolled around, only the Central Committee of the Communist Party of Ukraine issued a resolution outlining the commemoration program and restating the interpretation established in 1954.[7]

This new/old reunification paradigm took into account the Soviet treatment of Ukrainian history as a distinct subject and accepted the view that by the mid-seventeenth century there existed two separate East Slavic nations. But the attempt to merge pre-1917 and post-revolutionary historiographic concepts produced a contradiction. How could Ukraine reunite with Russia when, according to the official line, there had been no Russians, Ukrainians, or Belarusians in Kyivan Rus′? Soviet historians were discouraged from asking questions of that kind. The reunification concept became official doctrine in 1954, when the Central Committee of the Communist Party of the Soviet Union approved the "Theses on the Three-Hundredth Anniversary of the Reunification of Ukraine with Russia."

Scholarly discussion of the meaning and historical importance of the Pereiaslav Agreement resumed only in the late 1980s, following the advent of *glasnost*. Ukrainian historians overwhelmingly rejected the reunification paradigm, replacing the imperial- and Soviet-era "reunification" with the terms "Ukrainian Revolution" and "National-Liberation War" to denote the Khmelnytsky Uprising and its aftermath. Both terms stressed the national characteristics of the uprising. No less decisive in rejecting the term and the concept symbolized by it were Belarusian specialists in the early modern history of Eastern Europe. Their Russian colleagues remained much more loyal to the old imperial and Soviet interpretations of the Pereiaslav Agreement. One of them, a specialist in Russian diplomatic history named Lev Zaborovsky, supported the continued use of the reunification terminology by arguing that the desire of the Ukrainian population for union with Muscovy was apparent from the historical sources of the period. Yet Zaborovsky had no objection to calling the Khmelnytsky Uprising a "war of national liberation" as long as it was considered to have been anti-Polish.[8]

The reunification terminology seems to have made a comeback in Russian historiography after the fall of the Soviet Union. But was there indeed a reunification in Pereiaslav? And if there was, who reunited with whom? These are the questions I shall address, approaching them through a study of the construction and evolution of East Slavic group identities in the first half of the seventeenth century. An answer to this question must be based on a long view of Muscovite-Ruthenian relations and the Pereiaslav Agreement, going back at least to the turn of the seventeenth century.

The Origins

It was at the turn of the seventeenth century that a number of Orthodox intellectuals began to develop a view that prepared the way for what nineteenth-century historiography would call the "reunification of Rus´." That view was based on the notion of the dynastic, religious, and ethnic affinity of the two Rus´ nations. The origin of all three elements in the Ruthenian discourse of the time can be traced back to a letter of 1592 from the Lviv Orthodox brotherhood requesting alms from the tsar. The letter reintroduced Great Russian/Little Russian terminology into contemporary discourse. Its argument capitalized on the idea of religious unity between Muscovy and Polish-Lithuanian Rus´, employing the notion of one "Rusian stock" (*rod Rossiiskii*)—a community of peoples/nations (*plemia*) led by the Muscovite tsar, the heir of St. Volodymyr.[9] Thereafter, the Ruthenian Orthodox constantly employed all three themes in letters to Moscow as they sought ways to strengthen their case for alms and other forms of support from the tsar and the patriarch.

The idea of the ethnic affinity of the two Rus´ nations took on special importance in the writings of the new Orthodox hierarchy consecrated by Patriarch Theophanes in 1620. The hierarchs, who were not merely denied recognition but actually outlawed by the Polish authorities, could not take office in their eparchies and found themselves confined to Dnieper Ukraine. They needed all the support they could get, including support from Muscovy, and even contemplated emigration to the Orthodox tsardom—a plan later implemented by Bishop Iosyf Kurtsevych. Thus the famous *Protestation* of the Orthodox hierarchy (1621) asserted that the Ruthenians shared "one faith and worship, one origin, language and customs" with Muscovy.[10] The author of the Hustynia Chronicle (written in Kyiv in the 1620s, possibly by the archimandrite of the Kyivan Cave Monastery, Zakhariia Kopystensky) established a biblical genealogy for the Slavic nations that listed the Muscovites next to the Rus´ and called them *Rus´-Moskva*.[11]

The most compelling case for the ethnic affinity of the two Rus´ nations was made by the newly consecrated metropolitan himself. In a letter of August 1624 to Mikhail Romanov, Iov Boretsky compared the fate of the two Rus´ nations to that of the biblical brothers Benjamin and Joseph. Boretsky called upon the Muscovite tsar (Joseph) to help his persecuted brethren. "Take thought for us as well, people of the same birth as your Rus´ (*rosyiskyi*) tribe," wrote the metropolitan, using the latter term to denote both Ruthenians and Muscovites. A close reading of the texts indicates that the ethnic motif was a supplementary one in letters from the Ruthenian Orthodox hierarchs to Moscow, but it is of special interest for our discussion as one of the first instances of the use of early modern national terminology in relations between the two Ruses.[12]

How did the Muscovite elites react to the ideas put forward by the Ruthenian seekers of the tsar's alms? As might be expected, given the experience of the Time of Troubles, continuing military conflicts with the Commonwealth, and the general tendency of Muscovite society toward self-righteous isolation, the response was by no means enthusiastic. Patriarch Filaret was reluctant to accept and use in his correspondence the title of Patriarch of Great and Little Rus´ attributed to him by the Ruthenian bishop Isaia Kopynsky in 1622. In letters to the Orthodox in the Commonwealth, he would carefully style himself Patriarch of Great Rus´ (instead of all Rus´), apparently to avoid provoking a negative reaction from the Commonwealth authorities. The tsar did likewise. In 1634, Muscovite envoys assured Polish diplomats that the reference to "all Rus´" in his title had nothing to do with the Polish-Lithuanian "Little Rus´."[13] There was more understanding between the two parties on the issue of the Kyivan origins of the Muscovite ruling dynasty.

The Religious Schism

The attitude of the Muscovites toward Kyivan Orthodoxy is fully apparent in their insistence on the rebaptism of the Ruthenian Orthodox in their state. The Orthodox council of 1620 issued a pastoral letter entitled "Ukase on How to Investigate and on the Belarusians Themselves," which ordained the rebaptism not only of non-Orthodox but also of Orthodox Ruthenians in Muscovy. According to the "Ukase," those Ruthenian Orthodox who had been baptized by infusion (the pouring of water) and not by triple immersion, as was the custom in Muscovy, were to be rebaptized along with Catholics, Protestants, and Uniates. The policy was extended to cover those who did not know how they had been baptized or had received communion in non-Orthodox (including Uniate) churches. Only those who had been baptized by triple immersion (excluding confirmation) could be admitted to Orthodoxy by confirmation.

The "Ukase" led to the mass rebaptism of Orthodox Ruthenians who crossed the Muscovite border and entered the tsar's service between the 1620s and 1640s. Before rebaptism the converts were ordered to read (or have read to them, if they were illiterate) the text of an oath very similar to the one administered to those who entered the tsar's service. The convert promised to sacrifice his life, if necessary, for the Orthodox faith and the health of the tsar. He also swore not to leave the Muscovite state, not to return to his former faith, and not to instigate any treason in his new country.[14]

The "Ukase" and the policy promoted by it treated Orthodox Ruthenians not only as foreigners *(inozemtsy)* but also as either non-Christians or not entirely Orthodox (even those whose baptism was considered impeccable were allowed to join the Muscovite church only after making an act of contrition). But what was the reaction of those who accepted a second baptism, contrary to the laws of the church? Did they protest or call upon their fellow Christians and Eastern Slavs to come to their senses? We know of no such instances. The award given by the tsarist authorities to the new converts apparently silenced the Christian conscience of those who knew that there was something wrong with the practice. This, at least, is the impression given by the sources on the mass rebaptism of almost seven hundred Cossacks who entered the Muscovite service in 1618–19.

The vast majority of them were registered by Muscovite scribes as "Cherkasians" (meaning "Cossacks") in the Muscovite "table of ranks" and received a stipend commensurate with their status. But once they realized that non-Orthodox converts were getting a stipend twice as large for full rebaptism as the one paid to the Orthodox joining the Muscovite church by confirmation, more than half the Cossacks declared themselves non-Orthodox "Poles." Since the Muscovite scribes did not distinguish between Catholics and Uniates, the Cossack declarations, claiming either real or only imagined connection to the Union, were readily accepted. Moreover, declaring oneself a "Pole" entailed a larger salary for joining the tsar's service, because nobles, whom the Muscovite scribes usually treated as ethnic Poles, were paid better than rank-and-file Cossacks.

One of the former "Cherkasians" even proclaimed himself a noble of Jewish faith and descent and was registered as such by the Muscovite authorities upon his baptism. It would appear that the Cossacks (because of whom the ukase of 1620 had been adopted—it was also known as the "Ukase on the Baptism of Latins and Cherkasians") did not mind rebaptism as long as they were well paid for it. Besides, quite a few of them were joining the Muscovite service because they were married to Russian women whom they had met during the war, and ratification of their Orthodoxy by the local church also meant the recognition of their marriages, followed by integration into Muscovite society, sometimes with noble rank.[15]

The rebaptism of the Ukrainian Cossacks in Muscovy shows vividly that, while the Ruthenian Orthodox hierarchs could obtain alms by stressing religious affinity in their letters to the tsar and the patriarch of Moscow, the Muscovite authorities were by no means persuaded that they belonged to the same faith. Even if properly baptized, the Ruthenian Orthodox were tainted in the eyes of the Muscovites by their allegiance to a non-Orthodox ruler and everyday contact with the non-Orthodox. (Certainly they did not call upon their priests to reconsecrate the icons in their homes after every visit by non-Orthodox, as was the case with the Muscovite peasant described by Olearius).

What about the argument of ethnic affinity advanced by the Lviv brotherhood and its biblical interpretation presented by Metropolitan Boretsky in his story of Joseph and Benjamin? Here it would appear that the Ruthenian Orthodox had even less chance of being heard, or, if heard, of being understood. With regard to Orthodoxy, while they disagreed, at least they spoke the same language and used the same vocabulary. When it came to nationality, the Muscovites apparently lacked the language and vocabulary to deal with the issue. The Muscovite language of the time lacked terms not only for such Ruthenian phenomena as "church brotherhood" and "Uniates" but also for "nation." As noted above, the term *narod*, which served to render that concept in Ruthenian, meant just a group of people in Russian. Thus we know of no Ruthenian letter touching upon the national theme that was mentioned or acknowledged by the Muscovite side in any way.

In official correspondence, reference to the Ruthenians was made predominantly in political rather than national or religious terms, and they figured either as Poles or as Lithuanians. The Muscovite scribes who conducted negotiations and disputes with Lavrentii Zyzanii referred to his Ruthenian language as "Lithuanian." An exception was made only for the Cossacks, who were called "Cherkasians," but, as noted, this was a social rather than an ethnic or national designation. The situation was somewhat better with regard to ecclesiastical texts. There, as the title of the ukase of 1620 makes apparent, the term "Belarusians" was used to denote the Ruthenian population of the Commonwealth. But was it an ethnonational or an ethnoconfessional term? Its use in combination with the term "Cherkasian" indicates that it was not a marker of social status or identity.

The context in which it appears in ecclesiastical documents indicates that it was used to designate the Orthodox population of the Commonwealth. It could also be applied to Uniates, but Uniates often fell into the category of "Poles," the term used to denote either nobles or Catholics and Protestants of the Commonwealth irrespective of national background. Thus "Belarusian" was primarily an ethnonational term. It served an important purpose in distinguishing the East Slavic population of the Commonwealth from its Polish and Lithuanian neighbors. At the same time, it distinguished that population from the East Slavic inhabitants of Muscovy. The invention of a special term for the Ruthenian population of the Commonwealth, the treatment of that population as not entirely Christian, and the reservation of the term "Rusians" for subjects of the Muscovite tsar indicate that although the Muscovite elites recognized the Ruthenians as a group distinct from the Poles and Lithuanians, they also made a very clear political, religious, and ethnic distinction between themselves and their relatives to the west.

The Orthodox Alliance

A new stage in relations between Kyiv and Moscow began in the summer of 1648 at the initiative of the Cossack hetman Bohdan Khmelnytsky when he asked Muscovy to join forces with the Cossacks in the war against the Commonwealth. The situation of 1632 was repeating itself, with the difference that it was now the Cossacks, not the tsar, who were eager to obtain support. After the defeat of 1634, Muscovy was more than cautious. Besides, the specter of a new Cossack-led uprising that might spread to Muscovy and provoke a new Time of Troubles discouraged the Muscovites from becoming openly involved in the conflict. They adopted a compromise tactic: those of the Cossacks and rebels who wanted to cross the border were welcomed in Muscovy (on one occasion, Cossack troops were even allowed to launch a surprise attack on the Grand Duchy of Lithuania from Muscovite territory), but the tsar would not start a new war with the Commonwealth.

Not until 1651 was Muscovy finally prepared to change its policy of noninterference in Commonwealth affairs. Preparations were even made to convene an Assembly of the Land to sanction the war, but the Commonwealth army's defeat of the Cossacks at Berestechko put an end to the plan. By 1653, unable to obtain military assistance from the Ottomans and losing the cooperation of the khan, Khmelnytsky demanded that the Muscovite rulers finally make up their mind. That autumn, a special convocation of the Assembly of the Land decided to take Khmelnytsky and the Cossacks "with their towns" (meaning the territory of the Hetmanate) under the tsar's "high hand." An embassy led by the boyar Vasilii Buturlin was sent to Ukraine to administer an oath to the Cossack leadership and the rank-and-file Cossacks. In January 1654 the embassy met with Khmelnytsky in the town of Pereiaslav. After brief negotiations that were not very satisfactory to the Cossack side, a council was convened to formally approve Cossack submission to the tsar.

Historians still differ on what the Pereiaslav Agreement amounted to. Was it indeed an agreement? After all, no document was signed in Pereiaslav, and the tsar's approval of the conditions of submission was given much later in Moscow. If it was an agreement, was it a personal union, real union, alliance, federation, confederation, vassalage, protectorate, or outright incorporation? How did that arrangement compare with previous ones, such as the Zboriv Agreement of 1649 with the king, or agreements concluded by Muscovy with previously incorporated territories and peoples?[16]

Of greatest interest to us is not the legal status of the Pereiaslav Agreement but the discourse that accompanied its preparation and legitimized its conclusion. If Muscovy's involvement in the war with the Commonwealth was the main goal of Cossack diplomacy, what ideological arguments did Khmelnytsky and his associates use to convince the tsar to send his troops against Poland-Lithuania? Khmelnytsky's letters to the tsar and to his courtiers and voevodas provide sufficient information to answer this question. They indicate that, from the very beginning of that correspondence in the summer of 1648, the religious motif had a prominent place.

The tsar emerges from the hetman's letters as first and foremost an Orthodox Christian ruler duty-bound to assist fellow Orthodox Christians rebelling against Catholic persecution of their church. Khmelnytsky sought to lure the tsar into the conflict by invoking the mirage of a vast Orthodox empire including not only Cossack Ukraine and Polish-Lithuanian Rus´ but also the Orthodox Balkans and Greece. All the Orthodox—Greeks, Serbs, Bulgarians, Moldavians, and Wallachians—argued Khmelnytsky in his conversation with Arsenii Sukhanov, a Muscovite monk and one-time secretary of Patriarch Filaret, wanted to be united under the rule of the Muscovite tsar.[17]

Khmelnytsky also promised the tsar a rebellion in Belarus: as soon as Muscovy dispatched its troops to the front, the hetman intended to send letters to "the Belarusian people (*liudi*) living under Lithuania" in Orsha, Mahilioŭ, and other towns, setting off a revolt of forces two hundred thousand strong.[18] If the tsar refused to take the Zaporozhian Host "under his high hand," Khmelnytsky threatened to ally himself of necessity with the Muslim Turks and Tatars. Since the prospective alliance with the "infidels" would be directed first and foremost against Muscovy, such threats prompted the Muscovite authorities to reach a final decision in the autumn of 1653.[19]

How did the Muscovite authorities react to claims of confessional solidarity from people whom they regarded after the Time of Troubles not only as not entirely Orthodox but also as not entirely Christian, and whose representatives continued to be rebaptized once they crossed the Muscovite border? Surprisingly, given what we know about Muscovite religious attitudes of the earlier period, those appeals were heard, understood, and even welcomed. In fact, it was the common Orthodox discourse that created the ideological foundation for the Pereiaslav Agreement. How did that happen?

First of all, even after the Time of Troubles, Orthodoxy remained a potent weapon in the Muscovite foreign-policy arsenal. As noted earlier, Orthodox connections and rhetoric were put to use by Moscow during the Smolensk War of 1632–34 between Muscovy and Poland-Lithuania to attract Zaporozhian Cossacks to the tsar's side. Secondly, Muscovy entered into the union with Cossack Ukraine with very different views on Orthodoxy than those it had held in the aftermath of the Time of Troubles. Led by the new and energetic Patriarch Nikon, it was trying to open itself to the Orthodox world: the Kyivan Christianity once condemned by Patriarch Filaret could now serve as a much-needed bridge to that world. Nikon, bombarded by letters from Khmelnytsky, was in favor of extending a Muscovite protectorate to the Cossacks. But changes in the Muscovite attitude toward fellow Orthodox outside the tsar's realm had begun even before Nikon assumed the patriarchal throne in 1652.

An important stimulus for change was the debate over the marriage of Prince Waldemar of the Netherlands to Grand Princess Irina Mikhailovna. The event that ended the career of that admirer of Kyivan learning, Prince Semen Shakhovskoi, also prompted the Muscovite church to reach out to fellow Orthodox abroad. The debates with Lutheran pastors showed a lack of training, skills, and sophistication on the part of the Muscovite intellectuals. The church was in need of reform, and calls for it were coming not only from the capital but also from the regions. The movement of the Zealots of Piety was gathering strength in the provinces, and the ascension of Aleksei Mikhailovich to the throne in 1645 made its adherents influential at court as well. These new conditions called for a complete overhaul of Orthodox doctrine, and the formerly rejected Greek learning was now re-garded as the solution to the problem. But where could one find enough polyglots to translate from the Greek? The eyes of the Muscovite reformers turned to the learned monks of Kyiv.

In the autumn of 1648 the tsar wrote to the Orthodox bishop of Chernihiv, asking him to send to Moscow monks who could translate the Bible into Slavonic. In the summer of the following year, with the blessing of Metropolitan Sylvestr Kosov of Kyiv, the learned monks Arsenii Satanovsky (it would be interesting to know what the Muscovites made of his "Satanic" surname) and Iepifanii Slavynetsky arrived in Moscow, becoming the founders of the Ruthenian colony there. (It later counted such luminaries as Simeon Polatsky among its prominent members.) The years 1648–49 also saw the publication or reprinting in Moscow of a number of earlier Kyivan works, including the Orthodox con-fession of faith (*Brief Compendium of Teachings about the Articles of the Faith*) composed under the supervision of Petro Mohyla and approved by the council of Eastern patriarchs. The Muscovite Orthodox were clearly trying to catch up with their coreligionists abroad, who were moving quickly toward the confessional reform of their church. They hoped for enlightenment from Greece, but what they got was the beginning of the Ruthenization of Mus-covite Orthodoxy.[20]

The elevation to the patriarchal throne of Metropolitan Nikon, who was close to reformist circles in Moscow, strengthened the hand of those in the Muscovite church who were prepared to look to Kyiv for inspiration. At the last prewar negotiations with Commonwealth diplomats, the Poles maintained that the Mus-covites and the Orthodox Ruthenians were not in fact coreligion-ists, for the Muscovite faith was as far removed from Ruthenian Orthodoxy as it was from the Union and Roman Catholicism. The Muscovite envoys rejected their argument. They also ignored Polish accusations that Khmelnytsky had abandoned Orthodoxy and accepted Islam. Indeed, they turned the issue of the tsar's right to protect the liberties of his coreligionists into the main jus-tification for his intervention in Commonwealth affairs.[21] When the Assembly of the Land finally approved the decision to enter the war with the Commonwealth in the autumn of 1653, it did so not only to defend the honor of the Muscovite tsar, allegedly besmirched by Commonwealth officials' errors in citing his title (one of them consisted in calling the tsar Mikhail Filaretovich instead of Mikhail Fedorovich, as the secretaries used the monastic name of the tsar's father instead of his Christian name), but also "for the sake of the Orthodox Christian faith and the holy churches of God."[22]

The Muscovite embassy dispatched to Khmelnytsky scarcely missed an opportunity to visit a Ruthenian Orthodox church or take part in a religious procession along its way. It was met not only by Cossacks but also by burghers solemnly led by priests, who welcomed the embassy with long baroque-style speeches and sermons. The conclusion of the Pereiaslav Agreement itself was accompanied by a solemn church service. In his speech at Pereiaslav the tsar's envoy, Vasilii Buturlin, mentioned not only the Muscovite saints to whose support he attributed the success of the whole enterprise but also SS. Antonii and Feodosii of the Kyivan Cave Monastery and St. Barbara, highly venerated in the Kyiv metropolitanate, whose relics were preserved in one of the Kyivan monasteries.[23]

Together and Apart in Pereiaslav

What about ethnic motives for the "reunification"? Were they entirely absent from Cossack negotiations with the tsar? Although Khmelnytsky defined certain elements of the uprising in ethnic terms in his letters to Muscovy, it appears that the hetman and his scribes never made the seemingly natural link between the two Rus´ nations. In a letter to the voevoda Semen Bolkhovsky in the summer of 1648, Khmelnytsky complained about the persecution of "our Rus´ Orthodox Christians," but in his attempt to involve the tsar in the Cossack-Polish conflict he made no use of the theme of ethnic affinity between the two parts of Rus´; instead, he invited the tsar to seek the Polish throne, which was vacant at the time.[24]

That did not change in Khmelnytsky's subsequent letters to Moscow.[25] What changed was the way in which he referred to his homeland. If at first he called it Rus´ (the name he also used in his letters to the Polish king), from the spring of 1653 he began to refer to it as Little Rus´, thereby distinguishing between Ruthenia and Muscovy. In January 1654 he even introduced a corresponding change into the tsar's official title, addressing him not as "sovereign of all Rus´" but as "sovereign of Great and Little Rus´."[26] The tsar accepted this change in his title.[27] The beginning of the new war with the Commonwealth clearly freed him from the Muscovite envoys' claim of 1634 that the Polish Little Rus´ had nothing to do with the tsar's "all Rus´." Now the tsar claimed Little Rus´ as well, and his title was changed accordingly to avoid the ambiguity of 1634.

In accepting the formula "Great and Little Rus´," did the tsar and his Muscovite entourage also accept the ethnic affinity of the two Ruses as an important element in their conceptualization of events? Available sources indicate that this is extremely unlikely. The tsar's ideologists continued to think not just primarily but almost exclusively in dynastic terms. They saw the Cossack territories as just another part of the tsar's patrimony. In December 1653, the tsar's chancellery addressed the voevodas dispatched to Kyiv as "boyars and voevodas of the patrimony of his tsarist majesty, the Grand Principality of Kyiv." In April 1654, Aleksei Mikhailovich referred to Kyiv as his patrimony in a letter to Bohdan Khmelnytsky himself. His full title now included references to the principalities of Kyiv and Chernihiv.[28] We do not know how Khmelnytsky reacted to these manifestations of the tsar's patrimonial thinking. Nor are we certain of the meaning with which the hetman himself invested the terms Little and Great Rus´, for even after Pereiaslav he occasionally referred to his homeland as Rus´ (*Rosiia*) when writing to the tsar.[29]

A further complication is that most of Khmelnytsky's letters to Moscow are not available in the original but only in Muscovite translations "from the Belarusian." What strikes one about those translations is that they contain no references to the "Rus´ nation," whose rights Khmelnytsky was eager to defend in his Polish-language letters to the king. We know that Ruthenian authors of the period freely used the term "nation" (*narod*), which had the same meaning in Ruthenian as in Polish. Did Khmelnytsky consciously avoid such references in his letters to Muscovy, replacing them with such formulae as "Rus´ Orthodox Christians" or "the whole Rus´ Orthodox community of Little Rus´," which were contrary to Ukrainian practice at the time?[30] Or was the term lost in translation? Both possibilities suggest a breakdown of communication between the two parties.

Thus a nation-based dialogue was hardly possible, not least because of the lack of an appropriate vocabulary on the Muscovite side. If there was a reunion in Pereiaslav, it was an Orthodox one, declared but not yet implemented in numerous religious services, speeches, and pronouncements. In fact, it was not even a reunion (that did not happen in institutional, liturgical or other terms until the last decade of the seventeenth century and the first decades of the eighteenth) but an avowal of reconciliation. After the tumultuous struggle against the Union in the Kyiv metropolitanate and the shock of the Time of Troubles in Muscovy, the two sides had agreed to reestablish relations. The churchmen thereby provided the political elites with the common language required to begin a dialogue between the two nations, which by now were very different. It appears that lack of understanding in that regard was not the only disconnection between the two sides, as events in Pereiaslav demonstrated.

A major crisis was provoked by Buturlin's refusal to swear in the name of the tsar to the preservation of Cossack freedoms and liberties. Buturlin did his best to assure the Cossack officers that the tsar would not only preserve but actually increase their liberties, even though he refused to swear an oath in the name of his sovereign. Khmelnytsky left the envoy in church to await the results of his negotiations with the colonels. When it was conveyed to Buturlin that the Polish kings swore oaths to their subjects, the boyar stood his ground. He told his interlocutors that he represented the Orthodox tsar and autocrat, while the Polish king was neither; hence the two monarchs could not be compared.[31]

Khmelnytsky and the colonels were eventually obliged to consent. The Cossacks swore allegiance to the tsar without extracting an oath from the representative of their new sovereign. This was unprecedented in Cossack practice. Although the Polish king had indeed refused to sign agreements with them and recognize them as equals in negotiations, Polish commissioners took an oath in the name of the Commonwealth on whatever agreement they reached with the Cossacks, as was the case at Bila Tserkva in the autumn of 1651. The Cossacks would not swear their own oath otherwise. At Pereiaslav, they did. It was their introduction to the world of Muscovite politics.

Buturlin did not lie: tsars indeed never swore oaths to their subjects. At Pereiaslav the tsar's representative applied to his sovereign's new subjects the rules of steppe diplomacy—a set of principles inherited by Muscovy from the Golden Horde and practiced with regard to its eastern neighbors and vassals. As Andreas Kappeler has shown, those principles entailed "a loose protectorate, which was concluded by means of an oath, by installing a loyal ruler. From the Russian point of view that established a client status to which it could always refer in the future, whereas the other side saw it at the most as a personal and temporary act of submission."[32]

Indeed, if the Cossack elite viewed the oath and service to the tsar as conditional ("voluntary" [povol'ne], in their language) subordination to the ruler, with subsequent relations depending on the willingness of each party to keep its side of the bargain, Muscovite diplomacy regarded the oath as proof of eternal subjection. After all, the text of the standard oath included the following words: "And not to leave the Muscovite tsardom in treasonable fashion, and not to engage in double-dealing or treason."[33] Subsequent events showed quite conclusively that neither side in the Pereiaslav negotiations fully understood what it was getting into.

4.

Hadiach 1658: The Origins of a Myth

Few events in Ukrainian and Polish history have provoked as many "what ifs" as the agreement concluded between the Cossack hetman Ivan Vyhovsky and representatives of the Polish-Lithuanian Commonwealth near the city of Hadiach in the autumn of 1658. Long before the rise of virtual and counterfactual history, historians in Poland and Ukraine defied the maxim of positivist historiography that history has no subjunctive mood and plunged into speculation on how differently the history of both countries would have turned out if, instead of fighting prolonged and exhausting wars, Poland-Lithuania and the Hetmanate had reunited in a new and reformed Commonwealth. Would this have stopped the decline of Poland, the ruin of Ukraine, the interventions of the Ottomans, and the rise of Muscovy as the dominant force in the region?

The Union of Hadiach, as the agreement became known in historiography, had the potential to influence all those processes. It envisioned the creation of a tripartite Commonwealth—the Kingdom of Poland and the Grand Duchy of Lithuania, as well as a Principality of Rus´, with the Cossack hetman as its official head. The Union was the culmination of the activities of moderate forces among the Polish and Ukrainian elites and the embodiment of the hopes and dreams of the Ruthenian (Ukrainian and Belarusian) nobility of the first half of the seventeenth century. Nevertheless, the compromise embodied in the Union was rejected by mainstream forces on both sides. The Commonwealth Diet ratified the text of the treaty with a number of important omissions, but even in that form it was viewed with suspicion and rejected by the Polish nobiliary establishment, which could not reconcile itself to the prospect of Orthodox Cossacks enjoying equal rights with Catholic nobles. On the Ukrainian side, the Cossack rank and file rejected a treaty that proposed to give all rights in the new Principality of Rus´ to a limited number of representatives of the Ukrainian nobiliary and Cossack elite at the expense of the Cossack masses and the rebel peasantry, which would have to submit once again to the noble landlords' jurisdiction and control.[1] The Union was a disaster for its Ukrainian sponsor, Hetman Ivan Vyhovsky, who succeeded Bohdan Khmelnytsky in 1657 and was forced to resign in 1659. Vyhovsky was well aware that the Hadiach Agreement in the truncated form approved by the Diet was a virtual death sentence for him and his supporters. "You have come with death and brought me death," said Vyhovsky to the Polish envoy who delivered the text of the agreement to him. He himself survived the events that followed the ratification of the treaty, but his closest adviser and initiator of the Union, the general chancellor of the Cossack Host, Iurii Nemyrych, was captured and killed by insurgents who rebelled against the presence of the Polish troops brought to the Hetmanate by Vyhovsky's administration.[2]

Needless to say, the Union had its fair share of critics among Ukrainian scholars. The critical assessment of the Union by Viacheslav Lypynsky and Mykhailo Hrushevsky, the two most influential Ukrainian historians of the period, had a profound influence on the interpretation of the events of 1658–59 in twentieth-century Ukrainian historiography.[3] Nevertheless, it had to compete with the well-established tradition of treating Hadiach as a largely positive development in Ukrainian history. Quite a few Ukrainian political thinkers and historians of the second half of the nineteenth century tended to see the Union of Hadiach as a manifestation of Ukrainian autonomist and federalist aspirations. For example, the leaders of the Ukrainian movement in the Russian Empire, Mykhailo Drahomanov and Volodymyr Antonovych, were generally positive in their assessment of the Union. And scholars of the younger generation were particularly enthusiastic. Hrushevsky's student Vasyl Herasymchuk saw the Union not only as a major achievement of Ukrainian political thought but also as a step toward Ukrainian independence—a position shared by Ivan Franko, Ukraine's leading literary figure of the period.[4]

Indeed, since its inception in the early nineteenth century, modern Ukrainian historiography has been largely positive in its assessment of the Union of Hadiach and the actions and intentions of its authors. This applies particularly to the views of twentieth-century Ukrainian historians not subject to Soviet control. The revival of interest in Hadiach has been promoted, inter alia, by increasing attention to Polish historiography, which has traditionally been friendly to Hadiach. For many Polish historians, Hadiach remains a symbol of Poland's civilizing mission in the East, religious toleration, and ability to solve nationality problems within the context of a multiethnic state.[5]

After the fall of the USSR and the collapse of Soviet historiography, whose practitioners condemned Vyhovsky as a "traitor to the Ukrainian people" and cited the Hadiach Agreement as proof of that treason, positive assessments not only of Vyhovsky but also of the Union of Hadiach made their way into historical writing. One of the deans of contemporary Ukrainian historiography, Nataliia Iakovenko, sees the Hadiach Agreement as "a striking monument of the political and legal thought of its time, which, had it been realized, would indeed have had a chance of laying firm foundations for the future of the Polish-Lithuanian-Belarusian-Ukrainian community and renewing the Commonwealth by establishing new forms of coexistence for its peoples. This in turn would have guaranteed the protection of what had already been achieved—recognition of the right to freedom of the individual, property, and political expression."[6]

There are a number of reasons, both scholarly and political, for the persistence of the positive image of the Union of Hadiach in Ukrainian historiography. The goal of the present study, however, is not to examine those reasons but to look into the origins of the Ukrainian myth of Hadiach. When did it come into existence? What functions did it perform in the historical thinking of the Cossack elites and their Ukrainian heirs? These are the questions I propose to address.

In the second half of the seventeenth century, memories of the Union of Hadiach continued to flourish in Polish-controlled Right-Bank Ukraine. Just as the hetmans of Russian-ruled Left-Bank Ukraine always referred in their negotiations with the Muscovite court to the rights granted to the Cossacks at Pereiaslav in 1654, so every Right-Bank hetman tried to negotiate a deal reminiscent of the Union of Hadiach with his Polish counterparts.[7] One can only speculate on the role that the Union of Hadiach might have played in Cossack historical writing if it had developed in Right-Bank Ukraine, but Poland suppressed Ukrainian Cossackdom in the Commonwealth before such a tradition had been established there. Instead, the myth of Hadiach took shape in the works of the Left-Bank Cossack chroniclers, who had a generally negative attitude toward the pro-Polish hetmans and their political and diplomatic dealings with Poland.

Roman Rakushka-Romanovsky, a prominent Cossack officer, served both Left-Bank and Right-Bank hetmans. After becoming an Orthodox priest, he wrote the *Eyewitness Chronicle*—the first major monument of Cossack historical writing. Rakushka-Romanovsky, the first Cossack author to address the Hadiach Agreement as a historical subject, listed some of its prominent conditions in his chronicle but gave neither a positive nor a negative assessment of it. His summary of the conditions of the Union is useful for understanding how it was assessed by the Cossack officer elite of the period. Rakushka mentioned the granting of the office of Kyivan palatine to the hetman, the ennoblement of a few hundred Cossack officers in every regiment, and the creation of special courts for the Kyiv, Chernihiv, and Bratslav palatinates, which made it unnecessary to go to Lublin or attend Diet sessions in Warsaw in order to settle legal disputes. It would appear that the Cossack officers expected more from the agreement than it actually delivered, given that the number of Cossacks eligible for ennoblement was limited to one hundred in each regiment. It is also possible that these conditions were exaggerated in retrospect—after all, Rakushka wrote his account of the agreement many years after the event.[8]

By the turn of the eighteenth century, when Rakushka was completing his chronicle, the myth of Hadiach was already in the making. The Union's provisions were half-forgotten and half-exaggerated. The neutral or even positive attitude toward the Union was outweighed by the prevalent negative assessment of the hetmancy of one of its authors, Ivan Vyhovsky. Rakushka-Romanovsky himself treated Vyhovsky as a pro-Polish politician and a traitor to the tsar. For the author of the *Eyewitness Chronicle*, Vyhovsky symbolized "Liakh deceit and Latin depravity," manifested by his takeover of the hetmancy from Bohdan Khmelnytsky's son Iurii.[9] From Rakushka-Romanovsky on, Cossack historiography portrayed Vyhovsky and his alleged Polonophilism in an extremely negative light. The two contradictory aspects of the Hadiach myth—a positive attitude toward the Union and a negative one toward Vyhovsky—coexisted peacefully, demonstrating the complexity of the world in which the Cossack elites of the Left-Bank Ukraine reinvented their history and identity.

Rakushka-Romanovsky completed the *Eyewitness Chronicle* at the beginning of the eighteenth century, before Ivan Mazepa's revolt against Tsar Peter I in 1708 and the Battle of Poltava (1709). Mazepa's revolt dramatically changed the political atmosphere in the Hetmanate and, by all accounts, promoted the development of the Hadiach myth. The revolt raised the question of an alternative to the tsar's rule in Ukraine. It was approximately at this time that the Cossack officers rediscovered the text of the Hadiach Agreement and began a careful study of its provisions. Mazepa allied himself with Charles XII of Sweden and Stanisław Leszczyński of Poland. Whatever the shortcomings of the Union of Hadiach as compared with the Pereiaslav Agreement of 1654, it looked clearly superior to the limited Cossack autonomy that survived under Russian suzerainty in the first decade of the eighteenth century. Once again, the Treaty of Hadiach became attractive to the Hetmanate's elites, which had undergone "gentrification" in the ensuing half century and were dreaming of the noble status and rights associated with that process.

This new interest in the Union of Hadiach was short-lived but found its way into the Cossack chronicles written in the Hetmanate after the Battle of Poltava. Peter's encroachment on Cossack rights and the anti-Polish propaganda that he conducted from his new capital of St. Petersburg placed clear restrictions on the chroniclers' ability to express their thoughts on the subject. Nevertheless, it is clearly apparent that the post-Poltava chroniclers paid much more attention to the Union of Hadiach than did Rakushka-Romanovsky prior to Mazepa's revolt. Inspiration for the further development of the Hadiach myth came, not surprisingly, from Polish sources. Particularly influential in this regard was Samuel Twardowski's rhymed chronicle, *The Civil War*, four parts of which appeared in print in 1681.[10]

Twardowski discussed the Union in connection with the decisions of the Diet of 1659, which approved the agreement for the Polish side. He believed that the Union had resulted in the creation of a "third Commonwealth" in Ukraine (along with the Polish Kingdom and the Grand Duchy of Lithuania). For his narrative, Twardowski used the agreement as negotiated at Hadiach, not the final draft of the treaty approved by the Diet. Thus he referred to a Cossack Host of sixty thousand, not the thirty thousand stipulated by the Diet's decision. He also listed a provision on the liquidation of the church union, although it was reformulated in the final draft of the agreement to save the Uniate Church. Twardowski's characterization of the Cossacks was highly favorable for the most part. He regarded the creation of a "Cossack Commonwealth" in Ukraine as the fulfillment of a prediction allegedly made by the sixteenth-century Polish king Stefan Batory. Twardowski also compared the Cossacks' humble origins with those of the Macedonian Greeks, Romans, Ottomans, and even Polish nobles. He was clearly prepared to accept the Cossack officer elite as an equal partner in the Commonwealth.[11]

It was only to be expected that Twardowski's interpretation of the Hadiach Agreement would appeal to the Cossack chroniclers of the eighteenth century. Samiilo Velychko, a former secretary in the General Chancellery of the Hetmanate and the most prolific chronicler of the period, used Twardowski's account in his *Relation of the Cossack War with the Poles*, probably written in the 1720s. He translated Twardowski's verses from the Polish and used them almost verbatim, making reference to specific pages of Twardowski's work. Velychko's own contribution to the story consisted of a recontextualization of the Union of Hadiach, presenting it not as the outcome of the work of the Polish Diet of 1659 (as had Twardowski) but of negotiations conducted at Hadiach in September 1658. Velychko also supplied a lengthy commentary on the first provision of the agreement about the liquidation of the church union, arguing that it was an important measure intended to stop desertions from the Orthodox Church in Polish Ukraine. Finally, Velychko completely excluded from his account the speech delivered at the Diet by the Cossack representative Iurii Nemyrych.

When speaking of the Cossacks returning to the fold of the Polish king, Nemyrych had invoked the story of the prodigal son returning to his father. The first of Velychko's changes put the agreement into a Ukrainian rather than a Polish historical context, the second strengthened the Union's legitimacy from the viewpoint of the interests of the Orthodox Church, and the third helped deflect accusations that the Union was a mere surrender of Cossack Ukraine to the king. All these changes notwithstanding, Velychko's portrayal of Hadiach was inspired and heavily influenced by Twardowski's favorable treatment of the agreement. Like Rakushka-Romanovsky's account, Velychko's positive assessment of Hadiach coexisted peacefully with his largely negative characterization of Vyhovsky, whom he depicted as a Ruthenian noble "of one spirit with the Poles for the sake of passing vanity and well-being in this world."[12]

Especially interesting (and important for the present discussion) is the impact of Twardowski's interpretation of the Union of Hadiach on another major Cossack chronicle of the period, Hryhorii Hrabianka's *The Great War of Bohdan Khmelnytsky*, apparently written in the 1720s.[13] If Velychko's chronicle survived in a single copy, Hrabianka's circulated widely in eighteenth-century Ukraine and became the most influential historical work of the period. Hrabianka, who was well acquainted with the *Eyewitness Chronicle* and used it in his work, shared Rakushka-Romanovsky's negative attitude to Vyhovsky, calling him "an enemy and a blatant traitor."[14]

But in his discussion of the Union of Hadiach Hrabianka portrayed Vyhovsky as a victim of the Poles, who had made enticing promises to him. Thus, like Rakushka-Romanovsky and Velychko, Hrabianka did not extend his negative characterization of Vyhovsky to the latter's major diplomatic undertaking, the Union of Hadiach. He clearly liked the main ideas of the agreement and supplied additional details that enhanced his positive assessment of the Union. Some of those details were mere figments of the rich imagination of the Cossack elites, which were prepared to see much more in the Union than it had actually offered their forefathers.

Twardowski's work influenced Hrabianka's chronicle no less profoundly than it had affected Velychko's *Relation*. In some cases, Hrabianka was even less critical of his source than Velychko. For example, he failed to reconceptualize the history of the Union of Hadiach, introducing it to the reader in connection with the proceedings of the Warsaw Diet of 1659, exactly as Twardowski had done. Not unlike Velychko, Hrabianka used Twardowski's account of the conditions of the Union as the basis for his own account of the agreement. He also quoted from Twardowski's praise of the Cossacks, comparing their background to that of the ancient Greeks, Romans, Turks, and Poles.

Unlike Velychko, however, Hrabianka never named his source. He also introduced many more changes into Twardowski's account than had Velychko. Hrabianka dropped not only the account of Nemyrych's speech to the Diet but also the provision of the agreement that obliged the Cossacks to conduct a defensive war against Muscovy, as well as the amnesty to the Cossacks who had sided with the Swedes during their invasion of the Commonwealth. If Hrabianka's failure to mention Nemyrych can be explained by the same reasons as Velychko's, the other two changes reflect the new political sensitivities of post-Poltava Ukraine. In the wake of the defeat at Poltava, Hrabianka did not want to draw attention to the history of Cossack-Muscovite antagonisms or to past Cossack alliances with the Swedish king.[15]

If Hrabianka altered Twardowski's version of the treaty to eliminate items that he did not want his readers to know or remember, his additions to the text of the agreement give a good indication of what he wanted the Union of Hadiach to represent. First of all, Hrabianka introduced the concept of the Grand Principality of Rus′—a notion absent from Twardowski's work and probably borrowed from another Polish source, Wespazjan Kochowski's *Climacters*.[16] Thus Hrabianka referred to the Cossack hetman of the agreement (that is, Ivan Vyhovsky) variously in his text as hetman of the Grand Principality of Rus´-Ukraine, hetman of the Ruthenian nation, and Ukrainian or Little Russian hetman.

Hrabianka also added to Twardowski's text of the agreement the ideologically important statement that the Cossacks were joining the Commonwealth as "free men with free men and equals with equals," a formula that had entered Ruthenian political discourse in the first half of the seventeenth century and remained important in the eighteenth. Now, however, it was reintroduced to establish that the Cossack elites had enjoyed special rights under the Polish kings and to claim those rights from the Russian tsars. The same purpose underlay another of Hrabianka's additions to Twardowski's text—the statement that the king himself had signed the conditions of the Union, and then, as was the custom among monarchs, both sides had sworn to the agreement. Given the controversy over the refusal of the tsar's envoys at Pereiaslav to swear an oath in the name of the sovereign, this addition was also politically significant.[17]

The addition of Hrabianka's that had the most lasting impact on subsequent historiography and led to confusion in nineteenth-century historical writing pertained to the origins of the Hadiach Agreement. In his chronicle, Hrabianka claimed that the agreement had originally been submitted to the Poles by none other than Bohdan Khmelnytsky (the hetman's first name was not given in the chronicle, but "Khmelnytsky" was Hrabianka's standard form of reference to him).[18] Whether this was taken from a written source, garbled, or invented outright, it helped Hrabianka argue his case that the Union indicated the Poles' acceptance of a treaty originally proposed by the Cossacks. That could well explain why the Cossacks ultimately fell for a Polish trap.

However, in Hrabianka's scheme of things, neither the canniness of the Poles nor Cossack naïveté nor even treason on the part of Vyhovsky could undermine the good ideas put into agreement by Bohdan Khmelnytsky. The reference to Khmelnytsky, whose cult as hero and savior of Little Russia reached its peak in the 1720s, could not but add legitimacy to the Union of Hadiach.[19] Another factor that bolstered the reputation of the Hadiach Agreement in post-Poltava Ukraine was the opposition to the Union on the part of the Catholic hierarchy, registered by Twardowski and duly repeated by Hrabianka. In general, Hrabianka portrayed the Hadiach Agreement in a way that shielded it from accusations of disloyalty to the tsar or betrayal of the Orthodox Church.[20]

This was especially important, given that Hrabianka presented the Union of Hadiach as a viable alternative—and, one might conclude after comparing his texts of the Pereiaslav and Hadiach treaties, a more attractive one—to the Pereiaslav Agreement. The elites of the Hetmanate were fed up with Muscovite encroachment on their rights and privileges, which culminated in the abolition of the hetmancy in 1722 and the introduction of direct rule by the Little Russian College. They looked to history for alternatives to Russian rule, and the Union of Hadiach certainly fit the bill. Hrabianka's interpretation of Hadiach had a strong impact on the formation of Ukrainian historical identity in the Hetmanate. His chronicle was extremely popular among the Cossack elites, but even more popular were different variants of its condensed version, known as the *Brief Description of Little Russia*.[21] Together they contributed to the formation of a Hadiach myth that represented the Polish-Cossack agreement of 1658 as an alternative to Pereiaslav and helped form an identity rooted not only in Little Russia's experience under the tsars but also in its long tradition of existence under Polish kings.

This interpretation of Hadiach had little to do with the actual text of the treaty, which curtailed the Hetmanate's rights and Cossack liberties—a reality so obvious to Vyhovsky and his contemporaries. The popularity of the Hadiach myth can be properly understood only in the context of historical writing and the politics of memory. That myth was created and kept alive by generations of chroniclers and historians who desperately searched the past for an alternative to Russian rule. Despite the numerous flaws of the Hadiach Agreement, which were particularly glaring when compared with the Pereiaslav Agreement of 1654, it eventually began to be seen as a viable alternative to Pereiaslav and, even more importantly, to the subsequent Cossack-Muscovite treaties, which further curtailed the fragile autonomy of Ukraine.

5.

The Return of Ivan Mazepa

On the morning of 27 June 1709, two armies faced each other in the fields near the Ukrainian city of Poltava. One was led by the young and ambitious king of Sweden, Charles XII, the other by the not so young but no less ambitious tsar of Muscovy, Peter I. Both were backed by detachments of Ukrainian Cossacks—one led by Hetman Ivan Mazepa, who had rebelled against Peter and joined Charles, the other by Hetman Ivan Skoropadsky, appointed by the Russians to replace Mazepa. The ensuing battle has often been regarded as a significant turning point in Russian and, indeed, European history. Peter won, defeating his archenemy, saving his country, securing his hold over the Hetmanate (a Cossack polity subordinated to Moscow), and turning the tide of the long Northern War. Charles lost and had to seek refuge on the territory of the Ottoman Empire.

The Battle of Poltava is often perceived as a turning point in European history. At the end of the war Peter proclaimed himself emperor of Russia, and his country became a major European power. In time, Russia not only put an end to Swedish dominance in the Baltic region and Northern Europe but also embarked on a prolonged course of westward expansion that took its troops all the way to Paris during the Napoleonic Wars of the next century. Few scholars disagree with the conventional wisdom that Mazepa's revolt and the subsequent defeat of Charles had major negative consequences for the Hetmanate—the polity in which the battle was fought. While Mazepa had hoped to increase the autonomy of the Cossack state under the nominal rule of a distant sovereign, his defeat led to its severe curtailment. The hetman's right to appoint colonels was taken away by the tsar, who later availed himself of Hetman Skoropadsky's death to abolish the office altogether and place the Hetmanate under the rule of the Little Russian College.

The Battle of Poltava remains an important component of Russian and Ukrainian historical mythology. It also continues to generate interest among scholars, writers, and the public at large. If one understands myth in the broadest terms as a phenomenon that helps large collectivities define the foundations of their identity and system of values, then the term is clearly applicable to the verbal and visual presentation of the Battle of Poltava over the last three hundred years.[1] It can even be argued that the "Myth of Poltava" is one of the founding myths of the Russian Empire. Its origins can be traced back to the months, if not weeks, following the battle. Many elements of the imperial myth of Poltava were first laid down by Feofan Prokopovych in his sermon delivered before Peter I at St. Sophia's Cathedral in Kyiv on 22 July 1709, less than a month after the tsar's victory. Prokopovych's sermon includes themes that later became standard: the role of the tsar not only as a great military victor but also as the savior of Russia and father of his fatherland, and a portrayal of his enemy, Hetman Ivan Mazepa, as a traitor and instrument in the hands of foreign powers.

An essential element of the imperial myth of Poltava is the image of the "second Judas," the Cossack hetman Ivan Mazepa, first denounced with that epithet by Peter himself. The tsar ordered that Mazepa be anathematized after he learned that the hetman had sided with Charles XII in the fall of 1708, in the midst of the Northern War. This anathema, repeated every year in the churches of the vast empire, turned Mazepa into the most hated figure of the Russian political and historical imagination. The tsar even had an Order of Judas made, intending to bestow it on the elderly hetman once he was captured. Peter won the Battle of Poltava in June 1709, but the hetman was never caught. Instead, he became a symbol of treason to the ruler and the state; an object of government-sponsored hatred, association with whom was tantamount to sacrilege—a betrayal not only of secular authority but also of the Christian faith. Admiring Mazepa under such circumstances was extremely dangerous, but not everyone was prepared to cast aside the memory of the old hetman.[2]

Condemned by the tsar, abandoned by many of his followers, and anathematized by church hierarchs he had patronized in churches he had helped build, Mazepa was turned into a symbol of treason whose infamy outlasted that of the primary villain of Poltava, King Charles XII. But the power of imperial mythology had its limits. Simultaneously with the formation of the imperial myth of Poltava, its countermyth was born in Ukraine, presenting Mazepa not only as a protector of the Orthodox Church but also as a defender of the rights and freedoms of his people. Like the imperial myth, this countermyth of Mazepa began its life in the war of manifestos between Peter, Charles, and Mazepa on the eve of Poltava. It survived the most difficult post-Poltava years and took on new characteristics in nineteenth-century Ukraine.

In 1810, just over a century after the Battle of Poltava, Oleksii Martos, a young officer in the Russian military and a descendant of an old Cossack family, visited Mazepa's grave in the Moldavian town of Galați. Two years later his father, the celebrated sculptor Ivan Martos, best known for his statue of Kuzma Minin and Dmitrii Pozharsky in Moscow's Red Square, unveiled a monument to Catherine II at the Column Hall in the same city. While the father celebrated the empress who had put an end to the existence of the Cossack polity in Ukraine, his St. Petersburg-born son took a different attitude to the imperial past and its heroes. A few years after visiting Mazepa's grave, most probably around 1819, the year that Byron's *Mazeppa* was published, Oleksii Martos left the following record in his memoirs:

> Mazepa died far from his fatherland, whose independence he defended; he was a friend of liberty, and for this he deserves the respect of generations to come. . . . He is gone, and the name of Little Russia and its brave Cossacks has been erased from the list of nations not great in numbers but known for their existence and their constitutions. Besides other virtues, Mazepa was a friend of learning: he enlarged the Academy of the Brotherhood Monastery in Kyiv, which he renovated and embellished; he supplied it with a library and rare manuscripts. Yet the founder of the academy and of many churches and

philanthropic institutions is anathematized every year on the Sunday of the first week of Great Lent along with Stenka Razin and other thieves and robbers. But what a difference! The latter was a robber and a blasphemer. Mazepa was a most enlightened and philanthropic individual, a skillful military leader, and the ruler of a free nation.[3]

The Puzzle

Martos was not the only "dissident" who questioned the official line toward Mazepa and regarded him as a protector of the rights and freedoms of his homeland. On 3 June 1822, Mikhail Pogodin (1800–1875), then a twenty-one-year-old student at Moscow University, later a prominent Russian historian and one of the leaders of the Slavophile movement, recorded in his diary a conversation he had that day about the prevailing moods in "Little Russia"— the former Cossack lands of Ukraine. "Not a shadow of their former rights remains among them now. The Little Russians call themselves the true Russians and the others *moskali*. They do not entirely like them. Muscovy was thus something apart. They also call the Old Believers *moskali*. They love Mazeppa [*sic*]. Earlier they did not supply recruits but [Cossack] regiments. Thus, there were regiments from Chernihiv, [Novhorod]-Siverskyi, and so on. That was much better: they were all from one region and therefore more comradely, more in agreement. But now, someone from Irkutsk stands next to a Kyivan; a man from Arkhangelsk—next to one from Astrakhan. What is the sense of it?"[4]

What exactly did Pogodin have in mind when he referred to the Ukrainians' "love of Mazepa?" We shall answer this question by taking a close look at his Ukrainian acquaintances and the views of history to which they subscribed. We know that Pogodin discussed Ukrainian grievances and aspirations with Aleksei Kubarev, his older friend and mentor at Moscow University, and with Kubarev's close friend Mykhailo Shyrai, the son of Stepan Shyrai (1761–1841), a retired general, wealthy landowner, and marshal of the nobility of Chernihiv gubernia. It was from the younger Shyrai, also a student at Moscow University and Pogodin's rival in the dissertation competition for the university's gold medal, that Pogodin obtained the information on Ukrainian moods and their "love" for Mazepa. The rest of the conversation, as summarized by Pogodin, focused on "a certain Sudiienko, who, holding no civic office, governed the whole town merely by the respect that he commanded," and "Metropolitan Mikhail [of St. Petersburg]," who was "idolized in Chernihiv."

The impressions recorded by Pogodin came from Shyrai's family circle in Ukraine. The Sudiienkos were related to the Shyrais, and Mykhailo Shyrai's father, Stepan, was closely associated with Metropolitan Mikhail Desnitsky of St. Petersburg, formerly archbishop of Chernihiv, who had visited his family estate in Solova near Starodub on several occasions.[5]

Stepan Shyrai was an important figure in Ukrainian political circles of the first decades of the nineteenth century. A retired major general who had taken an active part in the Russo-Turkish wars under Aleksandr Suvorov, Shyrai was elected marshal of the Chernihiv nobility in 1818 and spent a decade leading the struggle for its rights and privileges. He became a strong critic of the high quotas of recruits whom the serf-owning landlords were required to contribute to the imperial army. Shyrai was also well known for his stories of the good old days. Around 1828, when he was about to leave office or had just left it, the sixty-seven-year-old Shyrai, at odds with Governor General Nikolai Repnin of Little Russia, took it upon himself to disseminate to the wider world arguably the most subversive text produced in nineteenth-century Ukraine, a history of the Cossacks entitled *Istoriia Rusov* (History of the Rus´).[6]

Although the manuscript is attributed to the long-deceased archbishop of Mahilioŭ, Heorhii Konysky (1717–95), and is supposed to have been completed in the late 1760s, its main ideas correspond closely to the list of Ukrainian grievances recorded by Pogodin. The author, whoever he was, and whenever he wrote his text, believed that the Cossacks, or the "Little Russians"—not the "Great Russians" or "Muscovites"—were indeed the true heirs of Rus´ and bona fide Rusians. He believed that Rus´ and Muscovy were different entities, disliked the Muscovites, and was a sworn enemy of the Old Believers. The unknown author argues that the Cossacks had not received due recognition for the services they had rendered to the empire. There seems to be almost a perfect match between the views of the Ukrainian elites of the 1820s and the historical manuscript that popped up in the libraries of local notables around that time. Whether the *History* influenced the mood of the Chernihiv nobility or simply reflected it, there is little doubt that the work offers unparalleled insight into the historical views held by descendants of the Cossack officers of the Hetmanate at a time when Ukrainian culture was entering the all-important stage of "heritage gathering," which led to the rise of the Ukrainian national movement in the mid-nineteenth century.[7]

There is, however, an important problem to be addressed before the thesis of a close correlation between the views of the Ukrainian nobility of the 1820s and those of the author of the *History* can be accepted without major reservations. This problem is expressed in Pogodin's phrase about the Ukrainian elites' "love of Mazeppa." Unlike Pogodin's Ukrainian landowners, the author of the *History of the Rus´* has an ambivalent attitude toward Ivan Mazepa and his actions, and his feelings for the old hetman would be hard to characterize as "love" or admiration. Could Pogodin have misunderstood his fellow student back in June 1822 or exaggerated what he had heard from him? Or did Mykhailo Shyrai accurately express the views of his father's circle, and does the problem lie with the author of the *History*? A first reading of the *History* offers no immediate answer to these questions. Depending on the nature and circumstances of the episodes described in the book, its author can be either critical or supportive of Mazepa, judgmental or forgiving. He appears to be seeking a balance between a frankly negative assessment of the hetman and an apology for him. In the process, he creates quite a contradictory figure who embarks on a dangerous path, "along which he was led by excessive courage and extreme bitterness into an immeasurable abyss."[8]

Reading Voltaire

On the surface, the overall assessment of Mazepa and his actions in the pages of the *History* is more negative than positive. To begin with, the anonymous author considers Mazepa an ethnic Pole (a nationality that he vehemently despises) whose actions are guided by wounded honor. This is the leitmotif of the author's treatment of the two Mazepa legends, one recorded by

Voltaire in his 1731 bestseller, *History of Charles XII*, and the other preserved as part of Ukrainian lore. According to both legends, Peter I provoked Mazepa's animosity by publicly humiliating him at one of his receptions. "The Czar, who began to be over-heated with wine, and had not, when sober, always the command of his passions, called him a traitor, and threatened to have him impaled. Mazeppa, on his return to Ukraine, formed the design of a revolt," wrote Voltaire.

Another version of this legend, apparently known to the author of the *History of the Rus'* from local sources, placed the same episode at a dinner hosted by Peter's close associate Aleksandr Menshikov, whom the author considered a sworn enemy of Ukraine. According to this version, Peter slapped Mazepa in the face as a result of the conflict. "Both these stories, taken together, show the same thing—that Mazeppa had a most harmful intent, inspired by his own malice and vengefulness, and not at all by national interests, which, naturally, ought in that case to have moved the troops and the people to support him, but instead the people fought the Swedes with all their might as enemies who had invaded their land in hostile fashion."[9]

Thus, the anonymous author basically accepted Voltaire's interpretation of Mazepa's actions as motivated by a personal desire for revenge. Writing after the French Revolution, the author was prepared to judge his protagonist's actions by the level of public support that they generated. Did he, however, approve not only the actions of the Cossack elites but also those of the popular masses? Throughout the *History of the Rus'*, its author shows very little regard for the masses as such, and his assessment of their behavior toward the Swedish army in the months leading up to the Battle of Poltava is no exception.

"The local people," he declares, making little effort to hide his contempt for the unenlightened and savage plebs, "then resembled savage Americans or wayward Asians. Coming out of their abatis and shelters, they were surprised by the mild behavior of the Swedes, but, because the latter did not speak Rusian among themselves or make the sign of the cross, they considered them non-Christians and infidels, and, on seeing them consuming milk and meat on Fridays, concluded that they were godless infidels and killed them wherever they could be found in small parties or individually." The masses emerge from this description as xenophobic, superstitious, and uncivilized, while the account itself exhibits all the characteristics of enlightened Orientalism.[10]

The anonymous author's characterization of Mazepa as an irresponsible leader driven to avenge a personal insult is certainly full of contradictions. On the one hand, he denounces Mazepa's actions in light of their reception by the Cossack elites (the Cossack Host) and ordinary people. On the other hand, he considers this reaction, especially on the part of the Cossacks, to be ill-informed, if not completely ridiculous. One way of explaining this contradictory attitude is to posit that the anonymous author inwardly sympathized with Mazepa and his cause, or, in Pogodin's words, "loved Mazeppa" but found it difficult to reconcile his feelings with the image of the hetman projected by official propaganda, which had an influence on him. For a variety of historical and political reasons, the author may also have been reluctant to manifest his true thoughts and feelings in the matter. If that was indeed the case, what was the source of his "love of Mazeppa"?

It would be futile to seek the answer to this question in those parts of the *History* where the author assumes the role of narrator. Speaking in his own voice, the author is more critical than supportive of the old hetman. His attitude changes when he allows his characters to speak on their own behalf, shielding the author from direct responsibility for what he has written; after all, he is only quoting existing sources without endorsing their views. More often than not, however, those sources are of the author's own invention, or at least a product of his heavy editing. This is particularly true of the speech allegedly delivered by Mazepa to his troops at the beginning of the revolt and cited at length in the *History*.

Letting Mazepa Speak

It is in this speech that the author of the *History* gives Mazepa an opportunity to present his case. The long speech was allegedly delivered at the moment, decisive for Mazepa and his homeland, when the hetman decided to switch sides and join Charles XII. In order to maintain the loyalty of his men, Mazepa had to convince the Cossack Host of the justice of his cause. Mazepa (or, rather, the anonymous author) makes the fullest use of this opportunity to explain his view not only of the revolt but of Ukrainian history in general. In his speech to the Cossack Host, Mazepa emerges as a protector of Ukrainian independence—the role ascribed to him by Oleksii Martos circa 1819. He also raises his voice in defense of the ancient rights and freedoms violated by the Muscovites, who allegedly deprived the Cossacks of their prior claim to the Rus´ land, of their government, and of the very name of Rus´—themes that, if one trusts the Pogodin diary, were dear to the hearts of the Ukrainian elites in the early decades of the nineteenth century.

Mazepa's call to arms is based on the dire circumstances in which his fatherland and the Cossack nation find themselves. "We stand now, Brethren, between two abysses prepared to consume us if we do not choose a reliable path for ourselves to avoid them," begins Mazepa's apocryphal speech, referring to the fact that two imperial armies are approaching the borders of Ukraine and that a clash between them is all but inevitable. The hetman tars Peter I and Charles XII with the same brush, depicting them as tyrants who rule arbitrarily over conquered peoples: "Both of them, given their willfulness and appropriation of unlimited power, resemble the most terrible despots, such as all Asia and Africa have hardly ever produced."

The hetman claims that the victory of either despot would bring nothing but destruction to Ukraine. The Swedish king would reestablish Polish rule over Ukraine, while the Russian tsar, who refused to confirm the rights and privileges guaranteed to Ukraine in the times of Bohdan Khmelnytsky, has treated the Cossack nation and its representatives in autocratic fashion. "If the Russian tsar is allowed to become the victor," argues the apocryphal Mazepa, "then threatening calamities have been prepared for us by that tsar himself, for you see that, although he comes from a line elected by the people from among its nobility, yet, having appropriated unlimited power for himself, he punishes that people according to his arbitrary will, and not only the people's will and property but their very lives have been subjugated to the will and whim of the tsar alone."

Mazepa's solution to the seemingly insoluble problem of choosing between the two despots is most unusual. He proposes to remain neutral in the conflict between them, but that neutrality is of a particular kind. Ukraine would accept the protectorate of the Swedish king and fight only against those forces that attacked its territory, which under these circumstances could only be Russian forces. The Swedish king, along with other European powers, would guarantee the restoration of Ukrainian independence. Mazepa's speech, at once passionate and highly rational, leaves no doubt that he is acting in defense of his nation (*natsiia*), which he wants to save from destruction and lead to freedom, restoring its independence and placing it on a par with other European nations.

Parts of his speech specifically counter the arguments of his critics, including the anonymous author's own claim that Mazepa betrayed the tsar for personal advantage. "And so it remains to us, Brethren," says the apocryphal Mazepa to his troops, "to choose the lesser of the visible evils that have beset us, so that our descendants, condemned to slavery by our incompetence, do not burden us with their complaints and imprecations. I do not have them [descendants] and, of course, cannot have them; consequently, I am not involved in the interests of our descendants and seek nothing but the welfare of the nation that has honored me with my current post and, with it, has entrusted me with its fate."[11]

The text of Mazepa's speech in the *History of the Rus´* is a product of historical imagination, but it is not completely divorced from the realities of Mazepa's era. The references in the speech to the Swedish-Ukrainian alliance of the Khmelnytsky era find clear parallels in the preamble to Pylyp Orlyk's Constitution of 1711. The passage in Mazepa's speech in which he argues the need for secrecy and denies any personal motive for switching from one ruler to another corresponds fully to the episode described by Orlyk in a letter to Metropolitan Stefan Iavorsky in 1721.

According to Orlyk, Mazepa told him in 1707: "Before God the Omniscient I protest and swear that it is not for my private gain, not for higher honors, not for greater enrichment, nor for other whims of any kind, but for all of you who remain under my rule and command, for your wives and children, for the general good of my mother, my fatherland, poor unfortunate Ukraine, for the whole Zaporozhian Host and the Little Russian people, as well as for the promotion and expansion of the rights and freedoms of the Host, that I wish to act, with God's help, in such a way that you, with your wives and children and our native land, along with the Zaporozhian Host, do not perish because of the Muscovite or the Swedish side."[12]

Mazepa's speech in the *History of the Rus'* presents an image of the hetman that not only directly contradicts the imperial depiction of him as a Judas, a traitor to the tsar and his own people, but also departs significantly from the image of him presented by most eighteenth-century Ukrainian chroniclers. Writers of the first half of the century, including the author of the Hrabianka Chronicle, preferred to steer clear of a detailed discussion of the politically dangerous age of Mazepa, limiting themselves to a few short, dispassionate entries on the events of 1708 and 1709. Authors of the second half of the century, including Petro Symonovsky and especially Aleksandr Rigelman, did not shy away from the controversial topic but accepted and promoted the official viewpoint in their treatment of Mazepa. Even so, the image of Mazepa as a defender of Ukrainian rights, which emerges—though not without difficulty—from the *History of the Rus'*, was not entirely without precedent in Ukrainian historical writing.

We know that a text of Mazepa's speech circulated in Ukraine in the first decades of the nineteenth century, but we do not have the text itself: Dmitrii Bantysh-Kamensky was promised a copy but never received it. Nevertheless, Mazepa's speech in the *History of the Rus'* finds parallels in certain extant sources. The main points of the speech correspond closely to the hetman's arguments as summarized in the *Brief Historical Description of Little Russia*. This narrative—written, according to a date on its title page, in 1789—is known today in a copy dated 1814. Its author claims that "Hetman Mazepa undertook to make use of the continuing war in Russia with the Swedish king in such a way as to renounce his subjection to the Russian sovereign and establish himself as an autocratic prince in the Little Russian regions with the help of Charles XII." The hetman "suggested to the Little Russian officers, first, that Little Russia had been subjected to destruction owing to the war with the Swedes, not for the sake of any interests of its own, but, in his opinion, even with impairment of its liberty; second, that the sovereign, exhausting it with taxes, would freely abrogate the treaties whereby it still prospered; third, that the present time offered a chance to think of the future; and, fourth, how difficult it was, having become accustomed to liberty, to endure never-ending bondage."[13]

What was certainly new in Mazepa's speech as rendered by the author of the *History of the Rus'* was the eloquence and persuasiveness with which the hetman presented his argument. Among the first to be persuaded was the anonymous author himself—assuming, of course, that he was not the author of the speech but the person who cited or edited an existing text. One can hardly imagine that he would have included such a text in his work if he were not at least partly sympathetic to Mazepa's argument and, by extension, to the hetman himself. Through the medium of Mazepa's speech, the anonymous author gave voice to many of his own ideas that he could not express on his own behalf. Despite the author's general verdict that Mazepa acted in his own interest, many of the prominent themes in the hetman's speech are picked up and further developed in those parts of the *History* where the narrator does not have to hide behind Mazepa in order to express his own views and ideas. The theme of Ukraine's neutrality in the Muscovite-Swedish conflict became a touchstone of the author's own reinterpretation of the Mazepa era, as well as the basis for his rejection of the anathema imposed on the old hetman.

Still, the strongest support for Mazepa's argument is not expressed by the author directly but through the medium of speeches by other characters, including the proclamation issued by Mazepa's ally, Charles XII. The king corroborates everything declared by Mazepa in his own speech and sounds the same themes of struggle against tyranny and the restoration of Rus´/Cossack independence (*samoderzhavie*) as does the apocryphal Mazepa. According to the *History*, Charles declares in his proclamation to the people of Ukraine:

> The Muscovite tsar, being an intransigent foe of all the nations on earth and desiring to make them bend to his yoke, having subjected the Cossacks as well to his dishonorable bondage; despising, revoking, and annulling all your rights and freedoms established by solemn agreements and treaties with you, has forgotten and shamelessly contemned gratitude itself, held sacred by all nations, which is owed to you Cossacks and the Rus´ nation by Muscovy, reduced to a nullity and almost to

nonbeing by its internal conflicts, by pretenders, and by the Poles, but maintained and strengthened by you. For the whole world knows that the Rus´ nation with its Cossacks was originally an autocratic nation—that is, dependent on itself alone, under the rule of its princes or autocrats. . . .[14]

The author of the *History of the Rus´* also gives voice to the other side, that of Tsar Peter I. Unlike Mazepa's speech and the proclamation of Charles XII, Peter's manifesto was not a product of the author's (or of a predecessor's) imagination but an actual document well known in Ukraine. But the extract quoted from it in the *History* is much shorter than the one from Charles's alleged proclamation, to say nothing of Mazepa's speech. The author quotes those parts of Peter's manifesto in which the tsar guarantees the rights and freedoms of Ukraine, not those in which he presents his main accusations against Mazepa. In the *History of the Rus´* Peter merely defends himself against accusations that he violated the rights of Little Russia and promises to protect those rights in the future: "One may say without flattery that no people under the sun can boast of such privilege and liberty as our Little Russian people, for we have ordained that not one *peniaz´* [small silver coin] be taken from it for our treasury, and we have made this a testament for our successors."

If Mazepa's statements are corroborated in the *History of the Rus´* by those of Charles XII, and vice versa, Peter's declarations are left with no narrative support or corroborating evidence, and what the author of the *History* says about the behavior of Russian troops in Ukraine raises serious doubt about the validity of the tsar's statements. Judging by the space allotted to Mazepa and Charles on the one hand, and Peter on the other, to present their cases, there is little doubt that the author's sympathies lay with the former, not the latter.[15]

Between Tsar and Nation

If the author of the *History of the Rus´* preferred to express his support for Mazepa's cause through speeches and texts attributed to others, he used his own voice to express his (and, by extension, his readers') loyalty to the Russian ruler and to declare his support for Peter. Where the author speaks on his own behalf, he takes a position that, unlike Mazepa's speech, does not tar both rulers with the same brush by depicting them as tyrants but differentiates them, favoring Peter at the expense of Charles. It is not that the author is uncritical of Peter's actions, but he certainly prefers him to Charles, whom he considers a frivolous adventurer.[16]

This becomes especially clear in the author's treatment of Peter's attempts to reach agreement with Charles on the eve of the Battle of Poltava by sacrificing Russian territorial acquisitions and claims, which the Swedish king brushes aside in humiliating fashion. The following passage leaves no doubt about the author's sympathies in this particular case:

> The Swedish king, drunk with the glory of a conqueror and with his constant victories, having rejected those offers [of peace], told those envoys of the tsar and foreign intermediaries striving to incline him toward peace that 'he would make peace with the tsar in his capital city, Moscow, where he would force the Muscovites to pay him 30 million talers for the costs of the war and show the tsar how and over what to rule.' Losing hope of achieving anything by peaceful means after such a brutal refusal, the sovereign began to rally his troops to the outskirts of Poltava, and at the council of war that was held there, the whole general staff decided to give resolute battle to the Swedes, come what may.[17]

Sympathizing with Charles and Mazepa on the strength of their arguments while remaining loyal to the ruler was no easy task, partly because the anonymous author disapproved of many of the tsar's actions and those of his Great Russian troops. He assuaged this dilemma by shifting responsibility to the tsar's advisers for those of Peter's actions of which he did not approve. To judge by the text of the *History*, Aleksandr Menshikov was the main culprit. He is depicted as the embodiment of absolute evil, especially in the vivid description of the Russian massacre of the defenders and peaceful inhabitants of Mazepa's capital, Baturyn. The author goes out of his way to describe the atrocities carried out by Menshikov's troops and to stress their commander's low social origins, apparently seeking not only to explain his cruelty but also to distance him as much as possible from the tsar.

> Menshikov assaulted the unarmed burghers, who were in their homes and had no part whatsoever in Mazepa's designs; he slaughtered them to a man, sparing neither sex nor age, nor even suckling infants. This was followed by the troops' plundering of the town, while their commanders and torturers executed the bandaged Serdiuk officers and civil authorities.[18]

The loyalty to the ruler expressed by the author of the *History* did not automatically translate into loyalty either to the tsar's satraps or—an especially important point for our argument—to his Great Russian army and, by extension, his Great Russian nation. This distinction between the ruler and Great Russia was not the anonymous author's invention. It had already been made very clearly in Semen Divovych's *Conversation between Great and Little Russia*, written in 1762, shortly after Catherine II's ascent to the throne. The Great Russia of Divovych's poem was forced to admit that Little Russia was not subject to her (Great Russia) but to the ruler who governed both polities. Great Russia says to Little Russia in that regard:

> I acknowledge that I myself am not your sovereign,
> But our autocrat is our common master.
> I do not dispute that he accepted you with honors;
> I see that he often made his own equal to yours.
> But say in peace, of which there was question above,
> Do you win the war, supposedly, without my forces?[19]

The distinction between Great Russia and Little Russia allowed the author of the *History* to take another contentious step and distinguish his loyalty to the ruler from loyalty to the ruler's troops. This distinction becomes particularly apparent in episodes where the anonymous author not only adopts a much more favorable attitude to the Swedish troops in Ukraine than to the tsar's army but also contrasts the benevolence of the Swedes toward the local population with the harsh treatment meted out by the Great Russians:

The incursion of the Swedes into Little Russia by no means resembled that of an enemy invasion and had nothing hostile in it, but they passed through the inhabitants' settlements and plowed fields as friends and humble travelers, touching no one's property and committing none of the misdeeds, licentious acts, and excesses of every kind that are usually perpetrated by our troops in the villages on the grounds that "I am a servant of the tsar! I serve God and the sovereign on behalf of the whole Christian community! Chickens and geese, young women and girls belong to us by military right and by order of His Highness!" The Swedes, on the contrary, demanded nothing of the inhabitants and took nothing by force, but wherever they encountered them, they bought goods from them by voluntary trade and for cash.[20]

In one case, referring to the massacres of Mazepa's supporters by the tsar's troops, the anonymous author even puts Russian persecution of the Little Russian (Rus´) nation on a par with its past persecution by the Poles. His attribution of the cruelty of those massacres to Menshikov does little to hide the fact that, in his mind, the Great Russian regime has proved as oppressive toward his nation as was the Polish one, which created the first Rus´ martyr, Severyn Nalyvaiko. Describing the massacre of Mazepa's supporters in Lebedyn, the anonymous author writes:

That punitive action was Menshikov's usual employment: breaking on the wheel, quartering, and impaling; the lightest, considered mere play, was hanging and decapitation. . . . It now remains to consider and judge—if, according to the words of the Savior himself, written in the Gospel, which are immutable and not to be ignored, "all blood spilled on earth will be required of this generation"—what requirement awaits for the blood of the Rus´ nation shed from the blood of Hetman Nalyvaiko to the present day, and shed in great streams for the sole reason that it sought liberty or a better life in its own land and had intentions in that regard common to all humanity.[21]

The figure of Mazepa, traitor to the tsar and defender of Ukrainian rights, presented the author of the *History of the Rus´*

with one more difficulty when it came to the anathema declared against him by the official church. Mazepa's relationship to Christianity was a significant problem that had to be dealt with one way or another, as it constituted a major obstacle to the hetman's historical rehabilitation. The author of the *History* coped with the anathema in a number of ways. Some of his methods exemplify his Enlightenment-era tolerance of other religions, while others display his romantic readiness to bend the facts and invent stories if they fit his paradigm. The anonymous author rejects as a form of superstition the popular conception of the Swedes as non-Christians. He also brands as fables stories about Mazepa joining the Swedes in rejecting Orthodoxy and desecrating Orthodox icons. Furthermore, he claims that Mazepa never spilled Christian—more precisely, Orthodox—blood.

In all these cases, the anonymous author is prepared to stand up for Mazepa, speaking now in his own voice and not hiding behind one of his characters. With regard to the spilling of Christian blood, the author first makes the apocryphal Mazepa declare neutrality in his speech to the Cossack Host, and then states that Mazepa maintained his neutrality during the Battle of Poltava, refusing to send his troops against the tsar's army. If Mazepa's declaration of neutrality was sheer invention on the part of the author, his troops' non-participation in the battle was not. They were too insignificant in number and too unreliable in military training and political loyalty to be used in combat.

This historical fact is interpreted by the anonymous author in a way that allows him to advance the thesis of Mazepa's neutrality, thereby undermining official accusations of political treason and betrayal of the Orthodox religion. According to the author of the *History*, Mazepa and his troops

> remained at their camps and the Swedish ones at all times, constantly avoiding engagements with the Russians and maintaining the strictest neutrality toward them, stipulated by Mazepa with the Swedish king and announced in his declarations throughout Little Russia. For Mazepa, as everyone knows, was a Christian, deeply pious, having built many monasteries and churches at his expense, and he considered it a mortal sin to

shed the blood of his compatriots and coreligionists, and he held to this with resolute firmness, yielding to no persuasions.[22]

The *History*'s emphasis on Mazepa's support of the Orthodox Church and the construction of Orthodox monasteries and shrines corresponds closely to the treatment of Mazepa by Oleksii Martos in his memoirs and was probably an important element of the Mazepa myth in early nineteenth-century Ukraine. Martos, who was close to the author of the *History of the Rus'* not only in his assessment of Mazepa but also in his treatment of the Pereiaslav Agreement of 1654 and other episodes of Ukrainian history,[23] may have had an opportunity to acquaint himself with the *History* between 1818 and 1821, when he was actively working on his own history of Ukraine. It is much more likely, however, that both authors utilized the same sources or reflected the same attitudes of the Ukrainian nobility (the Martos family, the Shyrais, and the anonymous author of the *History of the Rus'* either came from the Chernihiv region or had strong connections with it).

In any case, both Martos and the author of the *History of the Rus'* are highly critical of the anathema declared against Mazepa by the Russian Orthodox Church. The anonymous author characterizes the ritual declaration of anathema as "something new that had never yet existed in Little Russia; something terrible that was called 'Mazepa's companion to Hades.'" There can be little doubt that the author disapproved of Peter's presence at the ceremony, but, as always, he was prepared to shift the blame to one of the tsar's advisers, this time Feofan Prokopovych: "The numerous Little Russian clergy and the Great Russian clergy closest to these borders, deliberately summoned to Hlukhiv, under the leadership and inspection of the well-known bishop Prokopovych, having constituted itself as a so-called local synod, consigned Mazepa to eternal damnation, or anathema, on the ninth day of that same November. This dismal ceremony took place in the brick Church of Saint Nicholas in the presence of the sovereign, with a large assembly of officials and members of the public."[24]

In both the *History of the Rus'* and Martos's memoirs, Mazepa emerges not only as a defender of the interests of the Little Russian (Rus') nation but also as a proponent of its independence. The vision of an independent Ukraine, admittedly harking back to the past, is presented in the *History* as one of the goals of Mazepa and his ally, Charles XII. It must have been highly consonant with attitudes dominant in some segments of Ukrainian society, if Martos's memoirs are any indication. Given that the anonymous author's main strategy was to convince the imperial government to treat the Ukrainians as equals, Mazepa's references to independence should be regarded more as a threat than as a real political program.

The author of the *History of the Rus´* was caught between two contradictory imperatives: his loyalty to the ruler and the Romanov dynasty conflicted with his clear admiration for Mazepa as an embodiment of the Enlightenment ideals of struggle against tyranny, defense of human dignity, and protection of national rights. The solution to this seemingly insoluble problem was found in the concept of the nation, deeply rooted in Ukrainian historical writing of the previous era. While the anonymous author of the *History* remained loyal to the tsar in his description of the Poltava episode and shifted responsibility for Peter's ruthlessness and cruelty to his advisers, he found no difficulty in denouncing the tsar's Great Russian nation. If revolt against the tsar remained illegitimate for the author, the struggle of one nation against another in defense of its freedom and liberties certainly did not. The anonymous author was still faithful to Jean Bodin's notion that only God could judge and punish a ruler, but he was no less attuned to the ideal of national sovereignty as promoted by the leaders of the American and French revolutions.

In its interpretation of the Ukrainian past the *History* places the nation on a par with the ruler. The Rus´ nation of the *History* was first and foremost that of the Cossack officers and their descendants, but on occasion it could include the popular masses as well. The author of the *History* was dismissive of people of low social status and critical of the actions of uneducated peasants, but he had no qualms about using their deeds as an argument in his exposition when it suited his purpose. In his treatment of Little Russians and Great Russians, the anonymous author was unquestionably following in the footsteps of Semen Divovych and his

Conversation between Great and Little Russia, but he was prepared to go even further and treat their relations as those between separate nations, not just distinct historical and legal entities.

The anonymous author also emerges from the pages of his *History* as the first Ukrainian intellectual to struggle with the notion of the religious and ethnic closeness of Russians and Ukrainians. He recognizes the depth of the cultural association between the two nations but rejects the actions of the popular masses informed by that affinity. Instead, he turns the affinity into his principal weapon, claiming Ukraine's historical primacy as the Rus´ nation, attributing the Rus´ name almost exclusively to his compatriots, and trying to shame the Russian state and society into granting equal rights to their Little Russian brethren.

If one judges by the *History of the Rus´*, the Ukrainian elites of the early nineteenth century could not help admiring Mazepa despite their best efforts to remain loyal to the monarchy. Mazepa, however, never became an unambiguously positive character in Ukraine. Unable to resolve the problem of Mazepa's disloyalty to Peter, the elites had to conceal and qualify their admiration for the hetman. After all, according to Pogodin's diary, the Chernihiv nobility not only "loved Mazeppa" but also admired Osyp Sudiienko, a descendant of a prominent Cossack officer family who in 1811 donated one hundred thousand rubles to build a church commemorating Peter's victory at Poltava.

II

THE RED CENTURY

6.

How Russian Was the Russian Revolution?

There is probably no more important, though convoluted and often confusing, term for understanding Russian history than "Russian Revolution." The most confusing aspect of the term "Russian Revolution" is that it often obscures what actually took place in the multiethnic Russian Empire—a revolution of nations, of which the Russians were only one. The Russian Revolution understood as a multiethnic phenomenon fundamentally changed not only the economic, social, and cultural life of the former subjects of the Romanovs but also relations among the nationalities.

Nowhere were those revolutionary changes more dramatic than in the realm of imperial Russian national identity. From the mid-seventeenth century Russia was imagined by its elites as an entity composed of three Russias: Great, Little, and White. Since the mid-nineteenth century, Russian ethnographers and geographers had imagined the Russian nation itself as composed of three branches: Great Russian, Little Russian (Ukrainian), and White Russian (Belarusian). The emphasis was on unity, not diversity, and the imperial authorities were doing their best to ban the development of separate literary languages in Ukraine and Belarus, as well as to promote the Russian literary language as all-Russian or pan-Russian. But the concept of the pan-Russian nation and culture suffered a hard landing in the Revolution of 1917.

While Russia lost only part of its empire, the all-Russian nation fell apart completely, splitting into three separate nations: Russians, Ukrainians, and Belarusians. More than any other single event, the Russian Revolution set the Russians as a people on the path to modern nationhood, changing the geopolitics of the region for generations to come.

Vasilii Kliuchevsky treated the reunification of the Rus´ land as one of the driving forces of Russian history. The Russian Empire was never closer to the goal of reunifying those lands and forming one Russian nation than in April 1915, when Nicholas II visited Lviv and Przemyśl (Peremyshl). But the successful offensive of the Central Powers in May 1915 precipitated the rapid decline and subsequent disintegration of the Russian Empire. The Revolution of February 1917 made Poland and Finland free and began to split the core of the big Russian nation as well.

A key role in that process was played by Ukraine. Mykhailo Hrushevsky and the Central Rada unilaterally declared the territorial autonomy of Ukraine in June 1917. The genie of the federal restructuring of the Russian Empire and the concomitant partitioning of the big Russian nation was out of the bottle. The Provisional Government tried to put it back by sending its ministers to Kyiv, hoping to convince the Rada to withdraw its declaration of autonomy. Faced with the Rada's refusal, which was backed by Ukraine's minorities, including Jewish and Polish socialists, the ministers negotiated a deal in which they recognized the Rada and its government, the General Secretariat, as representatives of the Provisional Government in Ukraine. Thus Ukrainian autonomy, in curtailed form, survived its first encounter with the central government in Petrograd.

The Russian nationalists were outraged by what they interpreted as a surrender of Russian national interests by the socialist ministers of the Provisional Government. Vasilii Shulgin led the charge. He regarded the Provisional Government's recognition of curtailed Ukrainian autonomy as a betrayal of the Russian nation, of which Ukraine (Little Russia) and its inhabitants were an integral part. Shulgin insisted that Russians constituted the majority of the population in Ukraine. He defined Russianness on the basis of the written rather than the spoken language, and if one judged by the number of readers of the Kyivan press, it was the Ukrainians, not the Russians, who were in the minority. For Shulgin, the most important question was not the future structure of the Russian state but the "reclassification" of Little Russians as Ukrainians and Little Russia as Ukraine. In January 1918, Ukraine declared its independence from Russia, soon to be backed by the advancing German and Austrian armies.

The Central Powers not only backed the Ukrainians but also promoted Belarusian statehood. After German forces took Minsk in late February 1918, two groups of Belarusian activists, one assembled in Vilnius under the German occupation, the other formed in Minsk under Russian control, got together and decided, after heated debates, on the formation not of a Lithuanian-Belarusian but a separate Belarusian state independent of Russia. Their declaration of 25 March 1918 read as follows: "Today we, the Rada of the Belarusian National Republic, cast off our country the last chains of political servitude imposed by Russian tsarism upon our free and independent land."[1] The decision to declare Belarusian independence was passed by a slim majority of the assembly, and its significance was more symbolic than practical. The Belarusians were no longer claiming national and cultural autonomy or federal status in a future Russian state but outright independence.

It was in this period that Belarus acquired its insignia of statehood: a national flag with white stripes at the top and bottom and a red one in between, and a coat of arms featuring a mounted knight with a sword and shield—a symbol dating from the times of the Grand Duchy of Lithuania. The Rada established diplomatic representations in Vilnius, Kyiv, Berlin and other European capitals, issued Belarusian postage stamps, and supported cultural and publishing projects. In the course of just one year, from March 1917 to March 1918, the Belarusian national movement, like the Ukrainian, made a huge leap from demands for cultural autonomy to full independence.

The Whites under General Anton Denikin tried to put the genie of East Slavic independence back into the imperial bottle. When Denikin took Kyiv in August 1919, Shulgin got an opportunity to apply his solution of the Ukrainian question to the rest of Ukraine. He was the principal drafter of Denikin's programmatic appeal "To the Inhabitants of Little Russia," made public on the eve of his entrance into Kyiv. The appeal proclaimed Russian as the language of state institutions and the educational system but did not outlaw the "Little Russian language." It was to be allowed only in elementary schools to help students master Russian, as well as in private secondary schools. Its use in the court system was also permitted. This was very much in line with the program advocated by the Constitutional Democrats before the war and, in particular, with the thinking of Petr Struve, who opposed the prohibition of the Ukrainian language and culture but envisioned them as serving the lower classes of society, reserving the higher cultural spheres for the Russian language alone. But the Whites did not deliver even on those promises and attempted to suppress Ukrainian political and cultural activities completely.

The Bolsheviks under Vladimir Lenin were much more flexible and opportunistic. Lenin's thinking was rooted in his ideas on dominant and oppressed nationalities, first formulated on the eve and in the course of World War I, very much in response to Russian imperial mobilization under the banners of the Union of the Russian People and other nationalist organizations. Lenin, never a believer in the all-Russian nation, was prepared to treat the Great Russians, Ukrainians, and Belarusians as separate nations. According to him, the Great Russians were dominant, while the Ukrainians and Belarusians, former members of the privileged big Russian nation, were among the oppressed. In the summer of 1917, Lenin raised his voice in support of the Central Rada against what he perceived as the great-power chauvinism of the Provisional Government. But Lenin's stand on the nationalities was nothing if not contradictory.

As Terry Martin has noted, Lenin's nationality policies and pronouncements before October 1917 were designed with an eye to rallying support from the non-Russian nationalities for the overthrow of the existing regime, not for running the multiethnic country of which the Bolsheviks took control in the fall of 1917. The party that spoke Bolshevik now had to speak Ukrainian as well. Lenin spelled out the new policy in early December 1919 in a special resolution of the party's Central Committee on Soviet rule in Ukraine. He reminded his comrades that the Ukrainian language and culture had been persecuted and discriminated against under the tsarist regime and called on them to make it possible for the peasantry to speak Ukrainian in all governmental institutions, with no further discrimination. "Measures should be taken immediately to ensure that there is a sufficient number of Ukrainian-speaking personnel in all Soviet institutions, and that in future all personnel are able to make themselves understood in Ukrainian," wrote Lenin.[2]

What to do with the three East Slavic nations and their pro forma independence not only in cultural but also in political terms was decided in the fall and winter of 1922. As far as Lenin was concerned, Joseph Stalin's plan to include the republics in the Russian Federation, especially against the will of their leaders, put the Russians in the position of imperial masters, thereby undermining the idea of the voluntary union of nations. Lenin's thinking about the future of the republics was influenced by his concern for world-wide unity of the working classes of all nationalities. The survival of Soviet rule was closely linked in his mind with the success of world revolution, which depended on risings of the workers of Germany, France, and Britain, and then on nationalist movements in China, India, and Western colonies in Asia. The desire of those peoples for self-rule would have to be satisfied if the revolution were to triumph on a global scale.

Instead of an enlarged Russian Federation, Lenin proposed the creation of a Union of Soviet Republics of Europe and Asia. It was supposed to unite Russia and the existing formally independent republics as equals and establish all-Union government bodies. Stalin, recognizing that an enlarged Russian Federation would create a poor image for the multiethnic communist state as a community of equals, proposed simply to turn the Russian government bodies into all-Union ones. As he saw it, there was no need for another level of bureaucracy. But Lenin would not back down: for him, the Union was a matter of principle, not of expediency. Some way had to be found to accommodate rising non-Russian nationalism, but Stalin's model proposed a return to the ethnic inequality of the past, which had already brought down the Russian Empire and might topple the Soviet state as well.

Stalin was enforcing his control over the rebellious Georgian communists not only with party resolutions but also with fists. His point man in the Caucasus, Sergo Ordzhonikidze, had beaten up one of his Georgian opponents. When the Georgians complained, Stalin appointed a commission headed by his client Feliks Dzerzhinsky, the head of the secret police, which exonerated Ordzhonikidze. After a long talk with Dzerzhinsky on 12 December 1922, the highly agitated Lenin suffered a stroke that led to his partial paralysis a few days later. He was now lying in bed, trying to explain to the party leadership what was wrong with Stalin's policies and how they could be neutralized by reforming the Union that he had proposed, which had just been approved by the First All-Union Congress.

This was the leitmotif of the notes on the nationality question that the half-paralyzed Lenin dictated to his secretaries on 30 and 31 December. In Lenin's view, the main threat to the unity of his state was coming not from local nationalists, whom he hoped to accommodate by creating a federal façade for the future Union, but from the Great Russian nationalism that threatened to derail his plans. Dictating his thoughts, he argued for positive discrimination in favor of the non-Russian republics: "Internationalism on the part of the oppressor or so-called 'great' nation (although it is great only in its coercion, great only in the sense of being a great bully) should consist not only in observing the formal equality of nations but also in the kind of inequality that would redress, on the part of the oppressor nation, the great nation, the inequality that develops in actual practice."[3]

Lenin attacked the government apparatus, largely controlled by Stalin, claiming that it was mainly inherited from the old regime and permeated with Russian great-power chauvinism. The way to keep it in check was to take powers from the center and transfer them to the republics. Lenin was prepared to replace the Union he proposed and the model approved by the party congress with a looser union in which the powers of the center might be limited to defense and international relations alone. He felt that the republics' right of secession, guaranteed by the Union treaty, might be an insufficient counterweight to Russian nationalism and proposed that at the next congress the Union be reformed to leave the center with the aforementioned functions alone. The Union just approved by the congress gave the central government control over the economy, finance, and communications on top of military and international affairs.

Lenin did not get his way on the issue of confederation, and it is not clear whether he really wanted that model or simply used it as an argument in his polemics with Stalin. Nevertheless, he prevailed on the issue of the structure of the Union—a victory that had even larger consequences for the Russians than for the non-Russians of the former empire. Lenin's victory created a separate republic within the Union for the Russians, endowing them with a territory, institutions, population, and identity distinct from those of the Union as a whole. In the state planned by Stalin, the Russians would have continued to share all those features with the empire renamed as a union. In Lenin's state, they had no choice but to start acquiring an identity separate from the imperial one. Almost by default, Lenin became the father of the modern Russian nation, while the Soviet Union became its first cradle. Lenin's victory did much to fragment the prerevolutionary model of one big Russian nation. The result was a major shift in Russian self-perception and their perception by others, Ukrainians in particular.

7.

Killing by Hunger

On 14 December 1932, Joseph Stalin and Viacheslav Molotov, the former as head of the Communist Party, the latter as premier of the Soviet government, signed a decree "On the Procurement of Grain in Ukraine, the North Caucasus, and the Western Region." The country was in the midst of a food crisis that had already caused widespread hunger, but the decree was not concerned with the fate of the peasantry and the impending famine. Its purpose was to mobilize party cadres to continue extracting grain from the countryside so that, among other things, it could be sold abroad to pay for Soviet industrialization. Procurement quotas were not being fulfilled, and the collectivization of agriculture itself was in trouble, as was the reputation of Stalin and his team and, ultimately, their chances of staying in power.

The Soviet leaders demanded that their underlings in Ukraine and the North Caucasus—two of the three main grain-producing areas of the USSR—fulfill the grain-procurement plans for 1932 by January–February 1933. The decree of 14 December ordered the arrest and, if necessary, the execution of collective-farm heads and local officials who failed to fulfill the quotas. Some of the "saboteurs" were mentioned by name: fifteen regional officials were to be sentenced to hard labor for periods between five and ten years—the decree gave the Soviet judiciary a modicum of flexibility in that regard. In the Kuban region of the North Caucasus, the inhabitants of the Poltavskaia settlement were accused of sabotaging the procurement campaign, and the secret police was ordered to deport its entire population to the Soviet North.

The village would be resettled by Red Army veterans from central Russia.

But Stalin was not after bread alone. The decree of 14 December also dealt with the politics of culture. All "saboteurs" listed by name were Soviet cadres from Ukraine, and the population of the Poltavskaia village happened to be overwhelmingly Ukrainian as well. The decree ordered local officials in the Kuban to change the language of their official correspondence and of public education immediately from Ukrainian to Russian and to stop publishing Ukrainian-language newspapers and journals. In Ukraine, the decree demanded that the republic's leaders establish strict control over the "Ukrainization" policy instituted in the 1920s to promote the development of Ukrainian culture, and that they purge so-called nationalists and agents of foreign powers.

The December 1932 decree turned Stalin's all-Union "grain-extraction" campaign into a direct assault on the Ukrainian political elite and the cultural foundations of Ukrainian nation-building, thereby distinguishing the famine in Ukraine from that in other parts of the USSR. Now known in Ukraine as the Great Famine or Holodomor (killing by hunger), the famine of 1932–33 claimed the lives of close to four million people, more than half of those who starved to death in the Soviet Union during that period. The famine dramatically changed Ukrainian society and culture, leaving deep scars in the national memory. It also produced a vast literature on the subject and generated numerous debates in Ukraine and beyond. As the Soviet regime refused to admit the very existence of the famine, its recognition was hotly contested in the last decades of the Cold War. Subsequently it became a bone of contention between Ukraine and Russia, with the government of the former defining the famine as an act of genocide against the Ukrainian people and the latter stressing the all-Union character of the disaster.

With *Red Famine: Stalin's War on Ukraine* (2017), Anne Applebaum walks into the minefields of memory left by Stalin's policies in Ukraine and multiple attempts to conceal, uncover, interpret and reinterpret the Holodomor with new determination to set the record straight and new evidence that has become accessible since the fall of the Soviet Union. Her book is the most important English-language study of the famine since Robert Conquest's *Harvest of Sorrow*, published in 1986. She also uses a different set of lenses to evaluate the evidence provided by government documents and survivor testimonies.

Red Famine stands out from the existing English-language literature on the subject by its persistent focus on Ukraine as the place where the famine story not only takes on its salient characteristics and concludes but also where it begins. Applebaum recognizes and states repeatedly that the famine was not limited to Ukraine and was caused by policies that grew out of considerations and circumstances broader than what she defines as Moscow's "Ukrainian Question." But she is no less persistent in pointing out the uniqueness of the Ukrainian situation and the political and cultural factors—the strength of Ukrainian nationalism, the stubborn peasant resistance to the communist regime in Moscow and, last but not least, the fertility of the soil—that made the Ukrainian famine the deadliest of the Soviet famines of the time.

The time frame of the book is unusually broad for histories of the Great Famine. While the events of 1932–33 are central, Applebaum presents a brief survey of Ukraine's history before the twentieth century that illuminates her approach to the "Ukrainian Question." She also covers in detail the prehistory of the famine, starting with the Revolution of 1917, and her epilogue brings the interpretation of the Holodomor up to the present. This contextualization of the famine helps to explain its importance for the perennial historical debate on the Russian Revolution, understood in the book as comprising a number of national revolutions, the Ukrainian one in particular, and for the history of Russo-Ukrainian relations, so hostile today.

Ukraine's rich black soil has produced grain for international markets since the days of Herodotus, and the country became known as the "breadbasket of Europe" long before Germany occupied it in 1918 to feed its army and home front. In particular, the Bolsheviks were there before the Germans came. Applebaum documents the Bolshevik obsession with Ukrainian grain in striking detail. "For God's sake, use all energy and all revolutionary measures to send grain, grain, and more grain!" wrote Vladimir Lenin to his commanders in Ukraine in January 1918. "Otherwise Petrograd may starve to death. Use special trains and special detachments. Collect and store. Escort the trains. Inform us every day. For God's sake!" Lenin's troops were waging war against the socialist government of the Ukrainian Central Rada allegedly to crush counterrevolution, but at the top of Lenin's agenda was grain, without which the Bolshevik regime was doomed. The village, especially the Ukrainian village, was there to be robbed and exploited: communist colonialism was taking shape.

The Bolshevik regime survived civil war and economic collapse not only by being ruthless but also by making concessions to forces that its leaders were initially unprepared to tolerate, including Ukrainian nationalism and the Ukrainian peasantry. The first was appeased by the policy of Ukrainization, which offered support for the Ukrainian language and culture in exchange for giving up aspirations to political sovereignty. The second was pacified by the New Economic Policy, which allowed the peasants to hold the land they had acquired in the revolution and put an end to requisitions, introducing elements of the market.

Ukraine, or rather eastern and central parts of today's Ukraine that comprised the Ukrainian Socialist Soviet Republic during the interwar period, benefited from both policies, but the Bolsheviks considered them temporary. Their long-term objective was the elimination of both the peasantry and the nationalities. "The national question is purely a peasant question," declared Mikhail Kalinin, the formal head of the Soviet state and one of the very few Bolshevik leaders with a peasant background. "[T]he best way to eliminate nationality is a massive factory with thousands of workers." The connection established by the Bolshevik rulers between the peasant and nationality questions created a conviction that cost Ukraine millions of lives.

The Soviet Union entered the 1930s with a new sense of insecurity that prompted a drive to accelerate the revolutionary transformation of the economy and society. The Soviet leaders' hopes of using the Russian Revolution as a spark to ignite world revolution, first in Europe and then in the colonial East, never materialized and were replaced by the ruling elite's determination to build socialism in one country. The survival of the regime in a hostile capitalist environment necessitated a strong military-industrial complex to arm and mechanize the military, while mobilizing the population in defense of the "socialist motherland" required an ideology with deeper local roots than Marxist internationalism. The regime looked to the village to provide human and agricultural resources for industrialization and to Russian nationalism as a source of legitimization—policies that promised nothing good for Ukraine.

The first to feel pressure from the center was the village. Stalin's policy of forced collectivization, implemented in the fall of 1929, singled out Ukraine for especially rapid conversion to the supposedly more efficient model of agriculture. The collectivized farms were to produce more grain and sell it to the state for rock-bottom prices, providing resources for building the military-industrial complex. Those who questioned the new policy were declared to be kulaks (in Russian) or kurkuls (in Ukrainian)—a term that delegitimized the most entrepreneurial peasants, who had everything to lose from collectivization, as agents of counter-revolution. In March 1930, Moscow ordered the arrest of 15,000 kurkuls and the deportation to the North of more than 35,000 kurkul families from Ukraine alone.

The Ukrainian village, with its record of armed resistance to the Bolsheviks, rebelled. Two thousand "mass protests" were registered in Ukraine in March 1930 alone. Peasants in the Pavlohrad and Kryvyi Rih areas—the home base of the strongest warlord of the revolutionary era, Nestor Makhno—formed detachments but were soon outnumbered and outgunned by the regime's security forces. In areas neighboring on Poland, whole villages marched to the border in a futile attempt to cross it and leave the collectivization nightmare behind. Stalin sounded a retreat, blaming excesses in collectivization on overzealous local cadres. Peasants forcibly enrolled in the collective farms were allowed to leave them. That gave the peasants an incentive to work on their plots and, coupled with good weather, helped produce a record harvest in Ukraine in the summer and fall of 1930. It was a victory for the peasantry and a defeat for collectivization, but Stalin interpreted the good harvest differently.

With the harvest in the silos, Stalin moved his shock troops of party and Young Communist League activists and secret-police officers back into the countryside to push once again for collectivization and collect the grain. With rebel leaders of the previous year imprisoned or exiled and villages cleansed of kurkuls, the peasants returned to the collective farms, but they did not change their attitude toward the government and its policies. They were not eager to grow more than was needed for themselves and their families. The record harvest of 1930 would never be equaled again. Stalin and his aides in the Kremlin decided that peasants were simply hiding the grain they had grown. In the fall of 1931, they ordered requisitions that brought new famine to Ukraine in the spring of 1932. Hardest hit were the sugar beet-producing areas south of Kyiv, where the authorities tried to collect grain that was not there in the first place. The famine, limited at that point to Ukraine alone, had begun.

As people began dying en masse in central Ukraine in the late spring and early summer of 1932, the government in Moscow sent the republic new quotas for grain procurement in the fall of that year. As there was no sowing in regions already affected by famine, and the rest of the collective farms were in disarray, Ukrainian party officials sounded the alarm, pleading with Stalin for the reduction of quotas. He refused. Keeping the 1932 quotas in place and maintaining pressure on the peasantry, Stalin opened a new front in his war on Ukraine. His enemies were the Ukrainian party and government officials who were trying to defend the peasantry instead of toeing the party line and extracting grain no matter what.

The attack on the Ukrainian political leadership, allegedly colluding with the kurkuls in the countryside, was first conceived in the summer of 1932. Doubting the loyalty of the cadres in Ukraine, Stalin accused them of sympathizing with Ukrainian nationalism, a trend that he associated with Symon Petliura, a Ukrainian leader of the revolutionary era. He also suspected them of leanings toward Petliura's former ally, the leader of Poland, Marshal Józef Piłsudski. "If we don't make an effort now to improve the situation in Ukraine, we may lose Ukraine," wrote

Stalin to his right-hand man, Lazar Kaganovich. "Keep in mind that Piłsudski is not daydreaming. . . . Keep in mind that the Communist Party of Ukraine includes more than a few rotten elements, conscious and unconscious Petliurites as well as direct agents of Piłsudski. As soon as things get worse, these elements will not be slow in opening a front within and outside the party against the party."

Stalin wanted to purge the party leadership and top echelons of the Ukrainian secret police not only to facilitate increased grain requisitions but also to cleanse the party and government apparatus of cadres more loyal to their people than to their boss in Moscow. In November 1932 Stalin appointed a new chief of the Ukrainian secret police, Vsevolod Balytsky, who was experienced in combating Ukrainian nationalism. In the following month he opened one more front in his Ukrainian war, this time against the cultural elite. The decree signed on 14 December 1932 signaled the start of Stalin's offensive on all three fronts: against the peasantry, the local party elite, and the Ukrainian intelligentsia. It linked the failure to fulfill grain-requisition plans with kulak resistance to the regime, the alleged nationalism of the elites, the subversive activities of foreign governments, and policies to promote the Ukrainian language and culture. The political stage on which the Great Famine of 1932–33 would occur was now fully in place.

On New Year's Day 1933, Stalin sent a telegram to the Ukrainian party bosses ordering them to apply a recently adopted law on the theft of collective-farm property in order to prosecute those who did not fulfill grain quotas. From now on, every grain found in a peasant household could be considered stolen from the collective farm and thus from the state. As the procurement brigades, composed of party cadres from the cities, police officials, and local activists moved from one peasant household to another, confiscating grain and often taking all available food supplies as "fines" from the starving peasants, they left in their wake a devastated countryside bracing itself for the now inevitable famine.

The first cases of mass death from starvation were recorded that same January. Especially hard hit were regions of central Ukraine that had not recovered from the famine of 1932. Peasants there died at a higher rate than anywhere else, with Kyiv and Kharkiv Oblasts accounting for losses of over 1 million each.

Altogether close to 4 million people would die in Ukraine, most of them between March and June 1933, when food supplies were exhausted and early crops turned out to be too difficult for starving stomachs to digest. Government assistance arrived too late and was insufficient to stop the death spiral. It was distributed exclusively to the collective farms and shipped predominantly to the main grain-producing areas in southern Ukraine. People in the most severely afflicted areas of central Ukraine were left to die. As in the Gulag, the subject of Applebaum's earlier book, the regime was prepared to feed those still able to work.

As the peasants died of hunger, Stalin intensified his war on Ukraine on two other fronts: against the party elite and the cultural intelligentsia. The charge was led by Stalin's plenipotentiary Pavel Postyshev, who arrived in Ukraine in January 1933. Tens of thousands of Ukrainian communists were purged from the party during Postyshev's first year in Ukraine. In the commissariat of education close to 4,000 teachers were dismissed, and repressive measures were taken against most school administrators. Ukrainian writers were targeted for especially severe persecution. In May 1933, on hearing of the arrest of his friend, the writer Mykhailo Ialovy, Ukraine's leading communist author, Mykola Khvyliovy, committed suicide. "The arrest of Ialovy—this is the murder of an entire generation. . . . For what? Because we were the most sincere communists?" wrote Khvyliovy in his death note.

In July 1933, Mykola Skrypnyk, an old Bolshevik and architect of cultural policies in Ukraine, committed suicide to avoid imminent arrest. By that time, teaching and publishing in Ukrainian not only in the Kuban but also in other regions of the Russian Federation settled by Ukrainians was already banned. The largest ethnic minority in Russia was wiped out in cultural terms. In Ukraine itself, the promotion of Ukrainian culture among non-Ukrainians was stopped in its tracks, ensuring the dominance of Russian culture in the Ukrainian cities. Stalin's three-pronged assault on the Ukrainian peasantry and the country's political and intellectual elite produced a new Ukraine—subdued and silent but refusing to forget.

*
**

Anne Applebaum tells the story of the Great Famine not only with compassion but also with precision, using a wealth of official documents and oral testimony to reconstruct the events and reveal the thoughts, concerns, and feelings of those involved, both perpetrators and victims. Analyzing the famine in multiple political, economic, ethnic, and cultural contexts, she avoids reducing it to a chronicle of ethnic suffering or turning it into something that it was not.

"Stalin did not seek to kill *all* Ukrainians, nor did all Ukrainians resist," writes Applebaum in her conclusions. The Holodomor, she suggests, does not conform to the definition of genocide set forth in the United Nations convention of 1948, but it readily fits the definition produced by no less a figure than the father of the concept, the lawyer Raphael Lemkin, who emphasizes the Soviet attack on the Ukrainian political and cultural elite in his article of 1952, "Soviet Genocide in Ukraine." The UN convention, explains Applebaum, was shaped in large part by the Soviet delegates to that organization, who were eager to limit the definition of genocide to acts committed by proponents of fascist and racist ideologies. Applebaum leaves it to the reader to draw his or her own conclusions on the issue.

Red Famine, a book about an enormous tragedy, ends on a positive note. Applebaum suggests that Stalin, who succeeded in forcing the Ukrainian peasantry into collective farms and crushed the Ukrainian national renaissance of the 1920s, lost in the long term. People were killed, but their legacy lived on, as did the Ukrainian language, culture, and idea of independence. So did the memory of the Holodomor. "As a nation Ukrainians know what happened in the twentieth century," reads the last sentence of the book. *Red Famine* helps not only Ukrainians but the world at large to gain a better understanding of what the twentieth century brought to the world.

8.

Mapping the Great Famine

One of the most insightful and moving eyewitness accounts of the Holodomor, or the Great Ukrainian Famine of 1932–33, was written by Oleksandra Radchenko, a teacher in the Kharkiv region of Ukraine. In her diary, which was confiscated by Stalin's secret police and landed the author in the Gulag for ten long years, the thirty-six-year-old teacher recorded not only what she saw around her but also what she thought about the tragedy unfolding before her eyes.

"I am so afraid of hunger; I'm afraid for the children," wrote Radchenko, who had three young daughters, in February 1932. "May God protect us and have mercy on us. It would not be so offensive if it were due to a bad harvest, but they have taken away the grain and created an artificial famine." That year she wrote about the starvation and suffering of her neighbors and acquaintances but recorded no deaths from starvation. That all changed in January 1933, when she encountered the first corpse of a famine victim on the road leading to her home. By the spring of 1933, she was regularly reporting mass deaths from starvation. "People are dying," wrote Radchenko in her entry for 16 May 1933: "People are saying that whole villages have died in southern Ukraine."[1]

Was Radchenko's story unique? Did people all over Ukraine indeed suffer from starvation in 1932 and then start dying en masse in 1933? Which areas of Ukraine were most affected? Was there a north-south divide, as the diary suggests, and, if so, did people suffer (and die) more in the south than in the north? Were there more deaths in villages than in towns and cities? Were small towns affected? Did ethnicity matter? These are the core questions that the Harvard Ukrainian Research Institute's Digital Map of Ukraine Project is attempting to answer by developing the Geographic Information System (GIS)-based Digital Atlas of the Holodomor. The maps included in the atlas are based on a newly created and growing database that makes it possible to link different levels of spatial analysis from the raion to the republic level and to compare demographic, economic, environmental, and political indicators in relation to a given administrative unit.

Most of the questions we try to answer with the help of the GIS database have been informed by the vast literature on the Great Famine, with its focus on the causes of mass deaths from starvation, including environmental factors, levels of collectivization and, last but not least, nationality policy. By measuring the "footprint" of the Great Famine, we also seek to understand its dynamics, the intentions of the authorities, the fate of the survivors, and the consequences of mass starvation.[2]

The scope of our research has been determined by the availability of geo-referenced maps and "mappable" data. We have been working with a variety of maps of the Ukrainian Soviet Socialist Republic in its interwar borders prepared with the assistance of cartographers of Kartohrafiia Publishers in Ukraine, led by Rostyslav Sossa. Those maps served as a basis for the maps prepared specifically for this website by the chief cartographer of the Digital Atlas of Ukraine, Gennadi Poberezny, and its IT coordinator, Kostyantyn Bondarenko. They reflect administrative changes in Ukraine's external and internal borders, allowing us to compare the results of the 1926 and 1939 population censuses with data from the famine years of 1932–33. These maps help us answer many important questions, but they also impose limitations on our research, as most do not go beyond the raion level. They also stop at the boundaries of Soviet Ukraine and do not include the neighboring areas of Russia, Belarus, Poland, and Romania, thereby restricting our focus to questions that could be answered within the boundaries of interwar Soviet Ukraine.

Another set of limitations we had to face was the absence of reliable data on population losses in Ukraine at the oblast and raion levels. Such data were produced specifically for the purposes of this project by a group of demographers, including

Oleh Wolowyna (University of North Carolina at Chapel Hill), Omelian Rudnytsky, Nataliia Levchuk, Pavlo Shevchuk, and Alla Savchuk (all four from the Institute for Demography and Social Studies in Kyiv). Not all the results of our research to date have materialized in the form of GIS-based maps. Work is still continuing on many of the projects mentioned above. The maps that are currently available on the website, presented in the Map Gallery, reflect the first results of our research. All these maps are also available as parts of the interactive map of the Great Famine, which offers everyone using the website an opportunity not only to check the accuracy of our hypotheses but also to formulate his or her own questions and conduct independent research by comparing different layers of the map.[3]

What follows is the first attempt to make sense of the data we have collected and of the maps we produced on its basis. It is presented in the form of a chronologically based narrative that includes reference to the individual maps but is not and should not be viewed as an attempt at a comprehensive interpretation of the history of the Great Famine. Most of the archival documents used to discuss the meaning of the maps come from the most comprehensive collection of documents on the Great Famine, published in 2007 by Ruslan Pyrih.[4]

Where Did They Die?

Contemporary accounts indicate that Oleksandra Radchenko, whose diary was cited above, lived in one of the regions of Ukraine most severely affected by the Famine of 1932–33. Notwithstanding that, the rumor she recorded in her diary designated southern Ukraine as a region that suffered even more than her own. The rumor made perfect sense, given the experience of people who had lived through the revolution and the first years of Soviet rule. Southern Ukraine, administratively divided in the early 1930s into the Odesa, Dnipropetrovsk, and Donetsk (Stalino) Oblasts, had been the breadbasket of the Russian Empire and, subsequently, of the Soviet Union. Black earth made those lands especially fertile for growing grain in general and wheat in particular. But the Ukrainian steppe was also known for its occasionally harsh winters and, most of all, for the severe droughts that often afflicted the region, causing poor harvests, starvation, and sometimes famine.[5]

The famine of 1921–23 affected the southern parts of the republic, as did the famine of 1928, which was caused by a severe winter, massive loss of winter crops, and Soviet agricultural mismanagement.[6] Decades later, the famine of 1946–47 also ravaged the south more than any other part of Ukraine. While conditions of revolution and civil war and, later, government policies contributed to all three famines, the underlying factors were poor weather conditions and the resulting poor harvests in the black-earth steppe regions of Ukraine. For those who had lived through or knew of the famines of 1921–23 and 1928, it would be only natural to assume in 1932–33 that, whatever was happening in Kharkiv and other central regions of Ukraine, the situation was much worse in the south.[7]

This is not the picture that emerges from the maps produced by our project. According to the estimates of direct losses provided by the demographic group led by Oleh Wolowyna, the direct losses of the famine amounted to 3.9 million, with 0.6 million unborn children, bringing the overall toll of the famine to 4.5 million people.[8] The oblasts of Ukraine that suffered most were not the steppe regions, traditionally affected by drought, but the boreal-steppe zones of central Ukraine encompassing Kharkiv and Kyiv Oblasts. Traditional views on the geographic spread of the Famine of 1932–33, suggesting the south as the most affected area of Ukraine, have also been challenged recently by Stephen G. Wheatcroft and require reevaluation in light of the new demographic data.[9]

Let us start with a summary of the demographic data provided by Wolowyna and his group. Direct losses or total excess deaths, estimated as the difference between actual deaths and "regular" deaths during the non-crisis years, in Kyiv Oblast for 1932–34 have been estimated at 1.1 million; in Kharkiv Oblast, the estimate is 1.0 million. In southern Ukraine, by contrast, the estimates are considerably lower: 368,000 in Dnipropetrovsk Oblast and 327,000 in Odesa Oblast. The same applies if we look at direct losses calculated per thousand of population during all three years in which the effects of the Great Famine were felt. In 1933, the year that accounts for more than 90 percent of all losses, there were approximately 184 deaths per thousand in Kyiv Oblast and 176 per thousand in Kharkiv Oblast, while in Dnipropetrovsk and Odesa Oblasts the death toll was roughly half that level: 96 per thousand in Odesa Oblast and 90 per thousand in Dnipropetrovsk.

A comparison of the maps of the 1921–23, 1928, and 1932–33 famines suggests that the Great Famine had a different "footprint" than the two previous famines and cannot be considered to have been caused primarily by environmental factors or, at least, the same set of environmental factors. This cautious conclusion is supported by the prevailing trend in the historiography of the Great Famine, which emphasizes the human factor, especially government policies, as having caused the famine. It also puts the Famine into the category of "man-made" or, to use Oleksandra Radchenko's term, "artificial" famines.

Does this mean that environmental factors should be dismissed altogether in explaining the causes of the Great Famine? Our research demonstrates that it would be premature to do so. It also shows that environment did matter, but not in the same way as in the famines of the 1920s. On the eve of and during the Holodomor, environmental factors influenced human actions, particularly government policies that eventually contributed to the death toll of the famine.

Collectivization

The first in the long list of those policies was the collectivization drive, the centerpiece of the Soviet agricultural policy launched by the central authorities in the fall of 1928. The map of levels of collectivization shows significant differences among individual regions of the republic belonging to different ecological zones. By the autumn of 1932, 85 percent of peasant households in the steppe oblasts of Dnipropetrovsk, Odesa, and Donetsk had been collectivized, while the rest of the country lagged significantly behind—from 47 percent of households collectivized in Chernihiv Oblast to 72 percent in Kharkiv Oblast. In Kyiv Oblast, 67 percent of households had been collectivized.

What accounts for that difference? The main reason for the higher level of collectivization in the steppe oblasts was a policy designed and introduced by Joseph Stalin and his advisers in Moscow and implemented by the Ukrainian party authorities in Kharkiv. As shown on the map of ecological zones of Ukraine, the country is divided into four zones: two steppe and two boreal zones. It was the dividing line between the boreal and steppe zones that turned out to be the most important one in the eyes of the Moscow authorities as they produced plans for the collectivization drive.

For purposes of official reporting on the progress of collectivization, Ukraine was divided into four areas: Steppe, Left Bank, Right Bank, and Polissia. With the introduction of oblast administrative divisions in February 1932, the Steppe region encompassed the Moldavian Autonomous Republic and Odesa, Dnipropetrovsk, and Donetsk Oblasts; the Left Bank included Kharkiv Oblast and parts of Kyiv Oblast; and the Right Bank encompassed most of Kyiv Oblast and all of Vinnytsia Oblast. Polissia was originally divided between Kyiv and Kharkiv Oblasts, but in October 1932 most of it was included in the newly created Chernihiv Oblast. In July 1932 Donetsk Oblast was created, and it included the Donbas industrial region and the eastern parts of Kharkiv Oblast. Thus, while in the eyes of the central planners there was no clear oblast-based boundary between the boreal and boreal-steppe regions, there was one between the steppe and boreal-steppe areas.[10]

In the summer of 1930, the Central Committee of the Communist Party in Moscow decreed that the level of collectivization in the steppe areas of Ukraine was to reach the 65–75 percent mark by the end of the 1930/31 agricultural year. In other regions of Ukraine, a collectivization level of 35–45 percent was to be attained during the same period of time. The black-earth zones of the southern Ukrainian steppe were considered the principal grain-growing areas of the Soviet Union and were therefore supposed to be collectivized sooner and faster than the others in order to increase the grain yield for the government. As shown on the map of levels of collectivization, by the fall of 1932, according to official statistics, the Ukrainian authorities overshot the 75 percent target introduced for the previous year and reached the 85 percent mark in some of the southern areas. The other regions lagged behind by at least 10 percent.[11]

Stalin and his advisers in Moscow continually focused their attention on southern Ukraine. In March 1932, additional tractors were sent specifically to the Ukrainian steppelands to meet the quotas originally allocated by the Moscow authorities to Russia and Belarus. In April of that year, the general secretary of the Central Committee of the Communist Party of Ukraine, Stanislav Kosior, and other Kharkiv officials visited the southern regions of the Ukrainian steppe oblasts to oversee the sowing campaign firsthand. After the trip Kosior reported on his findings to Stalin. He was glad to note favorable weather conditions and a good crop of winter cereals in Odesa Oblast; he also predicted better sowing than in the previous year.[12]

Thus, by the spring of 1932 the Moscow government had created a new political, social, and technological situation in the southern oblasts of Ukraine. Those areas were more collectivized than the rest of Ukraine, had higher numbers of tractors and agricultural machinery, and, because of their ability to produce significantly more grain than areas to the north, were closer to the central concerns of the Moscow authorities than the rest of Ukraine.

The Advent of Famine

While the south was at the center of Moscow's attention, the Ukrainian government in Kharkiv had to deal with the entire republic. In the late spring of 1932 the attention of the Ukrainian leadership was focused on Kyiv, Vinnytsia, and Kharkiv Oblasts, which encompassed the boreal and boreal-steppe areas of Ukraine. What concerned them was the famine that engulfed the region in the first months of 1932.

Famine began to claim lives in central Ukraine and in the tiny Moldavian Autonomous Republic in the winter of 1931–32, about the same time as Oleksandra Radchenko recorded her first mention of famine in her diary. In 1932, there were 13.9 excess deaths per thousand of population in Kyiv Oblast, 9.4 in the Moldavian Republic, and 7.8 in Kharkiv Oblast. Judging by available official correspondence, the areas hardest hit were in southern Kyiv Oblast, around the cities of Bila Tserkva and Uman. Stanislav Kosior singled out those regions in his April letter to Stalin.

"What they now mainly expect from those regions is reports that there is nothing to eat; that they will not do any sowing," wrote Kosior, referring to the expectations of his underlings in Kharkiv. Judging by the tone and content of the letter, Kosior found himself between a rock and a hard place. On the one hand, he subscribed to the official line established in Moscow that there was no famine in Ukraine; on the other, he was sending clear signals that famine was already there.[13]

What were the causes of the 1932 famine in the southwestern parts of Kyiv Oblast? This area was known as a prime sugar-beet region and often referred to as such in official correspondence, with officials paying special attention not only to the grain harvest but also to the yield of beets and potatoes. In the late 1920s and early 1930s, in southern Kyiv Oblast, wheat—the main object of desire of the authorities in Moscow and Kharkiv—accounted for anywhere between 20 and 40 percent of the land allocated for growing grain. Still, the wheat and grain harvest was the top official concern, as in any other part of Ukraine. Moscow regarded the entire republic as a grain-producing region and assigned plan targets to the Ukrainian SSR as a whole, not to any group of oblasts belonging to a particular ecological zone of Ukraine. Kyiv Oblast came close to fulfilling its grain-procurement quota in 1931 but did so at a prohibitive cost.

In June 1932, the Ukrainian premier, Vlas Chubar, sent Stalin a letter in which he presented his understanding of the causes of famine in southern Kyiv Oblast. "The failure of legume and spring crops in those raions, above all, was not taken into account, and the insufficiency of those crops was made up with foodstuffs in order to fulfill the grain-requisition plans. Given the overall impossibility of fulfilling the grain-requisition plan, the basic reason for which was the lesser harvest in Ukraine as a whole and the colossal losses incurred during the harvest (a result of the weak economic organization of the collective farms and their utterly inadequate management from the raions and from the center), a system was put in place of confiscating all grain produced by individual farmers, including seed stocks, and almost wholesale confiscation of all produce from the collective farms."[14]

What that meant in practice was described in the private diary of Dmytro Zavoloka, a party official in Kyiv Oblast. "Grain was requisitioned right up to the top," wrote Zavoloka in May 1932.

> What they found in the granaries and the houses was taken, almost to the last pound (not everywhere, of course). And the poor or middle peasant or collective farmer often had his last pood [of grain] taken away because someone said that he was hiding kulak grain. In certain places grain requisition…turned into cruel treatment of the inhabitants, bordering on usurpation. Also, very often, they dekulakized "kulaks" who were never kulaks at all. But they came up with any odd reason and sold [the farm].[15]

At the time Zavoloka wrote his assessment of the grain-requisition campaign and its consequences, the famine was reaping its deadly harvest in the boreal-steppe oblasts of Ukraine. According to Chubar, those most severely affected by the famine were individual non-collectivized peasants whose property was requisitioned by the state for their failure to fulfill the procurement quotas. Next on the list were members of collective farms with large families. By March and April 1932, most villages had hundreds of people either starving or dying of hunger. In May 1932, a representative of the Kyiv Central Committee of the Communist Party picked seven villages in the Uman district at random. There were 216 registered deaths from starvation, and 686 individuals were expected to die in the next few days. In one of those villages, Horodnytsia, wrote the party official to Kosior, "up to 100 have died; the daily death toll is 8–12; people are swollen from starvation on 100 of 600 homesteads."[16]

The situation in neighboring Kharkiv Oblast was little better. The Ukrainian party official Hryhorii Petrovsky wrote to Stalin in June 1932, after his tour of Kharkiv Oblast, that "famine has engulfed a good part of the countryside." He requested assistance in the amount of two million poods of grain. "It will take a month or a month and a half for new grain to appear," wrote Petrovsky. "This means that the famine will intensify." A month earlier, officials in Moscow and Kharkiv had received a letter whose authors claimed to represent 5,000 peasants, mostly from Kharkiv Oblast, who were trying to board trains heading out of Ukraine in order to get bread and feed their families. "We can sign this declaration with our own blood," wrote the authors of the letter, "but we are not certain that there is any point in doing so. We inform you in all honesty that until the fruits and vegetables ripen, we are living on the refuse not needed as feed for the chickens, pigs, and dogs of Leningrad, Minsk, Homiel, and other oblasts in the vicinity of Moscow. . . ."[17]

In June 1932, when party officials in Kharkiv put together a list of raions most affected by the famine, Kyiv Oblast led with ten raions, followed by two other boreal-steppe oblasts, Vinnytsia with eleven raions and Kharkiv with seven. The steppe oblast of Dnipropetrovsk had five such raions, while Odesa Oblast did not make the list.[18] In the same month Chubar asked Moscow to send 1.5 million poods of grain to deal with famine in the central regions of Ukraine. Stalin was opposed. "As I see it, Ukraine has been given more than its due," he wrote to his right-hand man, Lazar Kaganovich. "There is no reason to give more grain and nowhere to get it from."[19] Eventually, Ukraine got 300,000 poods of grain from the all-Union reserves—one-fifth of the requested amount. That happened only because Chubar made a strong case that without such relief, the sugar-beet harvest in Kyiv and Vinnytsia Oblasts would be jeopardized. It worked, but only to a degree.[20]

Why did the boreal-steppe areas of Ukraine suffer more from the famine of 1932 than the steppe areas to the south and the boreal areas to the north? If one trusts official assessments (in particular, Chubar's letter to Stalin), those areas suffered as a result of a poor harvest of certain crops in 1931, official efforts to make up those losses by increasing grain-procurement quotas, and, last but not least, poor organization of labor on newly established collective farms. It should be noted that the famine was taking place in areas that usually did not lack food supplies. In an average year the stored quantity of grain and potatoes in that part of Ukraine amounted to anywhere between 500 and 750 kilograms per person. Both figures (of wheat production and storage of food supplies) were close to average for Ukraine.

Procurement Quotas

The famine in the boreal-steppe area of Ukraine in the spring of 1932 could not but impair the capacity of collective farms and individual peasants to carry out sowing for the next harvest. People who survived the famine did not have the seed stock, strength, or incentive to do what the authorities wanted them to do. Men, unable to feed their families at home, were going elsewhere in search of bread.

"There are almost no male collective farmers," wrote M. Demchenko, secretary of the Kyiv Oblast party committee, about his visit to a village. "People say that they have gone to get food, heading for Belarus and Leningrad Oblast." Dmytro Zavoloka recorded the same situation in his diary. "It's clear that after grain requisitions on that scale and such methods of work, the consequences have taken their toll," he wrote in May 1932. "Large numbers of peasants, including a good part of those on collective farms, have been left without grain. People have begun to flee en masse from their villages wherever their legs will carry them. Entire families are making their way to the farthest reaches of the republic just to avoid staying in their own villages. They avoid work, abandon the land, kill the livestock, and let the farms go to waste."[21]

There was little sowing in the regions most affected by the famine of 1932. By early May, only 18 percent of the planned sowing had been carried out in the Uman region of Kyiv Oblast. In early June Zavoloka recorded the results of sowing in Kyiv Oblast as a whole: only 51 percent of the fields had been sown, and potatoes had been planted only on 56.7 percent of the land allocated for them. "The right time has passed," wrote Zavoloka. "Sowing after 10 June is hopeless for growing and even more so for harvesting. This means that in Kyiv Oblast alone, almost two million hectares, perhaps more, have been left unsown." Zavoloka also wrote that with people going hungry, so were the animals. Between 40 and 50 percent of horses in the region did not survive the winter and spring of 1932. "The results of the spring sowing are more than catastrophic," wrote this party functionary, who tried to reconcile his communist beliefs with party policies in the pages of his diary but ultimately found it impossible to do so.[22]

The Kharkiv authorities tried to deal with the situation by sending their plenipotentiaries, emergency food supplies, and seed stocks to the raions and villages that had been hardest hit. They also tried to reduce the sowing plan assigned to Ukraine by the Moscow authorities. They failed on all counts. The plenipotentiaries could do little without food supplies, available assistance proved insufficient, and Moscow would not reduce the plan targets. On 5 May, the Soviet deputy premier, Valerian Kuibyshev, demanded that Premier Vlas Chubar of the Ukrainian SSR fulfill the centrally imposed plan and ensure the sowing of 11.331 million hectares instead of the 10.64 million hectares proposed by the Ukrainian authorities. While seed stocks for Kyiv and Vinnytsia Oblasts were at the top of the agenda in Kharkiv, Moscow was concerned with sowing in the south. On 29 May, Stalin personally intervened in the process of delivering seed stocks to Odesa Oblast. "Take steps to ensure that the corn dispatched from Rostov is used as directed. We await your reply," read Stalin's telegram to Kosior and Chubar.[23]

The failure of the sowing campaign in Kyiv and other oblasts located in the boreal-steppe region forced the Kharkiv authorities to ask Moscow to reduce the grain-procurement plan for the summer and autumn of 1932. They argued that 2.2 million hectares of land had been left unsown and that winter crops had perished on 0.8 million hectares. Moscow wanted Ukraine to deliver 356 million poods of grain that year. This constituted approximately 81 percent of the plan target assigned the previous year and 90 percent of the grain actually collected in 1931. As seen from Moscow, this probably seemed a reasonable reduction, but it took no account of the consequences of the famine of 1932 and the disruption of the regular agricultural process by the forcible establishment of collective farms.[24]

Stalin's aides, Viacheslav Molotov and Lazar Kaganovich, who visited Kharkiv in July, refused any further reductions. In the same month the party authorities in Moscow imposed a further increase of 4–5 percent to the plan at the raion level in order to make up for potential losses caused by planning errors. It was up to the authorities in Kharkiv to distribute grain-procurement quotas among the Ukrainian regions. They decided to shield the areas most affected by the famine of 1932 and shift the burden of the plan more to the south.[25]

The major beneficiaries of the new scheme were Kyiv and Kharkiv Oblasts, as well as the small Moldavian Autonomous Republic in the south. Moldavia, which had been hit as hard as Kyiv Oblast by the famine of the previous year, had its quota reduced to 46 percent of the grain turned over to the state in 1932. In Kyiv Oblast the new quota constituted 65 percent and, in Kharkiv Oblast, 74 percent of the grain delivered the previous year. The major loser was Odesa Oblast, whose quota was increased, probably because of good prospects for the new harvest, by 34 percent over that of 1931. In Dnipropetrovsk, Vinnytsia, and Donetsk Oblasts the reductions amounted to anywhere between 5 and 12 percent, in keeping with the average for Ukraine as a whole. Given the shift of grain-procurement quotas toward the south, the Kharkiv authorities had to change their original plans for collective farms and individual peasants by increasing targets for the former and decreasing them for the latter. Southern Ukraine was much more collectivized than the boreal-steppe region, and the increase in procurement quotas for the south meant that collective farms would have to deliver more grain.[26]

The Ukrainian government kept lobbying for reduced quotas for the areas affected by the famine of 1932 throughout the summer. In August, when Stalin agreed to reduce the procurement target for Ukraine by 40 million poods (a reduction of approximately 11 percent), Kyiv Oblast got a reduction of 11 million poods (close to 35 percent of its original plan); Vinnytsia Oblast, 9 million poods (23 percent); and Kharkiv Oblast, 8 million poods (11 percent). The quota for Dnipropetrovsk Oblast was reduced by 4 million poods (4.5 percent) and for Odesa Oblast by 2 million poods (2.3 percent). The south was now expected to bear an even heavier burden. The exception to that general rule was the highly industrialized Donetsk Oblast, where the plan target was reduced by 5 million poods, or 14 percent of the original plan. That decision was made in consultation between the Moscow and Kharkiv authorities.[27]

However, there were limits to how long the Kharkiv authorities could keep Kyiv Oblast at the top of their concerns. In October 1932, when, in the face of the failure to meet quota targets,

Molotov and then Stalin were forced to reduce the procurement plan for Ukraine by another 70 million poods (close to 20 percent of the original plan), Kharkiv Oblast was the first in line, asking for a reduction of its quota by 26.9 million poods (37 percent of the original plan). Kyiv Oblast asked for a cut of 5.7 million poods (18 percent), and Vinnytsia Oblast requested a reduction of 3.5 million poods (9 percent). It appeared that Kyiv Oblast was still very much in trouble, while Kharkiv Oblast had become a new leading disaster area. The major difference from August was that the southern oblasts began to ask for substantial reductions as well. Dnipropetrovsk Oblast wanted its quota cut by 16.4 million poods (19 percent), and Odesa Oblast by 14 million poods (16.6 percent).

There can be little doubt that the Kharkiv authorities were doing their best to reduce the procurement burden of the regions most affected by the famine of 1932, all of them in the boreal-steppe region of Ukraine. Through their efforts, they eventually succeeded in reducing the plan quotas—a measure that most affected the central oblasts of Ukraine. It soon turned out, however, that the regions affected by the famine of 1932 needed relief and reduced quotas of grain production.[28]

Grain Requisitions

In the fall of 1932, Kharkiv and Kyiv Oblasts, which were located in Ukraine's boreal-steppe belt, were leading among the Ukrainian regions in fulfilling their quotas for delivering grain to government depositories. In early November 1932, Mendel Khataevich, secretary of the Kharkiv Central Committee and also first secretary of Dnipropetrovsk Oblast, asked his Kharkiv and Moscow bosses to allocate 10 percent of all manufactured goods to reward collective farms and individual peasants in Kyiv, Kharkiv, and Donetsk Oblasts.

Khataevich was prepared to give to some areas and localities of Ukraine while taking from others. In the same telegram he proposed that there be no further deliveries of manufactured goods to those raions of Odesa and Dnipropetrovsk Oblasts that were lagging behind in the fulfillment of their quotas. Soon, the policy of blacklisting whole communities—collective farms and raions—was extended to all oblasts of Ukraine. It called for cutting off supplies of manufactured goods to settlements that failed to fulfill their quotas. Kyiv Oblast led in terms of blacklisted villages, while Dnipropetrovsk Oblast was in first place when it came to blacklisted collective farms. Among other things, this disparity reflected different levels of collectivization in the steppe and boreal-steppe regions of Ukraine.[29]

The lead taken by the boreal-steppe oblasts continued in the new year. By 1 January 1933, the collective farms of Kharkiv, Kyiv, and Vinnytsia Oblasts were ahead of their southern neighbors in fulfilling their plans, showing results from 85 percent and higher, with 100 percent fulfillment in Kyiv and Vinnytsia Oblasts.[30] The collective farms of the steppe oblasts and the newly created Chernihiv Oblast in the Polissia region lagged behind in plan fulfillment by a margin of at least 10 percent. In the steppe regions the failure to fulfill plan targets led eventually to their further reduction. In January 1933, their plan quotas were reduced by 12 million poods for Dnipropetrovsk and Odesa Oblasts. For Kharkiv Oblast, the quota was further reduced by 3.4 million poods; for Kyiv and Vinnytsia Oblasts, it remained the same.[31]

There are several factors that might account for the "leadership" of the boreal-steppe oblasts in fulfilling plan targets. One such factor is that those oblasts benefited from major reductions to their procurement quotas. The final plan for Kyiv Oblast reduced the quota by roughly half of the original amount of 31.2 million poods, while the original plan target itself constituted only 65 percent of the grain collected in 1931. The overall reduction was a whopping 68 percent. But the reduction of quotas is only one possible explanation of the "stellar" performance of Kyiv Oblast in fulfilling its plan.

Another is the ruthless efficiency of the local party machine in requisitioning grain from the peasantry. By the first months of 1933, when the party sent its people back to the villages in the boreal-steppe areas to collect grain for sowing, there was nothing to collect. If in Dnipropetrovsk Oblast, which was lagging behind in the fulfillment of its procurement plan, party workers collected 40 percent of what was required, in Kyiv, Kharkiv, and Vinnytsia Oblasts that number was between 13.4 and 20.5 percent.

For those peasants in the boreal-steppe zones who had survived the requisitions of 1931 and the famine of 1932, the new requisition campaign brought new suffering and claimed more lives. In her diary entry for 30 September 1932, Oleksandra Radchenko recorded the story of a peasant from the village of Piatnytske in Kharkiv Oblast who was detained by the authorities. They demanded grain, holding him captive the entire day, and released him only late at night. "They held me for grain procurement," the peasant told Radchenko, who met him as he returned home after nightfall. "Give, they say, but what is there to give? There are four sacks left; I have to do my sowing; I have to feed my children through the winter." The peasant was clearly distressed. "His voice shook; he might have burst into tears at any minute," wrote Radchenko in her diary. "Oh, poor, poor, tormented people."

The authorities were not only going after grain. They confiscated everything, treating all food supplies as potential "fines in kind" for unfulfilled procurement quotas. "[The] old man, who works on a rabbit farm, was 'robbed by the authorities,' as he reported," recorded Radchenko in her entry for 20 November 1932.

> That means they took all the cereal grains and fruit available. He has been dekulakized for two years and is almost indigent, just short of begging. He is 70 years old; the old woman is 65, and their crippled daughter lives in their apartment. And although they are destitute, everything they might have used to live on until February has been taken from them. The servant returned from leave…and cried out in despair, "What a horror this is! They are completely ruining individual farmers, taking everything away, going through trunks; cries and weeping everywhere. They shout, 'Take the children, too,' and there are five of them in the house."[32]

The hypothesis that it was pressure from above, not just reduced quotas that accounted for the exceptional performance of the boreal-steppe areas in meeting plan targets, finds corroboration in secret-police statistics. According to GPU (Main Political Directorate) data, in the first ten months of 1932, 300 cases of peasant "terrorism," a term used to denote violent resistance to the authorities, were registered in Kyiv Oblast, 255 in Kharkiv

Oblast, and 197 in Vinnytsia Oblast. Much larger oblasts in the south had rather modest totals: 58 cases in Donetsk Oblast, 80 in Dnipropetrovsk Oblast, and 170 in Odesa Oblast. If one also counts the 80 cases registered on territories controlled by border guard detachments, then the numbers for Vinnytsia and Kyiv Oblasts, bordering on Poland and Romania, should be increased even further. That tendency continued in the remaining months of 1932 and early 1933. Vinnytsia Oblast had 98 cases of "terrorism"; Kharkiv Oblast, 84; Chernihiv Oblast, 87; and Kyiv Oblast, 63. During the same months there were only 16 cases registered in Donetsk Oblast, 26 in Odesa Oblast, and 47 in Dnipropetrovsk Oblast.[33]

The Kharkiv authorities' efforts to deal with the situation by reducing quotas and shifting the main burden to the south did not change the situation on the ground. The central government demanded grain deliveries from the region whether or not the peasants had anything to eat. By early 1933, it was Kyiv, Kharkiv, and Vinnytsia Oblasts, the areas most affected by the famine of 1932, that seemed most vulnerable to the new wave of famine—one that threatened Ukraine as a whole on a much larger scale than that of the previous year.

Loans to the Dead

On 30 January 1933, Oleksandra Radchenko recorded the first death from starvation that she saw with her own eyes. "On the way to Zadorizhne, right next to the road, we saw a dead old man, ragged and thin. There were no boots on him. Obviously, he had fallen and frozen to death or died immediately, and somebody took the boots. On the way back we saw the same old man again. Nobody needs him." The famine soon decimated the population of Babanka. In a mere three days, between 24 and 26 April, 22 people starved to death in that village.[34]

The first official reports on the spread of the new famine began to arrive in Kharkiv in early February 1933. Most of them pertained to the boreal-steppe oblasts, especially Kyiv and Vinnytsia. But the first quantities of grain that Ukraine was allowed to take in order to cope with widespread starvation and growing famine did not go to Kyiv and Vinnytsia but to Odesa and Dnipropetrovsk

Oblasts. Kyiv and the boreal-steppe areas were overlooked by the center, which had control over grain depositories and supplies and, in the conditions of growing crisis, decided who or, rather, where people would live or die. Moscow needed peasants to live, or at least die at a slower rate in the areas that produced most of the grain—a policy that benefited the Ukrainian south. On 7 February 1933, the Politburo in Moscow decreed that Odesa and Dnipropetrovsk Oblasts could use 200,000 poods of rye each to deal with the food shortages. On 17 February, the party authorities in Kharkiv decreed that additional supplies of grain and flour be sent to the industrial Donetsk Oblast.[35]

The same "south first" policy continued in the second half of February. On 18 February, the Moscow Politburo decreed the release of a million poods of grain to Dnipropetrovsk Oblast, 0.8 million to Odesa Oblast, and 0.3 million to Kharkiv Oblast. As regards Dnipropetrovsk Oblast, the resolution corresponded to GPU statistics for March 1933, which indicated that 1,700 people had starved to death there—more than in all other oblasts of Ukraine combined. In Kyiv Oblast, according to GPU statistics, only 417 people had died by that time. While the clearly inaccurate GPU statistics can explain Moscow's particular attention to Dnipropetrovsk Oblast, they cannot do so in the cases of Odesa and Kharkiv Oblasts. According to the same GPU reports, 37 people starved to death in Kharkiv Oblast and 11 in Odesa Oblast.[36]

As the Union government focused on the south, it was left to the Kharkiv authorities to take care of the rest of the republic. The problem was that the resources at the disposition of the Ukrainian government were minuscule compared to those available in the center. By mid-March the party authorities in Kharkiv were swamped with reports of the skyrocketing mortality rate in Kyiv Oblast. "We have starvation and its consequences in 32–34 raions. In 16 raions we have 123 registered cases of cannibalism and eating of corpses (including 64 cases of cannibalism)," read one of the reports received by the Kharkiv Central Committee. "On the streets of Kyiv, the following numbers of corpses were picked up: January, 400; February, 518; in the first ten days of March, 249. In the most recent days, an average of 100 children [per day] have been left [in the city] by their parents." In February

1933, the Kharkiv authorities gave Kyiv Oblast 60,000 poods of grain, followed by 80,000 in early March.[37]

On 17 March 1933, the Central Committee in Kharkiv issued a special resolution on means of combating the famine crisis in Kyiv Oblast. An appeal was made to Moscow. This time the Moscow authorities reacted and allowed six million poods of grain to be taken from the central depositories to deal with the crisis. This famine relief measure had its effect. According to Oleh Wolowyna's research, the relative excess death factor (the number of excess deaths in an area or population divided by the relative total population) for Kyiv Oblast fell between mid-March and mid-May 1933 by roughly 30 points, from 80 to 53. But the impact was temporary. In May, the relative excess death factor began to rise again, exceeded the March peak by mid-June 1933, and reached 85 points.[38] In assessing the impact that the government's assistance, often offered in the form of loans with interest, had on the situation on the ground in the early spring of 1933, it is important to keep in mind that the rural population of Kyiv Oblast was almost twice as large as that of Dnipropetrovsk. There were close to 5 million people living in rural areas of Kyiv Oblast and 2.8 million in Dnipropetrovsk Oblast.[39]

The Kyiv crisis of March 1933 did not change the Union government's policy of offering assistance first and foremost to the main grain-producing oblasts in the south. On 28 May 1933, the Moscow Politburo adopted a resolution allowing the release of 0.3 million poods of grain each to Dnipropetrovsk and Odesa Oblasts. Donetsk Oblast received 0.1 million; the others—nothing at all. It was only after the Ukrainian leadership sent a special appeal to Stalin that Moscow agreed to give a fraction of the assistance it had provided to the steppe oblasts to those located in the boreal-steppe zone. Moscow allowed the provision of 200,000 poods of rye to alleviate famine in Kharkiv Oblast, 130,000 poods each in Kyiv and Vinnytsia Oblasts, and 30,000 poods in Chernihiv Oblast. For Kyiv and Vinnytsia Oblasts, Moscow cut the amount requested by the Kharkiv authorities by 15,000 poods.

This could not but have a direct impact on the worsening situation on the ground. In the following month the relative excess death factor reached its peak in the boreal-steppe oblasts, approaching 90 in Kyiv and Vinnytsia Oblasts, reaching 100 in

Kharkiv Oblast, and exceeding the 100 mark in Chernihiv—the oblast that received less assistance than any other in Ukraine. The difference between the boreal-steppe oblasts and those in the steppe zone could not have been more profound. The relative excess death factor in Odesa Oblast at that time was 50, while Dnipropetrovsk Oblast had a factor of 30, and Donetsk Oblast a factor of 15.[40]

The central government's policies favoring the steppe oblasts continued in the aftermath of the famine. In 1933, the Moscow authorities decreed the resettlement of the famine-ravaged areas of Ukraine by peasant families from Russia and Belarus. They wanted 6,679 households to go to Dnipropetrovsk Oblast; 6,750 to Odesa; 4,800 to Kharkiv; and 3,527 to Donetsk. The southern oblasts of Dnipropetrovsk and Odesa got the most attention from the center. The same pattern applied to horses shipped to Ukraine from other parts of the Soviet Union. Dnipropetrovsk Oblast received 5,719 head of livestock; Odesa, 6,812; and Kharkiv, 2,329. Moscow's neglect of the non-grain-producing areas of Ukraine during the spring and early summer of 1933 was among the factors that contributed to the higher than average death rate in the forest-steppe regions of the republic.[41]

Beyond Ecology

The dividing line between the boreal and steppe areas of Ukraine played an important role in defining the Moscow authorities' approach to planning their agricultural policies in Ukraine. As has been argued above, those policies contributed to the significantly higher death rate in the two boreal-steppe oblasts of Ukraine, Kyiv and Kharkiv. What that line does not explain is the difference in the death rate between those two oblasts and the boreal regions of Ukraine, which included the area north of Kyiv Oblast and all of Chernihiv Oblast, where the death rate was significantly lower than in the boreal-steppe areas. In Chernihiv Oblast in 1933 the death rate was 75.8 per thousand of population, compared with 183.5 deaths per thousand of population in Kyiv Oblast.

The map of losses by raion in 1933 leaves no doubt that while the sources we consulted give no indication that the line between the boreal and boreal-steppe areas mattered in the formulation of government policy, it clearly affected the inhabitants' chances of survival. Here we are dealing with a situation in which environment could have a direct impact, without the intermediacy of the political factor. One possible explanation of that fact could be the inhabitants' ability to feed and maintain domestic animals in wooded areas at the time of the famine, as well as their ability to survive on forest products that could not be confiscated by the authorities. Further research is needed to test these hypotheses.

The boreal-steppe divide also does not suffice to explain the lower death rate in Vinnytsia Oblast as compared with Kyiv and Kharkiv Oblasts, which lay within the boundaries of the same ecological zone. The raion data indicates that some raions of Vinnytsia Oblast suffered the same level of excess deaths as the boreal-steppe raions of Kyiv and Kharkiv Oblasts, but all those raions were in the central and eastern parts of the oblast. The western and southwestern parts, which happened to be closest to the Soviet-Polish and Soviet-Romanian borders, suffered significantly less.

An answer to this puzzle has been suggested by recent research on the history of Soviet border areas, which indicates that Moscow paid special attention to border regions, supplying them with larger quantities of consumer products than other regions of the Soviet Union. Back in 1930, entire villages in border areas had attempted to cross the Soviet-Polish border and find refuge from the horror of collectivization in neighboring Poland. Further research into government policies and strategies of survival in the border regions of Ukraine would be required, but there is little doubt that the death rate in those areas was lower than in the central and eastern parts of Vinnytsia Oblast—a factor that influenced the overall death rate in the oblast during the famine.[42]

Last but not least, the boreal-steppe divide does not explain differences in the death rate between the three steppe oblasts: Donetsk, Dnipropetrovsk, and Odesa. Donetsk Oblast suffered least, Odesa Oblast most. The high level of industrialization of Donetsk Oblast as compared with Odesa Oblast can partly explain this phenomenon: starving peasants could find employment and survive in major industrial centers that had centralized food supplies. Nor should one discount the Moscow authorities' differential treatment of individual oblasts with regard to famine relief.

This factor becomes especially apparent if one compares Dnipropetrovsk and Odesa Oblasts, the two main grain-producing areas of Ukraine. Throughout the spring of 1933 Dnipropetrovsk Oblast emerged as the main recipient of Moscow's assistance in the south, obtaining one million poods in February. Odesa Oblast received 0.8 million poods of grain. Between mid-March and mid-July the excess death factor in Dnipropetrovsk Oblast was significantly lower than in Odesa Oblast. In mid-May, for example, it reached 33 points, while that of Odesa Oblast stood at 60. The greater quantity of government relief undoubtedly influenced this major discrepancy between the two oblasts, which were quite similar in size of population, level of collectivization, and grain-producing capacity.[43]

In explaining the differences in the amount of aid received from the center, it is hard to overlook the role played by individual party officials in the history of the famine. Mendel Khataevich, who was appointed first secretary of the Dnipropetrovsk party committee in January 1933, maintained his position as secretary of the Central Committee in Kharkiv and had direct access not only to Stanislav Kosior and Vlas Chubar but also to Stalin's right-hand man in Moscow, Lazar Kaganovich. The personalities of oblast and raion party leaders mattered during the Great Famine, and in the spring and summer of 1933 the position taken by a senior party official and his ability to reduce plan targets and receive government assistance could make the difference between life and death for hundreds of thousands of starving people in the Ukrainian countryside.

There were limits, however, to what local officials could do independently of the Moscow and Kyiv authorities. Wheatcroft has suggested recently that Kyiv Oblast's higher death rate can be attributed to the actions of local officials, who imposed additional quotas on the peasantry in order to feed the cities of the oblast, which, unlike the industrial centers in the east and south of the republic, received few or no shipments from the central depositories. Thus far, this hypothesis has not been substantiated by documentary evidence with regard to special policies adopted by Kyiv officials. It also does not take into account that not all areas of Kyiv Oblast suffered equally, and many raions of Kharkiv Oblast suffered as much as the most affected areas of Kyiv Oblast.[44]

Let us now turn to the factors that apparently did not matter in the history of the Great Famine. A comparison of the maps of excess death rates with those of Ukraine's ethnic composition suggests that, while place of residence, defined in terms of ecological zones and border versus central location, influenced chances of survival, ethnicity did not. There is, however, one caveat pertaining to this general thesis. The maps indicate that the boreal-steppe regions hardest hit by the famine also happened to be those with the highest percentage of Ukrainians among the rural population. But we have no documentary confirmation that these areas were specifically targeted by the government or left without assistance because of their ethnic composition. Also severely affected were northeastern Kharkiv Oblast and concentrations of Jews and Poles outside the border regions of Vinnytsia Oblast. Furthermore, the map of urban losses indicates that small towns in Kyiv and Kharkiv Oblasts with significant Jewish populations were among the localities worst hit by the famine: this data is confirmed by official correspondence.[45]

Finally, one should address the impact on death rates of the official policy of denying supplies to villages and agricultural enterprises that failed to fulfill their grain-procurement quotas, otherwise known as blacklisted communities. Even though clusters of blacklisted villages can be found on the map within or close to areas with the highest rates of excess deaths, current data do not allow one to conclude or even suggest that blacklisting actually led to higher death rates. There can be a number of explanations for this phenomenon; lack of comprehensive data is one of them. The authorities' inability to enforce blacklisting of communities located near those that were not blacklisted—a "problem" addressed in official reports for December 1932—may be another.[46]

While GIS mapping of the Great Famine is only in its initial stages, and this essay is one of the first attempts to interpret the new data and the maps on which it has been plotted, we can already formulate some preliminary conclusions. Given the early stage of research, most of the conclusions are hypothetical and should be regarded more as an agenda for research than as the definitive word on the subject. In this context, it is important to bear in mind that GIS mapping is not only a way of presenting research results but also a way of posing new questions for research. For clarity's sake, I am presenting the preliminary results of the research discussed in this essay in point form.

ᴥ The geography of losses suffered by the population of Ukraine in the course of the Great Famine of 1932–33 sets it apart from the earlier famines of the 1920s, which occurred in the southern parts of the republic. During the Great Famine the death rate was highest in central Ukraine.

ᴥ An explanation for the distinct geography of the Great Famine should be sought in the different treatment of Ukraine's regions, first by the Soviet government in Moscow, and then by the Ukrainian leadership in Kharkiv. While Stalin and the members of his inner circle treated Ukraine as an entity with regard to grain procurement, they also distinguished the main grain-producing areas in the steppe zone of southern Ukraine from the boreal zones of central and northern Ukraine, which grew less grain or none at all.

ᴥ The steppe regions of Ukraine were more highly collectivized and supplied with tractors and other agricultural machinery on a priority basis. They were also the first to receive famine relief assistance and were the main beneficiaries of resettlement policy after the famine. The boreal-steppe regions of Ukraine, which included Kyiv, Kharkiv, and Vinnytsia Oblasts, had a lower level of collectivization and mechanization of agriculture.

ᴥ The central government's policy of forcing peasants to join collective farms by imposing higher procurement quotas on non-collectivized peasantry further disadvantaged the central and northern areas of Ukraine, which had a lower level of collectivized households than the steppe regions in the south.

ᴥ The famine began in the winter and early spring of 1932 in central Ukraine, particularly in the beet-producing areas of Kyiv Oblast, where, according to one version of events, local officials, forced by the central and republican governments to fulfill unrealistically high procurement quotas, took more grain than specified in plan quotas in order to make up for losses in the harvests of produce other than grain.

⧉ The famine of 1933 hit hardest those areas that had never fully recovered from the famine of the previous year. The famine of 1932, which affected Kyiv, Vinnytsia, and Kharkiv Oblasts, weakened and demoralized the peasants, who were unable or unwilling to stay on the collective farms or conduct the sowing campaign on their own. This resulted in the poor harvest of 1932 and the new and much more severe famine of 1933.

⧉ During the height of the famine in 1933, the central government in Moscow and the republican authorities in Kharkiv adopted different approaches to relief efforts. The Kharkiv government's priority was to provide support for the boreal-steppe regions of Ukraine hardest hit by famine, while Moscow's efforts were focused on the main grain-producing areas in the south.

⧉ Given that Moscow had more resources and overall control over the distribution of aid and grain loans, the central government's focus on the main grain-producing regions of Ukraine led to the neglect of the needs of the starving population in boreal-steppe areas. The central government was prepared to lower quotas for boreal-steppe areas on a number of occasions, but it was reluctant to provide those regions of Ukraine with food assistance, given their low standing in the pecking order of grain-producing regions.

⧉ The severity of the famine in the rural areas of Kyiv and Kharkiv Oblasts translated into an exceptionally high death rate among the urban population of those oblasts. Most of the urban dwellers who died in 1932–33 lived in small towns that had no centralized food supply and suffered the same fate as the countryside.

⧉ While Kyiv and Kharkiv Oblasts were hardest hit by the Great Famine, the losses in other parts of Ukraine were also in the millions, totaling 3.9 million deaths according to the latest estimates. This death toll set the Holodomor apart from the earlier famines not only in terms of geography but also in the absolute number of victims.

9.

The Call of Blood

On Thursday, 7 September 1939, as the shell-shocked Major Henryk Sucharski, commander of the Polish garrison of Westerplatte, surrendered the embattled fortress to numerically superior German forces, and Hitler's mechanized divisions rushed eastward, encircling Łódź, approaching Warsaw, and crossing the Narew River, Joseph Stalin summoned his military commanders to the Kremlin. On the agenda was Soviet entry into the war, which had already become global. Among its declared participants were Germany, Poland, Britain, France, and South Africa. The Molotov-Ribbentrop Pact, signed only two weeks earlier with Stalin's active participation, assigned parts of Poland east of the Narew to the Soviet sphere of influence, but the Soviet leaders were more than cautious about claiming their prospective booty.

On 5 September Viacheslav Molotov, chairman of the USSR Council of People's Commissars and people's commissar for international relations, had responded evasively to the German appeal of two days earlier to send the Red Army into Poland, saying that the time was not yet ripe. Now, with the Germans advancing, the Poles retreating, and the British and French doing little more than formally declaring war, Stalin wanted his military brass to speed up preparations for hostilities. The partial mobilization of reserves ordered the previous day was already taking effect. Soviet forces would cross the Polish border and seize the USSR's portion of war booty. But how to justify an act of open aggression against a neighboring state?

Stalin had his answer ready. Immediately after meeting with his commanders, he received in his Kremlin office the leader of the Communist International (Comintern), the Bulgarian communist Georgi Dimitrov. Also present were Viacheslav Molotov; the chief party propagandist, Andrei Zhdanov; and the chief Soviet representative in the Comintern, the Ukrainian communist Dmytro Manuilsky. Stalin told his visitors that the Soviet Union would take advantage of the world conflict to help the capitalist countries exhaust one another. He shared none of the admiration lavished by earlier generations of revolutionaries on Poland, which he characterized as a fascist state that was oppressing fellow Ukrainians and Belarusians. "The annihilation of that state under current conditions would mean one less bourgeois fascist state to contend with!" asserted Stalin. "What harm would result from the rout of Poland if we were to extend the socialist system to new territories and populations?" he asked his visitors, according to Dimitrov's diary.

One part of Stalin's argument was based on a Bolshevik-style class analysis and the logic of world revolution that had failed to materialize in the 1920s. Another had to do with national minorities—the non-Polish inhabitants of eastern Poland, which had been "allocated" to the USSR by the Molotov-Ribbentrop Pact. Indeed, it was the Ukrainian-Belarusian nationality card that would be used most broadly both at home and abroad as catchall justification for Soviet aggression. It would outlive the early days of the conflict, serving as the basis of the Soviet authorities' claim to their newly acquired territories until the end of the war.[1]

This essay looks into the development of the ethnic justification of Soviet aggression against Poland on three levels: diplomatic, propagandistic, and popular. It examines how the theme of ethnic minorities developed in Soviet-German negotiations in the weeks leading up to Soviet entry into the war and the signing of the Soviet-German Boundary and Friendship Treaty of 28 September 1939; discusses the use of the nationality card in Soviet domestic propaganda; and, finally, takes a close look at the impact of the nationality theme on Soviet public opinion. There are two questions of broader significance that I seek to engage in this essay. The first deals with the relationship between Soviet foreign and domestic policy, especially with the formulation and articulation of nationality policy. The second concerns the variety of responses to government policy available to the Soviet public under Stalinism.

I shall argue that 1) Stalin's vacillation on the new Soviet borders and the propaganda effort accompanying the Soviet invasion of Poland demonstrate that the Soviet leader and his advisers were surprised by the German offer of 23 August 1939 to divide Poland into spheres of influence, or occupation, and did not fully formulate their position on the scope of their territorial expansion until a month later, when the military campaign was all but over; 2) The Soviet authorities' view of the world not only as a community of states but also as a conglomerate of nationalities, as well as their understanding of the principle of national self-determination as possessing broad international legitimacy, had a profound impact on the formulation of Soviet foreign policy and defined the extent of Soviet territorial expansion in September 1939; 3) In the first weeks of the war, changes in Soviet foreign policy led to a change in government rhetoric on the nationality question, also opening the door to subsequent changes in nationality policy; 4) The change of nationality rhetoric helped the regime co-opt a sector of public opinion previously hostile to its policies both at home and abroad and prompted some segments of the Soviet public to formulate their relation to government policy in a way that does not fit the categories of resistance and compliance, which have received considerable attention in the recent literature on the subject.

The Geopolitical Crossword

Three days after Stalin's conversation with the Comintern leaders, one of the participants in the meeting, Viacheslav Molotov, was ordered to try the nationality argument for Soviet entry into the war on none other than the German ambassador to the Soviet Union, Friedrich-Werner Graf von der Schulenburg. On 10 September 1939, after telling Schulenburg that "the Soviet Government was taken completely by surprise by the unexpectedly rapid German military successes" and needed more time to prepare its own army for the invasion, Molotov mentioned to him a possible justification for the Soviet Union's prospective invasion of Poland.

"The Soviet Government," wrote Schulenburg, reporting the words of the Soviet foreign commissar to Berlin, "had intended to take the occasion of the further advance of German troops to declare that Poland was falling apart and that it was necessary for the Soviet Union, in consequence, to come to the aid of the Ukrainians and the White Russians 'threatened' by Germany. This argument was to make the intervention of the Soviet Union plausible to the masses and at the same time avoid giving the Soviet Union the appearance of an aggressor."[2]

The class analysis and export-of-revolution argument given by Stalin to Dimitrov had been dropped in Molotov's presentation to Schulenburg, while the nationality justification had survived, admittedly in somewhat different form. It was no longer the Polish state's poor treatment of the Ukrainians and Belarusians but their possible mistreatment by the Germans that was supposed to justify the Soviet invasion. On 14 September, Schulenburg reported to Berlin about his next meeting with Molotov. The Soviet foreign commissar was again preoccupied with the question of legitimacy. "For the political motivation of Soviet action (the collapse of Poland and protection of Russian 'minorities') it was of the greatest importance not to take action until the governmental center of Poland, the city of Warsaw, had fallen," reported Schulenburg on the new Soviet position. "Molotov therefore asked that he be informed as nearly as possible as to when the capture of Warsaw could be counted on."

To be sure, the Soviets were not simply awaiting the fall of Warsaw. They began to prepare their own population for war, and the ethnic explanation of the impending invasion played an important role. On 8 September, the day after Stalin's meeting with his military commanders and Dimitrov, the Polish military attaché in Moscow attended a public lecture in Gorky Park on the German-Polish war. The speaker asked whether his audience was prepared to observe impassively the sufferings inflicted by nobiliary Poland on Ukrainians and Belarusians. The audience responded with cries of "March, march on the evil Germans!"

On 11 September, the Red Army formed two fronts tasked with the invasion of Poland. They were based on the Kyiv and Minsk military districts but received "nationalized" names—Ukrainian and Belarusian. They also introduced the minorities theme in public propaganda. A few days later it appeared in the print media. Schulenburg concluded his report of 14 September by stating: "I would direct your attention to today's article in *Pravda*, carried by DNB [Deutsches Nachrichtenbüro—German Press Agency], which will be followed by a similar article in *Izvestiia* tomorrow. The articles serve [to prepare] the political motivation mentioned by Molotov for Soviet intervention."[3]

The two articles mentioned by Schulenburg ascribed the defeat of Poland to its mistreatment of its ethnic minorities and provided detailed information on the sorry status of Ukrainians and Belarusians in the prewar Polish state. The potential German threat was not mentioned, but Hitler's foreign minister, Joachim von Ribbentrop, finally became alert to the problem that might arise as a result of Molotov's desire to explain Soviet action against Poland by pointing a finger at the Germans. To forestall it, Ribbentrop wanted a joint Soviet-German statement stressing the desire of the two powers to "restore peace" in Poland.

On 15 September, the Reichskommissar cabled his ambassador in Moscow:

> We assume…that the Soviet Government has already given up the idea, expressed by Molotov in an earlier conversation with you, of taking the threat to the Ukrainian and White Russian populations by Germany as a ground for Soviet action. The assignment of a motive of that sort would be out of the question in practice. It would be directly contrary to the true German intentions, which are confined exclusively to the realization of well-known German spheres of interest. It would also be in contradiction to the arrangements made in Moscow and, finally, would—in opposition to the desire for friendly relations expressed on both sides—expose the two States before the whole world as enemies.[4]

When Schulenburg presented these arguments to Molotov at their meeting on 16 September, the day before the Soviet invasion of Poland, the Soviet commissar found himself on the defensive. Despite Ribbentrop's warning, he insisted on including a statement in the Soviet declaration on the causes of intervention arguing that "the Soviet Union considered itself obligated to intervene to protect its Ukrainian and White Russian brothers and make it possible for these unfortunate people to work in peace." According to Schulenburg's report, Molotov

conceded that the projected argument of the Soviet Government contained a note that was jarring to German sensibilities but asked that in view of the difficult situation of the Soviet Government we not let a trifle like this stand in our way. The Soviet Government unfortunately saw no possibility of any other motivation, since the Soviet Union had thus far not concerned itself about the plight of its minorities in Poland and had to justify abroad, in some way or other, its present intervention.[5]

As always, Molotov was acting on Stalin's instructions and was not at liberty to change anything in the declared position of the Soviet government. His superior, however, took Schulenburg's warning very seriously. At 2:00 a.m. on 17 September, Stalin summoned the German ambassador to the Kremlin not only to tell him that the Red Army was about to attack Poland but also to read him the note to the same effect that would be given to the Polish ambassador. "The draft read to me contained three points unacceptable to us," reported Schulenburg to Berlin. "In answer to my objections, Stalin with the utmost readiness so altered the text that the note now seems satisfactory for us." The note, which appeared in Soviet newspapers the next day, presented the defense of the Ukrainians and Belarusians as the main reason for the Soviet intervention, with no mention of a German threat. The relevant parts of the note were included almost verbatim in Molotov's address to the Soviet people, which was broadcast by radio a few hours after the invasion. In both cases, the Ukrainians and Belarusians were simply declared to have been left unprotected by the collapse of the Polish state.[6]

The main problem with their explanation of the invasion as an act of fraternal assistance to the Ukrainians and Belarusians was that, according to the secret protocol signed by Molotov and Ribbentrop in Moscow on the morning of 24 August 1939 (and dated the previous day), the Soviet sphere of influence extended beyond territories settled predominantly by Ukrainians and

Belarusians. The Soviet catch also included millions of Jews and Poles. If Jews were dispersed all over Polish territory, nowhere constituting a majority and consequently unable to claim a homeland of their own, the Poles had such a claim. They constituted an absolute majority of the inhabitants of lands between the Bug and Wisła Rivers who were to be brought forcibly into the Soviet sphere. Well aware of this, Stalin made preparations for dealing with the Polish question.

On the eve of the invasion, the commander of the newly formed Ukrainian front, Semen Tymoshenko, received instructions on how to facilitate the election of deputies to three popular assemblies—those of Western Ukraine, Western Belarus, and Polish regions east of the Wisła. These assemblies were to adopt resolutions requesting the incorporation of their territories into the USSR. Western Belarus and Western Ukraine would thereby join the existing Belarusian and Ukrainian Soviet Socialist Republics, while the Polish territories would join the USSR as a separate Polish Soviet Socialist Republic. On 15 September, Lavrentii Beriia, the people's commissar of internal affairs (NKVD), included a reference to the Polish assembly in the order he sent to his subordinates in Ukraine and Belarus. The order reflected current thinking at the very top of the Soviet pyramid of power.[7]

Beriia's instructions to NKVD officers in Ukraine and Belarus and the instructions to Tymoshenko show that on the eve of the Soviet invasion Stalin had no plans for creating a Polish buffer state between Germany and the USSR, an idea earlier entertained by the Soviet leadership. On 19 September, Molotov said as much to Schulenburg, who reported to Berlin on his conversation with the Soviet foreign commissar: "Molotov hinted that the original inclination entertained by the Soviet Government and Stalin personally to permit the existence of a residual Poland had given way to the inclination to partition Poland along the Neisse–Narew–Wisła–San Line."

That was the line defined by the secret protocol of the Molotov-Ribbentrop Pact of 23 August. Within the next few days, Stalin further developed his thinking on the issue. On 25 September, he told Schulenburg that he wanted to avoid "anything that in the future might create friction between Germany and the Soviet Union" and "considered it wrong to leave an independent Polish rump state." According to Schulenburg, Stalin proposed the following: "From the territory to the east of the demarcation line, all the Province of Lublin and that portion of the Province of Warsaw which extends to the Bug should be added to our share. In return, we should waive our claim to Lithuania."[8]

What was the logic of Stalin's new proposal? His desire to claim Lithuania might suggest that he wanted to regain a former Romanov possession. Besides, by swapping Polish territories for Lithuanian ones, Stalin straightened the line of his future defenses, moving the border farther away from Leningrad and eliminating the bulge in the south along the future western borders of Ukraine and Belarus. That is as far as the Lithuanian argument takes us, but Stalin's offer of the Lublin and Warsaw provinces to Germany clearly does not fit such an explanation, as those territories had largely belonged to the Russian Empire prior to 1917. Besides, Stalin was not willing to pass on the former Habsburg Galicia, which fell into the Soviet sphere of influence even though German representatives had expressed interest in the region in unofficial talks with the Soviet ambassador in Berlin in July 1939.

If the proposal was not solely an attempt to reclaim tsarist possessions or improve military defenses, what was it? A close reading indicates that the Soviet desire to recover lost territory and improve the geostrategic position of the state were adjusted to take into account ethnic boundaries and national identities of borderland populations. By getting rid of the ethnic Polish territories, Stalin was also bringing the new Soviet-German border into line with his propaganda thesis that Soviet forces had entered Poland primarily in order to liberate their fellow Ukrainians and Belarusians. He could thus explain the new border to the Soviet and foreign public much more effectively than the original one.[9]

There is also no reason to doubt the sincerity of Stalin's claim that he wanted to avoid anything in the new territorial arrangement that might make future German-Soviet relations more difficult. Getting rid of the Polish buffer state was one step in that direction. Getting rid of the Lublin and Warsaw provinces, settled largely by Poles, was another. Stalin had good reason for concern that Germany might use the cause of Polish reunification as a pretext to interfere in Soviet affairs and eventually go to war against the Soviet Union. A few months earlier, the world press had been full of suggestions that Hitler was going to use Transcarpathian Ukraine—the Czechoslovak province of Ruthenia—as a base for starting a war with Stalin for control of Soviet Ukraine.

In March 1939, Stalin declared from the podium of the Eighteenth Party Congress that he did not trust Western insinuations in that regard. Many regard Stalin's assertion as a signal to Hitler and Ribbentrop that he was prepared to make a deal. The deal he was negotiating now precluded the creation of a new "Transcarpathia," either Ukrainian or Polish. The proposed new Soviet-German boundary was to follow the San and Bug Rivers, roughly corresponding to the ethnic boundary in the region as defined by the Allied Supreme Council in Paris in December 1918, later known as the Curzon Line.[10]

On 28 September, Ribbentrop, who had flown to Moscow the previous day, signed the German-Soviet border agreement, which recognized the new line proposed by Stalin. In the course of negotiations, Ribbentrop tried to acquire the oil-rich Drohobych region of Ukrainian Galicia for Germany, but Stalin stood firm, agreeing to ship oil to Germany but not to give up the territory. He emerged from the negotiations not only as a protector of Ukrainian territory but also as a leader concerned about Ukrainians and Belarusians beyond the lands that were about to become part of the USSR. Molotov and Ribbentrop signed a confidential protocol that committed the Soviet government to raise no obstacle to the voluntary transfer of German inhabitants from the Soviet sector of partitioned Poland to the German sector. The German government promised to reciprocate with regard to Ukrainians and Belarusians. This privilege was not extended to Poles or Jews. Another protocol obliged each government to suppress Polish propaganda directed against the other party. In transferring Polish territories to Hitler, Stalin wanted to ensure that his new partner would not use the Polish card against the USSR.[11]

If the map accompanying the secret protocol of the Molotov-Ribbentrop Pact (23 August 1939) was largely the result of proposals made by Ribbentrop, the amendments made to it on 28 September originated with Stalin. Ribbentrop's proposal was based mainly on historical precedent and on the assumption that Stalin wanted to restore the old imperial borders in Eastern Europe. Stalin's amendments, by contrast, were based on ethnic criteria that dominated the thinking of the post-World War I era. In a mere three weeks—a brief period extremely rich in events and decisions—Stalin's nationality argument, which was first formulated, as far as we know, at his meeting of 7 September with Molotov, Zhdanov, Dimitrov, and Manuilsky, had developed from a theme intended to undermine the legitimacy of the Polish state into a propaganda tool and, finally, an important principle for determining the extent of Soviet territorial expansion and establishing the border with the Soviets' new German neighbor.

Stalin's uncertainty with regard to that border and his vacillation between creating a Polish buffer state, setting up a Polish Soviet Socialist Republic as part of the USSR, and transferring Polish territory to Germany indicate that he and his advisers were caught unprepared, first by the conclusion of the Molotov-Ribbentrop Pact and then by the rapid advance of the German panzer divisions into Poland. It was in the process of the September consultations and negotiations with Germany that they found a way not only to sort out their messy territorial relations with Germany but also to work out a language in which they could explain their actions both at home and abroad. The word "nationality" proved highly compatible with the words "borders," "security," "legitimacy," and "propaganda," linking them in a diplomatic crossword that preoccupied Stalin in the weeks leading up to the Soviet entry into World War II.

Soviet Propaganda

Of the two partners who signed the Molotov-Ribbentrop Pact in August 1939, it was the Soviets who were most concerned about its possible impact on public opinion in their country. When on the morning of 24 August Ribbentrop became too enthusiastic about the prospects of German-Soviet friendship, Stalin cautioned his guest with reference to public opinion. "Do you not think we have to pay a little more attention to public opinion in our two countries?" he asked the Nazi visitor. "For many years now we have been pouring buckets of shit over each other's heads and our propaganda boys could not do enough in that direction. Now all of a sudden, are we to make our peoples believe all is forgotten and forgiven? Things do not work so fast."

Stalin knew what he was talking about. When news of the pact broke in Germany, many in the Nazi leadership blamed Ribbentrop for betraying party principles by making common cause with the Bolsheviks. While most ordinary Germans eventually overcame the original shock and accepted the pact as a means of avoiding war on two fronts, many Nazi Party members found their deeply held anti-communist beliefs traduced. Some expressed their concerns to Hitler; others resigned from the party in protest.[12]

News of the sudden about-face in Soviet-German relations left the population of the USSR no less bewildered than that of Germany. People did not dare to resign from the Communist Party or voice their dissatisfaction publicly, but the NKVD registered mass disillusionment among the population, which had been fed for years on anti-fascist propaganda. Nikita Khrushchev, then first secretary of the Central Committee of the Communist Party of Ukraine, later remembered the embarrassment caused by the pact:

> We could not even discuss the treaty at party meetings. For us to have explained our reasons for signing the treaty in straightforward newspaper language would have been offensive, and besides nobody would believe us. It was very hard for us—as communists, as anti-fascists, as people unalterably opposed to the philosophical and political position of the fascists—to accept the idea of joining forces with Germany. It was difficult enough for us to accept this paradox ourselves. It would have been impossible to explain it to the man on the street.

Molotov admitted the problem caused by the Soviet public's reception of the pact in his speech to the Supreme Soviet on 31 August. Now the regime was faced with the task of explaining an even more treacherous move—the invasion of a neighboring state that had resisted a fascist attack.[13]

The Soviet use of the nationality issue to justify the invasion of Poland began in earnest with a publication in *Pravda* for 14 September that attracted the attention of Schulenburg and was picked up by the German Press Agency (DNB). It was in fact an editorial entitled "On the Internal Reasons for the Defeat of Poland." With regard to the fresh German victories on the Polish front, the editorial said: "It is hard to explain such a swift defeat of Poland solely by the superiority of Germany's military technology and military organization and the absence of effective assistance to Poland on the part of England and France." This was an implicit reference to an article that had appeared in *Pravda* only three days earlier.

On 11 September, in an essay entitled "The German-Polish War: A Survey of Military Operations," E. Sosnin enumerated four reasons for the collapse of Polish defenses: lack of fortifications on the country's western borders, German superiority in air power, the Wehrmacht's superiority in artillery, and lack of support from Poland's Western allies. Now the Soviet leaders were making an important corrective to Sosnin's assessment. The editorial stressed the "internal weaknesses and contradictions of the Polish state." It stated that "Poland is a multiethnic state. In the composition of the population of Poland, Poles make up only 60 percent, while the other 40 percent are made up of national minorities, mainly Ukrainians, Belarusians, and Jews. It suffices to note that there are no fewer than eight million Ukrainians in Poland, and about three million Belarusians." The Jews were thus relegated to secondary status. The editorial was really about the Ukrainians and Belarusians.[14]

The problem with the Polish state, according to the *Pravda* editorial, was not simply its multiethnic character but the way in which the Polish ruling circles treated their minorities—the subject broached by Stalin in his conversation with Dimitrov a week earlier. "Western Ukraine and Western Belarus," wrote *Pravda*, "regions of predominantly Ukrainian and Belarusian population, are the objects of the most flagrant, shameless exploitation on the part of the Polish landlords. The situation of the Ukrainians and Belarusians is characterized by a regime of ethnic oppression and lack of rights. The ruling circles of Poland, flaunting their supposed love of liberty, have done all they could to turn Western Ukraine and Western Belarus into a colony without rights, consigned for plunder to the Polish lords." The authors of the editorial went on to describe in detail the discrimination of the non-Polish nationalities on the legal and administrative levels. Special attention was paid to the sorry state of Ukrainian and Belarusian culture and the Polonization of the minorities. While the editorial allegedly dealt with the reasons for Poland's defeat, its implicit message was hard to miss: the Ukrainians and Belarusians were suffering under Polish rule and needed Soviet protection.[15]

The political significance of the editorial was not lost on foreign observers, and Schulenburg was not the only one to take note of it. With the benefit of hindsight, *Time* magazine (25 September) linked the *Pravda* editorial with the panic that Stalin and Molotov must have felt as they watched the German advance into Poland. In an article entitled "Dizziness from Success," which reminded the reader of Stalin's piece of 1930 about excesses in the collectivization of agriculture, the *Time* magazine writer argued that the editorial had been drafted by Stalin himself. "As the Germans reached Bialystok last week Comrade Stalin came out with his answer," went the article. The *Time* magazine author quoted liberally from the *Pravda* editorial on the mistreatment of Ukrainians and Belarusians and concluded with the following statement: "Thus with great circumspection the Dictator told the people what part of Poland Russia intended to get—i.e., the Polish Ukraine, the northeast area south of Lithuania."

In general terms, the argument used by the *Pravda* editorial was already familiar to observers of the European scene. Czechoslovakia had been dismembered in 1938–39, ostensibly to guarantee the rights and freedoms of minorities. The mistreatment of the German minority in Poland had served as a pretext for Hitler's attack on Poland only two weeks earlier, and Hitler had no qualms about exploiting Ukrainian nationalists either in Carpatho-Ukraine or in Poland to destabilize the situation and achieve his goals. If anything, Stalin was now taking a leaf from Hitler's book.[16]

When Viacheslav Molotov addressed the Soviet people on the radio in the late morning of 17 September, explaining why the country had entered the war, the nationality question was front and center in his argument. The Soviet foreign commissar began by claiming that the Polish state had collapsed, rendering existing treaties between Moscow and Warsaw invalid. The collapse of Poland had also created a vacuum on the borders of the USSR, threatening the security of the Soviet state. "The Soviet government," continued Molotov, "also cannot be expected to take an indifferent attitude to the fate of its blood relatives, Ukrainians and Belarusians residing in Poland who previously found themselves in the position of nations without rights and have now been completely abandoned to the vagaries of fate. The Soviet government regards it as a sacred obligation to extend a helping hand to its brethren Ukrainians and brethren Belarusians residing in Poland."

The importance of this ethnic justification of the invasion was further stressed in a statement later in the speech: "The Soviet government has directed the General Staff of the Red Army to order its troops to cross the border and take the lives and property of the population of Western Ukraine and Western Belarus under its protection." The "blood brothers," it seemed, had to be saved from the Polish government, even though it allegedly did not exist. There was no mention of the German threat or, for that matter, of the Jewish minority in Poland. The former had been edited out of the text of the Soviet note to the Poles by Schulenburg. Reference to the latter was probably omitted by the Soviets themselves.[17]

While lamenting the fate of national minorities was nothing new in European politics of the day, the *Pravda* editorial of 14 September and Molotov's speech of 17 September marked a major change in the Soviet use of nationality rhetoric at home and abroad. It was a shift from treating cross-border national minorities as a threat to the security of the Soviet Union to a rhetoric that allowed the regime to take advantage of those communities not only to advance Soviet interests in the international arena but also to extend Soviet borders at the expense of neighboring states. In a certain way it was a return to the policies of the 1920s, marked by the original optimism of the new communist regime, which had not yet abandoned its dreams of world revolution.

The policies of the 1920s, defined by Terry Martin as the "Piedmont principle," were designed to "exploit cross-border ethnic ties to project political influence into neighboring states." They were first formulated and promoted by the Ukrainian national communists who wanted Soviet Ukraine to serve as a beacon of hope for Ukrainians in Poland, Czechoslovakia, and Romania. Ukrainians abroad, went the argument, would be attracted to socialism and the USSR by the flowering of Ukrainian culture and society in Soviet Ukraine. This policy was ended during the Great Famine of 1932–33, which resulted in millions of innocent deaths. The beacon was extinguished. Ukrainian communists were accused of nationalist deviation and instigation of peasant resistance to the Soviet regime. The policy of cultural Ukrainization was curtailed and the "Piedmont principle" nullified.[18]

The new era became known for a different set of foreign-policy priorities and a different rhetoric that reflected a "besieged fortress" mentality. Ukraine and Belarus were now viewed as bulwarks of the Soviet state that were threatened by the capitalist West. The imperialists, argued the regime, were trying to exploit cross-border ethnic ties to spur non-Russian nationalism in the Soviet borderlands and create a fifth column in the USSR so as to prepare for a future invasion. The task of turning Ukraine into a "true fortress of the USSR" was formulated by Stalin himself in the months leading up to the Great Famine. Moscow's representatives in Ukraine were eager to oblige. "Comrades," said the newly appointed first secretary of the Communist Party of Ukraine, Nikita Khrushchev, to delegates at the party congress in June 1938, "we shall bend every effort to ensure that the task and directive of the Central Committee of the All-Union Communist Party (Bolshevik) and Comrade Stalin—to make Ukraine a fortress impregnable to enemies—is fulfilled with honor."

Khrushchev blamed the "difficulties that Ukraine underwent in the course of collectivization"—an indirect reference to the Great Famine—on the intrigues of the foreign enemies of the USSR, including Józef Piłsudski of Poland. Khrushchev's other references to Poland were intended to illustrate Soviet achievements in education and assert that the Ukrainian toiling masses would never tolerate the rule of the Polish lords. The rhetoric was defensive rather than offensive. The "Piedmont principle" was long gone. The "besieged fortress" mentality remained dominant until the appearance of the *Pravda* editorial on 14 September and Molotov's speech three days later.[19]

Molotov's speech was broadcast on Soviet radio at 11:30 a.m. on 17 September, less than seven hours after the two Red Army fronts crossed the Polish-Soviet border and began their offensive against dispersed and disoriented Polish troops. Since the broadcast was scheduled to coincide with the lunch break at government institutions, factories, and collective farms, hundreds of thousands of industrial and office workers, peasants, and students all over the Soviet Union gathered around radio transmitters to listen to the speech. They then participated in government-sponsored meetings featuring speakers who recapitulated Molotov's statements made a few minutes earlier and called on those present to give their full support to the newest party policy and the war effort. The next day, *Pravda* published a photo of a meeting attended by thousands at the Red Proletarian machine-tool factory in Moscow. It also ran an article on a gathering of professors and students of Moscow State University, reportedly with an attendance of six thousand, who welcomed the address delivered by a professor of party history, Vladimir Iudovsky. The professor characterized the invasion as "a sage act of world-historical significance."[20]

In Kyiv, the capital of Ukraine, *Pravda* correspondents registered an especially high level of political activity and rising popular enthusiasm. "Thousands of Kyivans crowded around transmitters on streets and squares," reported *Pravda* from the capital of a republic directly affected by the invasion and the change in the party's nationality rhetoric.

> With strained attention, they listen everywhere to the speech of Comrade V.M. Molotov. When Comrade Molotov speaks of the Soviet government's decision to offer assistance to Ukrainian and Belarusian brethren, stormy applause and shouts of "hurrah" resound. Comrade Molotov's words are lost in cries of "Long live Stalin!" "Long live the Party!" "Long live the Red Army!" Someone intones the proletarian hymn, and its sound carries far along the streets. In those minutes, two hundred draftees at the Stalin quarter recruitment office raised a fervent ovation in honor of the party and government. A meeting sprang up spontaneously. Someone took a red towel from a table, and in the hands of a draftee it turns into a scarlet banner under which the draftees swear to do their duty with honor to their homeland and to the proletariat of the whole world.[21]

Pravda and other Soviet newspapers were full of reports on public meetings at which workers, peasants, and representatives of the Soviet intelligentsia were encouraged by the regime to express their support for the intervention. Given the official nature of these meetings, it is not surprising that the language used by speakers and authors of resolutions was taken directly from Molotov's speech and other official pronouncements. Emphasis was placed on the national liberation of Ukrainians and Belarusians and the social liberation of the entire population of Poland's eastern provinces. Rhetoric that had characterized the "besieged fortress" mentality was abandoned almost overnight in favor of the language of national (and social) liberation. Not only was the fortress no longer besieged, but its walls were extended westward, necessitating a new terminology. The "national liberation" paradigm fit the bill. The Soviet authorities' claim that they had entered the war on behalf of their Slavic blood brothers, abandoned by their erstwhile Polish rulers, had limited impact on world opinion at best.

If one judges by Soviet media reports, Stalin and Molotov scored a major public-relations coup. But should one trust reporting in the Soviet media? The London *Times* wrote on 18 September regarding the events of the previous day in Moscow: "At 8 o'clock the Russian wireless broadcast a summary of the contents of the Note [to the Polish government], which stated that Soviet action was necessary to safeguard her own interests and to protect the White Russian and Ukrainian minorities in Eastern Poland. . . . It has been noted that the Soviet arguments bear a family resemblance to those invariably adopted by Hitler and as often demolished by the Soviet Press as pretexts for aggression. Accordingly, it was a bewildered Soviet population which listened to M. Molotoff's broadcast this morning." G. E. R. Gedye, the *New York Times* Moscow correspondent, reported on 17 September from the Soviet capital: "The Moscow population, recalling the reiterated declarations of leaders headed by Joseph Stalin that they did not desire a foot of anyone else's territory, went about today asking: 'What has happened now?' 'Are we at war; with whom and why?' 'What do we want in Poland?' 'What has gone wrong with the neutrality pact signed with the express purpose of keeping us from war?'"[22]

In the West, the Red Army's invasion of Poland was considered a stab in the back of a victim of Nazi aggression. Even politicians such as Winston Churchill in Britain, who gave limited support to the Soviet action, did so on the basis of arguments different from those invoked by Stalin and Molotov. But what was the impact of national-liberation rhetoric at home? Did it work, or did it fail? To answer this question, one has to deal with the difficult task of assessing Soviet public opinion. In the last few decades, popular attitudes toward international politics and, in particular, questions of war and peace have attracted a fair amount of attention from scholars of the Second World War.

Public opinion was an important factor in the formulation of foreign policy by democratic governments and an important consideration in the efforts of dictatorial regimes to mobilize public support for warfare. The Soviet Union certainly falls into the latter category, which creates additional problems in the acquisition and assessment of relevant data. It is difficult but not impossible to track major trends in the mood of the population under dictatorial regimes, partly because the regimes themselves allocated significant resources to monitoring those trends and changes.[23]

The NKVD Pollsters

Throughout Soviet history, the Communist Party leadership regularly received top-secret reports assessing the attitudes of the Soviet public to party policies. The reports came from two sources: party organs and the secret police. Whatever the circumstances, both types of reports always stated that the vast majority of the Soviet people welcomed, accepted, and endorsed the latest initiatives, thereby echoing newspaper coverage of those events. They then turned to the opinions of those who were doubtful of party policies or expressed opinions characterized as blatantly anti-Soviet. In that regard, both types of reports differed profoundly from the Soviet media.

The party reports tended to give less coverage of anti-Soviet activities, while the secret-police reports largely focused on just such activities. There was good reason for the difference. Emphasizing negative responses would not be in the interest of party officials preparing the reports, since it could be interpreted as an indication of deficiencies in their own propaganda efforts. Secret-police officials, on the other hand, could only benefit from focusing on negative responses. Dealing with existing or imagined opposition to the regime was the raison d'être of the secret police, and the reports provided, among other things, additional justification for maintaining an extensive and costly secret-police apparatus.[24]

The credibility of secret-police reports was at the core of the discussion about compliance and resistance under Stalinism in the first issue of *Kritika* (2000).[25] There is good reason to question the reliability of the information included in the reports, especially when they are mined exclusively for manifestations of opposition to the regime. There seems to be general agreement, however, that when it comes to "negative" statements—those critical of government policy—they certainly cannot be regarded as expressions of the only authentic feelings of the population but can be used to assess the range of responses offered by the Soviet public to a given initiative on the part of the Soviet state. But what about expressions of support for the regime and its actions? Should they be taken at face value or ignored?

One way to deal with this question is to distinguish two kinds of endorsements of official policy—those expressed in Bolshevik parlance of the period and those that did not mirror official pronouncements. Expressions of approval for Soviet entry into the war that used a vocabulary different from that of party declarations and media reports are of special interest. An added benefit of focusing on such expressions is the possibility of identifying sources of support for government policy beyond the party's own organizational base. The unexpected change of rhetoric in the Soviet media's justification of the coming military campaign is a case in which such a strategy may be applied to good effect.

I shall try to reconstruct the variety of positive and negative responses to the Soviet invasion of Poland on the basis of thirty-three reports about the reaction of the Soviet public to the outbreak of the war filed by officials of the People's Commissariat of Internal Affairs of Ukraine between 27 August and 15 October 1939. These reports have only recently become available to scholars as part of a publication project undertaken by historians from the Institute of Ukrainian Archaeography in Kyiv in cooperation with archivists of the Security Service of Ukraine, and with the support of a number of German governmental and public institutions. Most of the reports were prepared for Nikita Khrushchev, then first secretary of the Central Committee of the Communist Party of Ukraine, and for Lavrentii Beriia, people's commissar of internal affairs of the USSR, by the people's commissar of internal affairs, Ivan Serov, and his deputy, Mykola Horlynsky. They were based in part on reports that Serov and his assistants were receiving from the various regions of Ukraine and from NKVD officials in Red Army units posted in Ukraine. These, too, are included in my analysis.[26]

On 17 September, the date of the Soviet invasion of Poland and Molotov's speech to the Soviet people, Mykola Horlynsky sent an urgent request to his subordinates: "I propose that all heads of operational sections of the NKVD of the USSR with a secret service and intelligence in Kyiv present secret-service reports on the reaction of the population to Comrade Molotov's speech on the entry of our forces into Poland to the head of the Second Department of the NKVD of the USSR by 2:00 p.m. today. Thereafter draft versions of such reports are to be presented to Comrade Pavlychev every three hours." By the end of the day, Horlynsky had filed two reports assessing the mood of the Ukrainian population for Nikita Khrushchev. The first was based on the reactions of Kyivans, while the second was a follow-up memo including data telephoned to Kyiv from NKVD offices in the regions. Two more reports followed on the next day, and reporting continued on a regular basis until the very end of the campaign.[27]

What did the people of Soviet Ukraine think about the war? To begin answering this question, I shall present a spectrum of both "positive" and "negative" responses without trying to establish how widespread they may have been among the Soviet Ukrainian public in September 1939. In general, the NKVD reports agreed with the Soviet media, claiming that official efforts to convince the population of the legitimacy of government action had been largely successful. "A number of passages of Comrade Molotov's speech were accompanied by applause," wrote Mykola Horlynsky on 17 September.

The reaction of students was particularly enthusiastic. "At Kyiv University, Comrade Molotov's speech was met with shouts of 'hurrah' by students," reads the report. The following report suggested that young people in the provinces were just as enthusiastic: "A number of incidents have been noted of voluntary reporting to military recruitment offices, with requests for enlistment in the ranks of the RKKA [Workers' and Peasants' Red Army]. A group of students of the Mykolaïv Pedagogical Institute made a collective appeal to be enlisted as volunteers in the Red Army." While rank-and-file NKVD agents and their superiors were under pressure not only to find and record but also to fabricate positive responses to Communist Party initiatives, the episodes described above could hardly have been fabricated, as they were easily verifiable.[28]

What aroused such enthusiasm on the part of students? The information about Mykolaïv students volunteering for the Red Army was preceded in Horlynsky's report by the statement that "The action of the USSR is being assessed as a step in the direction of starting a world revolution and active struggle against the fascist aggressors." A student of the Vinnytsia Medical Institute named Benadsky allegedly told an NKVD informer that "our Soviet government will have to bear the red banner of revolution farther west. The defeat of Poland shows that one of the links of fascism has been broken." One might assume that the new crop of Soviet youth, born after 1917 and raised on notions of revolutionary romanticism, was welcoming an opportunity to follow in the footsteps of participants in the October Revolution and heroes of the Spanish Civil War, lionized by Soviet propaganda, in order to carry the torch of revolution to Central and Western Europe. The references to "fascist aggressors" and the breaking of "one of the links of fascism" echo Soviet anti-fascist propaganda of the years leading up to the conclusion of the Molotov-Ribbentrop Pact, which disappointed and disheartened idealistically inclined Soviet students. It appears that the students were prepared to see the Soviet invasion of Poland as a reversal of the policy initiated by the Molotov-Ribbentrop Pact.[29]

The report forwarded by Horlynsky to Lavrentii Beriia on 19 September included information from the regions indicating that not only students but also young workers and peasants were eager to take part in the war. In the city of Osypenko (present-day Berdiansk), "immediately after Comrade Molotov's radio address, eighty men presented themselves, twenty of them with their wives, and asked that they be directed to the Red Army to take part in military operations." Recruits in the Chernihivka region of Zaporizhzhia Oblast "began to demand their speedy enlistment in the army so that they might be in time to take part in military operations together with the whole Red Army."

It was not entirely clear to the population whether the Soviet troops would simply occupy Western Ukraine and Belarus without military action, fight the Poles, or engage the German army as well. R.P. Sheiner, the author of a letter intercepted by the NKVD, anticipated a war with Germany. "We had to take this action," he wrote about the invasion of Poland, "for the Germans would have attacked us in any event, so it is better to strike them on Polish territory than on ours." Some Red Army officers crossing the Polish border on the morning of 17 September believed that they were going to fight the Germans. "I thought that this was the beginning of war with Germany," remembered one of them later, "and many other officers thought the same."[30]

Most of the initial criticism of the Soviet invasion of Poland recorded by NKVD agents came from the ranks of the intelligentsia. Svitozor Drahomanov, the son of Ukraine's most influential political thinker of the nineteenth century, Mykhailo Drahomanov, and a translator at the Art Publishing House in Kyiv, allegedly stated in the presence of an NKVD informer: "In essence, this is the fourth partition of Poland, carried out by arrangement between Stalin and Hitler. . . . All that is going on may be called the victory of Hitlerism, which is the highest stage of the development of capitalist society." Drahomanov expressed his critique of official actions in language borrowed from recent Soviet propaganda and Vladimir Lenin's writings on the nature of imperialism. He was not the only one to attack the regime from the standpoint of Marxist orthodoxy and anti-fascism. A graduate student at the Institute of Folklore of the Ukrainian Academy of Sciences named Lanovy reportedly declared in the presence of a government informer: "And what will the whole world say? They will say that we are dividing Poland together with fascist Germany. England and France will declare war on us, which means that we will be fighting them together with Germany. What will the Western communists and the workers of the world say then?"[31]

The sudden U-turn embodied in the Molotov-Ribbentrop Pact certainly undermined the Soviet regime's credibility among many of its international and domestic supporters. For years the regime had attacked fascist Germany as the main threat to peace, prepared the population for a possible alliance with the Western democracies, and placed heavy propaganda emphasis on communist and proletarian solidarity in the world-wide fight against fascism. The USSR was at the forefront of that struggle—the greatest hope of all peace-loving peoples. Now all that was suddenly over. In the eyes of those Soviet citizens who linked the pact with the invasion of Poland, the regime stood condemned of complete disregard for its own political and ideological commitments. The Soviet Union was now making a mockery of its peace-loving rhetoric, becoming an aggressor, and betraying not only Britain and France but also its communist allies in the West—such were the themes of "negative" responses recorded by NKVD agents. There was also a good deal of criticism of the government's action from the viewpoint of *realpolitik*. Quite a few people from a variety of social backgrounds believed that Hitler would outsmart the Soviet leadership and eventually start a war with the USSR. These sentiments, widespread in Ukraine, were shared by many inhabitants of Leningrad, as indicated by the research of Sarah Davies.[32]

The apparent hypocrisy of the Soviet regime also drew strong criticism from students, who were the most enthusiastic supporters of the regime. "The shift in our policy has been too abrupt," said a student from Kyiv named Rybchynsky. "Only a month ago we were offering assistance to Poland against the aggressor, and now we are condemning it at every turn and have even taken over part of its territory." Some students resorted to irony. "Our papers cast fascism and Hitler in the darkest colors. Now it turns out that those were all lies. Hitler is conducting the war in most humane fashion; he is not devastating the population or cultural treasures," said a student of the Kyiv Construction Institute named Velednytsky.

Also questioned was the social component of the Soviet liberation paradigm. "It would have been better not to liberate the people of Western Ukraine and Western Belarus from the lords' oppression, for things are no better among us. They will feel that in a while," opined the medical student Gomerbarg. Even the least controversial claim, that of fraternal ties with the peoples of the newly occupied territories, was ridiculed. "It is very strange to hear assertions about our brethren in the West," said the Kyiv student Zalizniak. "Now we call them brothers, but if that brother had written you a letter earlier, you would have suffered for it." True believers from the ranks of the Red Army could also be quite critical. They were dissatisfied that their commanders had canceled a sharpshooting exercise known as "Shooting the Fascist."[33]

During the first few days of the invasion, Horlynsky reported to his superiors that there were no negative responses recorded among workers. Nor were there any reactions, either positive or critical, attributed to peasants in the reports. But soon reports began to arrive from the regions, and while they also focused largely on critical opinions attributed to the intelligentsia, there were growing references to critical statements by workers and peasants alike. Some of these repeated arguments noted in reports on the mood of the intelligentsia, but there were also new themes and arguments. Their underlying motives were protest against economic hardship, refusal to fight for Soviet rule in case of a German-Soviet conflict, and readiness to exploit the war in order to settle scores with the regime. A worker from Odesa named Tsukanov allegedly said in the presence of an NKVD informer: "Hitler is attacking Poland and will go on to attack our communists. The war is only a few days old, and we already have nothing."

A peasant named Hustovydyn in Sumy province allegedly tried to disrupt a meeting on the occasion of Molotov's speech, saying, "The Soviet government has stripped me bare and reduced me to poverty. Not a single idiot will go to the front." Kalynychenko, a peasant from Kirovohrad Oblast, told his fellow collective farmers: "The war will solve everything. We suffered for a long time; now there is less time to wait. Soon we will live without collectives." His attitude was shared by another peasant named Krosalo, who stated: "Even if the Germans take us over, we will be none the worse for that. On the collective farm, you are still hungry and threadbare. In 1933, Soviet power was guilty of starving many people to death."[34]

We cannot assess the popularity of either positive or critical opinions among the Soviet public presented in the NKVD reports. Many objects of NKVD surveillance managed to survive into the late 1930s precisely because they were able to keep their mouths shut or make neutral or pro-Soviet pronouncements when they suspected that they were dealing with an NKVD informer. A forty-eight-year-old Ukrainian woman who came from a dekulakized family and worked on the Soviet railroads commented as follows to interviewers of the Harvard Refugee Interview Project: "Generally, people in the Soviet Union worked hard and were silent; they were afraid to talk too much or to ask for some information because of the common terror and because many Soviet agents and spies were among the people. Especially former 'kulaks,' people like my husband and me, were silent and worked hard." Whether genuine or not, both positive and negative statements contained elements of people's real thinking, not constructed for the sake of the informer.[35]

What we do know, both from the reports and from other sources, is that resentment among the peasantry based on the outcomes of collectivization and the Great Famine of 1932–33 was an ongoing concern, and that the urban population, including that of Moscow, Leningrad, and capitals of the republics, suffered from shortages of food and manufactured goods that grew worse in August and September 1939. The public was generally confused by the recently signed Molotov-Ribbentrop Pact, not understanding on which side, if any, the Soviet Union was entering the war. Some of the people "polled" by the NKVD were concerned about what Britain and France would say regarding the Soviet invasion of an independent and embattled state.

The Nationality Card

The NKVD reports divided Soviet citizens into a number of categories, most notably by class, or social status, status and nationality. Judging by these reports, the strongest anti-Soviet statements were expressed by peasants and members of "other nationalities," which, according to the NKVD, generally meant Poles and Germans. Among the social groups, it was the intelligentsia, not the peasants or workers, that received most attention. If workers and collective farmers were allotted one category each, the intelligentsia had two: many reports included separate sections on "office workers and intelligentsia" and "academic circles." The special interest of NKVD officials in the opinions of the intelligentsia was also reflected in the number of statements quoted in NKVD reports.

The sections on the intelligentsia were two to four times longer than those on the working class or collective farmers. Some members of the intelligentsia quoted in the reports were under surveillance as part of ongoing investigations into the activities of illegal political organizations. Such people were already surrounded by informants, and it was relatively easy for NKVD agents to obtain information about their attitudes. Judging by the reports, it was the intelligentsia that provided the most sophisticated appraisal of changes in Soviet foreign policy, and it was the same group that reacted most actively to the dramatic change in Soviet nationality discourse on the eve and in the course of the Soviet invasion of Poland.

What was the intelligentsia's reaction to the changes in party rhetoric? If one trusts the NKVD reports, it was overwhelmingly positive. If one looks at statements and comments that did not reflect Molotov's address and media pronouncements, it appears that the national-liberation theme did indeed strike a chord with the intelligentsia. It was interpreted in two ways. The first was the old imperial view that regarded Ukrainians and Belarusians as part of a greater Russian nation and thus as Russians; their liberation meant the reunification of the Russian people and the return of the imperial borderlands to Russian control. The second approach was closer to the official government line, as it postulated the liberation and unification not of the Russian people but of the Ukrainian and Belarusian lands and peoples. Both approaches, the old imperial and the new national one, were reinforced by the class interpretation expressed in the official pronouncements: the Russians (alternatively, the Ukrainians and Belarusians) were to be liberated not only from national but also from social oppression.

The sentiments of those who subscribed to the old imperial vision of the Russian state and nation but were prepared to adapt it to the new official terminology were expressed by a professor of the Kyiv medical school named Romankevych, who allegedly stated in the presence of an NKVD informer: "The Soviet Union should restore the Russian lands—the Kholm region, Western Ukraine, and Western Belarus." A worker from Odesa named Liubchenko went even further in his claim to the lost imperial territories. "The Soviet government has acted properly," he said to an informer. "Western Ukraine and Belarus are settled by our people and constitute our territory. We should restore Bessarabia—it is ours too, after all." The treatment of Western Ukraine and Western Belarus as lands settled by "our people" was quite common in statements recorded by the NKVD, as were calls for the annexation of Bessarabia, the former imperial province that was annexed by Romania in the aftermath of the 1917 revolution and allocated to the Soviet sphere of influence by the Molotov-Ribbentrop Pact.

Interestingly enough, all these statements were quoted in the sections of reports devoted to positive responses. They were certainly in keeping with the notions of ethnicity held by the authors of the reports, who assigned the responses of Ukrainians and Russians to the sections on social categories but dealt with the reactions of "Galicians"—that is, Ukrainians who came from Galicia, formerly under the rule of Austria-Hungary—in the sections entitled "Among other nationalities."[36]

The old imperial interpretation of the invasion of Poland recorded in NKVD reports from Ukraine was apparently popular in Russia as well. G. E. R. Gedye reported for *New York Times* from Moscow on 18 September: "Privately, some confess confusion as to how the invasion is to be reconciled with Joseph Stalin's declaration that he did not want a foot of others' territory. Others again rationalize this casuistically, saying, 'But, of course, this was ours, inhabited by our kin, and torn from us by Poland in 1920.'" The academician Vladimir Vernadsky, one of the leaders of the Constitutional Democratic Party in the Russian Empire, the first president of the Ukrainian Academy of Sciences in 1918, and a major figure in the USSR Academy of Sciences in Moscow at the start of World War II, belonged to the latter group.

In his diary entry for 3 October, Vernadsky wrote that "The seizure of (Western) Ukraine and Belarus is approved by all. The course of history is amazingly spontaneous. The Poles are crazy. And the Czechs (incomparably milder in that regard) have also suffered because of it. But the policy of Stalin and Molotov is realistic and, it seems to me, correct—a Russian policy of state. In Poland, social revolution is a military force." Vernadsky considered the takeover of Western Ukraine and Belarus a manifestation of Russian policy and apparently had no problem with Stalin's export of revolution to Poland. His views were shared by other members of the all-Union Academy. On 18 October Vernadsky wrote that his colleague, the geochemist Aleksandr Fersman, was "constantly under the influence of the takeover of Ukr[aine]—a Russian policy."[37]

If intellectuals in Moscow saw the Soviet invasion of Poland as a manifestation of Russian policy, most of their colleagues in Ukraine interpreted it as evidence of the regime's Ukrainian policy. On 19 October, Vernadsky recorded in his diary a summary of his discussions with Leonid Iasnopolsky, a member of the Ukrainian Academy of Sciences who had moved to Moscow in 1931. "Iasnopolsky," wrote Vernadsky, "apparently like the overwhelming majority of those who find themselves here, sympathizes with Stalin's policy. Not so much because of the Germans as because of the restoration of the country's political significance and the 'liberation' of the Ukrainians and Belarusians from Poland." Vernadsky's observations on Iasnopolsky's views are echoed by the NKVD reports sent to Nikita Khrushchev and Lavrentii Beriia from Ukraine in September–October 1939. If one trusts those reports, most Kyiv academics subscribed to the modern, "Ukrainian" interpretation of the national- and social-liberation paradigm.[38]

Very few leading Ukrainian intellectuals refused to be swayed by official propaganda about benefits to the Ukrainian nation. Among the most critical was the renowned Ukrainian poet Maksym Rylsky, who was regarded by the NKVD as a Ukrainian nationalist. Rylsky argued that the invasion of Poland "runs counter to the humanity and justice about which we have always made so much noise." He continued: "And so I write verses every day praising the valiant Soviet forces and the wisdom of our policy, but there is no enthusiasm in my heart. We attacked the weak, after all, and it is very hard for an honest poet to justify such an action." The authorities refused to grant Rylsky permission to visit Western Ukraine in the fall of 1939. His opinion was shared by other Ukrainian writers. Semen Skliarenko told an NKVD informer: "In our time, you cannot believe anyone or anything. The strong falls upon the weak—that is an eternal law of life. Just yesterday we shouted that the Germans were barbarians, plunderers, and scoundrels, but now we are almost trading kisses with them. Such striking hypocrisy."[39]

If Ukrainian writers and poets were troubled by the injustice of the invasion and the duplicity of Soviet foreign policy and propaganda, academics took a much more forgiving attitude toward the regime. Some of them were genuinely excited about the new turn of events. Professor Mykola Hrinchenko of the Institute of Folklore at the Ukrainian Academy of Sciences allegedly told his colleagues: "I do not know whether there is any other foreign-policy measure of the Soviet authorities capable of arousing such joy among Ukrainians as this one. Ukrainians have reason to rejoice." Hrinchenko explained his excitement by noting that, with the Soviet takeover of eastern Poland, "the age-old hopes of the people of Western Ukraine, starving and suffering under the Polish yoke, have come true." It was a politically correct explanation of the enthusiasm generated by the realization of the principal goal of Ukrainian irredentism—the unification of the Ukrainian lands, to which the Ukrainian national movement had aspired since the latter half of the nineteenth century. Similar ideas were expressed by other Ukrainian intellectuals.

An analysis of responses to the Soviet invasion of Poland recorded by NKVD agents in Ukraine allows one to conclude that the regime's use of national-liberation rhetoric to justify its entry into World War II succeeded in extending its power base and co-opting dissenting views by appropriating nationalist discourse and presenting itself to society as a benefactor of the national cause. By and large, the Ukrainian intelligentsia was prepared to follow the government's lead in regarding the Red Army's invasion of Poland as a campaign of national liberation and unification of their native land, and not as their country's entry into global military conflict.[40]

*
**

The Soviet leadership's decision to justify its attack on Poland by invoking the liberation of that country's Ukrainian and Belarusian minorities helped mobilize support for the Soviet entry into World War II not only among those of its citizens who considered the Red Army's invasion of Poland justified in geostrategic and military terms, or were eager to promote world revolution, but also among those who considered it a just restoration of the old Russian imperial boundaries, a step toward the reunification of the Russian people and, last but not least, the unification of the Ukrainian and Belarusian nations. The broadening of popular support for Soviet foreign policy thus benefited the regime at a time when deteriorating economic conditions and a falling standard of living coincided with a sharp turn of Soviet propaganda away from its established anti-fascist attitude, which increased the number of critics of the regime.

An examination of the NKVD reports makes it quite clear that the Soviet people were not limited to clear-cut compliance or resistance in their dealings with the Soviet state under Stalinism. They were not merely "objects" of state policy but "subjects" in their own right who used their "subjectivity" not only to embrace the regime or learn how to "speak Bolshevik" in order to survive but also to lend or withdraw support from the state, depending on its policies. That was certainly true in the 1920s, and it appears to have been true for the late 1930s as well. The dictatorial state remained concerned about the attitudes of the population, classified along social and national lines. As the reaction of Ukrainian intellectuals to the Soviet invasion of Poland demonstrates, representatives of individual peoples were prepared to lend conditional support to the regime if it offered the realization of their objectives in return.

The initiative came from the state, but it was ultimately up to the particular group to accept or reject the government's offer. Besides, it was members of the Ukrainian intelligentsia who prepared historical, demographic, and other data on the newly acquired territories for the Soviet government and were thus in a position to influence the official position on a variety of issues. It is easy to assume that lengthy presentations to NKVD agents by the intellectuals under their surveillance were intended not only as manifestations of loyalty but also as attempts to influence party policy.

The Soviet regime had co-opted national-liberation discourse and policies in the 1920s. It embarked on a policy of co-opting Russian public opinion in the 1930s. Now it used similar tactics to co-opt those battered by its policies of the 1930s—the Ukrainian and Belarusian intellectual elites. Unlike in the 1920s, the government was prepared to offer them not only concessions at home but also opportunities abroad. The introduction of the ethnic theme into Soviet foreign-policy pronouncements initiated a change in Soviet nationality policy, documented in the Ukrainian case by the studies of Serhy Yekelchyk and Vladyslav Hrynevych. It was an obvious case in which foreign-policy considerations led to a shift in nationality policy at home.

If the "Piedmont principle," as Terry Martin has argued, was seen by the authorities as "an exploitable benefit of a domestically driven policy," and the "besieged fortress" mentality arguably reflected the regime's domestic and foreign-policy concerns alike, the "national-liberation" paradigm was formulated and implemented first and foremost in response to foreign-policy considerations. We see no attempt on the part of Soviet officials to employ national-liberation rhetoric or implement related policies either at home or abroad before the Stalin-Dimitrov meeting of 7 September 1939.[41]

Adopted quite unexpectedly in a desperate attempt to find justification for the coming aggression, the new national-liberation paradigm turned out to be a useful tool for the Soviet government in the course of World War II. It helped mobilize support for Soviet entry into the war in September 1939. For the next two years, it helped promote the Sovietization of Western Ukraine, Western Belarus and, in 1940–41, Bessarabia and Bukovyna. It also helped the Soviet leadership reclaim those territories in 1944–45. At the Yalta Conference in February 1945, neither President Roosevelt nor Prime Minister Churchill was able to refute Stalin's claims to Lviv and Drohobych, which were presented in ethnonational terms.

It was only with the start of the Cold War that the Soviet authorities were forced to abandon the national-liberation paradigm. Once again, as in the 1930s, ethnic contacts began to be regarded not as an opportunity to export Soviet influence abroad but as a channel through which the imperialist powers could corrupt the Soviet nationalities. From the late 1940s on, campaigns were launched against local nationalism, and contacts with cross-border ethnic communities and diasporas were severely curtailed. Once again, as in the 1930s, diasporas and compatriots abroad were condemned as enemies of the Soviet state and people.[42]

10.

The Battle for Eastern Europe

"The combination of Russian revolutionary sweep with American efficiency is the essence of Leninism," declared Joseph Stalin in 1924, the year of Lenin's death.[1] Stalin's fascination with American culture and business ethic was shared by many Bolsheviks of the 1920s. The last words read by Lenin's wife to her dying husband came from a short novel by the American author Jack London. While the United States was among the last countries to establish diplomatic relations with the Soviet Union, American companies were open for business with the Soviets earlier than their European competitors, supplying expertise and equipment for Soviet construction sites from Magnitogorsk in the Urals to the Dnieper Hydroelectric Station in Ukraine.

Franklin Delano Roosevelt's speedy recognition of Stalin's government in Moscow soon after his inauguration, along with his New Deal policies, helped create in the Soviet media an image of the American president as the kind of capitalist with whom one could do business. With Stalin fearing encirclement by Germany and Japan and mistrusting Britain and France, the United States emerged in Soviet public discourse of the 1930s as the least hostile, if not the friendliest, capitalist country in the world. US military intervention in the Far East during the Russian Civil War was largely forgotten, if not forgiven, by the Europe-obsessed Bolshevik leadership in the Kremlin.

When Hitler turned against Stalin in 1941, the Soviet leader found it much easier in historical, political, and psychological terms to ally himself with Roosevelt than with Winston

Churchill—in Bolshevik eyes, the embodiment of British imperialism since the 1917 revolution. Until Roosevelt's death in April 1945, he remained Stalin's favorite capitalist leader. The United States was not only the country on which the Soviet Union most relied during the war with Germany but also the one with which it was most comfortable when it came to building the postwar future: unlike the British, the Americans were not going to stay in Europe. In the Far East they were willing to accommodate Soviet territorial claims, and in the newly created United Nations Organization they treated the Soviets as equals, extending to them the right of veto reserved for major powers.

What went wrong in Soviet-American relations after 1945? This question, central to the debate on the causes of the Cold War, has been answered in various ways. Without dismissing the historical, cultural, and personal factors that led to the dramatic change in Soviet-American relations after World War II, I put the main emphasis on geopolitical factors. In the summary that follows I propose that it was Soviet expansion, or rather the return of Russia to Eastern and Central Europe, and direct American involvement in that part of the European subcontinent with the goal of protecting Western Europe and British positions in the region that spelled the end not only of the Grand Alliance but also of the relative friendliness of the interwar years and eventually led to the Cold War.

Interwar Eastern Europe was comprised of a number of young states that emerged on the ruins of the Ottoman, Habsburg, and (in part) Russian empires. The new states aspired to be national but grabbed more territory settled by minorities than they could assimilate to their titular nationalities. France and then Britain saw the region as a *cordon sanitaire* against the spread of communism. Stalin viewed it as a launch pad for capitalist attack not unlike that of 1920, when Polish and Ukrainian troops supported by the Entente captured Kyiv.

When in 1939 the French and British refused to allow Stalin to enter Eastern Europe militarily to deal with the German threat, the Soviet leader did so on the basis of the Molotov-Ribbentrop Pact. At the Teheran, Yalta, and Potsdam meetings with his new Western allies, Stalin insisted on keeping his gains of 1939 and claimed an East European sphere of influence that went beyond the one arranged with Churchill in 1944. At the Yalta conference, Roosevelt refused to recognize Stalin's claim to determine the political future of Eastern Europe, shifting the problem of spheres of influence to the arena of diplomatic negotiations, but at Potsdam Truman bowed to the seemingly inevitable Soviet control of the region.

Stalin had no clear idea of what to do with his new sphere of influence—whether to Sovietize it completely or leave some elements of democracy and free enterprise in place. He insisted, however, that it had to be part of the Soviet "sphere of security," as he called it in negotiations with Roosevelt and Churchill. He once went on record saying that the Russians knew how to fight but not how to negotiate. Stalin was determined to maintain Soviet political control over the territory taken by the Red Army during the war. He would compromise on Iran and Turkey, or even retreat from them, but dig in his heels on Eastern Europe.

After Britain's unexpected postwar implosion as a world superpower, American involvement in European affairs threatened Stalin's position in Eastern Europe. The threat, however, came not from US military power but from its economic potential, embodied in the Marshall Plan. Stalin could not compete economically. He responded militarily, as in the Berlin blockade, and politically, as in the communist coup in Czechoslovakia. One way or another, he sealed off Eastern Europe from the West to maintain his control over the region. The Cold War would eventually become global, but its beginnings and official end in Central and Eastern Europe in 1989 attest to the paramount importance of that region in Soviet-American Cold War rivalry.

Presuming that this reading of the fall of the Grand Alliance and the start of the Cold War correctly reflects Stalin's attitudes toward Eastern Europe and American involvement there, what lessons, if any, can be drawn for the current round of Moscow-Washington rivalry, often called Cold War II?

There are numerous parallels with the events of seventy years ago. Although the new rivalry seems to be global in scope, once again involving the Middle East, the eye of the new international relations hurricane is in the area known today as the "new Eastern Europe." It covers some former Soviet republics and extends from the Baltics through Ukraine, Belarus, and Moldova to the

Transcaucasus. Like most of the states that emerged on the ruins of the old empires in 1918, most of the newly independent states of extended Eastern Europe are economically and militarily weak, have major problems with democracy, and include significant ethnic minorities. Like their interwar predecessors, they are viewed in Moscow as a launch pad for Western aggression but are perceived in the West as the *antemurale* where Russian expansion into Europe can and should be stopped.

Putin's Russia is staging a return to its "near abroad" in a way that parallels the "return" of Stalin's Soviet Union to the lands that had been part of the Russian Empire or its sphere of interest. Some territories are being annexed outright, while others are being claimed as part of the Moscow-run economic and military union. As at the beginning of the Cold War, the main threat to Moscow's ambitions in the region is American economic power and the appeal of its democratic institutions rather than its military might. And, as before, Moscow's response to that economic and ideological challenge usually comes in military form. The Russians want a "new Yalta"—a division of Europe into spheres of influence. The Americans are resisting, as they did at Yalta.

There are differences as well. The most obvious one is that with the exception of parts of Ukraine, Georgia, and Moldova, the rest of the new Eastern Europe is not occupied or controlled by Russian troops, as most of Eastern Europe was seventy years ago. The countries in question are basically free to make their own choices with regard to form of government and participation in economic and even military alliances. This "openness" of the region creates both opportunities and challenges for the development of US-Russian relations, but challenges prevail as the dangers of open confrontation and proxy wars increase.

Can the history of the early Cold War help us understand the present-day problems of Russo-American relations? Yes, it can. The American political establishment spent a good part of the Cold War trying to answer the question of whether President Roosevelt sold out Eastern Europe to Stalin at Yalta. But however one answered that not very productive question, there was general agreement that "losing" Eastern Europe was a bad idea, and that ceding it to the Soviet sphere of influence did not prevent the Cold War. Another lesson drawn from those events was that the great powers could not decide the fate of the East European nations without inviting them to the negotiating table. These valuable takeaways from the past can be very useful today as the United States and Russia face new tensions in the part of the world that sparked the Cold War seventy-five years ago.

II.

The American Dream

On 15 February 1947, the Soviet Politburo approved a law "On the Prohibition of Marriage between Citizens of the USSR and Foreigners." Those found in violation of the new law were to be charged with anti-Soviet agitation and prosecuted according to article 58 of the Soviet penal code. In theory, a Soviet citizen could still marry a foreigner, but only after renouncing Soviet citizenship for that of a foreign country—an even greater crime, defined as "betrayal of the motherland" and punishable by execution, according to the same article 58.

The Iron Curtain was coming down between the Soviet Union and the outside world, breaking links established during the war and preventing the establishment of new ones. The state was laying exclusive claim to the loyalty of Soviet men and, more particularly, women, but the justification offered for the adoption of the law was as benign and humanitarian as it could possibly be. "Our women who have married foreigners and found themselves abroad in unaccustomed conditions feel bad and are subject to discrimination," read the text of the law adopted by the Supreme Soviet in March 1947.[1]

It has been argued that the reasons for the introduction of the new law included the dire demographic situation in the Soviet Union, which had lost tens of millions of its citizens in the war. Scholars also point to the regime's apparent desire to avoid recognition of dual citizenship and thus conflicting loyalties in families created during the war by Soviet citizens on German-occupied territories or in Germany itself, as well as to prevent the formation of such families in Eastern Europe, where there was now a significant Soviet military contingent. Finally, the Soviet law was adopted in the context of World War II laws and regulations prohibiting relationships between German soldiers and East European slave laborers and between American soldiers and German and Austrian women.[2]

In this essay, I consider the Soviet prohibition on marriages with foreigners in the context of growing Cold War tensions between the Soviet Union and its former World War II allies, Americans in particular. My focus is on one particular relationship produced by the presence of American airmen on the Poltava air base between April 1944 and June 1945. In the final year of the war, the US Air Force established three air bases in Ukraine behind the Soviet lines. The Poltava base (the other two were at Myrhorod and Pyriatyn) played an important role in American shuttle-bombing operations against targets in Eastern Europe. Thousands of pilots, airplane mechanics, and rank-and-file soldiers participated in the shuttle operations. Moreover, tens of thousands of citizens of the three Ukrainian towns were able to meet the Americans and, in some cases, establish close personal relations with US airmen stationed there for the duration of the war.

I discuss the story of the three airbases in my book *Forgotten Bastards of the Eastern Front* (2019), where I document Soviet efforts to break up relationships between American airmen and Soviet women. In this essay, I continue that story into the early Cold War era. The research presented in my book leaves little doubt that the Soviet practice of disrupting relations and prohibiting marriages between American and Soviet citizens, driven by ideological zeal, xenophobic distrust of the West, and cultural inferiority, began while the USSR and the United States were still allies. The story told in this essay, that of the Ukrainian woman Zinaida Tkachenko and the American airman John Bazan, demonstrates in great detail the extent to which the Soviet government and its secret police were prepared to go in order to deny Soviet citizens not only the right but also the opportunity to marry Americans. Although there were no basic changes of policy in that regard between 1944 and 1947, the Soviet attitude toward marriages with foreigners hardened significantly with the start of the Cold War.[3]

The love story of the thirty-three-year-old American airplane mechanic John J. Bazan and the twenty-four-year-old Ukrainian woman Zinaida Tkachenko began on a summer day in Poltava in 1944.

Zinaida Tkachenko had been born there in 1921 to the family of a blue-collar worker. Before the outbreak of the Soviet-German war in 1941, she managed to complete seven classes of secondary education, get married, and give birth to a baby girl named Liudmyla. She was twenty-three years old when the first Americans showed up in her native city. She soon met John. Born in New York City, John Bazan belonged to a family that counted seven sons and one daughter. Before the war the entire family lived at 867 Van Nest Avenue in the East Bronx. John was the oldest child, born on 4 February 1911. He joined the US Army on 17 April 1942. Army records identified him at the time as a single white male with no dependents. He had completed two years of high school, and his civilian occupation was listed as "technician." John was of medium height, 68 inches tall, and weighed 147 pounds.

A photo of John Bazan in military uniform that he gave Zinaida showed a man with an open face and a pleasant, somewhat shy smile. The chevrons on his left shoulder indicated that he held the rank of sergeant. Zinaida also kept another photo of John, pictured in warm winter clothing next to the American barracks at Poltava. Unlike many Ukrainian women who dated Americans, she did not conceal her relations with John from her friends or neighbors. They later recalled that he spoke fluent Russian. His family records indicate that Ukrainian was his mother tongue—the 1940 US Census gave Austria as the birthplace of John's mother, Catherine, who probably came from either Galicia or Bukovyna, two Ukrainian-speaking regions that belonged to Austria-Hungary before 1918. The two lovebirds could obviously communicate on a variety of topics, and their relations soon developed into something more than a chance sexual encounter. John often showed up at her house on the outskirts of Poltava with parcels of food and gifts. Zinaida spoke of John as her husband.[4]

Oddly, Sergeant Bazan's liaison with Zinaida Tkachenko attracted no attention from SMERSH officers in 1944–45. They probably had their eyes on bigger fish. But the Ministry of State Security (MGB) caught up with Zinaida Tkachenko in the fall of 1946, and in the spring of 1947 they opened a file on her. Three MGB informers, recruited from among women who dated Americans in 1944–45, testified that "While American aviators were based at the Poltava airfield in 1944, Tkachenko was widely acquainted with American servicemen, led a dissolute life, and had intimate relations with an American, John Bazan, whom she considered her husband." But no sooner had the Poltava MGB opened a file on her than Zinaida Tkachenko packed her belongings and moved out of the city. Both events took place in April 1947. The MGB soon learned that Tkachenko had moved to Zhovkva in western Ukraine, newly acquired from Poland. The local MGB there was busy fighting the Ukrainian nationalist underground that was active in the region and had no time or resources to deal with Tkachenko. It appeared that she had successfully escaped the attention of Soviet counterintelligence, which, once again, had bigger fish to fry.[5]

But the MGB officers were spurred into action in the spring of 1948, when John Bazan petitioned the American embassy in Moscow for an entry visa to the United States for his fiancée, Zinaida Tkachenko. He gave his old Bronx address. The MGB bosses in Kyiv wrote to their Zhovkva underlings, giving them three days to put together a plan to investigate Tkachenko. By the end of March 1948 they had established her address in Zhovkva and were reading her correspondence. In June they recruited a friend of Tkachenko's with whom she had come to Zhovkva in April 1947 and could report the first results of their work.[6]

Tkachenko had allegedly moved because she did not have a permanent job in Poltava and, to make ends meet, had had to sell all the dresses she got from Bazan. While in Zhovkva, she continued to correspond with Bazan and kept receiving parcels from him. She also tried to get an exit visa to the United States, but her correspondence with John came to an end in February 1948. Ironically, it was just when Bazan made his request to the American embassy that Tkachenko, having no news from him, decided to marry another man.

When an MGB informer ran into Tkachenko in mid-June 1947, Zinaida informed her that she had married. Her husband, a Red Army soldier who also came from Poltava, had been dismissed from the service earlier that year. "When I asked her how

John was," reported the agent, "Zina cursed, saying that there was no point in thinking of what could never be and that John had not written her for five months." According to the MGB report, Zinaida still held an "anti-Soviet and pro-American attitude" but "had become convinced that it was impossible to obtain an exit visa to America." In July, the Kyiv MGB sent their Lviv subordinates a copy of a letter to Tkachenko from the US embassy in Moscow. Two months later Tkachenko and her new husband suddenly left Zhovkva without informing anyone of their destination or new address.[7]

The MGB officers believed that Tkachenko had never given up hope of emigrating to the United States. She tried to visit Kaliningrad, the former Königsberg in East Prussia, by then under Soviet control, apparently in the hope of escaping to the West on a Soviet ship. She also expressed a desire to move to Sakhalin Island in the Far East, which had been divided between the Soviet Union and Japan before the war. None of those plans materialized, and by 1951 Tkachenko was back in Poltava, working as a seamstress at the local garment factory. It seemed that she had come full circle and that her saga was finally over. But the period of tranquility did not last very long.[8]

The Poltava MGB was actually waiting for Tkachenko. They were particularly interested in her visit to the American embassy in September 1946, which she had confided to a girlfriend who turned out to be a MGB informer.

The details of the visit sounded like an episode from a spy novel and must have quickened the pulse of the MGB agents. Tkachenko had a long conversation with one of the embassy officials, who questioned her thoroughly. After the meeting, instead of allowing Tkachenko to leave by the front door, they changed her appearance, put her in an embassy car, and drove her to a railway station outside Moscow, where she boarded a train for Poltava. Why did the Americans go to such lengths to conceal Tkachenko's identity if they had not recruited her as an agent? The question was anything but rhetorical to the Poltava MGB officers.[9] When investigating Tkachenko's plans to marry John Bazan and leave for the United States, they had not suspected him of working for American intelligence. But now that she had met secretly with an embassy official, she fell under suspicion as a potential spy.

The Kyiv MGB offered its subordinates in Poltava one of its own agents to help crack the case. The agent's code name was "Karenina," as in Leo Tolstoy's famous novel. She was introduced to Tkachenko as another unfortunate woman trying to get an exit visa to the United States to join her loved one. Karenina's main task was to find out what had happened to Tkachenko when she visited the embassy. What made the episode particularly suspicious in the eyes of the Kyiv and Poltava officers was that the MGB could not confirm through its informers in the embassy—Soviet citizens employed by the Americans—that Tkachenko had been there at all, as her name was absent from the register of visitors. Karenina, star agent that she was, succeeded where others had failed and provided an important new piece of information. After meeting with Tkachenko in June 1951, Karenina delivered the name of the US official who had interviewed Tkachenko—Roger Taylor. The MGB soon confirmed that there was indeed such a consular official at the embassy, but it was anyone's guess whether he had recruited Tkachenko to work for US intelligence.[10]

What concerned the MGB officers was Tkachenko's ability to establish contacts with Red Army officers. Their reports characterized her as a cunning individual who was good at establishing relations, especially with men. In the postwar Soviet Union, where so many men had died in the war, it was no easy task for women of Tkachenko's background to marry, but she seemed to have no problem in arranging her personal affairs. She had clearly captivated John Bazan, who was still trying to get her into the United States three years after their parting at Poltava. She got married within weeks after the correspondence with Bazan ended, and her plans to move to East Prussia in the hope of escaping from the USSR via the Baltic Sea were also associated with a man serving there in the Soviet Army. The fact that she eventually returned to Poltava made her an eligible bride to scores of Soviet military pilots posted at the bases previously used by the Americans.

The MGB had to do something to crack the Tkachenko case and establish whether she was spying for the Americans. They eventually decided to turn Tkachenko's alleged knack for establishing relations with Soviet military men against her and introduce her to "Romeo," an agent of military counterintelligence posing as an army officer. His code name was "Nikolaev." They designed a complex scheme whereby Nikolaev and Tkachenko would meet at the Poltava theater frequented by the Americans during their stay in the area. An MGB informer code-named "Rozova," who was closest to Tkachenko, would invite her to a performance, using two of four tickets purchased by the MGB. Rozova would explain that the tickets had been bought by her husband, but they had quarreled, so she was now happy to invite Tkachenko to come along.

Nikolaev, for his part, was to pretend that he had an extra ticket for a friend who had failed to show up. With one seat empty and another occupied by the MGB informer Rozova, Nikolaev would be free to exercise his talents as "Romeo" and establish contact with Tkachenko. He was supposed to invite the two ladies to a cafe after the performance and then "develop" his contact with Tkachenko. Nikolaev read his instructions on the day of the planned operation, 4 October 1952, and signed below the line that said: "Read, absorbed, and accepted for implementation." But the plan fell apart when Rozova told her handlers that she was busy that evening and refused to go to the theater. Then Nikolaev took a vacation. Eventually the operation had to be postponed until December 1952. With the "Romeo" scenario delayed, the MGB decided to bring back agent Karenina in order to find out as soon as possible whether Tkachenko was a spy. If not, they needed to recruit her as an agent for themselves.[11]

The Poltava MGB had high hopes of recruiting Tkachenko to help with the MGB's most important assignment of the early Cold War—uncovering an alleged Jewish plot against the Soviet regime. The anti-Semitic campaign in the USSR had picked up with the worsening of Soviet-American relations and the creation of the state of Israel in May 1948. From then on, Soviet Jews would be suspected of concealing their true loyalty to the new Jewish homeland and its American allies. The campaign against "cosmopolitans," a euphemism for Soviet Jewry, reached its height in 1952, with scores of luminaries of the Soviet medical profession, most of them Jewish, arrested on charges of poisoning or conspiring to poison the leaders of the Soviet government, including

Stalin himself. Anything smacking of a Jewish conspiracy, especially ties between Jews in the USSR and their counterparts in
the West, particularly the United States, became the subject of
the MGB's close attention and an absolute priority when it came
to the allocation of time and resources.[12]

To the MGB officers in Poltava, who were eager to respond
to signals from Moscow, it seemed that the Tkachenko case could
be adapted to fit the regime's new priority. The Poltava MGB
learned that while visiting Moscow to petition for an exit visa
from the USSR, Zinaida Tkachenko had made the acquaintance
of a Jewish woman, Rakhil Borisovna Kapova-Kagan. The MGB's
interest in Kapova-Kagan was much deeper than in Tkachenko.
Her husband had been arrested by the secret police back in 1931
and accused of dealing in foreign currency. He managed to leave
the USSR for the United States in 1933 and, as the relevant MGB
document expressed it, "betrayed the motherland" by refusing to
return. Ever since then he had been in correspondence with his
wife, and she had kept trying to get an exit visa to join him in
the United States.[13]

The MGB had information about Kapova-Kagan visiting the
American embassy back in 1935 and meeting informally around
the same time in a coffee shop with an American citizen suspected of spying on the USSR. MGB officers in Moscow were
now concerned about Kapova-Kagan's current activities, and their
Poltava underlings looked for ways to help answer that question
and advance their careers. The plan was to recruit Tkachenko
as an agent to spy on Kapova-Kagan. But what if Tkachenko
herself were an agent spying for the United States? The whole
thing could then backfire, ending the careers of the Poltava MGB
officers. Time was of the essence, and they finally decided to risk
inviting Tkachenko for questioning about her visit to the American embassy in September 1946. Depending on the results of the
interrogation and her willingness to cooperate, they would decide
whether or not to recruit her.

The head of the Poltava MGB approved a detailed plan of
recruitment. Lieutenant Panfilov was ordered to summon Tkachenko to the registration department of the local police, allegedly to discuss her emigration to the United States. He would then
drive her to MGB headquarters in Poltava for interrogation and

possible recruitment. The meeting was scheduled for 10:00 a.m. Since interrogation and recruitment might take up much of the day, and Tkachenko's long absence from home could alarm her relatives, it was proposed to send her two invitations, one for 10:00 a.m. and the other for 4:00 p.m., the second invitation allegedly to discuss the alimony case involving her daughter and her former husband. Panfilov would have the whole day at his disposal to complete the job.

Panfilov planned to start with questions about Tkachenko's contacts with the Americans and her ties with John Bazan. If she denied such ties, he would confront her with a photograph showing her together with Bazan. He would then discuss her visit to the US embassy in 1946. Panfilov had at his disposal the testimony of D. K. Gershanovich, a former Soviet employee of the US embassy, who had been arrested and sentenced on charges of anti-Soviet propaganda and agitation and betrayal of the motherland. Under interrogation, Gershanovich had testified that she remembered a girl from Poltava visiting the embassy in 1946. The problem was that she did not remember the girl's name and could not recognize Tkachenko from a photo provided by the MGB. But that was where Panfilov's interrogation skills would come into play. The recruitment plan was finalized by the end of February 1953 and approved for action on 3 March. But the next few days brought confusion into the ranks of the MGB.[14]

On 4 March, the day after the approval of the recruitment plan, Soviet newspapers carried disturbing news: Stalin was seriously ill. He died on 5 March, having been in a semi-conscious state since 1 March. Lavrentii Beriia, the Soviet security tsar, now emerged as a leading figure and put the brakes on Stalin's anti-Semitic campaign. On 10 March, the day after Stalin's funeral, Beriia invited Viacheslav Molotov to his office. Molotov's Jewish wife, Polina Zhemchuzhina, had been incarcerated since December 1948: she was arrested a month after befriending the Israeli ambassador to Moscow, Golda Meir. Molotov was in for a surprise. There in Beriia's office was his wife, released from the Gulag and free to go home. Times were changing.[15]

It is hard to tell what went wrong with the Poltava MGB plan to recruit Tkachenko. Whether changes at the top of the Soviet pyramid influenced the outcome or she was approached and refused to cooperate with the MGB, they never recruited her as an agent. They also did not believe that she was working for the United States. But the MGB had no doubt that she harbored anti-Soviet views inspired by the authorities' refusal to grant her an exit visa and exacerbated by the difficult financial situation in which she found herself afterwards. They did not expect to change her views but wanted her to abandon her plans to leave the Soviet Union. In July, they asked their bosses to send agent Karenina back to Poltava, as she had previously managed to elicit from Tkachenko the name of Roger Taylor, the US embassy official whom she had met in Moscow in September 1946. Now Karenina's task was "to convince Tkachenko of the futility of her efforts to leave for the USA."[16]

The task was carried out successfully, and in September 1954 the MGB, now called the KGB, archived its file on Tkachenko. Agent Rozova assured her handlers that Tkachenko had "completely renounced plans to leave for America." Rozova provided two additional pieces of information that supported her judgment and may have been partially responsible for Tkachenko's change of heart. Zinaida had found her first husband, whom she expected to support their daughter. She had also married again and had a child with her new husband.[17]

Zinaida Tkachenko's American dream was over. By the time the KGB archived her file, the 1947 law prohibiting Soviet citizens to marry foreign nationals had been annulled. That was done in November 1953, soon after Stalin's death. On paper, marriage to a foreigner ceased to be a crime, but that did not change the Soviet policy of preventing not only marriage but any unsupervised contact between Soviet citizens and foreigners. The authorities still insisted on deciding whom their citizens had the right to love. We do not know what happened to Zinaida Tkachenko after 1954. John Bazan continued to live in the Bronx until his death at the age of seventy in December 1981, with the Cold War still far from over.[18]

III

FAREWELL
TO THE EMPIRE

12.

The Soviet Collapse

The twentieth century witnessed the end of the world built and ruled by empires from Austria-Hungary and the Ottoman Empire, which fell in the final days of World War I, to the British and French empires, which disintegrated in the aftermath of World War II. This decades-long process concluded with the collapse in 1991 of the Soviet Union, the mighty successor to the Russian Empire, which was stitched back together by the Bolsheviks in the early 1920s, only to fall apart 70 years later during the final stage of the Cold War.

Although many factors contributed to the fall of the Soviet Union, from the bankruptcy of communist ideology to the failure of the Soviet economy, the wider context for its dissolution is often overlooked. The collapse of the Soviet Union, like the disintegration of past empires, is a process rather than an event. And the collapse of the last empire is still unfolding today. This process did not end with Mikhail Gorbachev's resignation on Christmas Day 1991, and its victims are not limited to the three people who died defending the Moscow White House in August 1991 or the thousands of casualties from the Chechen wars.

The rise of nation-states on the ruins of the Soviet Union, like the rise of successor states on the remains of every other empire, mobilized ethnicity, nationalism, and conflicting territorial claims. This process at least partly explains the Russian annexation of the Crimea, the war in Ukraine, and the burst of popular support for those acts of aggression in the Russian Federation. As the victim of a much more powerful neighbor's attack, Ukraine found itself in a situation similar to that of the new states of Eastern Europe formed after World War I on the ruins of the Austro-Hungarian, Ottoman, and Russian empires. Those states struggled with the enormous tasks of nation-building while trying to accommodate national minorities and defend themselves against revanchist powers claiming the loyalty of those same minorities.

Although the historical context of the collapse of empires helps us understand the developments of the last twenty-five years in the former Soviet space, it also serves as a warning for the future. The redrawing of post-imperial borders to reflect the importance of nationality, language, and culture has generally come about as a result of conflicts and wars, some of which went on for decades, if not centuries. The Ottoman Empire began its slow-motion collapse in 1783, a process that reached its conclusion at the end of World War I. The ongoing war in eastern Ukraine is not the only reminder that the process of Soviet disintegration is still incomplete. Other such reminders are the frozen or semi-frozen conflicts in Transnistria, Abkhazia, South Ossetia, Nagorno-Karabakh, and the semi-independent state of Chechnya.

A lesson that today's policymakers can learn from the history of imperial collapse is that the role of the international community is paramount in sorting out relations between former rulers and subjects. Few stable states have emerged from the ruins of bygone empires without strong international support, whether it is the French role in securing American independence, Russian and British involvement in the struggle for Greek statehood, or the US role in supporting the aspirations of former Warsaw Pact countries in Eastern Europe. The role of outsiders has been and will remain the key to any post-imperial settlement. Looking at the current situation, it is difficult to overstate the role that the United States and its NATO allies can play in solving the conflict in Ukraine and other parts of the volatile post-Soviet space. The fall of the Soviet Union, which carried the legacy of the last European empire, is still far from over.

13.

Chornobyl

In April 2016, as the world marked the thirtieth anniversary of the worst nuclear disaster in its history—the explosion and partial meltdown of the nuclear reactor at the Chornobyl (in Russian, Chernobyl) power station in Ukraine—there was a temptation to celebrate that date as well. The half-life of cesium-137, one of the most harmful nuclides released during the accident, is approximately 30 years. It is the longest "living" isotope of cesium that can affect the human body through external exposure and ingestion. The other deadly isotopes present in the disaster have long passed their half-life stages: Iodine 131 after eight days and cesium-134 after two years. Cesium-137 is the last of that deadly trio of isotopes.

These days, European tour operators offer trips to Chornobyl from Brussels, Amsterdam, or Berlin at the price of a mere 479.00 euros. Visitors are promised safety, comfort, and excitement while visiting the place where, on 26 April 1986, the explosion at Reactor No. 4 ended one historical era and started another. This hastened the end not only of the early, often barbaric stage in nuclear energy development but also of the political and social system that turned out to be less economically effective and more reckless with nuclear energy than its Cold War competitors.

That system was called communism, and the state that embodied it was known as the Union of Soviet Socialist Republics. The Chornobyl disaster marked the beginning of the end of a world nuclear superpower—a little more than five years later, that superpower would fall apart, doomed by the inefficiency of its managerial and economic system, as demonstrated by the Chornobyl disaster and the political and ethnonational movements that the disaster helped initiate. The Chornobyl accident took place at the fourth reactor of the Chornobyl power station, which exploded as a result of a turbine test that went wrong. That was the immediate reason for the accident, but its deeper causes should be sought in the confluence of two major flaws of the Soviet system.

The first was the militarization of the country's economy: the Chornobyl-type reactors were adapted from reactors created to produce nuclear bombs. Volatile under certain physical conditions, the Chornobyl-type reactor was pronounced safe and actively promoted by the leaders of the Soviet military-industrial complex, who then refused to take responsibility for what happened in Chornobyl. The second flaw was the violation of procedures and safety rules on the part of the operational personnel, who inherited the reckless "we can do it no matter what" attitude that characterized the first decades of the Soviet nuclear program and resulted in numerous accidents.

The Chornobyl accident was not the first major nuclear disaster in the Soviet Union. The first took place in the fall of 1957 at the nuclear plant near the town of Kyshtym in the Urals. This plant was tasked with producing plutonium for Soviet nuclear bombs. The explosion of the nuclear waste tank threw 160 tons of concrete lead into the air and released 20 million curies of radioactive material, including cesium-137. At least 80,000 square kilometers were affected by the radioactive fallout, but because of the secretive culture surrounding the program, the evacuation of close to 10,000 civilians in the environs of the plant did not start until one week after the accident. Information about the disaster itself and its consequences was suppressed and hidden from the Soviet public and the world. The suppression of that information helped the Soviet military-industrial complex to keep producing unsafe reactors and maintain the image of an absolutely safe industry not only among outsiders but also among the personnel operating the reactors.

One of the creators of the Chornobyl-type reactors, the then-president of the Soviet Academy of Sciences, Anatolii Aleksandrov, bragged that his reactors were safe enough to be installed on Red Square in Moscow. Instead, the Soviet government put a reactor 140 kilometers away from Kyiv and then denied reliable information about the accident to the city's two million citizens and the population of the country as a whole. But locating nuclear reactors in the European part of the USSR rather than in the Urals or Siberia meant that it was much more difficult to hide the scope of the accident. Indeed, within days after the Chornobyl explosion, winds brought the radioactive plume beyond the borders of the Soviet Union. During the night of the accident, the wind was blowing in a northwesterly direction, carrying the plume across Ukraine's border to Belarus, then to Lithuania, and finally across the Baltic Sea to the countries of Northern Europe.

The first to notice the high radiation levels caused by the Chornobyl explosion were nuclear experts in Sweden, 1,257 kilometers from Chornobyl. At 7:00 a.m. on 28 April 1986, Cliff Robinson, a twenty-nine-year-old chemist working at the Forsmark nuclear power plant near Uppsala, went to brush his teeth. In order to get from the washroom to the locker room, he had to pass through the radiation detector. The alarm went off. Soon the Forsmark workers were evacuated: it was originally assumed that something was wrong with the plant. In a few hours it became clear that the plant was not the cause of contamination. Because radioactivity was high at other nuclear power stations as well, officials concluded that the radioactivity was coming from abroad. Calculations and wind direction pointed to Soviet territory.

The Soviets first broke their silence fourteen hours after radiation was detected in Sweden. Soviet television aired a short announcement about the Chornobyl accident as part of its evening news program. The alarm in the West and the desire of the new Soviet leader, Mikhail Gorbachev, who had assumed power in the Kremlin only one year earlier, to establish some form of trust in relations between state and society created the first breach in the wall of secrecy surrounding the Soviet nuclear program. Still, the Soviets were reluctant to disclose all the information they had at the time and tried to hide the real state of affairs from their people and the world.

European leaders sounded the alarm. Sweden registered gamma radiation at levels 30 to 40 percent higher than normal. In Oslo, radiation levels were 50 percent higher than normal and in central and northern areas of Finland, six times the norm. But radiation levels had risen in other European countries as well, Austria being close to the top of the list. European political leaders reacted differently to the danger posed by the radioactive fallout. If German leaders (under pressure from the growing Green movement) demanded the closure of nuclear reactors, the French government (which was heavily dependent on nuclear energy) refused to recognize that Chornobyl clouds were bringing heightened radiation levels to their country as well.

Hans Blix, the head of the International Atomic Energy Agency, visited the accident site on 8 May 1986. Instead of traveling by car, in which case he would have detected high levels of radiation, Blix took a helicopter and flew over the station. He assured the world that the situation was under control and that the rumors spread in the West about thousands of people killed by the nuclear explosion were unfounded. As head of the organization responsible for promoting the peaceful use of nuclear energy, Blix was not interested in digging deeper into what had happened or what was going on in Chornobyl. He took the Soviets at their word. They in turn struggled to overcome their culture of secrecy, reinforced by fear that the truth about Chornobyl would spread panic among the population. They were also unable to free themselves from the legacy of anti-Westernism that saturated the Soviet establishment during the Cold War.

It took Gorbachev a full eighteen days to address the distressed Soviet people and the world, and even then almost half his address was dedicated to attacks on the West. Western media criticized the Soviet regime for continuing to withhold vital information, without which it was difficult to protect the population of Central and Western Europe from the Chornobyl fallout. But the Chornobyl accident had broken the Soviet regime's monopoly on this information. Moscow had to adjust to the new circumstances. That summer the Soviet scientist Valerii Legasov, who was in Chornobyl during the dangerous days following the accident and already suffering from radiation sickness, delivered a four-hour report at a conference organized by Hans Blix. Prepared despite objections from the leaders of the Soviet military-industrial complex, this report demonstrated to the world that the Soviet government was finally ready to lift the veil of secrecy from its nuclear program.

Mikhail Gorbachev later claimed that Chornobyl had changed him. More importantly, it changed Soviet society as a whole. The policy of glasnost, or openness, which gave the media and citizens the right to discuss political and social problems and criticize the authorities, had its origins in the post-Chornobyl days. During this time, the population demanded more and more information from the government, and the government was slowly changing its culture of secrecy. The Chornobyl disaster made the government recognize ecological concerns as a legitimate reason for Soviet citizens to create their own organizations and thereby broke the monopoly of the Communist Party on political activity. The first Soviet mass organizations and political parties began in the ecological movement, which engulfed the heavily polluted industrial centers of the Soviet Union.

While Belarus is by far the country most affected by the Chornobyl fallout, nowhere else has the connection between Chornobyl and political activism been more obvious than in Ukraine. The country is the second-largest post-Soviet state in terms of population and economic potential and was the site of the Chornobyl disaster. For Ukraine, the Chornobyl accident ended the love affair with nuclear power that began in the 1960s.

The idea of bringing nuclear energy to Ukraine belonged to Ukrainian Communist Party leaders who wanted to create new sources of electrical energy for the rapidly developing Ukrainian economy. By the time the Chornobyl nuclear power station went on line in 1977, Ukrainian intellectuals, including one of the country's leading poets, Ivan Drach, were welcoming the arrival of the nuclear age in their country. For Drach and other Ukrainian patriots, Chornobyl meant a step toward the modernization of Ukraine. He and other enthusiasts of nuclearization failed to notice that the project was run from Moscow. The republic was getting electrical energy but had little control over what went on at the plant. The plant itself and the accident that occurred there became known to the world under the Russian spelling of the nearest city—Chernobyl, not Chornobyl.

In the days following the Chornobyl accident, Ukrainian citizens suddenly realized how little control they had over their own destiny and that of their republic. The limits of the republican authorities' power over Ukraine became crystal-clear on the morning of 1 May 1986, when the winds changed direction and, instead of blowing northwest, turned south, bringing radioactive clouds to the capital of Ukraine. Given the quickly changing radiological situation, Ukrainian authorities tried to convince Moscow to cancel a planned parade marking International Workers' Day. They failed. "He told me: You will put your party card on the table if you bungle the parade," said the distressed Ukrainian party boss, Volodymyr Shcherbytsky, to his aides, referring to the telephone conversation he had had with Gorbachev. Despite the rapidly increasing radiation level, Gorbachev ordered his Ukrainian underlings to carry on as usual in order to show the country and the world that the situation was under control and that the Chornobyl explosion presented no danger to the health of the population. The parade went on as scheduled.

The explosion and partial meltdown of Chornobyl's fourth reactor released an estimated 50 million curies of radiation into the atmosphere—the equivalent of 500 Hiroshima bombs. In Ukraine alone, more than 50,000 sq. km. of land were contaminated—a territory larger than Belgium. The exclusion zone around the reactor alone accounted for 2,600 sq. km., from which more than 90,000 inhabitants were evacuated in the first weeks after the explosion. Most of them would never see their homes again. In Ukraine, 2,300 settlements and more than 3 million people were directly affected by the radiation fallout. Close to 30 million people who relied on the Dnieper and other rivers for their water supply were affected by the explosion.

The Chornobyl accident sharply increased discontent with Moscow and its policies across all party and social lines—radiation affected everyone, from members of the party leadership to ordinary citizens. As the Ukrainian party bosses mobilized the population to deal with the consequences of the disaster and clean up the mess created by the center, many asked themselves why they were risking their own lives and those of their family members. Around their kitchen tables, they grumbled about the center's failed policies but shared their frustration only with people they trusted. The only group that would not remain silent was that of the Ukrainian writers. In June 1986, at a meeting of the Ukrainian Writers' Union, many of those who had welcomed the arrival of nuclear power a decade earlier now condemned it as an instrument of Moscow's domination of their republic. Among those leading the charge was Ivan Drach, whose son, a student in a Kyiv medical school, had been sent to Chornobyl soon after the accident without proper instructions or protective gear. He was now suffering from radiation poisoning.

The Chornobyl disaster awakened Ukraine, raising fundamental questions about relations between the center and the republics, the Communist Party and the people, and fueling the first major public debate in a society struggling to regain its voice after decades of communist control. The Ukrainian writer Iurii Shcherbak not only wrote a book about the Chornobyl disaster that was exceptionally candid by the standards of the time but also organized an environmental group one year after accident. That group evolved into the Green Party—Soviet Ukraine's first legal political party since the 1920s. The ecological movement, which presented Ukraine as a victim of Moscow's activities, became one of the first forms of national mobilization in Ukraine during the years of the Gorbachev reforms. The new man in the Kremlin not only alienated the Ukrainian party leadership but also empowered democratically minded intellectuals and the nationally conscious intelligentsia to mobilize against that elite.

As things turned out, the two conflicting groups in Ukraine—the communist establishment and the nascent democratic opposition—discovered a common interest in opposing Moscow in general and Gorbachev in particular. In December 1991, when Ukrainians went to the polls to vote for the independence of their country, they also consigned the mighty Soviet Union to the dustbin of history: it was officially dissolved a few weeks after the Ukrainian referendum. While it would be wrong to ascribe the rise of glasnost in the Soviet Union or the rise of the national movement in Ukraine and other republics to the Chornobyl accident alone, it is difficult to overestimate the impact it had on those interrelated processes.

After the Maidan protests of 2013 and 2014, the Ukrainian parliament set up a commission charged with the task of removing any mention of communist leaders from the names of Ukraine's cities, towns, villages, and streets. The commission adopted recommendations with regard to the entire internationally recognized territory of the country, including the rebel regions in the east and the Crimean peninsula, which has been annexed by Russia. The only exception was the Chornobyl exclusion zone, which still remains a preserve of the Soviet past, captured by radiation and never released.

The city of Prypiat, which housed close to 50,000 construction workers and power-plant operational personnel, remains deserted even today—a modern-day Pompeii memorializing what would become the last days of the Soviet Union. Images of Vladimir Lenin and the builders of communism, along with slogans celebrating the Communist Party, still remain on the walls of Prypiat. The sarcophagus that European visitors can see on their trips to the exclusion zone stands today as a monument to the failed ideology and political system embodied in the Soviet Union. It is also a warning to leaders and societies who put military or economic objectives above environmental and health concerns.

While the thirty-year anniversary of the disaster marks the half-life of one of the deadliest isotopes released by Chornobyl, cesium-137, the harmful impact of the accident is still far from over. With tests revealing that the cesium-137 around Chornobyl is not decaying as quickly as predicted, scholars believe that the isotope will keep harming the environment for at least 180 years—the time it will take for half the cesium to be removed from the affected areas in Ukraine and beyond by natural means, weathering, and migration. Other radionuclides will stay in the region almost indefinitely. The half-life of plutonium-239, traces of which were found as far away as Sweden, is 24,000 years.

14.

Truth in Our Times

"Did it really happen?" "Was it really so bad?" "Is it true that they were so unprepared?" These are the questions I have been receiving again and again in the last few months in connection with the stunning success of the HBO/Sky miniseries *Chernobyl* (the Ukrainian city of Chornobyl became known to the world in its Russian spelling). The five-episode television drama took the world of entertainment by storm, becoming history's most popular miniseries in a few short weeks. It brought to life the tragedy of people who lived through, were affected by and, yes, caused the world's worst nuclear disaster.

My book *Chernobyl: The History of a Nuclear Catastrophe*, which was released in May 2018, one year before the airing of the miniseries, tells the story of the disaster on the basis of recently released archival documents, which I checked against people's diaries, memoirs, and interviews. Thus, on the factual level, both the book and I as its author can provide answers to many questions about the accuracy of the miniseries. But the inquiries that I have received in the last few months also made me think about the bigger question of what is true in our current understanding of the Chornobyl disaster, its causes, development, and consequences. That big "truth" about Chornobyl is at the very center of my current inquiry.[1]

On the one hand, we now know more than ever before about the history of the Chornobyl accident. We are also aware as never before of the dangers that nuclear energy poses to the world. But we are also confused more than ever before about the meaning of the Chornobyl experience and the closely related question of whether we can rely on nuclear energy in our efforts to deal with the challenges of economic growth and climate change. The answer to that question requires the attainment of a consensus on what happened in Chornobyl, the consequences of the disaster, and the lessons to be learned from it.

Finding common ground on these issues becomes more difficult with every passing day. We feel overwhelmed by the constant influx of information and find it hard to make sense of competing opinions. It is tempting to stop trusting anyone or limit the circle of trust to a few friends or social-media gurus, creating an echo chamber in which truth cannot be born and nurtured, let alone survive. Meanwhile, the nuclear age meets the post-truth era before our very eyes, testing our capacity to maintain life on the planet.

As "truth" becomes ever more compartmentalized and instrumentalized in the service of individual politicians, regimes, and countries, the threat of nuclear disaster remains global. Our survival in the nuclear age is possible only as a world community but, as noted, this requires a consensus on the facts and their meaning. The "truth" of our time must transcend private, political, and national compartments and become universal. Hiding the truth about problems with Chornobyl-type reactors and ignoring the truth about the flawed Soviet system of government led to the Chornobyl catastrophe; concealing the truth about its scope made the catastrophe much worse; inability to agree on the political and social reasons for the disaster may very well lead to new disasters in the future.

There are few places more suitable to start the search for universal truth than the Chornobyl exclusion zone. At its center is a modern-day nuclear Pompeii, the city of Prypiat, devastated by radiation and located only a few kilometers from the Chornobyl nuclear power plant. The city, which had been home to 50,000 construction workers and operators of the plant before the accident, is now completely overgrown with vegetation and inhabited by animals, offering a unique glimpse of what the planet would look like without us. The destruction of Prypiat is a story of the concealment of truth, first about science and technology, then about the scope of the disaster and, finally, about its consequences.

There are good reasons to believe that Prypiat would still be populated by humans and not animals if its inhabitants had known about an accident that happened seven years earlier at another Soviet nuclear plant in the settlement of Sosnovyi Bor, located 50 kilometers from Leningrad, now St. Petersburg. In the fall of 1975 the operators of the RBMK graphite-water reactor—the kind that exploded in Chornobyl—almost lost control of their nuclear "pot." A meltdown of the reactor and a Chornobyl-like catastrophe were avoided thanks only to pure luck and the professionalism of the operators. The reactor became unstable after running for some time at a low power level, and once the operators used control rods to shut down the reaction, they got the opposite of the expected reaction: the power level kept increasing. The operators managed to stop the reaction only by adding control rods manually.

Although a major disaster was avoided, a smaller one occurred. One of the fuel channels in the active zone of the reactor burst, releasing radioactive uranium into the core of the reactor. The management ordered the reactor to be "cleaned" with a release of 1.5 million curies of radionuclides into the environment. One curie suffices to make 10 billion quarts of milk undrinkable, but no one was informed about the release. The accident remained secret and, more important in the long run, its cause—the deficiencies of the reactor, which caused the emergency—remained highly classified. The control rods used by the operators to slow down the reaction were tipped with graphite, causing a spike in the level of the reaction when they entered the active zone. Information about the problem, known in the industry as a "positive void effect," was kept secret from the operators of similar reactors, including those in Chornobyl.

Since the truth about the Leningrad accident of 1975 was hidden, its lessons remained unlearned. The operators at other Soviet nuclear plants did not know and could not imagine that their reactors were prone to such problems, which might cause them to melt down and explode. When the next "positive void effect" occurred on the night of 26 April 1986 at the Chornobyl nuclear power plant, the Soviet nuclear industry ran out of luck. The combination of factors such as the inexperienced crew on duty that night at block no. 4 and the rush to complete the test program of the reactor's turbine before the start of the long weekend turned the "positive void effect" into a disaster that forced the inhabitants of Prypiat out of their city and left a good part of Europe to deal with the consequences of nuclear fallout.

The officials, institutions, and services in charge of dealing with the disaster were psychologically or physically unprepared to do so because they lacked information about previous accidents and were not trained to deal with new ones. The firefighters assigned to the power plant were never told that such things could happen and never trained to fight anything but regular fires. Safety instructors were not equipped with radiation counters that could accurately read the levels of radiation released by the explosion, and when they were finally ready to report the actual levels, their bosses were not psychologically prepared to accept their reports.

The director of the Chornobyl nuclear power plant, Viktor Briukhanov, was given two reports on the radiation level soon after the explosion and chose the one that gave significantly lower readings, pushing aside the safety inspector who insisted on the accuracy of his data. Briukhanov, who is somewhat unfairly portrayed in the miniseries as the embodiment of heartless official servility, was in fact a rather compassionate and competent technocrat. Nevertheless, he preferred "alternative facts" to those that turned out to be true, doing so for a variety of reasons, from psychological unpreparedness to deal with the grim reality to a desire to cover up his own mistakes or avoid the wrath of higher-ups about a situation for which he was not responsible and could not directly control.

The Soviet culture of secrecy, which overrode the emerging culture of safety, became a key factor not only in causing the Chornobyl catastrophe but also in magnifying its scope by concealing information about the accident from those most affected by it. The first thing that the KGB did after learning of the explosion was to cut the telephone lines and prevent all unauthorized communication between the power plant and the outside world. Even the members of the state commission sent to Prypiat by the

Kremlin to deal with the consequences of the disaster were not allowed to communicate by phone with their families or tell them where they had gone and what they were doing there.

The first terse information on the accident, which was allegedly under control, appeared in a Soviet television broadcast three days after the explosion, and that bulletin was released only because the Swedish authorities had expressed public concern about a possible nuclear accident in the Soviet Union that had sent clouds of radioactivity across Europe, causing safety alarms to go off at Swedish nuclear power plants. It took another ten days for health authorities to start issuing recommendations on what the public at large was supposed to do in order to minimize exposure to radiation.

Mikhail Gorbachev, who first addressed the country about the Chornobyl disaster eighteen days after the accident and waited almost three years to visit the site, explained the official silence by claiming that it had taken a long time for him and others in the leadership to learn what had actually happened and that they were unaware of the true extent of the catastrophe. His second in command, Prime Minister Nikolai Ryzhkov, was more open in his explanation of the cover-up: the authorities were afraid of causing panic. They were also concerned about losing face and compromising the prestige of the Soviet regime and its nuclear program. Those considerations turned out to be more important to the authorities than saving human lives. The citizens of Prypiat, who could see the exploded reactor building from the windows of their apartments, were evacuated a day and a half after the accident, but only after the decision to do so had been made at the highest level in Moscow.

The most horrific example of official callousness in dealing with the accident, coupled with criminal negligence with regard to the lives of citizens, was the May Day parade in Kyiv, ordered by the supreme authorities in Moscow (some sources suggest that the decision was made by Gorbachev personally). They were concerned, first and last, to create the impression that life was going on as usual in the capital of Ukraine, and that Western media claims to the effect that the Chornobyl explosion constituted a real and present danger to Kyivans were groundless. Moscow ignored the protests of local officials about rising levels of radiation and ordered the parade to go on. Among those marching and dancing in downtown Kyiv were folk ensembles and schoolchildren. When the suits in which the schoolchildren trained for their performance and then marched on 1 May were checked for radiation, they turned out to be radioactive. We have learned of this from recently released KGB reports: KGB officers oversaw the decontamination of the suits while keeping information about dangerous levels of radiation under wraps.

The truth about the causes and consequences of the Chornobyl disaster was fairly well known to the authorities by early July 1986, when Gorbachev convoked a session of the Politburo, the highest decision-making body in the USSR, to discuss the accident, punish the guilty, and decide what to do with the flawed reactors. Gorbachev knew about the design problem with Chornobyl-type reactors but remained silent about it, since an admission would have jeopardized the entire Soviet nuclear program, a good part of which relied on Chornobyl-type reactors. Gorbachev believed that he simply lacked sufficient funds to replace the dangerous reactors with safer ones. "Human error," meaning the managers and operators of the reactor, was declared the sole reason for the explosion.

Publicly admitting mistakes did not seem to be an option until Valerii Legasov, one of the key characters both in my book and in the miniseries, began the process of unveiling the truth about Chornobyl in his report to a conference called by the International Atomic Energy Agency in August 1986. People in Legasov's industry treated his action as a betrayal, but in fact even he was dealing in half-truths. He admitted the problems with Soviet safety culture and pointed to mistakes and safety violations committed by the personnel of the power plant, especially the operators in charge of the reactor during the explosion. Yet he remained silent about the "positive void effect" and the design problems with the reactors.

The real-life Legasov, unlike his character in the miniseries, never visited the trial of Viktor Briukhanov and other managers held responsible for the accident. It was a classic show trial designed to hide a significant part of the truth about Chornobyl and staged to reinforce the official party line: the managers and operators were solely responsible for the accident. Newly released KGB documents suggest that the KGB placed its agents in the prison cells of the accused to collect information on their mood and defense strategies and convince them to adopt the line favored by the authorities at their trial. This was especially important in the case of Anatolii Diatlov, an intelligent but arrogant techno-crat and one of the key characters in the miniseries, who based his defense on the argument that, while he had indeed violated some safety rules, the true culprits were the designers of the re-actor. What Diatlov said about the design flaws of the reactor in the Chornobyl courtroom remained secret from the public. The so-called "open" trial was conducted in a "closed" zone. Back in the summer of 1987, as is still the case today, one needed special permission to visit the city of Chornobyl, where the accused were put on trial.

Valerii Legasov committed suicide in April 1988, one day after the second anniversary of the Chornobyl disaster, crushed psy-chologically by the ire of his fellow scientists about his partial ex-posure of industry secrets. The industry's critical problems would remain under wraps for another three years, to be revealed only in the dying days of the Soviet Union, a country that was good at keeping secrets and bad at learning from mistakes.

There is general agreement among historians of the Soviet Union that the Chornobyl disaster contributed to profound change in Soviet politics and society by encouraging, if not forcing, Mikhail Gorbachev to launch his policy of glasnost or openness. The So-viet media finally got the right to deliver bad news and discuss economic, social and, eventually, ecological problems besetting Soviet society in the last years of its life. It is indeed hard to overestimate the role of the Chornobyl disaster in finally opening public debate, first on ecology and then on politics, although it would be more accurate to state that the change was caused and promoted not so much by the disaster itself as by the govern-ment's mishandling of its consequences, its addiction to secrecy, and its readiness to lie to its own people.

Glasnost began in 1987, the year after the accident, and was directly related to it. As Gorbachev, bruised by the Chornobyl debacle, began to introduce the first elements of glasnost into the Soviet media and public debate, early ecological activists concerned about the consequences of the disaster became the first to take advantage of the new policy and push its boundaries. Discovering the truth about Chornobyl became the life mission of the first Soviet ecological activists, among whom was Iurii Shcherbak, the author of the first oral history of the disaster. Shcherbak, who worked on his collection of interviews in the Chornobyl exclusion zone, could not publish it in his native Kyiv but managed to do so in Moscow, where control over information about the disaster was not as strict as in Ukraine and Belarus. Those were the republics most affected by radiation, where the authorities believed they had most to lose by initiating public debate on the disaster. The publication of Shcherbak's book in the liberal Moscow journal *Iunost´* (Youth) in 1987 was one of the first systematic attempts to get at the truth of what had happened at the station before, during, and after the explosion.

In 1988, Shcherbak founded Green World, an ecological association that would become the first independent political party in Ukraine in the following year. He and his friends turned their attention to the plight of areas especially hard hit by the disaster but officially pronounced safe for living and consumption of crops. The decision to draw a circle of 30 kilometers around the plant was made in early May 1986, long before the authorities knew what areas had been affected by the Chornobyl fallout. Meanwhile, radiation was spread by the wind and brought down to earth by precipitation. This meant that while some parts of the exclusion zone remained fairly clean, others, well outside the zone—sometimes as distant as the Austrian Alps—were affected. As the authorities ordered the evacuation of more than 100,000 people from the exclusion zone, some of the evacuees were settled in places even more affected by radiation than their native villages.

One of the areas that suffered most but received little government attention or assistance was the Narodychi district, located west of the reactor and outside the exclusion zone. Its fate and the future of its citizens became a concern of Alla Iaroshynska, a young journalist in the city of Zhytomyr, southwest of the Chornobyl nuclear power plant. She accidentally came across information suggesting that the authorities had built and were continuing to build housing for refugees from the exclusion zone in the Narodychi district. A kindergarten and school building were constructed in one of the most polluted villages. Iaroshynska wrote about her discovery, but her articles were never published, and she was subjected to intimidation by party officials in her city. Alerted by the disturbing news about Narodychi, Shcherbak helped to produce a documentary film about the area, but it had little chance of being shown—information about radiation fallout was considered a state secret.

It took the first relatively free elections to the Soviet parliament in the spring of 1989 for Iaroshynska, Shcherbak and others to make their concerns known to society at large. Both were elected to parliament, where they pushed, along with dozens of other activists-turned-politicians, to carry out their agenda of truth about Chornobyl. To that end, they made use of Soviet television channels broadcasting debates in the newly elected parliament. The secret of Narodychi was revealed, becoming an information bomb that destroyed what little trust the public still had in the government. Appalled by this development, Soviet officials maintained that the government was doing all it could to protect people, while activists such as Iaroshynska and Shcherbak were exploiting the tragedy to achieve their narrow political goals.

The anti-nuclear mobilization, powered by the demand for the government to tell the truth about Chornobyl, created fertile ground for the formation not only of the first political parties in the Soviet Union but also broader movements, "popular fronts" that raised the banner of political independence from the USSR in the Soviet republics. In Lithuania, the home of the Ignalina nuclear power plant—a twin station of Chornobyl where most of the HBO/Sky miniseries was shot—20,000 people created a living chain to protest the continuing operation of the power plant. Out of that protest came Sajūdis, the movement for Lithuanian independence. In March 1990, Lithuania became the first Soviet republic to declare full independence from the USSR.

In Ukraine, the anti-nuclear mobilization produced not only Iurii Shcherbak's Green World but also Rukh, the Ukrainian equivalent of Sajūdis, an organization that initially advocated perestroika but then shifted gears to demand the independence of Ukraine. Rukh was led by people who had cut their teeth in politics as ecological activists. One of them, Volodymyr Iavorivsky, became head of the newly created Chornobyl commission in the Ukrainian parliament. He also happened to be the first to read the declaration of Ukrainian independence from the floor of that institution in August 1991. The subsequent referendum on Ukrainian independence, held on 1 December 1991, produced a majority of more than 90 percent in favor. That pretty much finished the Soviet Union, which was dissolved on 8 December 1991 by the leaders of the three republics that had suffered most from the Chornobyl disaster.

The anti-nuclear mobilization in Lithuania, the first republic to officially leave the Soviet Union, and Ukraine, the republic whose decision sounded the death knell of the USSR, indicate the importance of the Chornobyl nuclear disaster not only in bringing elements of democracy to the Soviet Union but also in putting an end to that nuclear superpower. The Soviet Union collapsed under the weight of its mismanaged economy and mounting social problems, but also under the weight of the secrecy and lies surrounding Chornobyl. It was not the explosion of the reactor itself that did in the USSR but official efforts to hide the truth about the disaster and its consequences from the population.

The Soviet Union simply could not handle the truth about Chornobyl. The country that had developed the reactor, let it explode, and then dealt with the technological problems caused by the disaster much better than with the environmental and, most particularly, the human and social problems produced by it is no longer to be found on the world map. But the legacy produced by it will stay with us for generations to come. The new sarcophagus over the damaged reactor no. 4, completed in 2019 by an international consortium of companies at a cost of 1.5 billion euros, is designed to stay in place for one hundred years. After that a new solution and new investment will be required, as the spent fuel in the reactor will present a danger for centuries if not millennia to come.

What stands between us and the truth about Chornobyl today? Let us begin by noting the positive developments in the debate about the meaning of Chornobyl for the future of nuclear power. There is no longer a Soviet Union to monopolize information. Instead, we have as many parties and voices in the debate as one can imagine, as well as freedom to discuss different versions of the events and their possible consequences.

The debate on Chornobyl has become international on more than one level. While Ukraine houses the damaged reactor, its ownership is anything but absolute or exclusive, as even the thirty-kilometer exclusion zone is now divided between two sovereign states, Ukraine and Belarus. Besides, the money and expertise that were mobilized to construct the new sarcophagus and will be needed to run it for decades to come were supplied from abroad. The consequences of the disaster have been felt by many European countries, making them active participants in the debate. And the debate itself ranges far beyond Europe, especially after the Fukushima disaster. Almost anyone might be affected by the next nuclear catastrophe, and everyone looks at Chornobyl to grasp how that catastrophe might be avoided or, should that prove impossible, how its consequences could be mitigated.

Does this mean that we are closer to the truth about Chornobyl, meaning the understanding of its causes and consequences? I would suggest that we are. The internationalization of the debate and the progress of science allow us to better understand the causes of the accident, which should help to avoid future catastrophes. We also know more about the long-term impact of low doses of radiation on human beings and the environment. But there is still a long way to go, as the available data are quite fragmentary and opinions on the number of people affected extremely diverse, with estimates ranging anywhere between 4,000 and more than 90,000. The impact of the disaster on mental health, which includes emotional, psychological, and social well-being, is hard to assess, although we know that in self-perception the Ukrainians consider themselves the least healthy nation in Europe.

Thus, we are now better informed but want to know much more, and theoretically the openness of the debate should help in that regard. The irony is that technological progress creates unlimited possibilities for tampering with today's "openness," making it even more difficult to establish the "truth" about Chornobyl and assess the benefits and drawbacks of nuclear power. What the public thinks about Chornobyl and nuclear power is extremely important, since it is the public that votes in elections and influences political decisions on matters of energy and ecology. But the arrival of the age of "alternative facts" and so-called "post-truth," engendered by the explosion of social media and the resulting crisis of the mainstream media, makes informed debate extremely difficult. Uninformed opinion flourishes, as do conspiracy theories, with the result that science finds itself under attack, unable to win a fight without rules in a world shaped by Twitter.

Let me present a couple of examples of the ease with which conspiracy theories vitiate meaningful debate about Chornobyl and the pros and cons of nuclear energy. In 2015, *The Russian Woodpecker,* a documentary that promotes an "alternative" version of the Chornobyl explosion, received the World Cinema Documentary Grand Jury Prize at the Sundance Film Festival, lending international recognition and legitimacy to what is in essence a conspiracy theory of the disaster. The film introduces and promotes the view that the Chornobyl explosion had something to do with the super-secret Soviet Duga radar system, built a few kilometers away from the plant and abandoned after the disaster. I cannot count the number of questions raised about the possibility that it was the Soviet military that blew up the Chornobyl reactor.

If *The Russian Woodpecker* encourages the viewer to seek the causes of the accident in a secret Soviet military program, a new Chornobyl miniseries announced by the Russian television channel NTV points a finger at CIA operatives. The Russian production is first and foremost a response to the enormous success of the HBO/Sky *Chernobyl* drama, which received substantial but mostly negative attention in Russia. Many are upset that it was the British and Americans, not the Russians, who were the first to tell the world a story that the Russians consider their own in such epic fashion. Others saw the British-American production as an attack on the prestige of the Russian state in its Soviet incarnation or as a Western plot to undermine Rosatom, the Russian monopoly enterprise producing reactors and equipment for the nuclear industry, and its prospects of obtaining lucrative contracts outside Russia.

While the effort of the Russian miniseries to pin the blame for the Chornobyl disaster on the CIA strikes one as bizarre, there is little doubt that it will gain currency in Russia. The KGB seriously considered such a possibility immediately after the explosion, and attacks on the West for political exploitation of the disaster were commonplace in the Soviet media for weeks and months afterwards. Ironically, Mikhail Gorbachev, the father of glasnost himself, led the way in anti-Western propaganda at the time. Almost two-thirds of his first address to the country on the Chornobyl catastrophe, which he delivered in mid-May 1986, consisted of attacks on the United States and its Western allies. It would appear that when it comes to the nature of debate in Russia, we have come full circle to the beginning of our story about the pursuit of truth concerning Chornobyl. In Moscow today, as in 1986, before Gorbachev's glasnost and perestroika, the main values to be promoted and defended are the prestige of the state and its nuclear program, while the main enemy from whom those values must be protected is once again the West.

Critics of the HBO/Sky miniseries point to the inaccuracies in the miniseries' portrayals of the individual episodes and characters as well as misrepresentation of some of the realities of the Soviet life. They are often correct. But what is missed in that critique of the television drama is that the creators of the HBO/Sky *Chernobyl* did a much better job of accurately recreating and visualizing that reality than any other Western and most post-Soviet television productions. While making mistakes here and there, they grasped the big truth about the political and social conditions that caused Chornobyl better than any other film-makers before them. That masterful and evocative presentation of the big picture is the main contribution of the miniseries to our common understanding not only of the Chornobyl story but also of the challenges we face together as a world community in dealing with nuclear energy.

Today we are witnessing a global revolt against globalization and a revival of populism and nationalism reminiscent of interwar Europe. The "America First" sentiment in the United States, Brexit in the United Kingdom, and Putinism in Russia are aspects of a major shift away from the universal and back to the particular. Many look at the world around us from ever more narrow vantage points, geographic, political, social, and cultural. But nuclear disasters recognize no international, social, or cultural borders. They affect people and countries that had nothing to do with the construction of this or that nuclear plant, and their consequences stay with the human race forever—after all, the half-life of the plutonium-239 released by Chornobyl and spotted in Sweden is 24,000 years.

An essential truth about Chornobyl is that we cannot live with conflicting "truths" about the same event created and disseminated within isolated national, social, or cultural spaces. It was just such "truths" that created the monstrous Chornobyl disaster: authoritarian control over economy and society, lack of free discussion and distribution of scientific information, and disregard for human life and health in the pursuit of allegedly higher economic or political goals, to name a few. Improving reactors and making them safer is important but not sufficient. We must reach agreement on the political, economic, and social conditions that produced disasters in the past if we are to prevent future catastrophes that may threaten the existence of humankind as a whole.

Maps

Figure 1. Fragment of Radvila map with depiction of Volhynia and area on the right bank of Dnieper River referred to as "Vkraina." Joan Bleau, *Le Theatre Du Mondou Novel Atlas* (Amsterdam, 1649).

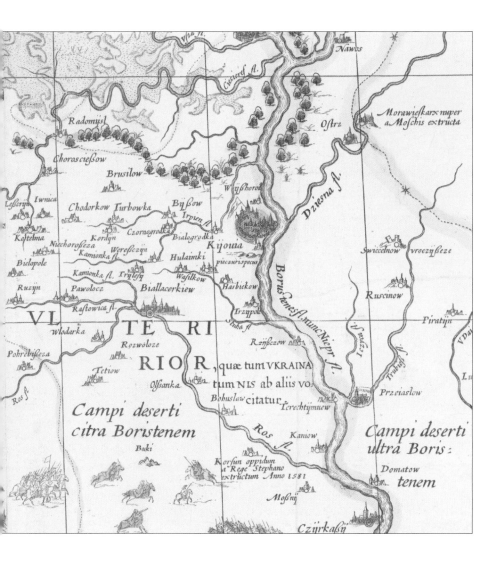

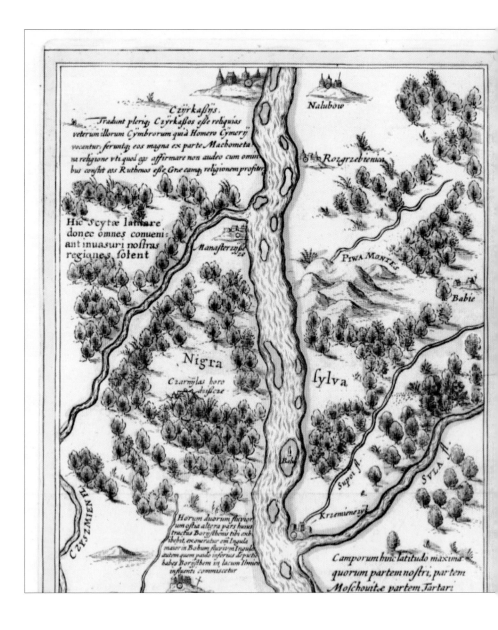

Figure 2. Fragments of Radvila map depicting part of the Dnieper River with Cossack settlements. Joan Bleau, *Le Theatre Du Mondou Novel Atlas* (Amsterdam, 1649).

E. *Nienasytecz poroh*

F. *Susfki poroh*

G. *Woluij poroh*

H. *Walkonowa zaboia poroh*

I. *Tœwutzany poroh alias limes*

Chortica

Locus est ad Borysthenem, Demetrÿ
Wisniowiecÿ antiquiſſimæ Proſapiæ Heroiis
œconomia militari clariſſimus hic enim ſedem
ac firmamentum ſui roboris ſtatuerat dimi
diumq̃ eius loci muro cinxerat, qui natura
adeo munitus extitit vt Ducis vel Chami
Perekopenſis ac totius illius Hordæ vires et
impetum tamdiu ſuſtinere potuerit donec
longa obſidione carens Wisniowiecciuſ
rebus advictum nece ſſarÿs equos coge
retur abſumere ad extremum nauiculis
conſcenſis Porohos ſuperauerit ſaluiſq̃
ſuis omnibus incolumis Czyrkaſſos
peruenerit.

Chorticki ostrov

KONSHA WODA FL.

Hoyran

Tomackoho ostrov

Tomakowka

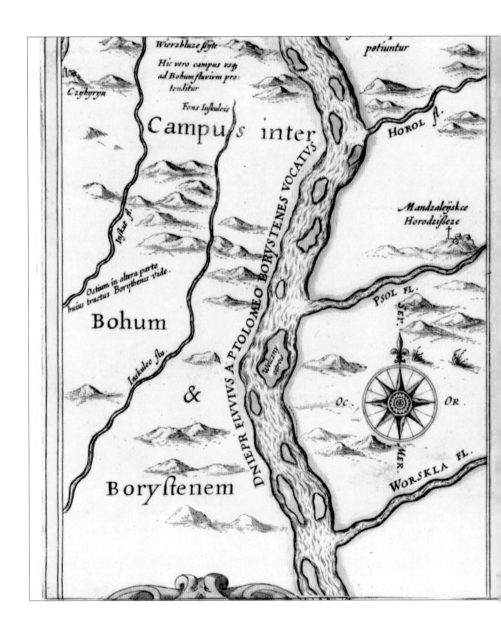

Figure 2, cont.

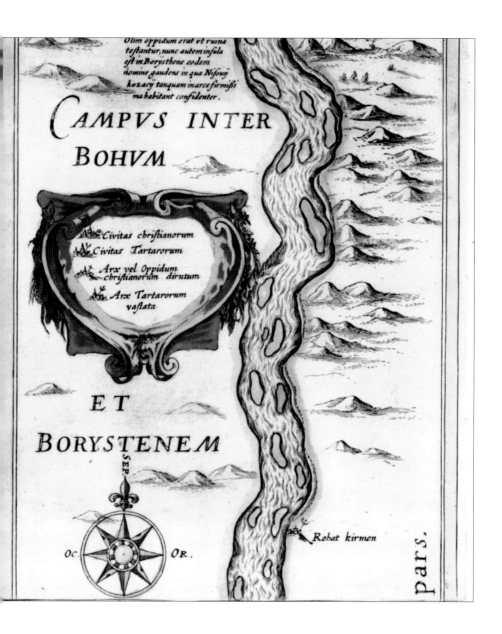

Olim oppidum erat vt ruina
testantur, nunc autem insula
est in Borysthene eodem
nomine gaudens in qua Nisouij
kozacij tanquam in arce firmißi
ma habitant confidenter.

CAMPVS INTER

BOHVM

Civitas christianorum
Civitas Tartarorum
Arx vel Oppidum
christianorum dirutum
Arx Tartarorum
vastata

ET

BORYSTENEM

SEP.

OC. OR.

Rohat kirmen

pars.

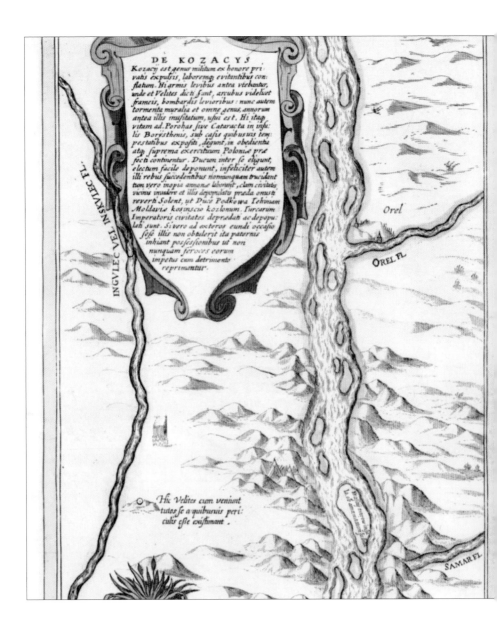

Figure 2, cont.

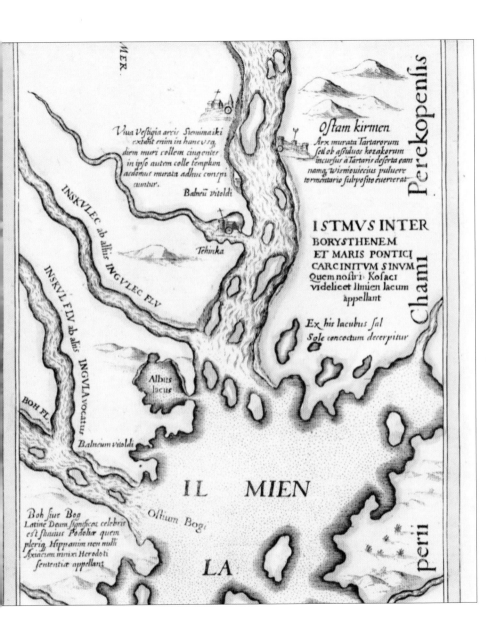

Viua Vestigia arcis Siemimaiki exstat enim in hanc vsq; diem muri collem cingentes in ipso autem colle templum acdemut murata adhuc conspi cuntur.

Balneū vitoldi

INSKVLEC ab aliis INGVLEC FLV

INSKVL FLV ab aliis INGVLA vocatus

Tehinka

BOH FL.

Albus lacus

Balneum vitoldi

Boh siue Bog Latine Deum significat celebris est fluuius Podoliæ quem pleriq; Hippanim non nulli Axiacum innixi Herodoti sententiæ appellant

Ostium Bog

IL   MIEN

LA

Ostam kirmen

Arx murata Tartarorum sed ob assiduos kozakorum incursus à Tartaris deserta eam namq; wisniouiecius puluere tormentario subpositio euerterat

Perekopensis

ISTMVS INTER BORYSTHENEM ET MARIS PONTICI CARCINITVM SINVM Quem nostri Kosaci videlicet limien lacum appellant

Chami

Ex his lacubus sal Sole concoctum decerpitur

perii

Figure 2, cont.

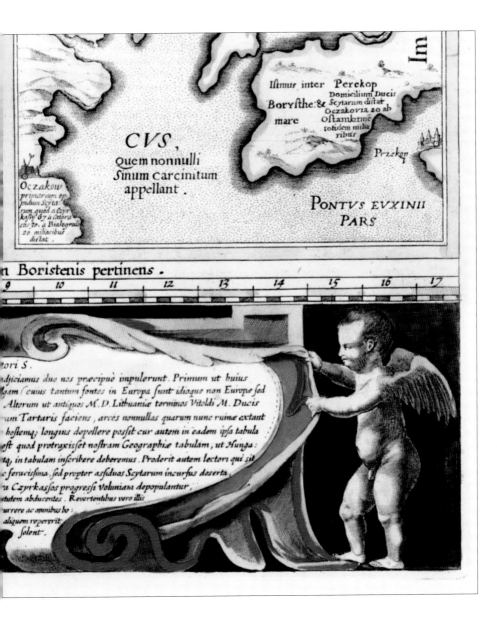

Ismur inter Perekop
Borysthe & Domicilium Ducis
mare Scytarum distat
Oczakovia 20 ab
Oftamktmē
totidem milia
ribus

Przekop

CVS,
Quem nonnulli
Sinum carcinitum
appellant .

Oczakow
primarium op.
pidum Scyta.
rum quod a Czyr
kasiu 67 a Catars
cis 70. a Bialogrula
20 miliaribus
distat .

PONTVS EVXINII
PARS

Im

n Boristenis pertinens .

9 10 11 12 13 14 15 16 17

tori S.
...ndjiciamus duo nos præcipuè impulerunt. Primum ut huius
...gam (cuius tantum fontes in Europa sunt) idioque non Europæ sed
...Alterum ut antiquos M. D. Lithuaniæ terminos Vitoldi M. Ducis
...um Tartaris faciens , arces nonnullas quarum nunc ruinæ extant
...hostemq; longius depellere posset: cur autem in eadem ipsa tabula
...est quod protraxisset nostram Geographiæ tabulam, ut Hunga-
...tq, in tabulam inscribere deberemus . Proderit autem lectori qui sit
...c feracissima, sed propter assiduas Scytarum incursus deserta,
...a Czyrkassos progressi Voluniam depopulantur ,
...stitutem abducentes . Revertentibus vero illis
...urrere ac omnibus bo-
...aliquem repererit
...solent .

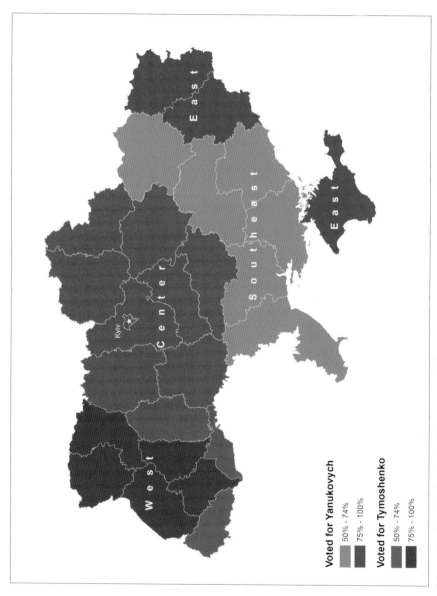

Map 1. Presidential election in Ukraine, 2010. Map source: *MAPA: Digital Atlas of Ukraine*. Ukrainian Research Institute, Harvard University.

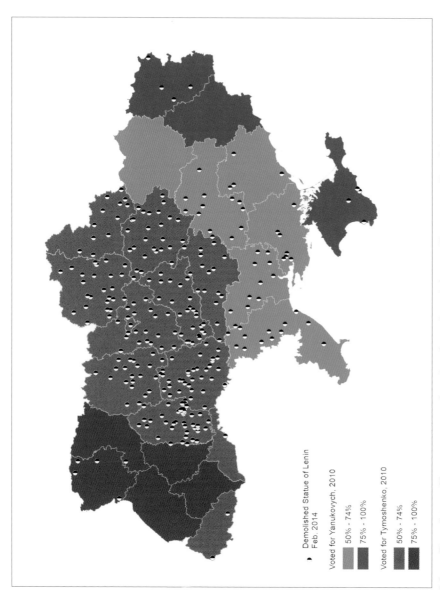

Map 2. Demolition of Lenin statues and results of presidential election. Data source: Den. Map source: *MAPA: Digital Atlas of Ukraine.* Ukrainian Research Institute, Harvard University.

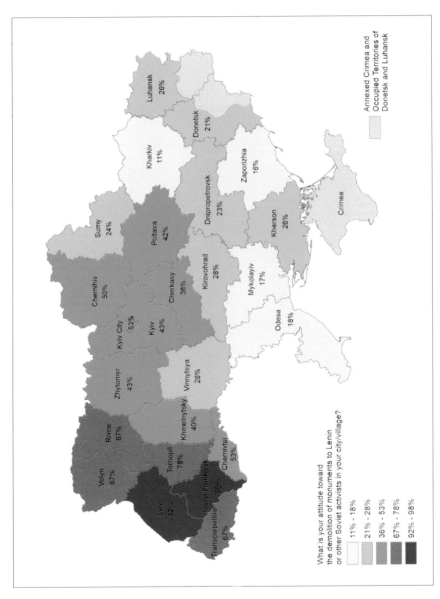

Map 3. Support for the demolition of Lenin statues, March 2015. Map source: *MAPA: Digital Atlas of Ukraine*. Ukrainian Research Institute, Harvard University.

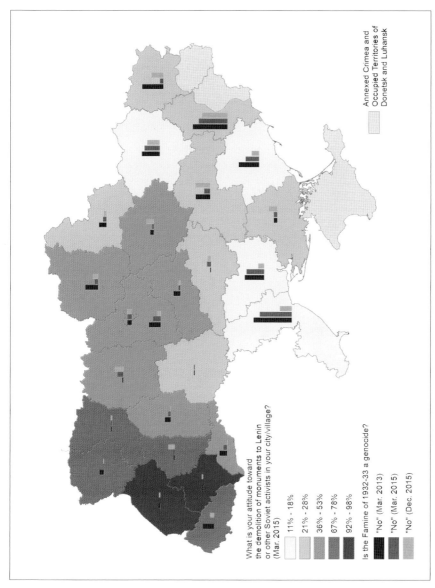

Map 4. Demolition of Lenin statutes and the Holodomor as genocide. Map source: *MAPA: Digital Atlas of Ukraine*. Ukrainian Research Institute, Harvard University.

Annexed Crimea and
Occupied Territories of
Donetsk and Luhansk

What is your attitude toward
the demolition of monuments to Lenin
or other Soviet activists in your city/village?
(Mar. 2015)

11% - 18%
21% - 28%
36% - 53%
67% - 78%
92% - 98%

Is the Famine of 1932-33 a genocide?

"No" (Mar. 2013)
"No" (Mar. 2015)
"No" (Dec. 2015)

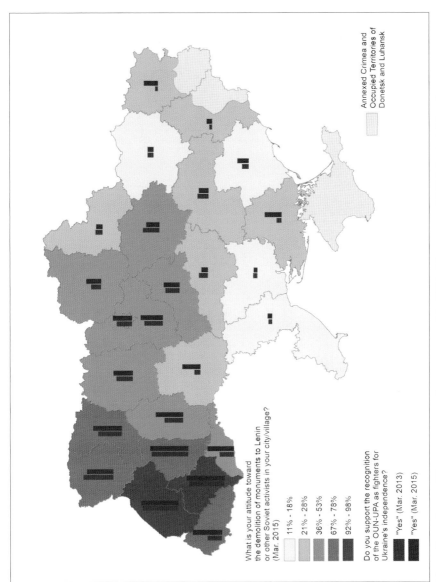

What is your attitude toward
the demolition of monuments to Lenin
or other Soviet activists in your city/village?
(Mar. 2015)

11% - 18%

21% - 28%

36% - 53%

67% - 78%

92% - 98%

Do you support the recognition
of the OUN-UPA as fighters for
Ukraine's independence?

"Yes" (Mar. 2013)

"Yes" (Mar. 2015)

Annexed Crimea and
Occupied Territories of
Donetsk and Luhansk

Map 5. Demolition of Lenin statues and recognition of the UPA. Map source: *MAPA: Digital Atlas of Ukraine*. Ukrainian Research Institute, Harvard University.

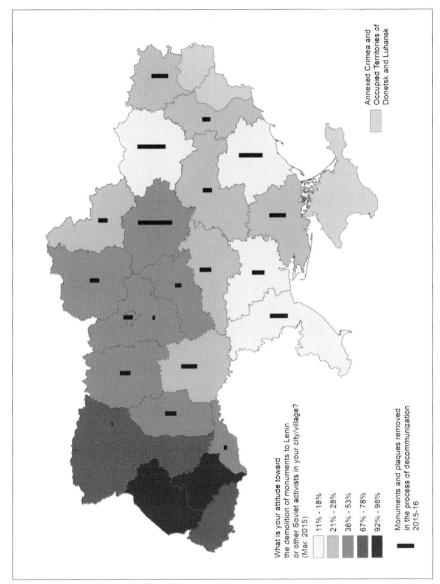

Map 6. Demolition of Lenin statues and removal of monuments. Map source: *MAPA: Digital Atlas of Ukraine*. Ukrainian Research Institute, Harvard University.

What is your attitude toward
the demolition of monuments to Lenin
or other Soviet activists in your city/village?
(Mar. 2015)

11% - 18%
21% - 28%
36% - 53%
67% - 78%
92% - 98%

Monuments and plaques removed
in the process of decommunization
2015-16

Annexed Crimea and
Occupied Territories of
Donetsk and Luhansk

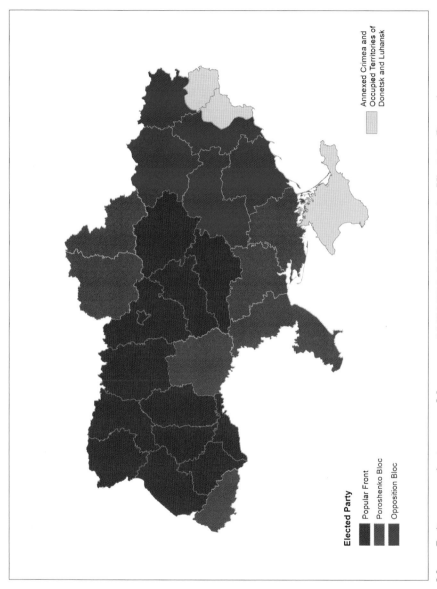

Map 7. Parliamentary elections, 2014. Map source: *MAPA: Digital Atlas of Ukraine*. Ukrainian Research Institute, Harvard University.

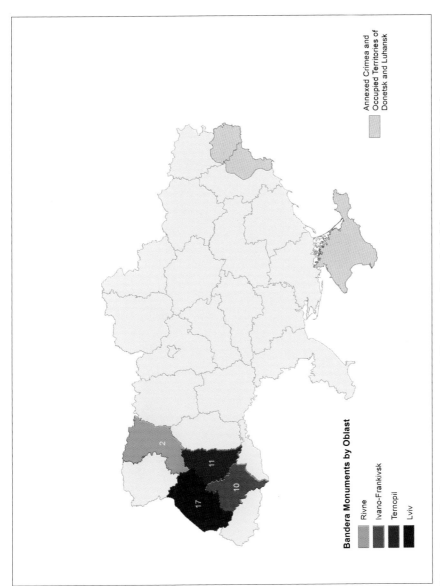

Bandera Monuments by Oblast

Rivne

Ivano-Frankivsk

Ternopil

Lviv

Annexed Crimea and
Occupied Territories of
Donetsk and Luhansk

Map 8. Stepan Bandera monuments, 1991–2016. Data source: Dyvys.Info. Map source: *MAPA: Digital Atlas of Ukraine*. Ukrainian Research Institute, Harvard University.

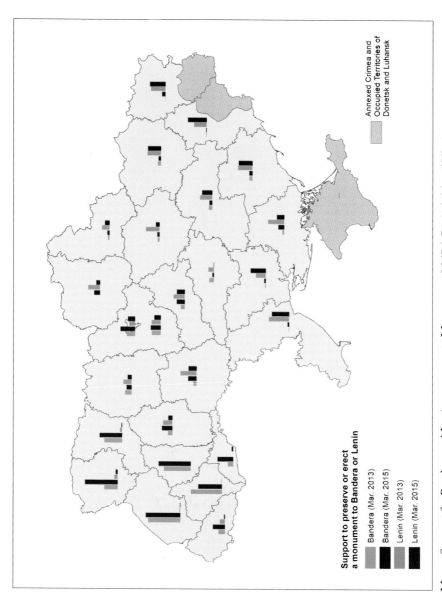

Support to preserve or erect a monument to Bandera or Lenin

Bandera (Mar. 2013)
Bandera (Mar. 2015)
Lenin (Mar. 2013)
Lenin (Mar. 2015)

Annexed Crimea and Occupied Territories of Donetsk and Luhansk

Map 9. Support for Bandera and Lenin monuments. Map source: *MAPA: Digital Atlas of Ukraine.* Ukrainian Research Institute, Harvard University.

15.

The Empire Strikes Back

On 18 March 2014, President Vladimir Putin addressed the Russian Federal Assembly with a most unusual request, asking the legislature to annex part of the territory of a neighboring state. The territory was the Crimean Peninsula, the neighboring country Ukraine. He hailed the annexation of the Crimea—an act to be undertaken in violation of the sovereignty of Ukraine, which had been guaranteed by Russo-Ukrainian treaties and ensured by the Budapest Memorandum of 1994—as a triumph of historical justice.

Much of Putin's argument was historical and cultural in nature. Putin, who has never concealed his regret and even bitterness about the fall of the Soviet Union, referred specifically to the Soviet collapse in a speech delivered on the occasion of the Russian annexation of the Crimea in March 2014. "The Soviet Union fell apart. Things developed so swiftly that few people realized how truly dramatic those events and their consequences would be," said Putin, recalling the events of 1991. "It was only when the Crimea ended up as part of a different country that Russia realized that it had not only been robbed but plundered." He continued: "And what about the Russian state? What about Russia? It humbly accepted the situation. This country was going through such hard times then that, realistically, it was incapable of defending its interests." Putin's speech was meant to remove all doubt that the "hard times" were over and that Russia was back, prepared to undo the "injustice" inflicted on it by the disintegration of the USSR.[1]

What exactly that would mean, and how far Russia was prepared to go in order to undo perceived injustice, were the questions on the minds of many world leaders. After a telephone conversation with Putin, Chancellor Angela Merkel of Germany said in apparent disbelief that he was living "in another world." The former American president, Bill Clinton, provided clarification of what world that was, suggesting that Putin wanted to reestablish Russian greatness in nineteenth-century terms. Prime Minister Arsenii Yatseniuk of Ukraine repeatedly accused Putin of wanting to restore the Soviet Union. The Russian president denied the charges, stating that he was not trying to bring back either the empire or the USSR. Technically, he was right. During the past decade, Russia has been waging open and hybrid wars, annexing territories, and using its virtual monopoly on energy supplies to the countries of Eastern Europe as a weapon, the goal being to establish a much less costly and more flexible system of political control over post-Soviet space than was available either to the Russian Empire or to the Soviet Union. Yet many policies of the present-day Russian leadership have their origins in the last years and months of the existence of the USSR.[2]

By far the most important of those policies has been the Russian leadership's early decision to maintain Moscow's political, economic, and military control over the "near abroad," as the Russian political elite and media dubbed the former Soviet republics. As early as the fall of 1991, advisers to Boris Yeltsin envisioned Russia gathering in the republics on its borders within the subsequent twenty years. Like many other former imperial powers, Russia opted out of the empire because it lacked the resources to keep the costly imperial project going. Unlike most of its counterparts, however, it took along the rich oil and gas resources of the empire—most of the Soviet oil and gas reserves were located in Russian Siberia.

Thus Russia had more to gain economically than to lose from the collapse of the USSR. Russian control over oil and gas resources made the divorce with the empire in 1991 easier in economic terms and prevented armed conflict between Russia and the republics that declared independence. We now know that such conflict was not eliminated but merely postponed. Over the last decade, rising oil and gas prices have made it possible for Russia to rebuild its economic potential and military might, allowing it to reopen the question of disputed borders and territories and step up its efforts to gather back the Soviet republics more than twenty years after the Soviet collapse.

Ukraine, the second-largest post-Soviet republic, has played a crucial role in preventing successive Russian attempts to reintegrate the "near abroad" in economic, military, and political terms. Back in 1991, Russo-Ukrainian relations were the key factor in deciding the future of the Soviet Union. In August 1991, once the Ukrainian parliament declared the republic's independence, the Russian government of Boris Yeltsin threatened Kyiv with partitioning of its territory. Fingers were pointed specifically at the Crimea and the Donbas (Donets Basin), which became a battleground twenty-three years later. Despite threats from Moscow, Ukraine pushed forward with its quest for independence, and in December 1991 the Soviet Union was replaced by the Commonwealth of Independent States, which was the result of a Russo-Ukrainian compromise. In his speech on the annexation of the Crimea, Putin claimed that many in Russia regarded the Commonwealth as a new form of statehood. But that was not the position of the Ukrainian leadership, which took its own independence and that of the other former Soviet republics with the utmost seriousness.[3]

In the 1990s, Ukraine turned the Commonwealth into an instrument for a "civilized divorce"—a term coined in Kyiv—as opposed to one for Russian control over the "near abroad." Ukraine worked hard to ensure recognition of its borders by Russia. In 1994, Kyiv gave up its nuclear arsenal in exchange for a guarantee of territorial integrity and independence given by Russia, the United States, and Great Britain. In 1997, the Ukrainian government agreed to lease the naval base in Sevastopol to the Russian fleet in exchange for a treaty that recognized the inviolability of Ukrainian borders. It took the Russian parliament two years to ratify the treaty that formally recognized the Crimea and Sevastopol as integral parts of Ukrainian territory. It seemed that the two countries had finally resolved all outstanding issues in their relations resulting from the Soviet collapse.[4]

The next decade demonstrated the limits of the Russo-Ukrainian understanding and the degree to which Russia was prepared to recognize Ukraine as an independent state. In the late 1990s, Ukraine began its drift toward the West, declaring integration into the European Union as the goal of its foreign policy and refusing to join Russian-led economic, military, and political institutions. Domestically, Ukraine managed to remain a much more pluralistic society than Russia, with a strong parliament, competitive politics, and an influential opposition.

In 2004, Ukrainian civil society refused to accept the results of a rigged election and endorse the Russian-backed candidate, Viktor Yanukovych, as the country's new president. After a long and peaceful protest that became known as the Orange Revolution, the outgoing president of Ukraine agreed to a new round of elections that brought to power a pro-Western candidate, Viktor Yushchenko. From that time on, Moscow treated Kyiv's orientation toward the West not only as a growing external danger but also as a threat to its own increasingly authoritarian regime. As far as the Kremlin was concerned, Ukraine's rejection of rigged elections and resistance to a corrupt regime were setting an example to Russia's own struggling civil society and had to be stopped at all costs.[5]

The current crisis in Russo-Ukrainian relations began on the night of 21 November 2013 with a Facebook post by Mustafa Nayyem, a Ukrainian journalist of Afghan descent. He was disturbed by news that the government of Viktor Yanukovych, who had come to power in 2010, had refused to sign a long-awaited association agreement with the European Union that envisioned the creation of a free economic zone including Ukraine and EU and stipulated the reform of Ukrainian legislation, democratic procedures, and business practices according to the standards of the European Union. "Fine," wrote Nayyem in his Facebook account, "Let's be serious. Who is ready to show up on the Maidan by midnight tonight? 'Likes' will be ignored. Only comments on this post with the words 'I'm ready.'" There were six hundred "I'm ready" responses. At 9:30 p.m. Nayyem typed another post: "Dress warmly, bring umbrellas, tea, coffee, a good mood, and friends."

Shortly after 10:00 p.m., he was on Kyiv's central square, known in Ukrainian as the Maidan, where the Orange Revolution had begun ten years earlier. About thirty people had gathered by the time he arrived. By midnight, there were more than a thousand young, educated urbanites. For them, the expected association agreement with the EU was the last hope that Ukraine might finally embark on a European course of development, overcome corruption, modernize its economy, and provide a decent standard of living for its people. Those hopes were now being crushed. Nayyem and his friends could not remain silent.[6]

The protest began like a festival, with singing and dancing to brave the cold weather of late November. It soon became known as the Euromaidan—the largest pro-European rally in history. President Yanukovych, for his part, had learned from the Orange Revolution of 2004 that the sooner one got rid of protesters, the better. Thus, in the early hours of 30 November, riot police were ordered to attack the students camping on the Maidan. They did so with the utmost brutality under the pretext of clearing the square to allow the construction of a huge Christmas tree in preparation for New Year's celebrations that were still one month away. Once images of police beating unarmed students were posted on the Internet, dormant Ukrainian civil society reacted sharply. The next day was Sunday, and close to 350,000 people showed up in downtown Kyiv to protest police brutality. The Euromaidan, which had begun with protests against the postponement of the signing of the EU association agreement, turned into what became known as the Revolution of Dignity. Hundreds of thousands of people would join the protests that continued through December 2013 into January and February 2014.

With the United States and EU countries applying pressure on President Yanukovych for a peaceful resolution of the crisis, Yanukovych turned to Russia. Ever since his election in 2010, the Kremlin had wanted him to stop Ukraine's drift toward the West, refuse to sign the association agreement with the EU, and join the Russian-led customs union whose members included Belarus and Kazakhstan. Yanukovych was at first reluctant to do so, but the Kremlin raised the stakes by starting a trade war with Ukraine in the summer of 2013. In November, Yanukovych gave up. He refused to sign the agreement with the EU and went to Russia instead to negotiate a US $15 billion loan needed to keep his kleptocratic government afloat until the next presidential elections, which were scheduled for 2015. The Russian government granted the loan and delivered the first installment. The task now was to keep Yanukovych in power, and the Kremlin thought it could best be done by suppressing the Maidan protests—an option advocated publicly by Putin's adviser Sergei Glazev. In January 2014, as protests continued, Yanukovych forced laws through parliament allowing him to do just that. But the new laws, condemned by the opposition as draconian, only brought more people onto the streets.

Clashes between protesters and police began in late January, reaching their peak on 18 February 2014, when dozens of protesters and policemen were killed by gunfire. That day the government ordered snipers to shoot at the protesters, and fatalities among them soon exceeded one hundred. Those killed by the police and hired thugs became known as the "heavenly hundred." The European Union imposed sanctions, including travel bans and asset freezes, on members of the Ukrainian government responsible for the use of force against the protesters. The Ukrainian parliament, dominated by big-business oligarchs who did not want to lose access to money stashed in Western banks, passed a resolution prohibiting the government from using force against citizens.

That was the end of the Yanukovych regime, which could not survive without reliance on brute force. On 21 February 2014, EU delegates led by the Polish minister of foreign affairs, Radosław Sikorski, negotiated a deal between Yanukovych and the leaders of the opposition. One of its conditions was a new presidential election before the end of the year. But Yanukovych, who had no illusions about its outcome, fled his mansion near Kyiv the same night, reportedly taking hundreds of millions of dollars and leaving behind a private zoo and a fleet of vintage cars. The next day parliament voted to remove him from office. He drove with his bodyguards to the Crimea, and then, by some accounts, boarded a Russian ship to make his way to the Russian Federation, where he was granted citizenship.[7]

The Russian government was extremely displeased with the turn of events in Kyiv. On 21 February 2014, the Russian representative at the negotiations conducted by Sikorski refused to sign the agreement on behalf of his state, but after Yanukovych fled Kyiv, Moscow accused the West and the Ukrainian opposition of not honoring the agreement. It declared the Kyiv events a coup and branded the new Ukrainian government unconstitutional.

As the world watched the closing ceremonies of the Sochi winter Olympic Games on 23 February 2014, the corridors of European foreign ministries were rife with speculation about what Russia might do once the games were over. Vladimir Putin later admitted that on that day he gave his subordinates an order to begin the takeover of the Crimea. On 27 February, four days after the end of the Olympics, Viktor Yanukovych, now safe on Russian territory, issued a statement claiming to be the legitimate president of Ukraine, and a detachment of heavily armed men in unmarked uniforms seized the buildings of the Supreme Council and government of the Crimea and flew Russian flags atop both centers of power.

On the same day, with the "green men" firmly in control, the Crimean parliament held a closed session that lacked a quorum, according to numerous reports, and dissolved the Crimean government. As the new prime minister it appointed Sergei Aksenov, the leader of the Russian Unity Party, which had obtained only 4 percent of the vote in the Crimean parliamentary elections. On 1 March, Aksenov appealed to Vladimir Putin to help ensure "peace and order" on the peninsula. The next day, Russian military units moved out of their barracks in Sevastopol and, with the support of troops brought from Russia, seized control of the Crimea. They were assisted by specially trained groups of Russian Cossacks and mercenaries from Russia, as well as local militias. Vladimir Putin and the members of his government, who had originally denied allegations of Russian military intervention in the Crimea, eventually admitted the participation of the Russian military in its takeover.

The Russian annexation of the Crimea was given a veneer of legitimacy by a referendum hastily organized on 16 March 2014. Officials declared that more than 83 percent of eligible voters had taken part in the referendum, with close to 97 percent voting in favor of joining Russia. Unofficial reports, including those from the Human Rights Council subordinate to the Russian president, cut both numbers almost in half, estimating the turnout at under 40 percent and the vote for joining Russia at under 60 percent. Those figures find support in a poll conducted in the Crimea in February 2014, when not many more than 40 percent of those polled were in favor of joining Russia. But the new authorities clearly did not want to take any risks and went for outright falsification. In the city of Sevastopol, they reported a turnout that amounted to 123 percent of registered voters. The referendum was boycotted by the 250,000-strong Crimean Tatar community and declared illegal by the government of Ukraine. Its results were not recognized by the international community. But on 18 March 2014, Russia officially annexed the peninsula. In his speech on the occasion, Vladimir Putin claimed that the Crimean referendum had been held "in full compliance with democratic procedures and international norms."[8]

It turned out that the annexation of the Crimea was just the beginning of Russian aggression against Ukraine. In April, veterans of the Crimean campaign from the ranks of Russian Cossacks, nationalist activists, and undercover intelligence officers moved from the Crimea to the cities and towns of southern and eastern Ukraine. Their targets were government administration buildings, as well as headquarters of police and security services in the cities of Kharkiv, Luhansk, Donetsk, Mykolaïv, and Odesa, as well as in the smaller towns of southeastern Ukraine. The goal, many believe, was to proclaim a number of separatist republics that would then unite as one Russian-backed state of *Novorossiia*, or New Russia—the name originally used for one of the imperial provinces in southern Ukraine after the Russian annexation of the Crimea in the late eighteenth century. Participants in anti-government rallies were often bussed across the border from Russia and the Russian-controlled Transnistria region of Moldova.

The new revolutionary government in Kyiv was completely unprepared to deal with the Russian annexation of the Crimea and the hybrid war that the Kremlin had begun in the eastern Ukrainian Donbas. For months, the leaders of the new government had led the opposition in its street war against the police and now could not rely on the latter's support in dealing with the foreign-inspired insurgency. In fact, many policemen joined the Russian mercenaries and the local rebels. The Ukrainian army was virtually nonexistent. It was in transition from a conscript army to a professional one, severely underfunded, with no combat experience. The Russians had been fighting their war in Chechnya since 1991, and the Ukrainians were no match for the well-trained Russian regular troops and special forces. It soon turned out that they had major problems in dealing even with Russian-trained local militias. The troops initially could not bring themselves to shoot at paramilitaries who were firing on them and taking over their barracks and equipment.

Kyiv began to put its act together only in mid-April. It was then that one of the leaders of the Maidan protests and the new minister of the interior, Arsen Avakov, managed to reclaim the regional administration building in his native Kharkiv, and Igor Kolomoisky, a Ukrainian oligarch, returned from de facto exile in Switzerland to lead the government of his native Dnipropetrovsk region. Avakov, an ethnic Armenian, and Kolomoisky, an ethnic Jew, emerged as the "saviors" of Ukraine from the Russian hybrid-war offensive, dispelling the myth of the nationalist or even fascist leanings of the new government in Kyiv and its supporters disseminated by Russian propaganda. By mid-May, it was clear that the Russian attempt to raise a revolt throughout southeastern Ukraine and create *Novorossiia*, a state that would divide Ukraine in half and provide the Russian government with land access to the Crimea and Transnistria, had failed.

The Russian strategists of the hybrid war were much more successful in the Donbas industrial region on Ukraine's eastern border with Russia, where Russian-backed separatists declared the formation of the Luhansk and Donetsk "People's Republics." On 12 April, armed men led by Igor Girkin (nom de guerre Strelkov), a former colonel in Russian military intelligence and a veteran of the Yugoslav wars of the 1990s, seized the government and police headquarters in the city of Sloviansk in the northeastern Donbas. By the end of the month, militias led by former Russian intelligence officers and reinforced by Cossacks, volunteers, and Chechen fighters brought in from Russia and funded with Russian money had seized administrative buildings in most cities and towns of the region, including its two major centers, the cities of Luhansk and Donetsk. They also seized radio and television stations, cutting off Ukrainian channels and bombarding listeners and viewers with misinformation about the new Kyiv government, which was called a "fascist junta," and its plans, which allegedly included the desire to ban the Russian language in the region. Viewers and listeners were promised Russian salaries and pensions, which were significantly higher than those in Ukraine, and citizenship either in Russia or in the new state of Novorossiia, which would include a good half of Ukraine.

The propaganda was effective: significant numbers of unemployed and semi-employed youth joined the rebel militias, where they were paid for their services. The resistance of the pro-Kyiv activists was crushed, and some of them were kidnapped and killed, while help from Kyiv failed to arrive. There were several reasons why the covert Russian invasion met little resistance in the Donbas. A major industrial powerhouse in Soviet times, it had become an economically depressed area with the switch from a command economy to the market after 1991. Like cities in rust belts throughout the world, Donetsk became a criminal capital. Many of its new elites had criminal backgrounds or connections, with the region's best-known politician, Viktor Yanukovych, having served two prison sentences in his youth.

While dependent on subsidies from Kyiv, the region had a strong sense of local pride and identity. Its ethnic composition differed from that of neighboring regions of Ukraine, as ethnic Russians constituted majorities in Donetsk and some other towns of the area. In 2001, only 24 percent of the inhabitants of Donetsk Oblast and 30 percent of those in Luhansk Oblast identified Ukrainian as their native language, as compared with 67 percent in neighboring Dnipropetrovsk Oblast. Although ethnic Ukrainians made up 47 percent of the population of Donetsk, only 27 percent of the city's children received their education in Ukrainian. Russian was the dominant language on the streets of the Donbas, and the local elites exploited that fact to mobilize their electorate, claiming that the new Kyiv government was a threat to the Russian language.

Despite their strong sense of local identity, in early April 2014, 85 percent of Donetsk residents were opposed to the seizure of government buildings and installations by militias, and more than 60 percent favored the arrest of separatist activists. But the local political and business elites refused to act against the Russia-led insurgents. They either remained neutral or even tacitly supported the protests in the hope that the new government in Kyiv would be more willing to make a deal with them if the region was in turmoil. It was a short-sighted tactic. They would soon lose control over the rapidly developing crisis.

As the leaders of the Russian-inspired and funded insurgency took a page from the local elite's playbook and used the theme of protecting the allegedly threatened Russian language and culture, the region's political and business elites decided to go with the flow. In the local referendum that took place on 11 May 2014 and was not recognized by Kyiv, voters were asked whether they supported the *samostoiatel'nost'* of the republic—a term that could mean either autonomy or independence. The leaders of the Donetsk "republic" declared that 89 percent of voters favored independence, and the corresponding figure in Luhansk was 96 percent, but these figures were as fraudulent as the ones released in the Crimean referendum, and many of those who voted later claimed that they wanted broad autonomy, not independence. The referendum took place without the presence of international observers and was not recognized by the international community.

The Ukrainian government launched a counteroffensive against the separatist takeover of the Donbas in mid-April, without apparent success until after the presidential election of 25 May 2014. It brought to power one of the leaders of the Euromaidan protests, the Ukrainian business tycoon Petro Poroshenko, who won more than half the vote in the first round. On 26 May, the Ukrainian army recaptured the Donetsk international airport; on 13 June, it took control of the port city of Mariupol on the Sea of Azov; and on 5 July, it took the city of Sloviansk, forcing the units of Colonel Igor Girkin, who by then had declared himself defense minister of the "Donetsk People's Republic," to retreat to Donetsk. With the Ukrainian forces on the offensive, Russia increased its support for the separatist insurgents, now led by two Russian citizens with close links to the Russian government and security services—Colonel Girkin and the self-proclaimed prime minister of the Donetsk People's Republic, Aleksandr Borodai. In the second half of June, the Ukrainian government claimed and NATO intelligence confirmed the continuing influx from Russia to Ukraine not only of trained militants but also of heavy military equipment, including tanks and multiple-rocket launchers.

On 17 July 2014, the war in eastern Ukraine became truly international as Russia-backed separatists shot down Malaysian Airlines Flight MH 17, killing all 298 people on board. The destruction of a civilian airliner produced a flood of protests throughout the world, forcing US and EU leaders to step up sanctions against Russian political and business elites associated with the undeclared war against Ukraine. But sanctions, which have an impact over time, had no immediate effect on Russian behavior. If anything, Russia increased its involvement in Ukraine. In July, Russian artillery and missiles began bombarding Ukrainian territory from the Russian side of the border, and in August regular units of the Russian army crossed the border not just to reinforce Russian mercenaries and local militias but also to take the lead in fighting the Ukrainian armed forces and volunteer battalions. Thousands of Russian regular troops took part in the offensive launched by the separatists during the last week of August 2014. Some of them were captured by the Ukrainian military and paraded before television cameras as proof of Russia's invasion of Ukraine. By sending regular troops into a battle previously fought under the command of Russian military officers and with Russian equipment, Moscow stopped the Ukrainian advance and saved the self-proclaimed Luhansk and Donetsk "republics" from imminent defeat.

In early September 2014, with the participation of Russia and the Organization for Security and Cooperation in Europe (OSCE), the two sides signed an agreement that resulted in a shaky ceasefire. In February 2015, a new ceasefire was negotiated in Minsk (Minsk II) by the leaders of Germany, France, Russia, and Ukraine, only to be violated in the next few weeks when Russian-backed militants took over the strategic railway centre of Debaltseve, previously held by the Ukrainian side. In 2015, despite the Minsk II agreement, Russia continued to provide military support for its puppet regimes in the Donbas, sending not only supplies and weapons but also its military personnel, and causing the continuation of the sanctions introduced by the West to discourage Russia from aggravating the conflict.[9]

The Russian Empire, the Soviet Union, and then post-Soviet Russia all associated international power and security with control over territories along their borders. If they could not control such territories completely, they would partition them and control what they could. This was the rationale behind the partitions of Poland in the second half of the eighteenth century and the division of Germany after World War II. The "New Russia" project, launched by the Russian government in 2014, had as its primary goal the partitioning of Ukraine and the creation of a Russian-controlled state in the southern and eastern parts of the country. That project failed, as Russia managed to destabilize and control only a small part of the projected state of New Russia. While the Crimea was annexed right away, the covert Russian war in the Donbas created conditions for the establishment of another enclave of "frozen conflict" unrecognized by the rest of the world, not unlike Transnistria on the territory of Moldova and Southern Ossetia and Abkhazia on the territory of Georgia. These enclaves are used to apply pressure to Western-leaning republics. Chances are that this will be the primary function of the new frozen-conflict area in eastern Ukraine.

Many in Russia and around the world believe that the crisis is far from over, mainly because Vladimir Putin did not achieve most of what he wanted when he began his aggression against Ukraine. "Putin wanted to tie Ukraine to Russia, to encourage its entry into the Customs Union. He got the exact opposite," wrote the Russian opposition leader Boris Nemtsov in October 2014. "He wanted Ukraine to maintain a neutral status. He failed miserably. . . . He wanted to win the respect of the Ukrainian people. He created a long-term enemy. . . . Putin wanted a 'Novorossiia' stretching from Donetsk to Odesa. He got a small section of the Donetsk and Luhansk Oblasts. . . . [H]e wanted a corridor to the Crimea via Mariupol. He raised awareness and resistance among the locals and spurred Russian residents in Mariupol to dig trenches around the city. . . . He wanted to seize land without firing a single shot, as in the Crimea. He got 4,000 people killed on both sides. . . . Putin wanted to be recognized as a strong leader in world politics. He became an outcast." Indeed, short of the annexation of the Crimea, few of the original goals set by the Russian leadership in the winter and spring of 2014 were achieved by the end of that year. And even that came at a huge cost to the Russian economy and international prestige.[10]

In the wake of the Russian aggression against Ukraine, Vladimir Putin's (and, by extension, Russia's) stock in the West fell to an unprecedented low. Relatives of those who perished in the shooting down of Malaysian Airlines Flight MH 17 held him responsible for the deaths of their loved ones. Many began speaking of a return of Cold War relations between Russia and the West. Some American politicians, including Hillary Clinton, compared Russia's readiness to use the rhetoric of protecting Russian-speakers abroad as a pretext for the invasion and annexation of foreign territories with the policies of Nazi Germany on the eve of World War II. The Russian invasion of Ukraine and annexation of the Crimea was indeed the first case of forcible takeover of territory in Europe since the end of World War II. Parallels were also drawn between the actions of Slobodan Milošević in Yugoslavia in the 1990s and Vladimir Putin in 2014—both had used the national minorities card as a pretext for war.[11]

Ukraine's movement away from its former imperial master toward an international center of gravity finds numerous parallels in the history of the disintegration of empires and the emergence of national states. The French helped the British colonies of North America free themselves from London; the British, Russians, and French helped the Greeks free themselves from Istanbul; and in 1918, the Germans backed the Ukrainian nation-building project against Bolshevik Moscow. What makes the Ukrainian situation different is that the European Union, the pole that attracts Ukraine most, is not a united polity or a state at all. The strength and attractiveness of the EU lie in its values and in the models of political, economic, and social organization of its member states. Its weaknesses are its cumbersome structure and difficulty in formulating a coherent foreign policy. Nor is the EU equipped to deal with military threats and war situations like the one in Ukraine. The EU has the ability to attract but currently no political will to accept new members and no military muscle to defend those aspiring to join it.

The Ukrainian crisis reminded the world once again of the importance of the United States as a major stakeholder in European security and prosperity—the role it played for most of the twentieth century. The United States, whose involvement in East European affairs diminished significantly in the wake of Second Gulf War, began its return to the region's political scene with the start of the Euro-Revolution in Ukraine. Washington, whose relations with Moscow have been tarnished by tensions in the Middle East in the wake of the Arab Spring of 2010 and suffered a further setback with Putin's return to the office of Russian president in the spring of 2012, has provided leadership in formulating a joint Western response to the crisis. That response, which included diplomatic pressure and economic sanctions against Russia, as well as financial and limited military assistance to Ukraine, helped to stop Russian aggression in the fall of 2014.

With the United States and the European Union drawing closer, and Russia on the other side of the divide, what we see today is not a reenactment of the Cold War or a new version of the Great Game, a superpower rivalry that played out in Central Asia in the nineteenth century and in East-Central Europe through most of the twentieth century. Both the United States and the European Union are at best reluctant participants in the current crisis. The Cold War years of trying to haul any Western-leaning country out of Moscow's net are long gone. Neither the United States nor the EU is trying to gain control of Ukraine or keep the country in its sphere of influence. The need to respond to Russian aggression comes from the simple fact that such blatant violation of bilateral and multilateral agreements signed by that country has shaken and continues to threaten the foundations of the post-World War II and post-Cold War political order, raising the specter of arbitrary border revisions, regional conflicts, and global instability.

The origins of the crisis that caught both Washington and Brussels by surprise lie in Ukraine's desire to transform itself by choosing a Western model of development and Russia's determination to stop that from happening and keep the former province in its embrace. To be sure, what happens in Ukraine depends mainly on the actions of the Ukrainians themselves. But historical contextualization of the current crisis suggests that Ukraine's desperate attempts to free itself from the suffocating embrace of its former master have a much greater chance of success with strong international support. The goal should not be to move Ukraine from one sphere of influence to another but to reject imperial and post-imperial forms of domination, which should be relegated completely to the past, where they belong.

16.

When Stalin Lost His Head

A chain saw cut through a thin layer of aluminum alloy with much whining but little difficulty—the monument's neck was hollow. Then someone hit the top of the monument with a metal rod, and the head fell off, hitting the concrete floor. The rest of the monument remained intact. It was the dark winter evening of 28 December 2010. Several young men made their way into the gated area around a three-story pink stucco office building in downtown Zaporizhzhia. They blocked the doors, making it impossible for the guard to get out. They then proceeded to the monument next to the building entrance and started the chain saw. Once the job was done, they left the severed head on the stairs to the building and departed.

The young men belonged to Tryzub (Trident), a Ukrainian nationalist organization named after Stepan Bandera, the leader of a faction of the Organization of Ukrainian Nationalists (OUN) during World War II. The statue they beheaded was a monument to Joseph Stalin. On the following day, 29 December, Tryzub claimed responsibility for what had happened in Zaporizhzhia. The statement released by the organization read: "On 28 December an unidentified mobile group belonging to the Stepan Bandera Tryzub in Zaporizhzhia successfully carried out a national defense action, liquidating the Stalin-Dzhugashvili illegally erected on the territory of the Zaporizhzhia Oblast committee of the CPU [Communist Party of Ukraine]." Although the communists denied that anything of that nature had befallen the monument, their bluff was soon called when a video appeared on YouTube documenting the decapitation. The young men from Tryzub had taped the whole procedure, which has now been viewed almost sixty thousand times (including a few times by this author).[1]

This essay discusses the significance and broader implications of events that happened in Zaporizhzhia on the night of 28 December 2010 and in the days and months preceding and following the event. Its immediate goal is to explain why a monument to Stalin appeared, of all places, in Ukraine, a recent poster child for the Western democratic project in Eastern Europe; why it was damaged by people associated with the name of Stepan Bandera, the leader of the most radical group of Ukrainian nationalists during World War II; and what this tells us about political and memory wars in contemporary Ukraine. The essay's ultimate goal is to contribute to our understanding of the interrelation of politics and memory in post-communist societies.

The Post-Soviet Hero

The return of Joseph Stalin to the public sphere in post-Soviet space began in Russia soon after the disintegration of the Soviet Union. It was championed by two political forces, the Russian communists and Russian nationalists, and came on the heels of the liberal anti-Stalin campaign that was a hallmark of Gorbachev's perestroika. Disillusioned with the liberal agenda in the first post-Soviet decade, which witnessed economic collapse, political chaos, and loss of the Soviet empire and superpower status, Russian society embraced the values and symbols offered by communists and nationalists. According to polling data collected by the Levada Center, only 10 percent of those polled in 1989 considered Stalin a great leader. That figure increased to 20 percent in 1994 and 35 percent in 2000. Stalin's popularity reached its peak during Vladimir Putin's first tenure as president of Russia, crossing the 50 percent threshold in 2004, and hovering around 50 percent ever since.

While most Russians condemn Stalin-era terror and repressions, many of them see in Stalin an effective economic manager and a great leader who won the war and turned his country into a superpower. As the Soviet victory in World War II developed into a key historical myth in post-Soviet Russia, it gave special prominence to Stalin, who, according to the myth created in his lifetime, was most responsible for the victory. Nostalgia for the lost Soviet past with its social stability and imperial grandeur helped to propel Stalin to celebrity status in Russian media and society. Some observers believe that by embracing Stalin, the Russian public also embraced authoritarianism as the only effective way of governing their country.[2]

While the return of Joseph Stalin to prominence began in Russia, it did not stop at its borders. Ukraine, sharing much of the Soviet past with Russia, underwent similar political and economic turmoil after the fall of the USSR, and on many levels it remains part of the Moscow-centered informational space. It experienced the spillover effect of Stalin's rehabilitation in Russia. In Ukraine, however, the return of Stalin was modest at best. In 2010, only 28 percent of the population considered him a positive figure, while 64 percent had negative attitudes toward him. Yet Stalin's popularity differed significantly from one region of Ukraine to another. In western parts of the country only 7 percent viewed Stalin positively, but in its eastern oblasts, bordering on Russia, the number of those with a positive attitude toward Stalin reached 44 percent, which was comparable with the Russian numbers.[3]

If in Russia Stalin emerged as a hero for communists and nationalists alike, in Ukraine, while communists, or some of their leaders, embraced Stalin, Ukrainian nationalists rejected him as a symbol of the suppression of Ukrainian statehood and culture and a perpetrator of crimes against the Ukrainian nation. It is not surprising that the monument was erected by communists in eastern Ukraine, while the organization that destroyed the monument had its main backing in western Ukraine.

The Warlord

The Zaporizhzhia communists officially unveiled the bust of Stalin on 5 May 2010, a few days before the 65th anniversary of VE Day. On 9 May, in the eastern Ukrainian city of Luhansk, a monument was unveiled to the victims of atrocities committed by the Bandera faction of the OUN during and after World War II. The two events were either initiated or supported by the same political force—the Communist Party. They manifested the arrival of Stalin as a new resource in Ukraine's memories of World War II and underlined the importance of those memories as a battleground between different political forces in the country.

The Zaporizhzhia ceremony was attended by numerous Red Army veterans. Some of them, wearing military uniforms decorated with combat awards, formed an honor guard next to the monument. "We built the monument at the request of our veterans," stated Aleksei Baburin, the first secretary of the Zaporizhzhia regional committee of the CPU and a deputy of the Ukrainian parliament. The inscription on the monument identified Stalin not only as head of the Soviet state but also as a generalissimo. The depiction of Stalin in a marshal's uniform and epaulettes, along with the date of the ceremony, the uniforms of the honor guard, and the inscription on the monument left no doubt that the communists were seeking to legitimize the monument to a figure extremely controversial in Ukraine by linking him with the well-established Soviet narrative of the victory of the Soviet people in the Great Patriotic War of 1941–45, as the Soviet-German segment of World War II became known in the USSR. The reference to Red Army veterans was a crucial element of that legitimization. "Only those who do not honor their grandfathers and fathers can get involved in a discussion of whether this is needed or not," asserted Baburin with regard to the monument. "We are carrying out the will of our veterans."[4]

One of the main speakers at the event was Ivan Shekhovtsov, who donated the largest sum for the construction of the monument: 50,000 hryvnias (close to US $7,000) out of the total cost of 106,000 hryvnias. Shekhovtsov, a retired Soviet-era criminal prosecutor from Kharkiv, first made a name for himself in the late 1980s when he initiated his first lawsuit in defense of the honor and dignity of Joseph Stalin. Altogether Shekhovtsov filed close to twenty suits defending his hero's reputation against attacks on him by such people as the Belarusian writer Ales Adamovich. Even now, he continues to claim that it was the Germans, not Stalin's NKVD, who executed the Polish officers in Katyn Forest, and that the Great Ukrainian Famine of 1932–33 had nothing to do with the policies of Stalin and his associates. His advocacy of Stalin caused a breach in his family. Shekhovtsov's wife of many years and his two children, both lawyers, broke all relations with him, but he continued his activities after the disintegration of the USSR.

In 2004 Shekhovtsov published a four-volume study entitled *Delo Stalina-"prestupnika" i ego "zashchitnika"* (The Case of Stalin the "Criminal" and of His "Defender"). To publish the book he turned for money to his wealthy children, but they refused to support the project. Shekhovtsov eventually found a sponsor in Russia to whom he promised to return the loan. It is not clear who the sponsor was and what happened to the loan, but in 2012 Shekhovtsov unexpectedly came up with 50,000 hryvnias for the construction of the Stalin monument. He claimed to have made the donation out of his pension. Given that the average pension in Ukraine does not exceed US $300.00, and most of that money goes for food, Shekhovtsov's donation was nothing short of a miracle. But so was the installation of a monument to Stalin in a country that had celebrated the victory of the Orange Revolution five years earlier.[5]

Shekhovtsov welcomed those gathered at the ceremonial unveiling as citizens of the Soviet Union. He then praised Stalin as a great leader and military commander. He emphasized the link between Stalin and the Soviet-era myth of World War II by making reference to the heroism of Zoia Kosmodemianskaia, a member of the Communist Youth League who was sent by the NKVD to burn villages behind the German lines during the battle for Moscow in the winter of 1941. Russian peasants, who were not partial to the idea of dying in the open fields, captured Zoia and turned her over to the Germans, who executed the young saboteur.

The Soviets, for their part, turned her into a war hero. According to the propaganda myth, before her execution Zoia allegedly exclaimed: "Stalin is with us! Stalin will come!" It was the myth of a life given in service to Stalin that captured the imagination of the young Ivan Shekhovtsov, then a private in the Red Army. Addressing the Zaporizhzhia gathering, Shekhovtsov added another important element to the old myth: Stalin, it was said, had personally visited the grave of Zoia Kosmodemianskaia. The reference to Stalin paying tribute to one of his fallen soldiers reinforced the connection between the Stalin monument and the theme of the Great Patriotic War.[6]

That theme found its reflection in the comments that the Zaporizhzhia communists began to collect in June 2010 in a special book dedicated to the Stalin monument. At first, most of the visitors who were asked to leave their comments in the book were from outside Ukraine. A certain Afinogenov, a retired major from the Arkhangelsk region of Russia, concluded his laudatory comment on the brave Zaporozhians who had dared to put up a monument to Stalin with the war-era slogan "For the Motherland, for Stalin!" The retired Colonel A. Lugansky from Odesa wrote that without Stalin there would have been no victory in the war. He also concluded his comments with a war-era slogan: "Victory will be ours!" Aleksandr Belenky from Israel stressed Stalin's role in the construction of socialism and in winning the "Great Victory." He also wrote that his grandfather, a Red Army artillery soldier, had been killed in the "Great Patriotic War."

Eventually, as locals were also invited to leave their comments in the book, they indicated victory in the war as Stalin's major achievement. The Reverend Vasilii, a retired archbishop of the Ukrainian Orthodox Church in the jurisdiction of the Moscow Patriarchate, thanked the regional committee of the Communist Party for keeping alive the memory of a "great person." He was especially moved by Stalin's alleged order to take an icon of the Kazan Mother of God into the skies over Moscow and Leningrad in order to entreat divine protection of the capitals from a German takeover. Many stressed in their comments that this was a monument to Generalissimo Stalin.[7]

Stalin vs. Bandera

Not everyone in Zaporizhzhia was happy with the installation of the monument to Stalin or accepted the notion that anyone showing respect for veterans of World War II had to put up with the monument. Among the most vocal opponents were members of Ukrainian nationalist organizations. Their members were not allowed to approach the monument at its unveiling, but they promised that it would not last very long. On 28 December, it looked as if they had delivered on their promise. But the communists put on a brave face. Instead of turning to the police and claiming that someone had destroyed the monument, which they had installed without proper permission from the authorities, they placed the head back on the metal bust, claiming that the vandalism had resulted in the loss of a couple of letters of the inscription. But the worst for the monument still lay ahead.[8]

Half an hour before midnight on 31 December 2010, a blast shook the environs of the communist headquarters. It was the time of night when people were opening bottles of champagne and setting off fireworks, but the sound that came from the compound had nothing to do with New Year's celebrations. It accompanied a blast that destroyed the Stalin bust hastily repaired only a few days earlier. Although the base survived, the bust itself was blown to bits. The largest fragment was that of the generalissimo's left hand, holding a marshal's epaulette. The glass was blown out of the windows, and the hammer and sickle above the entrance to the building hung at a crazy angle. Who had blown up the monument? The opinions of readers of the Internet publication *Ukraïnska pravda*, known for its liberal nationalist views, were divided. It could either have been the nationalists finishing the job or the authorities themselves, pursuing their own political agenda. "Whatever it is, it's a delight all the same! Happy New Year, gentlemen!" remarked a reader in the discussion column.[9]

As had been the case a few days earlier, there was an organization prepared to claim responsibility for the attack. The difference was that no one had ever heard of the "Movement of 1 January" that did so. The statement released in the name of that organization read: "In honor of the 102nd anniversary of the birth of the Leader of the Ukrainian people, Stepan Bandera, a special combat unit of the Movement of 1 January blew up a shrine to the butcher of Ukraine, Stalin (Dzhugashvili). This is only our first action to destroy the enemies of the Ukrainian nation. Our next targets will be anti-Ukrainian officials, policemen, bandits of the 'SBU' [Security Service of Ukraine], prosecutors, and judges who persecute Ukrainian patriots. We shall destroy all Zionists and their wretched synagogues on our sacred Ukrainian land; there will be no mercy for them! We call on all patriots to band together in autonomous combat units, undergo training, and study military science and explosive materials. Our time has come: the National Revolution is not far off! Liberty or death!"[10]

Although the statement used some of the language employed by nationalists, its calls for terrorist acts and anti-Semitism had no parallels in recent Ukrainian history. The authorities termed the demolition of the Stalin monument an act of terrorism. The search for the perpetrators began. It did not take very long to find the members of Tryzub who had claimed responsibility for decapitating the monument—they were soon arrested, interrogated, and put behind bars—but it was much more difficult to pick up the trail of those who had blown up the monument a few days later and issued a statement calling for violence and ethnic hatred. Many in the nationalist and liberal camps believed that the task was impossible, as the authorities themselves were behind the act. Suspicions of that nature intensified as the authorities arrested leaders of the largest nationalist party, Svoboda (Liberty), which had its power base in western Ukraine but was gaining strength in the center and east of the country. A regional governor declared that the organization's leaders were preparing a coup d'état and planning to shoot down President Viktor Yanukovych's airplane. Many believed that the authorities had staged a provocation that could lead to the declaration of a state of emergency and postponement of parliamentary elections.[11]

Whoever was behind the explosion that destroyed the Stalin monument in Zaporizhzhia, the fact that responsibility for its previous decapitation was claimed by an organization named after Stepan Bandera immediately placed the event into the context of Ukrainian memory wars, which, ever since the Orange Revolution, had pitted Red Army veterans against veterans of the Ukrainian Insurgent Army, a World War II partisan formation led by members of the OUN. The statement of the "Movement of 1 January" highlighted the issue of anti-Semitism and violence as a common feature of nationalist thinking and actions. The two competing narratives of World War II—the Soviet-era myth of the Great Patriotic War versus that of the Ukrainian nationalist underground's heroic resistance to both communists and Nazis—again came crashing into the Ukrainian public sphere. By no coincidence whatever, the first narrative was embodied by the figure of Stalin, the second by that of Bandera.

According to a poll taken in the fall of 2010, Bandera was the second least popular figure in Ukraine after Stalin. If Stalin was viewed negatively by 64 percent of those polled, Bandera scored 51 percent. Supporters of both historical figures were equal in number—28 percent of those polled. As in the case of Stalin, Bandera's supporters and opponents were divided along geographic lines. While Bandera was favored by 58 percent in the west, his support reached only 9 percent in the east of the country.[12]

The division of Ukrainian historical memory of World War II along the Stalin-Bandera line found its most vivid representation in two developments that took place in January 2010, the last full month of President Viktor Yushchenko's tenure. On 13 January, a Kyiv court declared Stalin and other leading members of the communist regime in Russia and Ukraine guilty of the crime of genocide, as they had created conditions for the Great Ukrainian Famine of 1932–33. The court's finding became law on 21 January. On the following day, in his speech marking a Ukrainian national holiday, Unity Day, President Yushchenko announced that he had a signed a decree bestowing the title of Hero of Ukraine on Stepan Bandera. In a period of less than ten days, Stalin had officially been pronounced a criminal and Bandera a hero. With Yushchenko due to leave office within weeks, and Viktor Yanukovych of the Party of Regions, which enjoyed the support of communist voters, poised to take his place, everyone understood that these last official actions of Yushchenko would be challenged by the new administration.[13]

The Zaporizhzhia monument to Stalin was in many ways a response to the erection of numerous monuments to Bandera in the western regions of the country during the previous decade. The largest of them, in the city of Lviv, was unveiled in 2007. After Yanukovych's victory, the communists believed that they could get away with a monument to their anti-Bandera, Stalin. They were not entirely alone in their desire to do so. Asked about the monument to Stalin, Vasyl Khara, a member of parliament from the ruling Party of Regions, called Bandera and the commander of the Ukrainian Insurgent Army, Roman Shukhevych, "enemies of our people, scoundrels and traitors who destroyed the people." He then asked a rhetorical question: "So why could they put up monuments to those scoundrels, but there can be no monument to Stalin?"[14]

The destruction of the Stalin monument on New Year's Eve 2010 led to a new escalation of memory wars in Ukraine and the partition of Ukrainian memory space along the Stalin-Bandera line. Petro Symonenko, the leader of the Communist Party of Ukraine, called on his cadres to "show solidarity and unite for struggle against neo-Nazi nationalist evil and oligarchs who sponsor fascist organizations and parties." He also called on President Yanukovych to revoke the awards bestowed on the war-era nationalist leaders by his predecessor. "If the most decisive measures are not taken to end the terrorism of the Svobodaites, the Tryzubites, and other nationalist bands and formations, it may end in tragedy for the people of Ukraine," intoned Symonenko. "I address myself to the president of Ukraine: cancel immediately the illegal decrees of your predecessor, Yushchenko, awarding the title of Hero of Ukraine to the traitors and Hitlerite lackeys Shukhevych and Bandera."[15]

Symonenko was not the only communist to counterpose a good Stalin to an evil Bandera. Quite a few of the communists who wrote their comments in the book at the Stalin monument in Zaporizhzhia did likewise. One of them claimed in the summer of 2010 that Stalin was a true leader, not like Yushchenko, Tymoshenko, and Yatseniuk, then Ukraine's political leaders, who had allegedly betrayed their people as Bandera, Shukhevych, and the eighteenth-century Ukrainian hetman Ivan Mazepa, who raised a revolt against Peter I, had done before them. The communist demands were eventually heard in Kyiv. The blast created the right political atmosphere for taking the award of Hero of Ukraine away from the nationalist leader. Eleven days after the destruction of the Stalin monument, the Yanukovych administration declared that the title of Hero of Ukraine awarded to Bandera had been officially rescinded. The Ukrainian courts did so on a technicality—by law, the award could not be given to a noncitizen of Ukraine, and Bandera, who was killed on KGB orders in October 1959 while in exile in West Germany, had been a citizen of Poland but never of Ukraine.[16]

The Liberal Dilemma

President Yushchenko's decree bestowing the title of Hero of Ukraine on Bandera took the Ukrainian liberal elite by surprise. For years its most prominent representatives had been associated in one way or another with the national-liberal camp in Ukrainian politics—the coalition of nationalist and liberal forces that brought about Ukrainian independence in 1991 and fueled the Orange Revolution of 2004 that brought Yushchenko to power. His Bandera decree indicated that the coalition was all but dead. Yushchenko's decree was treated with understanding by intellectuals with nationalist leanings but rejected by their liberal counterparts.

For one, argued the liberals, Bandera was too controversial a figure to be treated as a national hero. He divided Ukraine instead of uniting it. Politically, the decree allowed the Russian leadership to claim that the Orange camp had pro-Nazi sympathies; it also alienated the Polish elites, which until then had been among the strongest supporters of Yushchenko's attempt to join the European Union. That was one reason for the liberal rejection of Yushchenko's effort to make a hero of Bandera. The radical nationalism of Bandera's ideology, as well as the xenophobic and anti-Semitic views of the OUN leadership, were equally important.[17]

While they did not welcome the decree, many liberals also did not believe that the new president's revocation of the title of hero was the right way to proceed. As Iaroslav Hrytsak, one of the leading intellectuals of the national-liberal camp, explained in his blog in the Lviv Internet publication Zaxid.net, while Yushchenko's decree had divided Ukraine, the revocation could not stitch it back up. Many in the national-liberal camp did not welcome the February 2010 resolution of the European Parliament that called on the new president of Ukraine to annul his predecessor's decree. The Ukrainian intellectuals were especially disappointed by the support for that resolution on the part of the Polish members of the European Parliament, who, they believed, had failed to appreciate the complexities of the political situation in Ukraine and, by passing such a resolution, strengthened the hand of the new authoritarian leaders of Ukraine and their Russian backers.

Hrytsak suggested that the ideal solution for Ukraine would be to agree on some form of historical amnesia. Not very optimistic in that regard, he called on his readers to accept a situation in which minorities had the right to their own historical narratives and heroes. Hrytsak cited London, with its monuments both to Cromwell and to Charles I, as a possible model for the implementation of such politics of memory.[18]

While anti-Semitism featured prominently in the statement of the nonexistent "Movement of 1 January," and both communists and liberals touched upon it in their debates on the participation of members of the Bandera faction of the OUN in the Holocaust, the subject remained marginal. It moved much closer to the center in the debate on Bandera's legacy that was provoked by the Yushchenko decree among students of Ukrainian history in North America. The debate split a group of scholars, formerly maintaining something of a consensus in their assessment of Ukrainian history, who were associated in one way or another with the Canadian Institute of Ukrainian Studies at the University of Alberta. Most of those who took part in that debate during the first half of 2010 stressed the close relation between the ideological premises of the Bandera organization and European fascism, putting the emphasis on the anti-Semitic element of nationalist ideology and nationalist collaboration in the Holocaust. One of the participants in the debate, John-Paul Himka, referred particularly to the results of his recent study of the Jewish pogrom in Lviv immediately after the German takeover of the city in late June and early July 1941.[19]

Many of the contributions to the Canadian debate appeared the same year in Ukrainian translation in a book compiled by Tarik Amar, Ihor Balynsky, and Iaroslav Hrytsak but had limited impact on the discussion of Bandera's legacy in Ukraine. The very division of the memory camps in Ukraine along the Bandera-Stalin line made the Holocaust theme marginal at best.

The Return of the Tyrant

The Zaporizhzhia communists felt it a matter of honor to restore the monument to Stalin. Indeed, on 7 November 2011, slightly more than ten months after the first monument was blown up by still undetermined perpetrators, they unveiled a bust of Stalin on the anniversary of the Bolshevik Revolution of 1917. This time they encountered more obstacles on the part of the civic authorities than they had with the original installation. The authorities in Kyiv and Zaporizhzhia alike were opposed to the monument, and the city council finally agreed to its installation only as an interior feature of the building that housed the local headquarters of the Communist Party.

The communists placed their new bust of Stalin in a bay window of their reconstructed building. There was another change as well. Along with Stalin, in the other wing of their building, the communists installed a monument to none other than Zoia Kosmodemianskaia, the heroine of Ivan Shekhovtsov, the pensioner from Kharkiv who had donated 50,000 hryvnias to build the original monument. This time, apparently, Shekhovtsov had run out of funds but not out of ideas. He was not mentioned among the major donors to the reconstruction, but Kosmodemianskaia featured as prominently in the Zaporizhzhia pantheon as Stalin. The dictator's association with the history of the world war and the legitimization of his cult by means of Great Patriotic War mythology were strengthened in the new version of the monument.[20]

With the perpetrators who had blown up the original monument still at large (the authorities had to release the leaders of the nationalist Svoboda Party after it proved impossible to link them to the blast), and the Tryzub members who had cut off Stalin's head a few days previously behind bars, no one seemed willing to launch another assault on the monument. The new attack on it came from unexpected sources and was carried out in an unusual manner. Local journalists got together to produce and display on a downtown billboard a poster challenging the legitimacy of the Stalin monument in the context of the same historical mythology that legitimized it—the mythology of World War II. The poster, which went on display in December 2011, depicted the figure of Adolf Hitler, his hands spread in apparent disappointment. The text read: "What makes me any worse than Stalin? Give me a monument as well." A line in smaller print at the bottom of the poster explained the reason for the action: "Let's rid the city of its shame!" The reference was of course to the Stalin monument.[21]

The communists challenged the display of the poster on legal grounds. Ukraine has a law against fascist propaganda, and the portrait of Hitler was interpreted as such. The Hitler poster was soon removed, but a new one, sponsored by the same group of journalists, took its place. It bore an image of Stalin (Ukraine did not, at that time, have a law against the propaganda of Stalinism). The text of the new poster read: "I killed millions of Ukrainians, and what have you done to deserve a monument?" The line at the bottom in smaller print remained unchanged: "Let's rid the city of its shame!" This time the installation of the monument to Stalin was challenged on the basis of a different historical myth—that of the Great Famine of 1932–33.[22]

While the heroization of Bandera left the Ukrainian national-liberal intellectuals divided and disoriented, attempts to glorify Stalin by building him a monument in Zaporizhzhia offered grounds for solidarity across national-liberal lines. Comparing Stalin to Hitler and presenting him as a criminal responsible for the death of millions of Ukrainians during the Great Famine were two main themes on which liberals and nationalists agreed with one another. In November 2011, as a district court in Zaporizhzhia was deciding the fate of Tryzub members accused of decapitating the Stalin monument, Valentyn Nalyvaichenko, the new leader of Viktor Yushchenko's party, Our Ukraine, was reported in the media to have "reminded both representatives of the procuracy and judges deciding the case that by decision of the Kyiv Appellate Court of 13 January 2010, Stalin and his henchmen were found guilty of organizing the famine-genocide of the Ukrainian people." Nalyvaichenko, himself a native of Zaporizhzhia, stated: "I remind all officials who tolerated the erection of a monument to Stalin in Zaporizhzhia that the criminality of the Stalin regime has been acknowledged by the parliamentary assemblies of the CSCE and the Council of Europe, and that their resolutions should be carried out by our state."[23]

On 12 December 2011, a court in Zaporizhzhia sentenced nine members of the Tryzub organization, most of them young men from eastern Ukraine, to prison terms ranging from one to three years. The implementation of the sentence was postponed, meaning that those sentenced were released from prison after the court ruling. They were ordered to compensate the Communist Party for 106,000 hryvnias spent on the construction of the monument, 50,000 of them donated by Ivan Shekhovtsov. Those sentenced appealed the court's decision, but in June 2012 the regional court of appeal left the sentence without change. The same court ruled that the erection of the Stalin monument was an illegal act.

The Tryzub members were tried and sentenced for causing damage to property that happened to belong to the Communist Party. In an interview given to media outlets after the court proceedings, the perpetrators showed no remorse for what they had done. They declared that, with the Yanukovych administration's assumption of office, Ukraine had come under foreign occupation, and the installation of the monument to Stalin was an insult to the Ukrainian nation. To the disappointment of many liberals, there was no trace of liberal ideology in the statements of those who had toppled the symbol of the liberals' main embodiment of evil—Joseph Stalin.[24]

The War That Failed to End

In Ukraine, the history of World War II continues to serve as a battleground of two different versions of its past. The first is represented by proponents of the well-developed Soviet-era myth of the Great Patriotic War, revised after 1991 to restore the original centerpiece of that myth—the image of Joseph Stalin as victor. The alternative offered to that old myth is the heroic image of the nationalist underground fighting on two fronts, against the Nazis and the Soviets. While World War II mythologies serve as a consolidating factor for all of Ukraine's neighbors, including Russia, Belarus, and Poland, they continue to divide Ukrainian society along political and geographic lines. The myth of the Great Patriotic War with Stalin at its center unites Ukraine with Russia and Belarus in its memory of World War II. The myth of heroic nationalist resistance against communism brings Ukraine closer to the countries of East-Central Europe.

The struggle over the Stalin monument in Zaporizhzhia pitted two diametrically opposed political forces and visions of history, communist and nationalist, against each other, leaving scant middle ground for interpreting the history of World War II in Ukraine on the eve of the Maidan protests of 2013 and Russian aggression and annexation of the Crimea in 2014. As shown by the analysis presented here, the debates over Stalin and Bandera, as well as over the Soviet and nationalist legacies, divided Ukrainian society between two versions of the past. Neither side seemed to realize at the time that both versions were little more than politically constructed myths.

17.

Goodbye Lenin!

Sunday, 8 December 2013 witnessed by far the largest public protest to take place in the city of Kyiv since the Orange Revolution of 2004. About 800,000 people poured into Independence Square (Maidan) and Khreshchatyk Boulevard in the city center to protest actions taken by the government of President Viktor Yanukovych.

The protests had been initiated eighteen days earlier, on the night of 21 November, by a few hundred people appalled at the abrupt change in the policy of the Ukrainian government, which, under pressure from Russia, had refused to sign the long-awaited association agreement between Ukraine and the European Union. The EuroMaidan, or the European Maidan protests, as they became known in the media, were started by Kyiv yuppies—a relatively small group of Western-oriented journalists, businessmen, political activists, and students—who saw in the association agreement their last hope of reforming Ukrainian politics and society in order to liberate them from the Soviet legacy and the corrupt Russian-backed regime of President Yanukovych.

The EuroMaidan turned into what became known as the Revolution of Dignity on Sunday, 1 December, after government riot police brutally dispersed student protesters encamped on the square. Close to 350,000 Kyivans took to the streets of the capital. The orientation toward Europe and signing of the association agreement with the EU remained among their slogans and goals. But the new protest was fueled first and foremost by their refusal to countenance the regime's brutality as a way of solving political problems. The people rejected the increasingly authoritarian government, which they now wanted to bring down.

On the following Sunday, 8 December, the number of protesters more than doubled, their ranks increased by sympathizers from other parts of Ukraine, above all from the country's pro-European west. Emboldened, those leading the protests called on their followers to blockade the Presidential Administration. The Revolution of Dignity was about to enter a new stage. The government knew that and was preparing troops to crush the revolt. Violence was in the air.[1]

Lenin Falls

Sometime after 5:00 p.m. on 8 December 2013, when the main rally was over and winter darkness had fallen on the streets of Kyiv, a column of approximately 200 men, most of them wearing balaclavas, began to proceed from the Kyiv city administration building, the protesters' headquarters on Khreshchatyk, to the intersection of that boulevard with another one named after Ukraine's most famous poet, Taras Shevchenko. The column was headed for the monument at the foot of Shevchenko Boulevard across the street from the Besarabka (Bessarabian Market), the city's main agricultural bazaar. The monument, which honored Vladimir Lenin, had been erected in December 1946, as the Soviet authorities were "cleansing" and reclaiming the symbolic space after the defeat of the Nazis, who had occupied the city from 1941 to 1943.

Ever since Ukraine's declaration of independence in 1991, followed by the removal of a much larger statue of Lenin from the city's main square, many in Kyiv had wondered whether the Lenin monument on Shevchenko Boulevard should go as well. Why should there be a monument to the founder of the Russian Communist Party and godfather of the brutal Soviet regime on the boulevard named after Shevchenko, whom many considered the spiritual father of the Ukrainian nation? The statue was also an eyesore to those less concerned with the Ukrainian nation than with belief in the market economy—a belief symbolized by the Bessarabian Market across the street from the monument. It stood as proof that even the Bolsheviks could not fully crush market forces. Among the Kyivans who wanted the monument to stay in place were members of the Communist Party of Ukraine, who were prepared to defend it with their bodies if need be. The civic authorities decided to play for time, citing the artistic value of the marble statue as an excuse to keep it where it was.[2]

As monuments to Lenin were removed by city councils in other parts of Ukraine, the Kyiv authorities took a pause on the monument that lasted more than twenty years. That seemed excessive to Ukrainian liberals and intolerable to Ukrainian nationalists. The latter decided to take the initiative into their own hands. The first attempt to demolish the monument was undertaken by members of the Ukrainian nationalist organization Tryzub (Trident) on 30 June 2009, the anniversary of the declaration of Ukrainian independence by nationalists in 1941 and the birthday of one of the icons of Ukrainian nationalism, Roman Shukhevych. The attackers managed to damage the monument before they were arrested and put behind bars. As justification of their action, they cited the decree on the Soviet regime's responsibility for the Holodomor, the Great Ukrainian Famine of 1932–33, signed a few days earlier by President Viktor Yushchenko. When the pro-Western and anticommunist Yushchenko was replaced in early 2011 by the pro-Russian President Yanukovych, who was friendly to the communists, the perpetrators were prosecuted, but their sentences were suspended. The Lenin monument was restored soon after the attack. The pause taken by the civic authorities continued.[3]

The start of the EuroMaidan protests in November 2013 presented a new threat to the monument, and the government dispatched a special detachment of riot police to protect it from any eventuality. With a column moving toward the monument on the evening of 8 December, the police knew what to expect. They had already fought off an attack on the monument the previous Sunday, 1 December, later claiming it had been so violent that eight officers had had to seek medical attention. This time they decided to do nothing. The large column and the mass character of the protest earlier in the day may have been one reason. But it is equally possible that the authorities did not mind the impending demolition and were preparing to use that act of symbolic violence to justify the very real violence they intended to unleash in the coming days. One way or another, the column of men in balaclavas got a free hand to do what they had come to do—demolish the monument to Vladimir Lenin.[4]

Demolish they did. While the organizers of the action cheered on the crowd gathered around the monument with nationalist and anticommunist slogans, young men in balaclavas attached a tall ladder to the monument—together with the pedestal, it was more than 10 meters in height—put a loop around the neck of the communist chief and, with considerable effort, pulled the monument off the pedestal. Lenin fell headfirst, crushing a granite plate near the base of the monument. His neck did not survive the impact, and the head broke off, to the further excitement of the crowd. In front of the cameras the attackers, some armed with heavy hammers, descended on the demolished idol, trying to split off pieces of the marble body as revolutionary souvenirs. A representative of the largest Ukrainian nationalist party, Svoboda (Freedom), which claimed responsibility for the action, compared the fall of the monument to that of the Berlin Wall.[5]

Leaders of the mainstream political parties were less enthusiastic. Andrii Shevchenko, a prominent Ukrainian journalist, member of parliament, and future Ukrainian ambassador to Canada, made a statement on behalf of the leadership of the EuroMaidan coordinating committee, claiming that the demolition had not been sanctioned by that body. But Shevchenko also refused to condemn the toppling of the monument, stating that there was no place in downtown Kyiv for a monument to Lenin. A few weeks later Ukraine's most celebrated composer, Valentyn Sylvestrov, expressed the opinion of many when he stated: "They brought down the monument—a dubious achievement of the revolution, but an achievement." Many Kyivans, as well as people in other parts of Ukraine, did not welcome the manner of the removal or share the nationalist ideology of those who carried it out, but they did not doubt that it was high time for Lenin to go.[6]

The toppling of the Lenin monument in Kyiv on 8 December 2013 is considered the start of what became known as the *Leninopad*, or Leninfall—the mass demolition of Lenin monuments in Ukraine in late 2013 and the first half of 2014. Indeed, television coverage of the demolition of the most recognizable Lenin monument in the country triggered similar attacks in the Ukrainian provinces, but the process was slow to gather speed, and the impact of the Kyiv toppling became clear only in retrospect. Only three monuments were demolished or vandalized elsewhere in Ukraine between 9 and 30 December 2013. Nine more were attacked in January 2014, and an additional five in the first half of February 2014. Given that there were hundreds of monuments to Lenin all over Ukraine, the immediate impact of the fall of Kyiv's Lenin was modest at best.[7]

But then, all of a sudden, anti-communist hell broke loose. On 21 February alone, more than 40 Lenin monuments and statues were either demolished or attacked by activists in small towns and villages of Ukraine. By the next day, more than a hundred monuments and statues were gone. Altogether the month of February 2014 witnessed the demolition of 320 statues and monuments to Vladimir Lenin. The term "Leninfall" was born. The chronology of the Leninfall, not unlike its beginnings in December 2013, was closely associated with the main stages of the Revolution of Dignity protests. The dramatic spike in attacks on Lenin monuments on 21 February came in the wake of the violent clashes and mass killing of protesters on the Maidan one day earlier. To the crescendo of violence on the Maidan, the pro-Maidan forces in the Ukrainian provinces responded with attacks on the symbols of the erstwhile communist regime, which came to be seen as a proxy for the corrupt administration of President Yanukovych.

While no other month matched February 2014 in number of demolished or vandalized monuments to Lenin and other prominent figures of the communist regime, the Leninfall continued for the rest of the year, further fueled by the Russian annexation of the Crimea in March 2014 and the beginning of open warfare in the Donbas in April and May 2014. Altogether in 2013–14 more than 550 monuments to Lenin were removed in Ukraine by local activists and by decisions of local councils.[8]

The Leninfall of 2013–14 had a less dramatic but in many ways even more consequential continuation in the following year. In April 2015, the Ukrainian parliament passed a set of four "Decommunization Laws." In the following month, President Petro Poroshenko, elected to office in the middle of the Crimean and Donbas crises in May 2014, signed the legislation into law. One of the laws established a six-month deadline for the removal of all monuments to Lenin and leaders of the communist regime. It decreed the renaming of thousands of Ukrainian cities, towns, villages, and streets in order to remove all communist-related names. By early 2017, close to 1,300 additional Lenin monuments and statues were gone. The Leninfall had attained its ultimate objective. Out of approximately 5,500 Lenin monuments and statues in Ukraine in 1991, all but a few were gone by October 2017, the month marking the centenary of Lenin's October Revolution of 1917. In Ukraine, the century of V.I. Lenin was over.[9]

Interactive Mapping

What should one make of the Leninfall story? Was the demolition of the Lenin monuments just an unfortunate episode, a passing spasm of symbolic violence fueled by social upheaval and resulting in the loss of part of the country's cultural heritage (some of the monuments, such as the one removed in Kyiv, had unquestionable artistic value)? Or did it reflect a broader change in society and its perception of itself and its past? And if the latter is truer than the former, then what does that memory shift tell us about the direction taken by Ukrainian politics and society since the time of the EuroMaidan and the Revolution of Dignity?

None of these questions can be adequately addressed without taking into account the spatial dimension of the Leninfall. Taking place in the midst of Ukraine's most profound political crisis since the demise of the Soviet Union, the Leninfall was as much the outcome of political strife as were the wars of historical memory. Politics and memory had been closely interlinked in Ukraine at least since the Orange Revolution of 2004, and both have had very strong regional components. Regionalism in Ukrainian politics and memory had been strengthened by the Revolution of Dignity and the loss of the Crimea and parts of eastern Ukraine to Russian-led separatist projects, which also mixed politics and memory, as evidenced by the "Novorossiia" project, rooted in the imperial past, and the creation of the Donetsk and Luhansk "people's republics," inspired by the Soviet experience and endowed with the Soviet legacy.

The exploration of the regional dimensions of Ukrainian historical identity and the politics of memory based on that regionalism is the main objective of the "History and Identity" module of the MAPA: Digital Atlas of Ukraine Project developed by the Ukrainian Research Institute at Harvard University. This module is the result of collaboration with two main partners: the project entitled "Region, Nation, and Beyond: An Interdisciplinary and Transcultural Reconsideration of Ukraine" under the leadership of Professor Ulrich Schmid at the University of St. Gallen, Switzerland, and a project undertaken by the Razumkov Center in Kyiv under the title "The Formation of the Common Identity of Ukrainian Citizens in New Circumstances: Peculiarities, Prospects, and Challenges." Some information for the module was provided by the Institute of National Memory of Ukraine.[10]

The maps developed by MAPA Project Manager Kostyantyn Bondarenko and MAPA Research Fellow Viktoriya Sereda are based on a spatial analysis of the data produced by two surveys conducted in Ukraine in March 2013 and March 2015 by the University of St. Gallen Project with the support of the Swiss National Foundation and the Wolodymyr George Danyliw Foundation, as well as a December 2015 survey conducted by the Razumkov Center and funded by the Swedish International Development Cooperation Agency, the Konrad Adenauer Foundation, and the Ministry of Foreign Affairs of the Netherlands under the auspices of the "Social Transformation in Ukraine and Moldova" project. The first two surveys included 6,000 respondents aged 18 and above, while the third covered more than 10,000 respondents of the same age category.

The discussion that follows is based on the data and maps produced on the basis of the above-mentioned surveys. Both the maps and the databases, including the formulation of survey questions and responses to them, expressed as percentages of all responses, may be consulted on the module page of the MAPA website. The MAPA maps reproduced in this collection (see pp. 216–24) represent one or more layers of the spatial information available on the website. Although the MAPA-produced maps and layers of information provide the basis for this discussion, it also draws on maps and data produced by other mapmakers and projects acknowledged in the notes. While this essay focuses mainly on the Leninfall and seeks to offer preliminary answers to the questions formulated at the start of this section, it is also prepared as a demonstration of the possibilities inherent in GIS-based mapping and spatial analysis based on it and is presented as an invitation to further research into the spatial dimensions of Ukrainian memory politics and Ukrainian society at large.

The Geopolitics of Memory

Ever since the Orange Revolution of 2004, memory wars have shaken Ukraine almost without interruption. The battle has been fought by proponents of two historical narratives: one post-Soviet, strongly influenced by the Soviet-era Russocentric and pro-communist interpretation of the past, the other ethnonational, with strong anti-communist and often anti-Russian overtones rooted in the nationalist resistance to Soviet rule during and after World War II. The Ukrainian liberal camp, represented by a significant group of Ukraine's leading historians and backed by pragmatic elements in the Ukrainian government and political elite, found itself embroiled in this struggle between two radically different visions of the Ukrainian past. The liberal narrative of Ukrainian history, with its inclusive attitude toward citizens who were not ethnic Ukrainians, helped lead the country toward independence in the late 1980s and early 1990s but was unable to regain ground lost after the polarization of Ukrainian politics, including the politics of memory, in the course of the Orange Revolution.[11]

The polarization of Ukrainian politics after 2004 had a clear regional dimension, pitting the east of the country, nostalgic for the Soviet period, against the west, which was anti-communist and oriented toward Europe. Under the circumstances, the politics of memory became an important instrument for political parties trying to mobilize their regional electorates. But "lived memory," rooted in the actual history of a given region, began to be modified by current politics in this period. The city of Kyiv, for example, which had been under some form of Russian control since the mid-seventeenth century, accepted many elements not only of liberal national but also nationalist narratives of Ukrainian history, as did the population of other urban centers in predominantly rural central Ukraine. In regions east of the Dnieper, elements of national and nationalist narratives made inroads not only in rural regions such as Poltava but also in industrial centers like Dnipro (formerly Dnipropetrovsk).

Given the close connection between memory and politics in Ukraine, it is only natural to start our discussion of the present-day geography of memory by considering the country's regional political preferences, as shown on Map 1 (p. 216). Political scientists and sociologists who study Ukraine have come up with various divisions of Ukrainian political space into macroregions, usually based on voter behavior but also including historical and cultural components, especially linguistic preferences. The number of macroregions typically varies from two to five. This discussion identifies four macroregions, but the regional map that we have chosen differs somewhat from generally accepted political-science models.[12]

For the purposes of our analysis, we found most useful the regional division of Ukraine based on a map of the 2010 presidential elections. The map reproduced above divides Ukraine into two parts and then splits those zones into two additional segments, yielding a division of the country into four macroregions. The basis for this division is the number of votes cast for the two major contenders in the 2010 presidential elections, Viktor Yanukovych and Yulia Tymoshenko. The areas where more than 75 percent voted for Tymoshenko constitute one macroregion, and those where she received between 50 and 74 percent of the vote are another. Two more macroregions consist of those areas where more than 75 percent voted for Yanukovych and those where he gained 50 to 74 percent of the vote. The two regions in which Yanukovych and Tymoshenko achieved majorities constitute superregions dividing Ukraine into eastern and western halves. To a large degree, the divisions indicated on the map came into existence in the 2004 presidential elections that produced the Orange Revolution.

For the purposes of this discussion the regions marked on the map can be labeled West, Center, Southeast, and East, the latter being a composite region that includes the Donetsk and Luhansk Oblasts of eastern Ukraine and the Crimean peninsula. Since I find this map and its regional divisions by far the most useful geographic tool for analyzing the data produced by the surveys, I shall use the four regional names just mentioned in my further discussion.

The Revolt of the Center

Let us now discuss the geographic dimensions of the Leninfall as it occurred between December 2013 and the summer of 2014, keeping in mind the map of the 2010 presidential elections.

Scholars and political activists in Ukraine have made several attempts to map the Leninfall. By far the best-known map, which takes in the period up to the end of February 2014, was produced by the newspaper *Den* (The Day). The *Den* map, reproduced above (Map 2, p. 217), includes the monuments removed in the East—the Crimea and the Donetsk and Luhansk Oblasts of Ukraine. The map leaves little doubt that the original Leninfall—the demolition of Lenin statues within the first few months after the fall of the Lenin monument in Kyiv—had a clear regional dimension.[13]

The "eye" of the Leninfall "hurricane" is clearly visible in Ukraine's Center, making significant inroads into parts of the Southeast. The virtual exclusion of the West from that map has a fairly simple explanation: most of the monuments there were demolished either in the months leading up to Ukrainian independence or in the first years of independence. The exclusion of the East—the Crimea and a good part of the Donbas—is a more complex phenomenon associated with the Russian annexation of the peninsula and the start of the hybrid war in eastern Ukraine. The lack of enthusiasm for demolishing Lenin monuments there is reflected in the results of the 2013 survey and, for non-occupied parts of Ukraine, in the surveys of 2015, as will be discussed below.

What happened in the Center in late 2013 and early 2014, and why did that macroregion emerge as the driving force of the Leninfall? Was a shift in the attitudes of the local population responsible for that change?

Our data from the March 2013 survey along with research done by scholars in Ukraine suggest that even before the start of the EuroMaidan, support for retaining Lenin monuments in the Center was lukewarm at best. Kyiv Oblast, where attitudes more or less reflected those of the Center in general, had 23 percent of respondents wishing to keep such monuments in their towns and villages. The strongest support for the status quo was registered in Poltava Oblast, where 34 percent of respondents favored monuments to Lenin in their settlements. These figures set the Center apart from both the West and the Southeast, its immediate regional neighbors. Ternopil Oblast in the West had the lowest level of support in the entire country—no respondents at all—in favor of Lenin monuments. Odesa Oblast in the Southeast had the country's highest level of support, with 51 percent of respondents favoring Lenin statues.[14]

That was before the start of the Leninfall. The EuroMaidan, the Revolution of Dignity, and the outbreak of warfare in the East produced a major shift in the historical attitudes of the Center, sharply reducing enthusiasm for Lenin. In Kyiv Oblast, support for Lenin monuments fell from 23 percent to 16 percent, while in Poltava it dropped from 34 percent to 10 percent, turning one of the most pro-Lenin regions in the Center into one of its most anti-Leninist.

Map 3 (p. 218) uses shades of color to show the level of support for the demolition of Lenin monuments in March 2015 (the more intense the color, the stronger the desire to get rid of Lenin). In the city of Kyiv there was a majority (53 percent) in favor of demolition, while Kyiv Oblast was on par with Poltava Oblast: in both cases, 42–43 percent of respondents favored demolition. Once again, the Center stood apart from the Southeast, where support for demolition did not exceed 28 percent of those surveyed, with the lowest level of support (11 percent) registered in Kharkiv Oblast. An important aspect of the Leninfall story that emerges clearly from Map 3 is that, by March 2015, in terms of desire to rid itself of Lenin monuments, the Center had effectively joined the West to create a joint "Lenin-free" space in Ukraine.

For all its drama, the iconoclastic demolition captured by television cameras in Kyiv and elsewhere was not a sudden rupture in the Center's narrative of memory but the culmination of a process that had begun earlier. In the course of the 1990s, close to 2,000 Lenin monuments had been demolished in the Western regions of Galicia and Volhynia. The process continued into the next decade, spilling over into the Center. In those two macroregions more than 1,200 statues were removed in the 2000s. Compared to those figures, the Leninfall, which accounted for about 550 statues, was a rather modest development.[15]

The 2013 and 2015 surveys, the first taken before the Euro-Maidan, the second afterwards, allow one to suggest that the Center has joined the West in more than the rejection of Lenin and communism. Obscured by the drama of the demolition was the culmination of a process whereby, in the minds of the population at large, Soviet-era mythology was replaced with elements of the Ukrainian national narrative, which represented Ukraine as a major, if not the principal, victim of the Soviet regime. Since the Orange Revolution of 2004, that narrative has come to include the interpretation of the Holodomor, or the Great Ukrainian Famine of 1932–33, as an act of genocide perpetrated by the communist regime in Moscow against the Ukrainian people. Although the Ukrainian parliament voted in 2006 to recognize the Holodomor as an act of genocide, the issue soon became contested, as Russia mounted an international campaign against the genocide interpretation of the Famine, while President Yanukovych, elected in 2010, dropped the reference to genocide from his official pronouncements.[16]

President Yanukovych's change of rhetoric does not appear to have had much impact on attitudes toward the Holodomor in the Center, where, as shown on Map 4 (p. 219), the majority continued to regard it as an act of genocide. That map shows the percentage of respondents who rejected the interpretation of the Holodomor as genocide in March 2013, March 2015, and December 2015. The level of denial is shown by columns, while the color map in the background indicates levels of support for the demolition of Lenin monuments in March 2015.

As may be assumed on the basis of this map, as early as March 2013, the Center was forming a common memory space with the West when it comes to the popular attitude toward the Holodomor and, by extension, toward the overall record of the communist regime. This trend gained new impetus with the EuroMaidan, with a further decline of naysayers in March 2015. The adoption of the decommunization laws in April of that year produced a slight rise in the numbers of naysayers in the Center and even in some parts of the West but did not change the overall picture: the West and Center stood together in recognizing the Holodomor as an act of genocide. The number of skeptics was already low in March 2013. In Chernihiv Oblast, for example, they declined from 15 percent in March 2013 to 4 percent in March 2015, and a slight rise of that number to 7 percent in December of that year did not change the overall picture.

That interpretation of the Holodomor set the West and Center apart from the Southeast, where in December 2015 the nay-sayers, while not constituting a majority, still showed significant strength. Their percentage was highest in the Ukraine-controlled areas of Donetsk Oblast, reaching 30 percent of respondents. The decommunization laws revealed the difference in the attitude toward the Holodomor between the combined Center-West and Southeast, reducing the number of naysayers in the Southeast and slightly increasing it in the Center and West. The two memory spaces were clearly marching to different drums.

The common memory space of the West and Center was formed not only by the rejection of the communist regime and the condemnation of its crimes but also by the joint adoption of elements of the new nation-based historical discourse. The significant element here is the popular attitude toward the fighters of the UPA—the World War II-era nationalist-led Ukrainian Insurgent Army, which has been a hot-button issue in Ukrainian politics since 2004. The UPA, whose soldiers are as much praised for their resistance to the communist regime as they are criticized or even vilified for participation in the ethnic cleansing of Poles, fought in the western regions of Galicia and Volhynia and has been part of the living memory of the local population. Those living in the West saw the UPA condemned under the Soviet regime and celebrated during the years of independence. The Center, which had no direct exposure to living memory of the UPA, has been slow to accept the relevant historical mythology as part of its own narrative.

This is one of the features of memory politics in Ukraine reflected by Map 5 (p. 220). Its shades of color show levels of support for the demolition of Lenin monuments, while its columns show varying degrees of support for the proposed official recognition of UPA soldiers as fighters for Ukrainian independence. Ternopil Oblast, the West's leader in terms of anti-Lenin sentiment, also led in acceptance of the pro-UPA narrative. Support for the recognition of UPA soldiers as fighters for Ukrainian independence increased there from 94 percent in 2013 to an overwhelming 98 percent in 2015.

Map 5 also shows, that in enthusiasm for the UPA, the Center has been catching up with the West, and the EuroMaidan produced a boost in that regard. In March 2015, more respondents were in favor of the UPA in the Khmelnytskyi region in the Center than in Volyn (Volhynia) Oblast in the West: 72 percent vs. 69 percent. Support for UPA recognition increased most dramatically in Transcarpathia, where it grew from 37 percent to 75 percent of respondents. In Kyiv Oblast the rise in support was less dramatic but increased from 47 percent to a majority of 57 percent. While support for the UPA had been negligible in the Southeast before the EuroMaidan, it grew in that region as well, especially in oblasts affected by the Russo-Ukrainian war: in Luhansk from 7 percent to 35 percent and in Kherson from 13 percent to 44 percent of respondents—still quite low in comparison to the Center.

Thus the Leninfall is best understood as the culmination of a relatively long process fueled by two parallel developments—the condemnation of communist crimes and the acceptance of a nationalist alternative to the communist historical narrative. Both developments began in the West in the 1990s and made inroads into the Center in the 2000s. The creation of a common West-Central memory space was sealed in symbolic terms by the public toppling of the Lenin statues, but it had begun to develop in the decades following Ukrainian independence and the Orange Revolution of 2004.

The maps reproduced in this collection indicate that the memory shift that brought the West and Center together also highlighted differences in historical attitudes between the Center and the Southeast. Under the influence of the EuroMaidan and, especially, the Russo-Ukrainian war, the Southeast began to move closer to the Center in condemning the crimes of the communist regime but in many ways remained outside the new common West-Central memory space. Few things better demonstrated the memory gap between the West and Center on the one hand and the Southeast on the other than the hundreds of Lenin monuments still standing in prominent public spaces in the Southeast after the triumph of the Leninfall in the Center in 2013–14. But change was coming there as well.

The Center Rules

The "Southeastern" chapter in the history of the Leninfall began in earnest in May 2015, when President Poroshenko signed the decommunization laws. Adopted by parliament in the previous month, those laws decreed the removal not only of Lenin monuments but also of all forms of commemoration of historical figures and events associated with the communist regime. One of the laws bestowed on UPA soldiers the symbolic status of fighters for Ukrainian independence.[17]

As the local authorities began to implement the new laws, they put to shame the activists of the original Leninfall, removing 1,320 monuments and statues by January 2017, more than double the number of those eliminated in 2013–14. With the Center already cleansed of most of its Lenin monuments and statues, the brunt of the new policies was borne largely by the Southeast, where support for such demolition was significantly lower than in the Center. The data from the March 2015 survey, taken only a month before parliament's adoption of the laws, highlights the differences between the two macroregions. If in Kyiv and Poltava Oblasts of the Center support for demolition was about 42 percent, in Kharkiv Oblast of the Southeast it stood at only 11 percent, not significantly lower than in Odesa, where 18 percent of respondents supported demolition. Even in Dnipropetrovsk Oblast, the center of Ukrainian mobilization at the start of the Russo-Ukrainian war in 2014, support for the removal of Lenin monuments did not exceed 23 percent.

Map 6 (p. 221) combines data on attitudes toward the demolition of Lenin monuments (shown, as on previous maps, in shades) with data on the number of monuments and plaques to communist leaders removed as a result of the decommunization laws (represented by blue columns). The map leaves little doubt that, with the curious exception of Poltava Oblast, most of the remaining monuments and plaques were demolished or removed in 2015 and 2016 in the Southeast of the country, where support for demolition had been lowest before the adoption of the laws.

Why did the parliament pass and the authorities in the Southeast accept and duly implement laws not favored by the majority of the local electorate? The main explanation lies not in the EuroMaidan, which triggered the original Leninfall, but in the outcome of Russia's aggression, which dramatically changed the political map of Ukraine. Here it is useful to return to the map of the 2010 presidential elections. According to it, the Ukrainian electorate was split down the middle, with the blue areas electing Viktor Yanukovych with approximately 49 percent of the overall vote, while the orange areas supplied the lion's share of the 46 percent of the overall vote received by Tymoshenko. Thus the voting power of the two halves of Ukraine, West and Center against Southeast and East, was approximately equal. But the annexation of the Crimea and the hybrid war in the Donbas removed the East—the Crimea and the most populous parts of Donetsk and Luhansk Oblasts—from Ukrainian political space, dramatically reducing the voting power of the "blue" areas of the country.

Electoral politics were soon translated into the politics of memory. In the October 2014 parliamentary elections, parties based mainly in the West and Center received 68 percent of the national vote, reducing the Opposition Bloc, based exclusively in the Southeast, to a mere 10 percent of the vote. Map 7 (p. 222), which shows the results of those elections, reflects the new political reality. It represents the oblasts that elected candidates of the pro-presidential bloc (dominated by local administrators, business elites, and center-right pragmatists) in red; Prime Minister Arsenii Yatseniuk's Popular Front (dominated by national liberals) in dark red; and the Opposition Bloc, led by former members of President Yanukovych's administration, in blue.[18]

In the crucial vote on the decommunization laws in April 2014, the Opposition Bloc deputies refused to support the legislation. But their support was not needed, and their opposition could be ignored, as 69 of the 82 Popular Front deputies voted in favor, as did 106 of the 146 members of Petro Poroshenko's bloc. The greater number of defections in the president's camp than in the prime minister's might be explained by the fact that, unlike in the Popular Front, many of the president's allies came from the Southeast, including the Odesa region, where support for demolition did not exceed 18 percent of those polled in March 2015. If the Leninfall in the Center was prompted from below, in the Southeast it proceeded from above.

While the population of the Southeast was not eager to get rid of Lenin, it also had no desire to fight in order to preserve him. One possible reason is that the demolition was carried out by the local authorities in a lawful and orderly manner. Another reason was that, as indicated by Map 4, which shows the change of attitudes toward the Holodomor, the Euromaidan helped move the Southeast closer to the historical narrative accepted in the Center, a tendency reinforced and solidified by the decommunization laws. The most striking decline of skepticism toward the interpretation of the Holodomor as an act of genocide was registered in Odesa Oblast, where the number of naysayers fell from 45.0 percent in March 2013 to 38.0 percent in March 2015 and then to 14.0 percent in December 2015.

The "Lenin-free space" dramatically expanded by the decommunization laws has been defined in memory terms by a growing rejection of the Soviet-era historical narrative, but there is no consensus on the narrative that should replace it. While the Southeast partakes in the national interpretation of the Holodomor with the Center and the West, it is reluctant to accept the heroization of the UPA fighters emanating from the West, which has made significant inroads in the Center. Between 2013 and 2015 there was growing recognition throughout Ukraine of the UPA soldiers as fighters for Ukrainian independence, but the numbers in the Southeast are minuscule as compared with those in the other two other macroregions (see Map 5, p. 220). If in Kyiv Oblast such recognition increased from 47 percent to 57 percent, in Odesa Oblast the increase was more modest, growing from 10 percent to 15 percent of the respondents. In Kharkiv Oblast the level of support remained at 15 percent, and in Dnipropetrovsk Oblast the number actually decreased from 28 percent to 25 percent of those polled. Decreased support was also registered in Kirovohrad Oblast in the Center.

The King Is Dead

"The king is dead, long live the king!" is a saying that can be applied only partially to the Leninfall both in the Center and in the Southeast of the country. Lenin, the king of the communist narrative, expired symbolically in the two successive waves of the

Leninfall, his monuments toppled and his plaques removed, but his vacated central position in Ukrainian public space remains contested. One potential contender for the vacancy is Stepan Bandera, who emerged after independence as one of the country's most celebrated historical figures. The most idolized figure by far is Taras Shevchenko, with 1,256 monuments and plaques. But Bandera seems to be the most celebrated political leader, with 40 monuments erected in his honor since 1990. As noted in the media, some of them reminded viewers of the Lenin monuments of the past.[19]

Is Ukraine indeed, as some argue, undergoing not only the decommunization but also the simultaneous "Banderization" of its historical memory and public spaces? Yes and no—here again, geography is the key. The Bandera cult and its reflection in the building of monuments is limited in geographic scope. As shown on Map 8 (p. 223), as of October 2016, all forty Bandera monuments were located in the West, most of them in three Galician oblasts. The Volhynia region, which was also part of the UPA theater of operations, had only two monuments in Rivne Oblast, while Volhynia Oblast had no monument at all.[20]

Map 9 (p. 224), and the data on which it is based, suggest that the situation will not change anytime soon. While there is an appetite for erecting more monuments to Bandera in Volhynia—a spike in that regard has been registered since the EuroMaidan in the "Bandera-free" Volhynia Oblast—the drive is still limited to the West, while the Center and Southeast remain largely immune to the Bandera cult. Although support for the erection of monuments to Bandera (indicated by the blue columns on the map) increased throughout Ukraine between March 2013 and March 2015, it remains as low, or even lower, than support among opponents of the Leninfall for maintaining or rebuilding monuments to Lenin—the trend shown by the red columns on the map.

The decline of public support for Lenin monuments and the rise of support for monuments to Bandera is an all-Ukrainian phenomenon, with a few exceptions such as the city of Kyiv in the Center and the Mykolaïv region in the Southeast, where rising support for Bandera monuments occurred simultaneously with rising support for Lenin monuments. While in Kyiv, in March

2015, more people wanted a monument to Bandera than to Lenin (38 percent vs. 18 percent), respondents in the Sumy, Poltava, and Kirovohrad regions in the Center still favored monuments to Lenin over those to Bandera. The Southeast produced no oblast preferring Bandera to Lenin, even though support for maintaining Lenin monuments had declined significantly between March 2013 and March 2015. In Kharkiv and Dnipropetrovsk Oblasts more respondents wanted a monument to Bandera in 2013 than in 2015, but the numbers were very low to begin with. In the case of Kharkiv, they dropped from 8 percent to 6 percent of respondents, and in Dnipropetrovsk Oblast from 9 percent to 7 percent.

When it comes to public support for monuments to Bandera, the Center finds itself in the same memory space as the Southeast, and both differ significantly from the West in that regard. The lack of enthusiasm for Bandera in the East and, partially, in the Center was confirmed by Volodymyr Viatrovych, the director of the Institute of National Memory and one of the main sponsors, promoters, and implementers of the decommunization laws. According to him, out of 51,493 streets renamed in Ukraine when the laws were implemented, only 34 received the name of Bandera. With the number of demolished Lenin monuments standing at 1,320, only 4 monuments to Bandera were erected before January 2017. While the decision to get rid of communist symbols was made by parliament in Kyiv, the question of what new names to give the now "decommunized" cities, towns, villages, and streets rested with local authorities in the Center and Southeast of Ukraine, and Bandera clearly was not among the favorites there.[21]

Neither the Center nor the Southeast is rushing to replace one toppled political leader with another. That reluctance was already apparent after the demolition of the first Lenin monument in downtown Kyiv in December 2013. Back then, Ukrainian national and nationalist banners, as well as those of the European Union, were placed on the now empty pedestal to fill the void in the symbolically important public space. Kyivans interviewed for the St. Gallen project in early February 2014, a few weeks before the start of the actual Leninfall, were opposed to replacing Lenin with a monument to another political leader.

"In my personal opinion, that space should simply be sanctified for a long time, and a little chapel should be erected there or, I don't know, a memorial to the victims of the Holodomor or of communist terror," said one respondent. "I would not place anything there for now. . . . I think there should be a public discussion about whom to place, some national hero or national genius, or an artist or writer," commented another Kyivan. Yet another respondent supported the idea of temporary installations in place of a permanent monument: "I liked the idea of one of the artists of establishing it as a kind of permanent monument. Giving an artist a month, say, to put up some kind of installation or sculpture there. It stands for a month and is then replaced by something else." A floral installation at the base of the old pedestal became a temporary solution to the Kyiv monument problem in May 2017.[22]

In September 2017, a petition was circulated about replacing the remnants of the monument with a fountain, while the top of the pedestal was decorated with the trident emblem (the centerpiece of Ukraine's coat of arms) and with Ukraine's national blue-and-yellow and nationalist red-and-black banners. Radical opponents of the new, post-Yanukovych government attached a plaque to the pedestal commemorating two participants of the EuroMaidan who were killed by the secret service and police loyal to the new government after the Revolution of Dignity. One of those commemorated was a radical leader with alleged criminal connections, the other a Buddhist guru from the Donbas. The Soviet-era inscription citing Lenin's words about a free Ukraine being possible only in union with the Russian proletariat still remained on the pedestal. With the Lenin statue gone, the pedestal had become an ideologically contested space. But the nature of the main debate had changed: it no longer concerned loyalty to Lenin or Russia but the future of the Ukrainian nation.[23]

The Center and parts of the Southeast found a different solution to the problem posed by the remaining pedestals. In the city of Chernihiv, the surviving pedestal of the Lenin monument was turned into a Ukrainian national shrine, with a poem by the early twentieth-century poet Lesia Ukrainka inscribed on it, and the trident painted in the blue-and-yellow colors of the Ukrainian national flag and augmented with the motto "Ukraine or death." The pedestal became part of a public space dedicated to the heroes of the Heavenly Hundred—victims of the police shootings on the Kyiv Maidan in February 2014—and Ukrainian soldiers who died in the war in the Donbas, officially called an anti-terrorist operation (ATO). The square where the Lenin monument had stood was renamed the Square of the Heavenly Hundred. In Poltava and in the southern city of Kherson, pedestals of Lenin monuments were also turned into shrines to the Heavenly Hundred and soldiers of the ATO.

Thus, in many cities of the Center and parts of the Southeast, Lenin monuments are being replaced not with monuments to a single historical figure but with memorials to heroes of another rising cult—defenders of democracy in the Revolution of Dignity and defenders of Ukrainian independence and territorial integrity in the war with Russia. In urban centers of the East—parts of the Donbas recaptured by the Ukrainian army, where Lenin monuments were removed mainly by Ukrainian volunteer battalions fighting in the war—attempts to turn the remaining pedestals into shrines to the heroes of the Heavenly Hundred did not take root, and supporters of the pro-Russian rebels have taken the opportunity to cover the pedestals with anti-Ukrainian slogans and graffiti. In the West, where Lenin monuments were removed in the late 1980s and early 1990s, the public spaces were reappropriated long ago, leaving little space in symbolically important city centers for memorials to the Heavenly Hundred.[24]

The Catch-Up Game

The nationalist activists of the Revolution of Dignity, who began the Leninfall in November 2013 with the removal of the Lenin monument in Kyiv, achieved their immediate goal of cleansing Ukraine of monuments that embodied the Russocentric Soviet interpretation of Ukrainian history but failed to replace them with a hero or historical narrative of their own. While the public either supported or raised no objection to the toppling of the Lenin monuments, it refused to replace him with a new demigod, indicating a level of maturity in a society that is still emerging from Soviet-era authoritarianism. But that refusal also indicates another feature of the Ukrainian situation—the lack of a historical narrative and historical figures equally acceptable to all parts of the country. This is a task that Ukraine has yet to address in a variety of ways, including the process of reimagining and re-dedicating its public spaces.

This spatial analysis of recent shifts in the historical attitudes of Ukrainian society indicates that region, in particular macrore-gion, remains a key component in the formation of the country's new political and historical identity. The Leninfall of 2013–14 had a clear regional footprint marking the shift of historical memory in central Ukraine. The toppling of Lenin monuments in the Center was the culmination of a relatively long process of re-thinking the recent and distant past, resulting in a new readiness to condemn the communist regime for its crimes, the rejection of Soviet and neo-Soviet historical narratives, and the ascription of greater value to past struggles for independence—a phenomenon reflected in the growing perception of UPA soldiers as fighters for Ukrainian sovereignty.

The toppling of Lenin monuments in the Center helped cre-ate a common memory space shared by the Center and West, where the monuments had been removed a decade or two earlier and the communist narrative replaced with a national or even a nationalist one around the same time. The creation of a common memory space was a catch-up process in which the shift of public memory matched the political shift that had occurred a decade earlier. The map of Ukrainian historical memory created by the Revolution of Dignity in 2014 finally became congruent with the political map of 2010, which reflected the political frontline that first emerged during the Orange Revolution of 2004. This inter-pretation of the origins of Ukraine's memory shift suggests the primacy of electoral politics over the politics of memory.

The revolt of the Center during the Revolution of Dignity not only altered the memory landscape of the region but also produced a major change in the politics of memory throughout the country. The combined political power of the Center and West enabled those two regions to impose their new consensus with regard to the rejection of communism on the Southeast, which was not only disoriented by the Revolution of Dignity and the ongoing hybrid war with Russia but also outnumbered in parliament because of the loss of the Crimea and the most populous parts of the Donbas. The Center thus became the law-giver in the realm of historical memory politics. It also served as a moderator and creator of a new national narrative in which the pro-independence struggle represented by the UPA fighters was promoted, while nationalism as an ideology embodied by Stepan Bandera was rejected.

The story of the Leninfall provides new insights not only into the changing memory landscape of contemporary Ukraine but also into the country's profound political shift. The political consensus achieved in parliament on the issue of decommunization by deputies representing the West and Center, as well as the political decline of the Southeast, which lost its traditional allies from the Russian-occupied eastern parts of Ukraine, herald the end of the division of Ukraine into two virtually equal parts along the line established during the Yushchenko-Yanukovych elections of 2004 and replicated in the Yanukovych-Tymoshenko presidential contest of 2010. A new majority supported by the Yushchenko and Tymoshenko electorate—a conglomerate of nationalists and liberals united by the idea of a pro-Western political course—has emerged in Ukraine and shown its ability to define the country's domestic and foreign policy. As in memory politics, so in electoral politics the role of the Center has increased both as moderator between the West and Southeast and as generator of policies capable of uniting all parts of Ukraine.

IV

EUROPEAN HORIZONS

18.

The Russian Question

The fall of the USSR exposed the confusion between the Russian (later Soviet) empire and the Russian nation prevailing throughout Russian history. In 1991, Russia abandoned the non-Slavic components of its empire but has found it difficult to part ways with the Slavic ones. Russia today has enormous difficulty in reconciling the mental maps of Russian ethnicity, culture, and identity with the political map of the Russian Federation, especially when it comes to neighboring Ukraine and Belarus.

The Russian question, understood as a set of problems facing the Russian nation during and after the disintegration of the Soviet Union, was first placed on the public agenda by Aleksandr Solzhenitsyn, Russia's best-known author of the second half of the twentieth century, in a series of essays published between 1990 and 2008. One of those works, *The Russian Question at the End of the Twentieth Century* (1994), includes a survey of Russian history from the era of Kyivan Rus´ to the first post-Soviet years. The Russian question, according to Solzhenitsyn, was really about the survival of the Russian nation. He discerned threats from various quarters, including moral decay, economic degradation, the rising influence of Western values and institutions, and the partitioning of Russia by newly created state borders. Solzhenitsyn looked back to the final decades of imperial rule as a paradise lost for the Russian Empire and the Russian nation.

Solzhenitsyn claimed that he was not an imperialist. Indeed he was not. He was a Russian nation-builder. As early as 1990, he called on the Russians to separate themselves from the non-Slavic republics, even if they wanted to stay together with Russia. Solzhenitsyn imagined the Russian nation as consisting of a Great Russian core and an East Slavic periphery including Ukrainians and Belarusians, as well as Russian-speakers residing in other republics. His ideal solution was the creation of a "Russian Union" consisting of Russia, Ukraine, Belarus, and northern Kazakhstan. As this vision of Greater Russia failed to materialize in 1991, Solzhenitsyn advocated an enhanced role for the Russian state in providing legal protection for Russians and Russian-speakers abroad, as well as the formation of Russian ethnic autonomies in parts of foreign states where Russians and Russian-speakers constituted a majority.[1]

Half Ukrainian by birth, Solzhenitsyn was especially bitter about Ukrainian independence and questioned the sovereignty of the Ukrainian state over its eastern and southern regions, where Ukrainians constituted a majority, but the dominant language on the streets was Russian. "Its burdensome error," he wrote with reference to Ukraine, "lies precisely in that inordinate expansion on territory that was never Ukraine until Lenin: the two Donets provinces and the whole southern belt of New Russia (Melitopol–Kherson–Odesa) and the Crimea. . . . That primal psychological error will produce ineluctable and deleterious effects in the inorganic union of western provinces with eastern ones, in the division into two (now three) religious branches, and in the resilience of the oppressed Russian language, which 63 percent of the population has hitherto regarded as its mother tongue. How much ineffective, useless effort will have to be expended to cover those cracks! As the proverb has it, stolen goods stick out a mile."[2]

Solzhenitsyn's words became a self-fulfilling prophecy. An ardent opponent of communism, he saw most if not all the troubles besieging the Russian nation as the result of Soviet ideology and practice. For him, progress actually meant going back to pre-Soviet times. To overcome its profound political, economic, and cultural crisis, Russia would have to return to its roots, which included the big Russian nation of imperial times, encompassing Ukrainians and Belarusians as well as Russians. The conservative utopia of Russian nation-building that Solzhenitsyn proposed to the new Russian state and society was a time bomb that went off with the outbreak of the Russo-Ukrainian conflict. Vladimir

Putin, who had repeatedly expressed his admiration for Solzhenitsyn and his writings in public, used much the same language
in trying to convince President George W. Bush at the NATO
summit of 2008 that Ukraine was "not even a state" and that most
of its territory had been "given away" by Russia. In 2014, Russia
forcibly annexed the Ukrainian Crimea with its ethnic Russian
majority and began a military confrontation in the Donbas region
of eastern Ukraine with its ethnic Ukrainian but predominantly
Russian-speaking majority.[3]

The Russo-Ukrainian conflict reprised many of the themes
that had been central to political and cultural relations in the region for the previous five centuries. These included Russia's great-
power status and influence beyond its borders; the continuing
relevance of religion, especially Orthodoxy, in defining Russian
identity and conducting Russian policy abroad; and, last but not
least, the importance of language and culture as tools of state
policy in the region. More importantly, the conflict reminded the
world that the formation of the modern Russian nation is still far
from complete. The Russian question, formulated in those terms,
still awaits solution. Will the hostilities in Ukraine open cracks in
the pan-Russian identity based on concepts rooted in the Russian
imperial era? Will it be replaced with the model of a Russian
political nation limited to the borders of the Russian Federation?
Clear answers to these questions are elusive, but a journey into
the history of the pan-Russian idea can help us explore its origins
and explain how it managed to survive for so long and why it has
proved inadequate as a foundation for a viable modern state.[4]

The Kyivan heritage has been central to Russian identity since
the rise of the Grand Duchy of Moscow as an independent state
in the mid-fifteenth century. Over the centuries, it has become
nothing short of the foundation myth of modern Russia. The
Kyivan roots of the Muscovite dynasty and church helped form
a powerful myth of origin that separated Muscovite Rus´ from
its immediate Mongol past and substantiated its claim to the
Byzantine heritage. There has been a long tradition of regarding
the Russian tsars, starting with the fifteenth-century founder of

the independent Muscovite state, Ivan III, as embodying two traditions, those of the khan and the *basileus*—the Mongol and Byzantine rulers.

What has been taken for granted in that interpretation of tsarist rule is its princely origin, which is reflected not only in the title of the Muscovite rulers. They all imagined themselves as members (later continuators) of the Kyivan ruling dynasty known today as the Rurikids, and Tsar Ivan the Terrible used the Kyivan dynastic connection with Byzantium to present himself as an heir of the Roman emperor Augustus. Even more important was another element of dynastic continuity between Kyiv and Moscow—the one that allowed the Muscovite rulers to lay claim to the patrimony of the Kyivan princes. This patrimonial right, first fully formulated in the late fifteenth century during the Muscovite subjugation of the Republic of Novgorod, was used to claim not only ethnically Russian but also Belarusian and Ukrainian territories in the sixteenth and seventeenth centuries.[5]

At the end of the eighteenth century, Catherine II, who had neither Rurikid nor Romanov blood in her veins, found no better argument to justify the partitions of Poland than to strike a medal with the inscription "I returned what was torn away," referring to the restoration of the Kyivan patrimony lost in the previous centuries. During World War I, Tsar Nicholas II celebrated the short-lived reunification of the Rus´ lands under his scepter by traveling to the city of Lviv in 1915. The theme of Moscow's gathering of the Rus´ heritage survived the collapse of the empire and was revived in Stalin's takeover of western Ukraine in the course of World War II. Moscow's struggle to reclaim the historical and territorial legacy of the lost kingdom of Kyivan Rus´ lasted half a millennium, ending only with the annexation of Transcarpathian Ukraine to the USSR in 1945. Moscow lost Transcarpathia along with other Ukrainian territories less than half a century later with the disintegration of the USSR in 1991, turning the dream of Rus´ reunification into an ever-moving target.[6]

Another important element of modern Russian culture and self-identification that goes back to Kyivan times is religion. An absolute majority of Russians associate themselves with the Orthodox Church—the brand of Christianity brought to what is now Russia from Kyiv during the medieval period. The construction of the monument to St. Volodymyr in downtown Moscow in 2018 underlines the importance of that connection not only for Russian history but also for present-day Russian self-identification. Moscow was the early winner in the age-old contest for the religious mantle of Kyiv. In the first decades of the fourteenth century, when the political center of Northeastern Rus´ was located in the town of Vladimir, the junior branch of the Rurikid princes in Moscow managed to convince the metropolitan of Rus´, who had fled Kyiv in the wake of the Mongol invasion, to settle there. Later metropolitans never left Moscow, helping the Muscovite rulers claim supremacy in the contest for power between the princes of Northeastern Rus´ and then extend their control over other Orthodox lands of the former Kyivan realm.

Beginning with the emergence of the independent Muscovite (Russian) state in the second half of the fifteenth century, the Russian Orthodox Church, with its headquarters in Moscow, helped the Russian rulers set their realm apart not only from the Muslim successors to the Mongol Empire but also from the rest of the Christian world. When the Muscovite church refused to accept metropolitans from Constantinople after Byzantium entered into an ecclesiastical union with Rome at the Council of Florence (1439), it effectively cut its ties with both Eastern and Western Christianity, turning Muscovite Orthodoxy into a purely Russian faith and institution. The division cut through the former Kyivan lands, leaving Ukraine and Belarus, which remained under Constantinople, on one side of the border and the independent Muscovite church, unrecognized by other Christians, on the other. This not very splendid isolation had a profound impact on Muscovite society and identity, which still manifests a symbiosis between Russianness and the native form of Orthodoxy.

It was only in the seventeenth century, after the creation of the Patriarchate of Moscow (1589) and the reestablishment of ties with the Orthodox East, that Muscovy managed to overcome the isolationism of its religious world view and employ Orthodoxy as a tool for the "gathering of the Rus´ lands." In the mid-seventeenth century, when Tsar Aleksei Mikhailovich took the Ukrainian Cossack state led by Bohdan Khmelnytsky under his "high hand," the decision was justified by the need to protect coreligionists—a powerful legitimizing argument in the age of the Protestant Reformation and Catholic Reform. As Muscovite and then Russian imperial armies moved west in the course of the next century and a half, the Moscow patriarchs not only blessed the troops but also presided over the forcible religious conversion of the tsars' new subjects—a development that proceeded apace after the subordination of the Kyivan metropolitanate to Moscow in the last decades of the seventeenth century. The problem was that many inhabitants of the Polish-Lithuanian Commonwealth who ended up within the Russian Empire after the partitions of Poland were Uniate Catholics who accepted the jurisdiction and dogmas of Rome.

The "return" of the Uniates to the "faith of their fathers" was a leitmotif in the activity of the Russian Orthodox Church throughout the nineteenth century: the Uniates of Belarus and Ukraine were brought under its control at the Council of Polatsk in 1839. It continued into the twentieth century, when in the last months of World War II Joseph Stalin gave his blessing to the forcible "reunification" of former Uniates, now known as Greek Catholics, in western Ukraine. The revival of the Ukrainian Greek Catholic Church in the last years of the USSR challenged the Moscow Patriarchate's control over the Eastern Christians of Ukraine, as did the rise of independent movements among the Ukrainian Orthodox, who created two autocephalous (self-ruled) churches—the Ukrainian Autocephalous Orthodox Church and the Ukrainian Orthodox Church of the Kyiv Patriarchate—in what Moscow claimed as its canonical territory. The religious unity of the former Kyivan realm under Moscow's auspices was also shattered in Belarus by the rise of the Roman Catholic and Greek Catholic churches.[7]

The European concepts of empire and nation came to Russia at the same time, during the rule of Peter I, who gained considerable success in his efforts to reform his realm along Western lines and turned the Tsardom of Muscovy into the Russian Empire. As far as Peter was concerned, the new terms "empire" and "emperor" were just Western equivalents of the old Russian terms "tsardom" and "tsar." The complete merger of the notions of empire and nation took place in Russian discourse during the eighteenth century. It was then that the marriage of empire and nation was accomplished in the minds not only of the Russian elites but also of the world at large. That was also the period in which Russian geographers moved the eastern border of Europe from the Don River (established by Strabo) to the Ural Mountains, and the Russian Empire began to be imagined as part of the European family of nations. That conception was fully developed during the long rule of Catherine II. Emulating European models but also considering themselves rivals of Europe, the Russian imperial elites began to think of their empire as a nation-state.

Among the first to promote the concept of nationhood were the tsar's recently acquired subjects in Kyiv and Ukraine, who had been exposed to European "national" thinking of earlier times. The Kyivan clerics who published the *Synopsis* (1674), the historical narrative that became the first textbook of Russian history, believed that not only Muscovy's dynasty and religion but also the idea of the Rus´ tsardom and the Rus´ nation had come to Moscow from Kyiv. Few readers of the *Synopsis* in Muscovy understood at the time what a "nation" was. Thus it was with the help of alumni of the Kyiv Mohyla Academy that the concept of the imperial nation of Rus´, including inhabitants of both Great and Little Rus´, came into existence. It became the cornerstone of the idea of Russianness that received full expression in the nineteenth century in the works of one of the founders of modern Russian literature, the Ukrainian-born Mykola Hohol (Nikolai Gogol). Imperial Russia made little meaningful distinction between the different branches of the Eastern Slavs and closely associated Russianness, broadly understood, with dynasty, state, religion, and language, all originating in Kyiv.[8]

The Russian imperial elites of the eighteenth century used the notion of dynastic, religious, and cultural commonality to build a new model of Russian imperial identity. It was pan-Russian in historical, cultural, territorial and, last but not least, ethnic terms. It included the ancestors of modern Russians, Ukrainians, and Belarusians, and from the perspective of later proponents of Russian unity it constituted a paradise lost. The first significant challenge to this conception came from an enemy defeated on the battlefield: Poland tried to regain its place on the map of

Europe by reinventing itself as a modern nation, while claiming the loyalty of the Ukrainian and Belarusian subjects of the tsars.[9]

The Poles rose in the revolt in 1830 and then in 1863. But the weapons used were not guns alone: history, education, and religion became important instruments in the struggle. Count Sergei Uvarov not only formulated a new vision of Russian identity based on autocracy, Orthodoxy, and nationality in its pan-Russian incarnation but also helped make Kyiv an outpost of Russian learning by establishing a university there in 1834. The naming of the new university after St. Volodymyr was followed by the erection of a monument to him on the slopes of the Dnieper—a new symbol of the region's Russian identity. The Russian imperial project contended with its Polish opponent for the loyalty of Ukrainians and Belarusians not only by opening Russian educational institutions but also by closing Polish ones and forcing Uniates into the Russian Orthodox Church. Backed by the vast resources of empire, pan-Russian identity appeared invincible in its progress.

But the same period witnessed the incipient fragmentation of the pan-Russian model of identity. The rise of literary Russian, best manifested in the writings of Aleksandr Pushkin, removed Church Slavonic, the language of most eighteenth-century writing, from the center of imperial cultural life, doing away with the common East Slavic literary medium of communication and cultural expression. Ukrainians began to write and publish in their vernacular, while some Polish or Polonized writers residing in Belarus began to experiment with the Belarusian idiom. The development of linguistics, along with growing interest in the common people and the rise of folklore studies, took many proponents of pan-Russian identity by surprise. It turned out that "Russians" all over the empire were using different languages and dialects and following different, if related, customs and folk traditions. First Polish and then Russian and Ukrainian authors began to voice the opinion that various "Russians" not only spoke different languages but also belonged to different ethnic groups. The academic and cultural legitimacy of the pan-Russian nation was now in question. It was only a matter of time before it would be challenged politically as well.[10]

The first to declare the pan-Russian nation obsolete were the members of the first Ukrainian political organization, the Brotherhood of SS. Cyril and Methodius, which was led by the historian Mykola Kostomarov and included Ukraine's leading poet, Taras Shevchenko. These were intellectuals mobilized by the empire to fight for the pan-Russian idea against the Polish threat. Instead of being inspired by loyalty to the empire, these Romantics imagined Ukraine as the cornerstone of a federation of Slavic nations, on a par with Russia and Poland. Although they were arrested and exiled, they did not give up on their ideas.

In the 1860s, they took advantage of the liberalization that followed the Russian defeat in the Crimean War (1853–56) to establish the journal *Osnova* (Foundation), begin the publication of Ukrainian primers, and push for the introduction of the Ukrainian language in the schools. The new Polish revolt of 1863 and the readiness of its leaders to use the Belarusian language for propaganda purposes further undermined the Russian imperial project in the western borderlands. Politics and culture came together to question not only the unity of the empire but also the validity of the pan-Russian conception of Eastern Slavdom. The authorities fought back by prohibiting publications in Ukrainian—a deliberate effort to arrest the development of an alternative to Great Russian culture and identity.

The intellectual response to the growing cracks in the pan-Russian edifice was formulated by the Russian publicist Mikhail Katkov, who placed rising Russian nationalism at the service of the empire. In the 1860s, he put together the elements of the model of imperial identity that would survive, with some modifications, until the fall of the empire in 1917. If Ukrainian activists such as Kostomarov believed that there were two Rus´ nationalities—the Northern or Great Russians, including the Belarusians as a subgroup, and the Southern Russians or Ukrainians—Katkov claimed that there were three such nationalities: Great, Little, and White, all members of a big Russian nation. Each had the right to a local dialect and folklore, but all were supposed to use one literary language and develop one higher culture—the Great Russian language and culture. The primacy of the Great Russian language, literature, and culture was often presented as a common accomplishment of all three branches of the pan-Russian nation.

This policy found its embodiment in a new round of prohibitions of the Ukrainian language in the last quarter of the nineteenth century.[11]

The Revolution of 1905 removed the prohibition on Ukrainian-language publications but also awakened radical Russian nationalism, which began mobilizing the Ukrainian and Belarusian peasantry in support of the empire and against Poles and Jews. Official support for Russian nationalist organizations helped turn the formerly Polish-ruled regions of Ukraine and Belarus into hotbeds of Russian nationalism. Ukrainian and Belarusian activists, for their part, were sidelined and marginalized in the years leading up to World War I. The outbreak of war gave one more boost to Russian nationalist patriotism, and the success of Russian arms in Galicia briefly brought two ancient centers of Kyivan Rus′, Lviv and Peremyshl (Przemyśl), under tsarist rule. One more push into what is now Ukrainian Transcarpathia was expected to complete the age-old process of gathering the Rus′ lands. But Russian defeat at the front and economic collapse at home brought the empire and its dreams to an abrupt end. By the time Nicholas II was forced to resign in March 1917, not only Lviv and Peremyshl were lost to the enemy but also a good portion of the Ukrainian and Belarusian lands acquired during the partitions of Poland.[12]

The concept of the pan-Russian nation suffered a hard landing in the revolutionary year 1917. In the course of that year, Russia ceased to be an empire and was proclaimed a republic, while Ukraine declared its autonomy as part of the Russian republic and then established its own statehood, to be associated with Russia by federal ties. The following year brought declarations of independence of the Ukrainian and Belarusian republics and their occupation by the Germans. The Bolshevik government, which fought hard to regain control of Ukraine and Belarus, was forced to make a number of political and cultural concessions, recognizing their de jure but not de facto independence and the distinctness of their languages and cultures. Traditional pan-Russian nationalism, championed by the White Movement, challenged the Bolshevik claim to power and thus was no ally of the new Bolshevik regime in St. Petersburg and then in Moscow. The revolution brought about the complete delegitimization of the pan-Russian nation, identity, and culture. Russians, Ukrainians, and Belarusians, the former branches of the pan-Russian nation, were recognized as separate peoples, formally equal in status and rights.

What to do with the three East Slavic nations and their pro forma independence not only in cultural but also in political terms was decided in the fall and winter of 1922. During his last months in power, Vladimir Lenin convinced Stalin to abandon his project of bringing the formally independent states of Ukraine and Belarus into the Russian Federation and insisted that they be recognized as republics of the Soviet Union on a par with Russia. Lenin was trying to keep Russian nationalism in check, apprehensive that it would repel not only existing Soviet republics but also potential new members in Europe and Asia. Lenin's victory over Stalin led in December 1922 to the formation of the Soviet Union, which provided the non-Russian republics with institutional foundations for the development of their cultures and identities.[13]

In all three East Slavic republics, the new national identities became closely associated with the communist experiment, which linked them together. If for Russia communist rule meant the loss of people and territory, for Ukraine and Belarus it brought along an anti-colonial momentum linking the ideas of social and national liberation. In search of political support during his struggle for power in Moscow, Stalin made an alliance with the national communists in Ukraine, Belarus and other republics, allowing the anti-colonial momentum to last until the end of the 1920s. The active phase of Ukrainization and Belarusization, which brought affirmative action promoting local cadres, languages, and cultures, ended with criminal prosecutions and trials of the champions of those policies. The Ukrainian Famine of 1932–33, in which close to four million people died, was an assault not only on the village, which refused to be collectivized, but also on the non-Russian political and cultural cadres that had promoted national identity beyond the limits of Moscow's tolerance.[14]

Russian national identity was dominant on the all-Union scene by the 1930s. Stalin's increasingly secure monopoly of power allowed him to dispense with support from the elites of the Union republics. The industrialization drive made it necessary to centralize economic planning and production, which proceeded in tandem with the growing prominence of Russian as the lingua franca of the Soviet Union. The Bolshevik leadership, which was preparing the country for the coming war, regarded non-Russian cultural nationalism as a threat to unity. The authorities would increasingly treat Russian nationalism as their best hope for survival in the coming conflict: they were eager to stop discrimination against Russian culture in the non-Russian republics and use it as an instrument of mass mobilization in support of the regime. Hitler's accession to power in 1933 and the signing of the Anti-Comintern Pact by Germany and Japan in 1936 were milestones in Stalin's efforts to promote Russian nationalism in the USSR. Russia was dominant again, although the pan-Russian garb of the imperial era was gone, and the Russian Federation was portrayed as prima inter pares. To play down the extent of Russian control, limited support was given to other cultures—a policy that became known as the Friendship of Peoples.[15]

World War II brought some adjustments but no substantial change to the growing alliance between Russian nationalism and the political leadership of the Union that began in the 1930s. The partial rehabilitation of Ukrainian and Belarusian nationalism at the beginning of the war was used by the Kremlin to legitimize the invasion of Poland and the seizure of its eastern, largely Ukrainian and Belarusian territories assigned to Stalin by the Molotov-Ribbentrop Pact of 1939. Hitler's invasion of the USSR in the summer of 1941 pushed Russian nationalist propaganda into high gear. All three East Slavic nationalisms were promoted by the regime in the first and most difficult years of the German-Soviet War, which Soviet propaganda called the Great Patriotic War of the Soviet People.

But after the victories at Stalingrad and then Kursk in 1943, the party leadership took a more cautious approach toward the promotion of non-Russian nationalism—a policy that it ended completely in 1945. What followed was a crackdown on the more liberal elements in the Russian cultural establishment, the leaders of the Jewish movement, and the champions of Ukrainian and Belarusian culture. Also under attack were cultural figures in other Soviet republics. By the time of Stalin's death in 1953, Russian nationalism was dominant again, as was the Russian Orthodox Church, and an anti-Semitic campaign, disguised as a struggle against "rootless cosmopolitanism," was under way.[16]

The non-Russian cultures revived somewhat in the late 1950s with the de-Stalinization campaign and the liberalization of Soviet political and cultural life initiated by Nikita Khrushchev. But Khrushchev also launched a utopian project of constructing communism, along with the formation of a new Soviet man and the forging of a new historical entity, the Soviet people. This was in keeping with inherited dogma about the disappearance of nationalities at the communist stage of human development. The only cultural foundation for such a merger was the Russian language and Russian culture. Khrushchev's successor, Leonid Brezhnev, abandoned the utopian idea of building communism but promoted linguistic and cultural Russification under the slogan of the formation of the Soviet people. It gathered speed in the 1970s and came to an end only in the late 1980s, having produced lasting effects in the East Slavic core of the Soviet Union. While Russification efforts encountered serious resistance in the Baltics, the Caucasus, and Central Asia, they bore fruit in Ukraine, and especially in Belarus, where the Belarusian language was pushed out not only from the streets of the big cities but also from the offices and corridors of educational and cultural institutions.[17]

The goal of creating a pan-Slavic nation was much closer to realization on the eve of the fall of the USSR than it had been on the eve of World War I and the fall of the Russian Empire. While Ukrainians and Belarusians were recognized as distinct peoples, the level of their cultural Russification, which increased with urbanization and the movement of village dwellers to the Russian-speaking cities, the Russification of the educational system, especially at the university level, and the growth of mass media, was much higher than it had been seventy years earlier. The fall of the Soviet Union resulted from political rather than ethnocultural mobilization, which crossed linguistic and cultural lines, particularly in Ukraine. But the fall of the USSR promoted the development of distinct political and cultural identities in each of the new East Slavic states.[18]

Russia was ready to shake off the economic burden of the non-Slavic empire, but the disintegration of the Slavic core caught its leadership by surprise. The shock caused by the loss of empire was compounded by the challenge of building a new political nation on territory carved out of a much larger linguistic and cultural space considered to be Russian. Modern Russian identity is probably best imagined as a set of *matrëshka* nesting dolls. At the core is the doll of Russian ethnic identity, followed by the doll of Russian citizenship, which includes not only ethnic Russians, then by the doll of East Slavic identity and, largest of all, the doll of participants in Russian culture—the Russian-speakers of the world.

When it comes to official policy, initially the civic model of the Russian nation emerged victorious over the project of restoring the Soviet empire or Solzhenitsyn's vision of a big Russian nation. But failure to maintain control of the post-Soviet space either through the Commonwealth of Independent States or through the more flexible project of forming a Russian "liberal empire" provoked the new Russian leadership to revive the pan-Russian nation as a means of restoring Russia's great-power status and mobilizing support for its foreign-policy ventures in the "near abroad." As in Eastern Europe after World War II, Moscow lacked the resources to build a liberal empire in open competition with the West. Thus it turned to imperial symbols and concepts of the pre-1917 era, using them as instruments of soft and then hard power in the region.[19]

The Russo-Ukrainian conflict has been characterized on the Russian side by a return to outdated ways of thinking about nations and their relation to language and culture, coupled with a nineteenth-century model of great-power behavior in the international arena. Paradoxically, that conflict was initiated at a time when nostalgia for former unity was in decline both in Russia and in other post-Soviet states. While the Russian government was quite successful in mobilizing support among the largely ethnic Russian population of the Crimea, the outcome of Russian propaganda in the Russian-speaking but for the most part ethnically

Ukrainian regions of eastern and southern Ukraine was mixed at best.

The pan-Russian idea was brought to Ukraine by armed militias along with authoritarian rule and the concept of a nation monolithic in ethnicity, language, and religion—a proposition that was always a hard sell in the historically multiethnic and multicultural borderlands of Eastern Europe. Thus, Russia succeeded in annexing or destabilizing areas where the majority or plurality of inhabitants considered themselves ethnic Russians but failed in culturally Russian areas where most of the population associated itself ethnically and politically with Ukraine.[20]

The Russian question, formulated as a set of issues involving historical and modern Russian identity, is far from resolved. Lack of clarity in defining Russian nationality and the country's cultural and territorial boundaries helped turn the virtual identity conflict between the Russian and Ukrainian nation-building projects into a shooting war. It pitched the nineteenth-century model of a language-based nation against the modern model of a political nation united by values. The long-term outcome of the conflict and its impact on nation-building in the region are still unclear, but, contrary to the wishes of its authors, it accelerated the disintegration of one big Russian-dominated cultural space and promoted the development of separate identities on the ruins of the pan-Russian projects of the past. The solution to the Russian question lies not in territorial expansion but in the formation of a law-based democratic society capable of living in harmony with its neighbors and playing a positive role in the modern world.

19.

The Quest for Europe

As the Orange Revolution of 2004 confirmed Ukraine's democratic credentials and focused world attention on it, Ukraine's democratically elected leaders launched a peaceful "offensive" in Brussels and other European capitals, trying to put their country on a fast track to membership in the European Union (EU). But the "old Europe," dragged into talks on the resolution of the Ukrainian crisis in late 2004 by the countries of the "new Europe," was more than reluctant to send encouraging signals to Kyiv. In fact, the Brussels bureaucrats were trying to discourage the newly elected Ukrainian president, Viktor Yushchenko, and his team from submitting an application for Ukraine's membership in the EU.

In May 2005, Ukraine's representative to the EU made the following comment on the EU's recent attempts to stop Ukraine from applying for membership: "We consider that the decision to apply for EU membership is the sovereign right of any European state that 'respects principles of freedom, democracy, human rights, fundamental freedoms and rule of law.' Notably, it is envisaged by Article 49 of the EU Treaty."[1] Indeed, the EU has no right to ignore an application from a "European state." But is Ukraine a European state? The Brussels bureaucrats had some doubts in that regard. Emma Udwin, the spokeswoman for EU External Relations Commissioner Benita Ferrero-Waldner, noted in January 2005 with regard to Ukraine's prospects of membership that "implicitly, there will first have to be a discussion of whether a country is European," implying that Ukraine's self-identification as a European state was far from universally accepted. "The bloc," wrote a Radio Free Europe/Radio Liberty correspondent reporting on Udwin's comments, "has yet to decide where the borders of Europe lie."[2]

The importance and urgency of that task can hardly be exaggerated, given that in December 2004 the EU invited Turkey to begin membership talks, and by mid-2005 voters in a number of West European countries, most notably France, had defeated the draft EU constitution, which was explained as a protest against future EU enlargement. While the general mood in Western and Central Europe opposed eastward expansion of the Union and favored strengthening its eastern borders, the countries of Eastern Europe, many of which had just joined the EU, were in favor of continuing enlargement of the most prestigious European organization. Arguments in favor of the latter option were best articulated in November 2006 by the EU's enlargement commissioner, Olli Rehn. In his report on the future of the EU, Rehn opposed attempts to define the borders of Europe and called instead for thinking about Europe's frontiers—a concept that suggests both challenge and opportunity. To strengthen his case, Rehn quoted the historian Eric Hobsbawm, who once stated: "Geographically, as everyone knows, Europe has no eastern borders and the continent therefore exists exclusively as an intellectual construct."[3]

Indeed, Europe is actually a peninsula with a very broad eastern frontier. It is not easy to draw the line separating Europe from Asia, even where the two continents are divided by water. After all, according to Greek legends, the princess Europa, who gave her name to the peninsula, was forcibly taken to the future "European" Crete from Phoenicia (in present-day Lebanon). At least Crete is divided from the mainland by a substantial body of water, but there is nothing comparable to the Mediterranean Sea between Lisbon and Vladivostok, or, for that matter, Singapore. Where one draws the line dividing the Eurasian land mass depends on one's notion of where Europe ends; hence the geographic puzzle facing opponents of the eastward enlargement of the European Union. Perhaps they would prefer to deal with the concept of Christendom, which was replaced by the secular idea of Europe around the turn of the eighteenth century. By that criterion, Turkey would readily be denied membership on the basis of its Muslim religion and culture. It might even be possible to draw a line dividing Western and Eastern Christendom, thereby excluding not only Romania and Bulgaria, which joined the extended EU on 1 January 2007, but even the Greek homeland of the European idea.

But that approach would not work with Ukraine, which Samuel Huntington defined in his bestselling study of modern civilizations as a "cleft" country divided between the Orthodox East and the European West. Back in the 1990s, Huntington seriously considered a scenario of Ukraine's disintegration along the East-West civilizational line. Ukraine survived the post-Soviet chaos of the 1990s and managed to turn its weakness into a strength, emerging as one of the most democratic and tolerant societies of the post-communist world. The name "Ukraine" means "borderland," reflecting not only the country's position on the civilizational divide but also its historical capacity to serve as a contact zone between Eastern and Western Christianity, Judaism and Islam. For centuries, Ukraine was also divided between the Russian Empire and its Central and East European rivals, the Polish-Lithuanian Commonwealth and the Ottoman and Habsburg Empires. Each of those powers promoted and advanced its own religious and civilizational project.

The history of Ukraine as a borderland reflects the long struggle of its inhabitants to transcend political boundaries and forge an identity that would distinguish them from their immediate neighbors to the east, west, and south. First Western Christianity and later the secular cultures of Europe served as important "others" against whom the Ukrainians defined themselves and their country as part of Orthodox-Byzantine civilization. Even more significant for the present discussion is that these Western cultural influences were among the major factors that helped define Ukraine's identity: through long association with them, the Ukrainians came to see themselves as part of the West, distinct from their Orthodox neighbors to the east.

How does this age-old tradition of complex and often contradictory relations with the Christian and European West influence Ukraine's present-day identity, and how does it affect the attitude of Ukraine's political and cultural elites toward the European project of the last fifty years? This essay puts the efforts of the Ukrainian leadership to join the EU into broader historical and cultural perspective, sketching the development of Ukraine's European idea from the early eighteenth century to the first decade of the third millennium. It argues that Ukraine's current quest for EU membership has important cultural and national dimensions, apart from diplomatic, political, and economic ones. There is a long and well-established intellectual tradition of defining Ukraine through its close association with Europe, its culture and values.

Ukraine's past and present quest for inclusion in Europe cannot be properly understood without taking into account the other pole of Ukrainian cultural identity, that of Russia. Russia's dominant role in the region has been and continues to be regarded as a potential threat to the survival of the Ukrainian language, literature, culture, and identity. This encourages Ukrainian elites to think of Europe not only as a political and economic but also a cultural counterweight to their powerful eastern neighbor. Judging by the title of a book published in 2003 by the then president of Ukraine, Leonid Kuchma—*Ukraine Is Not Russia*—today's Ukraine is at pains to define itself vis-à-vis its northern neighbor, and the importance of Europe's role in that process can hardly be exaggerated.

From very early on, the lands of present-day Ukraine were considered part of Europe. Medieval and early modern geographers, following their Greek and Roman predecessors, drew the eastern boundary of Europe along the Tanais River—that is, the Don, which "flows quietly" through the modern Russo-Ukrainian borderland. The eighteenth-century Russian historian Vasilii Tatishchev drew the line even farther to the east, along the Ural Mountains, which he saw as marking the division between Russia proper and its Asian colonies, including Siberia. The mountains were, of course, no match for an ocean, and Russia failed to become a "normal" European state with a clear distinction between the mother country and its colonies. But the notion that Europe ended at the Ural Mountains was accepted by eighteenth-century Europeans. Russia was a major actor on the European stage and thus a European state, at least in the eyes of the German-born empress Catherine II, the French encyclopedists with whom she corresponded and, indeed, the educated European elite in general.

Throughout the eighteenth century, there were probably no more enthusiastic promoters of the European identity and calling of the Russian Empire than the alumni of the Kyiv Mohyla Academy in what is now Ukraine. Educated in Kyiv and in European universities such as those of Rome, Göttingen, and Königsberg, Ukrainians in the Russian service, from Feofan Prokopovych to Oleksandr Bezborodko and Viktor Kochubei, were in the forefront of the Europeanization of the Russian psyche. But what about their native Ukraine? By the mid-nineteenth century, which saw the first stirrings of the Ukrainian national "awakening," Ukraine was considered a cultural backwater of the Russian Empire. Its role as a bridge between Europe and Russia, played so successfully in the seventeenth and eighteenth centuries, was relegated to the past. The capital city of St. Petersburg, which Ukrainians had helped build and populate with bureaucrats and intellectuals, including such luminaries of Russian literature as Mykola Hohol (Nikolai Gogol), had supplanted Ukraine as Russia's window on Europe. Since then, Ukraine's attitude to Europe has largely been determined by its attitude to Russia—still the two poles of Ukrainian collective identity and self-image.

For most of the nineteenth century, European influences were channeled to Ukraine through Russia. This allowed Russians intellectuals such as Vissarion Belinsky to read their own cultural situation back into the early modern era and claim that the Pereiaslav Agreement of 1654, which placed Cossack Ukraine under a Muscovite protectorate, had opened the doors of European civilization to Ukraine—a statement repeated in many Soviet-era museum exhibits in Ukraine. The fact that it had been the other way around did not bother Belinsky, who denied Ukrainians the right to develop their own literature, or his twentieth-century Russian and Ukrainian admirers. In the 1830s, Hohol (Gogol) still thought of Ukraine in the all-European context, considering the history of the Cossacks more interesting than that of any of the independent nations of Europe. But his Russian contemporaries had serious doubts in that regard. To be fair, they were not sure of their own identity either, with Slavophiles fighting Westernizers and vice versa. Until the arrest in 1847 of the members of the clandestine Brotherhood of SS. Cyril and Methodius, the first Ukrainian national organization, the Slavophiles seemed favorably disposed to Ukraine and its cultural strivings. Not so the Westernizers.

Vissarion Belinsky opposed the development of a separate Ukrainian literature on the grounds that it was not European, as was, in his opinion, Russian literature, whose finest poetic achievements were the result of Russia's historical proximity to Europe and the assimilation of European elements into Russian culture. According to Belinsky, Ukrainian literature could develop only if the Ukrainian elites eliminated European elements from their culture, leaving the "non-European" Ukrainian element at its core. He wrote in that regard:

> As far as the Little Russians are concerned, it is laughable even to think that anything could now develop out of their folk poetry, which, by the way, is wonderful: not only can nothing develop from it, but it has stood still ever since the days of Peter the Great; one could set it in motion only if the best, noblest sector of the Little Russian population gave up the French quadrille and began dancing the *trepak* and *hopak* once again, exchanged the tailcoat and frock coat for the jerkin and the homespun mantle, shaved its head and let down its topknot—in a word, reverted from a condition of civilization, education, and humanity (the acquisition of which Little Russia owes to its union with Russia) to its former barbarism and ignorance. . . .[4]

Thus, in the eyes of the Russian Westernizers, Russia was Europe and Ukraine was not, and the development of a distinct Ukrainian culture was a step away from Europe and the associated ideals of progress and liberty. Indeed, Belinsky and the nineteenth-century Russian Westernizers could be considered the forefathers of the concept promoted until recently by the pro-Russian lobby in Ukraine and epitomized in the slogan "To Europe together with Russia." If Belinsky wanted to halt the development of a distinct Ukrainian poetry, literature, and culture, the proponents of this slogan wanted Ukraine to follow in the wake of Russian foreign policy—a course that could easily lead to curtailing the revival of the Ukrainian language, literature, and culture and threaten the development of a distinct Ukrainian identity.

On the Ukrainian side, the most prominent nineteenth-century thinker to turn the tables on Russian intellectuals in the debate on the European character of Russia and Ukraine was Mykhailo Drahomanov. In his article "The Lost Epoch: Ukrainians under the Muscovite Tsardom, 1654–1876," he took issue with Russian claims that Muscovite rule over Ukraine was responsible for abolishing the old "disastrous" Cossack way of life and introducing new European mores. The Muscovite tsars, he argued, did not introduce European methods of government but absolutism and arbitrary bureaucratic rule. Discussing the Pereiaslav Agreement and the conditions negotiated by the tsar and the Cossack officers in the spring of 1654, Drahomanov wrote: "When we compare the rights which were guaranteed to the Ukrainian Cossacks with the despotism that existed in the Muscovite tsardom, there is no doubt that the Cossack constitution had more in common with the free European constitutional governments of today than the Muscovite tsardom had, or than even the present Russian Empire has."[5]

In Drahomanov's view, Europe stood for the rights of man and Russia for absolutism and arbitrary government without the consent of the governed. He believed that Bohdan Khmelnytsky's revolt against Poland in 1648 was consonant with the ideas of freedom that were then developing in Europe. According to Drahomanov, Ukraine had good prospects of developing its own freedoms and liberties from the modest beginnings apparent in the Europe of that day. Those prospects were cut off by Muscovy, which was responsible for Ukraine's "lost epoch" of more than two hundred years—centuries in which Ukraine could have joined Europe on its path to freedom. "No wonder," wrote Drahomanov, "that, during the years when Ukraine was united to Muscovy, with its autocratic tsar and legal serfdom and non-existent education, Russian despotism gradually brought about the destruction of Ukraine's freedom. . . . A wall of tsarist and bureaucratic despotism was erected to prevent the free political ideas then current in Europe, which Ukraine had always welcomed, from penetrating."[6] For Drahomanov, Europe equaled freedom, and on that scale freedom-loving Ukraine was Europe (or close to it historically and mentally), while Russia was not. In fact, it was preventing Ukraine from becoming part of Europe. But if Russia was not Europe, what was it?

Ukrainian thinkers and historians of the second half of the nineteenth century were in no doubt about what Russia represented. In their eyes, Russia, with its authoritarianism and lack of respect for collective and individual freedoms, stood for Asia, with all the negative connotations characteristic of the nineteenth- and early twentieth-century discourse of Orientalism. Drahomanov's former colleague at Kyiv University and founder of modern Ukrainian historiography, Volodymyr Antonovych, shared the ideas of Polish historians, who often denied the European character of Russia. No less critical of Russia's "Asianism" was Antonovych's student Mykhailo Hrushevsky, the creator of the national narrative of Ukrainian history and the first head of the independent Ukrainian state in 1918. Hrushevsky believed that, when it came to national culture and character, Ukrainians were much closer to Europe than Russians.

Not unlike their European neighbors, Ukrainians had respect for personal dignity and established forms of life, while Russians, in his opinion, lacked those "European" characteristics and idealized some questionable characteristics of their own culture. Among the latter, Hrushevsky listed "lack of human dignity in oneself and disrespect for the dignity of others; lack of taste for a good, comfortable, well-ordered life for oneself and disrespect for the interests and needs of others in such a life and the achievements of others in that sphere; lack of will to establish an organized social and political life; a disposition to anarchism and even social and cultural destructiveness."[7] In an essay on "Our European Orientation" (1918), Hrushevsky underlined those elements of Ukrainian history that linked it with Western and Central Europe, establishing Ukraine's "European" credentials and stressing the differences between its historical development and that of Russia.

After the defeat of the Ukrainian Revolution, Hrushevsky, not unlike Drahomanov before him, saw the future of Ukraine in a European federation of democratic states. After his return to Ukraine in 1924, Hrushevsky fought vigorously against the channeling of European cultural achievements to Ukraine through Moscow. He protested Moscow's attempts to limit translations from European languages into the languages of the Soviet nationalities, reserving for Russian literature the role of "window on Europe" for the non-Russian literatures and cultures. Hrushevsky insisted on direct access to European scholarship and culture for the Ukrainian academic and cultural elites. These efforts of Hrushevsky's echoed the struggle against Russocentrism and for a European orientation waged inside Ukraine's communist establishment by the writer and publicist Mykola Khvyliovy. According to the Soviet constitution, the Soviet Union was not Russia writ large but a union of independent republics, and Khvyliovy and his colleagues insisted on treating it that way. They refused to orient their culture toward Russia and insisted on access to West European culture and literature, denying Moscow the role of intermediary in that intercultural dialogue.

Writing in 1926, Khvyliovy asked his readers a rhetorical question: "Is Russia an independent state?" and answered it: "It is! Well, in that case we, too, are independent." "By which of the world literatures should we set our course?" he continued his argument.

> On no account by the Russian. That is definite and unconditional. Our political union must not be confused with literature. . . . The point is that Russian literature has weighed down upon us for centuries as master of the situation, as a literature that has conditioned our psyche to play the slavish imitator. And so, to nourish our young art on it would be to impede its development. The proletariat's ideas did not reach us through Muscovite art; on the contrary, we, as representatives of a young nation, can better apprehend these ideas, better cast them in the appropriate images. Our orientation is to Western European art, its style, its techniques.[8]

As is apparent from the quoted excerpt, Khvyliovy justified his advocacy of the dramatic turn of Ukrainian culture from Russia to Europe with reference to the two dominant Soviet discourses of the time. The first was the idea of proletarian revolution, the second that of the national-liberation struggle of "young" nations against "old" imperial ones. In that context, Europe figured as the homeland of the proletariat, while young Ukraine was better equipped to understand proletarian culture than "old" Russia. Thus Ukraine's quest for Europe was cast in Marxist and revolutionary terms.

The Russian response to Khvyliovy's argument was formulated by none other than Joseph Stalin, once a promising Georgian poet and later a ruthless Soviet dictator, who easily defeated the Ukrainian Marxist writer at the game of Bolshevik dialectics. In his letter of April 1926 to the Ukrainian Politburo dealing with nationalist deviations in the Communist Party of Ukraine, Stalin specifically attacked Khvyliovy and his writings. He wrote that, in calling for the reorientation of Ukrainian culture from Russia to the West, Khvyliovy was in fact turning his back on the homeland of the first proletarian revolution and allying himself with the bourgeois West. Stalin's line of argument, which ignored Khvyliovy's national-liberation paradigm and turned his class-based argument upside down, was adopted by party officials in Ukraine. One of them, People's Commissar of Education Oleksandr Shumsky, who was accused of leniency toward Khvyliovy, later attacked him, making full use of Stalin's insistence on an orientation toward Moscow not as the capital of Russia but as the capital of the international workers' movement. Shumsky argued that "Red Moscow has also been created by the will, effort and blood of Ukrainian workers and peasants. Moscow is the capital of our Union. Moscow is the center and brain of the proletarian cause throughout the world. This is our Moscow."[9]

Stalin's argument won the day and determined the fate of Ukraine's European discourse for generations to come. Khvyliovy shot himself in 1933 to avoid arrest. Hrushevsky was exiled to Moscow, the capital of the world revolution, and died in Russia under suspicious circumstances in 1934. Khvyliovy's reluctant critic, Oleksandr Shumsky, was assassinated on Stalin's orders in 1946. The Second World War and especially the subsequent Cold War promoted the notion of a hostile bourgeois Western Europe in official Soviet discourse. That discourse presented Ukrainian national aspirations as manifestations of Ukrainian bourgeois nationalism, while proponents of Ukrainian national culture were portrayed as stooges of the capitalist West.

From the 1930s on, Soviet Ukraine was effectively cut off from the West, while anything resembling a European identity of Ukrainian elites or a European orientation of Ukrainian culture was not only discredited in the state-controlled public discourse but also suppressed and persecuted in the institutions associated with Ukraine's European orientation. That was the case with the Ukrainian Greek Catholic Church, which was dissolved and "reunited" with the Russian Orthodox Church in 1946 in order to break its link with Rome. Still, there were limits to what the Soviet totalitarian state could control, especially with regard to processes going on beyond its borders. Between the two world wars, significant parts of Ukraine remained outside Soviet control. Galicia and Volhynia constituted parts of the Polish state, while Bukovyna was part of Romania and Transcarpathia of Czechoslovakia.

Those countries and their Ukrainian lands became known in world politics of the time as Eastern Europe—a term applied to the newly independent European states from the Balkans in the south to the Baltics in the north and from the borders of Germany in the west to those of the Soviet Union in the east. "Eastern Europe" replaced the First World War-era term *Mitteleuropa*, coined by the German strategist Friedrich Naumann to denote the lands "between Germany and Russia" that he expected to constitute the German sphere of influence after the war. Contrary to his expectations, the war resulted in the complete or partial disintegration of the empires that controlled those territories, creating a new zone in Europe that needed a new identity and a new name.

Among those who promoted the concept of Eastern Europe, while stressing wherever possible the new region's connections with Western Europe, was the Polish historian Oskar Halecki. He and other Polish authors advocated the inclusion in East European geographic space not only of Poland but also of Belarus and Ukraine. This was partly a response to the geopolitical reality of the time, as western Ukraine and western Belarus constituted parts of the interwar Polish state. It was also a tribute to the long-standing Polish historiographic tradition of referring to Poland in its pre-1772 borders when discussing it as a historical entity. Back then, before the first partition of Poland, which wiped the Polish-Lithuanian Commonwealth off the political map of Europe, that state had included all the Belarusian territories and all of Ukraine west of the Dnieper.

Ukrainian cultural elites in interwar Galicia also considered their land part of Europe, not because it had been ruled for centuries by Poland but because, for almost a century and a half, it had been part of the Habsburg Monarchy and, later, Austria-Hungary—a multiethnic conglomerate that extended from Brussels in the west to Venice in the south and Lviv in the east. In fact, some Ukrainian literary figures of the period believed that the interwar Polish state had cut them off from the continent and therefore promoted the slogan "back to Europe." Political commentators and historians, however, were less convinced of the exclusively European character of their nation. In the 1920s, opposing the general trend among social scientists and historians of the region to regard their newborn countries as part of a historical and cultural space between the Eurasian East and the European West, the Ukrainian geographer Stepan Rudnytsky and the historians Stepan Tomashivsky and Viacheslav Lypynsky began to treat Ukrainian history and culture as products of the country's situation at the crossroads between East and West.

Not unlike Polish and Romanian intellectuals, the Ukrainian authors emphasized the Western (European) influences on their national culture. In so doing, they not only followed in the footsteps of their Central European colleagues but also countered opposing claims from the Russian Eurasianists and Pan-Slavists. The interwar tradition of applying the East-West paradigm to the interpretation of Ukrainian history and culture was continued in North America in the second half of the twentieth century by such scholars as Ivan L. Rudnytsky, Omeljan Pritsak, and Ihor Ševčenko.

The Second World War brought about substantial changes in the political geography of Europe. Not only did the former Polish possessions of Galicia and Volhynia become parts of the

Ukrainian Soviet Socialist Republic, but the formerly Czechoslovak Transcarpathia was annexed to it as well, along with other Ukrainian lands. All of Eastern Europe ended up in the Soviet sphere of influence, including Germany's eastern lands, adding to the *Mitteleuropa* once conceived by German strategists not only the lands between Germany and Russia but part of Germany itself. The response of the East European intellectuals who emigrated to the West after the war was to stress even more the historical and cultural links of their region with the countries of Western Europe.

In 1950, Oskar Halecki, who immigrated to the United States, published a book entitled *The Limits and Divisions of European History*. There he developed some of his earlier ideas on the history of Eastern Europe and suggested a new name, East-Central Europe, which stressed the region's close relation to the West. Halecki divided Europe into three parts: western, central, and eastern. He further divided Central Europe into West-Central and East-Central segments. The former term was used to denote Poland, Hungary, and Czechoslovakia, known during the interwar period as Eastern Europe. As had been the practice before the war, Poland was treated not within its new political borders but within its historical ones, including some if not all of the Ukrainian and Belarusian territories, which were considered to be part of East-Central Europe.

The term "West-Central Europe" has never gained acceptance in scholarly and political discourse, but "East-Central Europe" has become current in scholarship, if not in politics. While politicians and the media continued to speak and write about the countries of the Soviet bloc as parts of Eastern Europe, academics proved more willing to adopt the new name for the region. It was promoted mainly by historians of Poland, including Halecki himself, Piotr Wandycz, and others. The University of Washington Press published a multivolume series on the history of East-Central Europe, and a number of chairs in history departments of North American universities have dealt with the history of East-Central Europe. The term made its way into political discourse in the countries of the region, especially Poland, after the velvet revolutions of 1989.

In the academic sphere, the strongest promoter of the concept has been the Institute of East-Central Europe in Lublin, led by Professor Jerzy Kłoczowski. Over the last fifteen years the institute has held scores of conferences and published dozens of volumes dealing with the history of the region. For Polish political and academic elites, the concept helped keep alive the long tradition of treating Poland and its former Commonwealth territories of Lithuania, Belarus, and Ukraine as parts of one region. There is certainly a connection between the role that Poland plays today in promoting Ukrainian interests in the West, including its bid for membership in the EU, and the perception of its role as a leader in the lands that once constituted the Polish-Lithuanian Commonwealth and now, in Polish eyes at least, make up part of East-Central Europe.

In Ukraine, the idea of East-Central Europe found support among historians first and foremost. The early 1990s saw the establishment of a Society of Historians of East-Central Europe chaired by Professor Natalia Yakovenko, and in 2001 a *History of East-Central Europe* was published in Lviv under the editorship of Leonid Zashkilniak. Historians and literary scholars were among the few Ukrainian intellectuals who pointed out European elements of Ukrainian culture long before the dissolution of the USSR. Research on early modern Ukrainian culture and the multilingual (Ukrainian, Polish, and Latin) literature of the period could hardly avoid stressing the differences between Ukrainian and Russian culture and the closeness of the former to European literary and cultural trends. But that argument was never fully articulated in the USSR, given prevailing circumstances, nor did it make a major impact on Ukrainian political thought of the period. Soviet censorship bears only part of the responsibility for that situation.

Given the division of Europe, the rise of the United States to prominence in international affairs, and the creation of the United Nations, the postwar period was often characterized by a discourse in which the concept of Europe as Russia's traditional "other" was replaced by a notion of the West that included not only Western Europe and North America but also such a remote and southeastern part of Western civilization as Australia. The Ukrainian dissidents of the last decades of the USSR's existence oriented themselves not on specifically European values but on universal values and human rights promoted by Western countries. One of them, the literary scholar and publicist Ivan Dziuba, writing in the 1960s, decried the lack of translations of world literature into Ukrainian. Protesting suggestions that Ukrainians "could reach the world's intellectual life through the medium of Russian culture rather than directly," Dziuba followed in the footsteps of Hrushevsky and Khvyliovy, the difference being that it was not just Europe but the whole world from which Ukraine was cut off by Russia. The signing of the Helsinki Final Act on Security and Cooperation in Europe (1975) gave international legitimacy to the dissident movement in the USSR and the countries of the communist bloc, but, when it comes to Ukrainian political and cultural thought of the period, Europe as such remained part of the broader category of the American-led West.

After the dissolution of the USSR, independent Ukraine found itself at the crossroads of different cultural and political trends. Should the new Ukrainian nation go west and try to join the EU, play a more active role in the Commonwealth of Independent States, or become a major actor in the region that Polish intellectual and political elites called East-Central Europe? Or should it, perhaps, seek to lead the group of former Soviet countries of the Black Sea region? Ukraine under President Leonid Kuchma eventually adopted the model of a multivector foreign policy. Finding no welcome in the West, given their corrupt political and economic practices, and not wanting too close an association with Russia and its much more powerful oil tycoons, the Ukrainian political elites were also restrained by the conflicting political and cultural sympathies of the Ukrainian population—pro-European in western Ukraine and pro-Russian in the eastern parts of the country. As a result, Ukrainian foreign policy lacked a clear orientation for most of the 1990s and early 2000s, unless one can consider as such repeated attempts to play Russia off against the West and vice versa in order to achieve tactical goals.

The first years of the new millennium showed quite clearly that Ukraine's intellectual elites and some of its political leaders were growing weary of the ineffectiveness of the Kuchma regime. Its balancing act between East and West not only in terms of foreign policy but also with regard to political, economic, and social development was leaving the newly independent nation further and further behind its western neighbors, who had reformed their political and economic systems in preparation for joining the EU. Disappointment was especially pronounced in western Ukraine, where it found expression in a revival of the cult of the "grandmotherly" Austria-Hungary, which had ruled the region prior to 1918, and in a particular kind of Galician cultural isolationism. Some of the region's most prominent intellectuals were prepared to toy with the idea of Galicia's leaving Ukraine and "returning" to Europe.

More a dream than a plan, and more a cultural than a political project, those ideas found their reflection and inspiration in the writings of Ukraine's most popular novelist, Yurii Andrukhovych. Frustrated with the corruption and ineptitude of the Kuchma regime in Kyiv, Andrukhovych defined his new cultural space not within the boundaries of Ukraine as a whole, as in his writings of the early 1990s, but in Galicia, historically rooted in its Austrian past and conceived as part of a common space with countries of Central Europe—the imagined world created prior to 1989 in the writings of Milan Kundera and Czesław Miłosz. It took the Orange Revolution to bring Andrukhovych back to his post-independence belief in Ukraine as a country that was parting ways with its colonial past and setting out on the path of European integration.

What was the response of the European West to the Ukrainian elite's post-1991 attempts to declare their country part of Europe? Although experts at the Deutsche Bank predicted that Ukraine would become the most prosperous of the former Soviet republics, the EU never took Ukraine seriously as a potential member. In 1993, when the Council of Europe first looked into the possibility of its eastern expansion, the only post-Soviet republics considered for future membership were the Baltic states of Estonia, Latvia, and Lithuania. The disastrous performance of the Ukrainian economy was certainly one of the reasons for such lack of interest in the country responsible for the disintegration of the once mighty Soviet Union. But Ukraine's dispute with Russia over nuclear weapons, Russia's claims to the Crimea and the Black Sea Fleet, and lack of international recognition of Ukraine's borders also could not fail to influence the EU's position on Ukraine. Meanwhile, the newly independent country was struggling to assert its independence. It did not obtain support in the international arena, as the West did not want to antagonize the wounded Russian bear lest the political situation slip from Boris Yeltsin's control and the nuclear-armed post-Soviet states follow the example of the former Yugoslavia, with much more disastrous consequences for the whole world.

Thus the Americans made common cause with the Russians, forcing Ukraine to give up its nuclear arsenal. The Poles and other East Europeans, on whom Ukraine was counting to form an anti-Russian bloc, were eager to join the EU and did not want to associate themselves too closely with a potentially failed nation or further antagonize Russia, which was in the process of withdrawing its troops from the former Soviet-bloc countries. Thus, in the summer of 1994, Ukraine had no choice but to agree to sign a document offered to it by the EU. The Agreement on Partnership and Cooperation between the EU and Ukraine was supposed to take effect only in 1998, almost four years after its signing, and its true purpose was to help Ukraine achieve political and economic stability, not to become a member of the EU.

In 1998, at the first meeting of the Council for Cooperation between Ukraine and the EU, created to oversee the implementation of the 1994 agreement, Ukraine requested associate membership, only to receive a polite "no." This occurred less than a year after the EU had not only initiated negotiations on future membership with such East European countries as Poland and Lithuania, with which Ukraine had been linked culturally and historically for many centuries, but also welcomed applications from countries like Romania and Bulgaria, whose political regimes and economic situation were hardly better than those of Ukraine. The document offered to the Ukrainian authorities, entitled "The Common Strategy of the EU toward Ukraine," made no provision for future membership.

In 2004, following the largest ever expansion of the EU, which extended it to the western borders of Ukraine (with Hungary, Slovakia, and Poland gaining membership), Ukraine was offered a new document entitled "The Action Plan" and designed for countries neighboring with the EU. Brussels was thus treating Ukraine on a par with such "neighbors" as Israel and Morocco. The entire world watched the drama and triumph of the Orange Revolution in Kyiv in November and December 2004—an event inspired by Ukrainian society's desire to part ways with Russian-sponsored authoritarianism and join the democratic family of European nations. It was then that the EU decided to open membership negotiations with Turkey.

When the new Ukrainian government of President Yushchenko approached the EU in the aftermath of the Orange Revolution, asking for a "clear European perspective," or the prospect of membership, it was offered nothing more than an additional ten-point program that did not change the substance of its relations with the EU and held out no hope of membership even in the most distant future. As a goodwill gesture, Ukraine introduced visa-free entry in 2005 for citizens of the member states of the EU. For its part, the EU forced its new members to reintroduce strict Cold War-era controls on their borders with Ukraine. This was the case, for example, in the Slovak village of Szelmenc. "A 10-foot-high wire fence means that villagers on the Ukrainian side have to travel 416 miles to buy a 30 Euro visa (a fortune in that part of the world) to meet a relative on the other side of the street," reported the *Wall Street Journal* in September 2005 in an article entitled "The 'Apartheid Wall.'" The author noted that "It's hard to forge an 'Alliance of Civilizations' when Europe's so busy putting up walls."[10]

The stagnation of the Ukrainian economy in the 1990s and the corruption of the Kuchma regime were of course major reasons for the EU's reluctance to consider Ukraine as a prospective member. Ukraine's failure to introduce strict controls on its borders with Russia could not but influence the EU's decision to "fortify" its new eastern boundary. Another reason is Ukraine's size and the concern that its admission would cost the EU too much in agricultural and infrastructure subsidies. But that is only part of the story. The Brussels bureaucrats felt most comfortable with those forces in the Kuchma administration, including former Prime Minister Viktor Yanukovych, who showed little initiative concerning Ukraine's integration into Europe and oriented themselves on Russia. As Winfried Schneider-Deters pointed out at the time, Russia remained the EU's major concern. After all, the agreement signed in 1999 by the leaders of the EU and Russia on the development of mutual relations in the decade 2000–2010 included recognition of Russia's leading role in creating a new system of political and economic relations in the Commonwealth of Independent States.

While the old Europe welcomed the Orange Revolution and the resulting prospects for Ukraine's democratic development, it remained uneasy about Russia's reaction to Ukraine's growing ties with Europe. Quite telling in that regard was the statement made in September 2005, when Viktor Yushchenko was chosen as the first recipient of the Chatham House Prize: he was given the award in part for leading the Orange Revolution in such a way that Ukraine, Russia's largest partner, brought about no serious deterioration in Europe's relations with Moscow.

The EU's reluctance to admit that Ukraine is a European state even as it opens membership negotiations with Turkey, a country predominantly non-European in geography, history, and culture, may be viewed with amusement by outside observers, but it clearly annoys the Ukrainian political elite. Ukraine's claim to the European character of its state, based on its geography, history, and culture, was once summarized by Oleh Zarubinsky, acting chair of Ukraine's parliamentary commission on European integration.

In September 2005, addressing a conference in Washington, D.C., he made the following statement:

> I would like to remind you of one thing which is self-evident. I can't stop repeating it, and I won't get tired of repeating it. That is: Ukraine is a European state. First of all, Ukraine is geographically situated in Europe, and moreover, the geographic center of Europe is situated in Ukraine—in Transcarpathia, near the village of Rakhiv. The history of Ukraine is not a topic of conversation today, but one may remember that Kyivan Rus´ was one of the most developed countries in Europe over 1,000 years ago. One of the ancient trade routes crossed the territory of

Ukraine—"from the Varangians to the Greeks." Over time our links with Europe were cut off due to historical circumstances beyond our control. Therefore, one should admit that Ukraine has always been a European state in terms of geography, history, and culture. Now it is time Ukraine regained its place in Europe in terms of developed institutions of democracy and political system. It is high time Ukraine joined the family of well-developed democratic European states.[11]

The lukewarm reaction of the old Europe to prospective Ukrainian membership in the EU brought profound disappointment and disillusionment to those activists in Ukraine who most strongly promoted President Viktor Yushchenko's pro-European course. The feelings of that part of the Ukrainian intellectual elite were best expressed by Yurii Andrukhovych, an enthusiastic promoter of Ukraine's European choice during and immediately after the Orange Revolution. By the spring of 2006, he was so disappointed with the lack of support for Ukraine's bid for EU membership on the part of the old Europe that he vented his frustration with the state of Ukrainian-European relations at the Leipzig Book Fair, where he was awarded the Prize "For European Understanding."

In his Leipzig speech, delivered on 15 March 2006, Andrukhovych directed the attention of his audience to a recent statement by a senior official of the European Commission who claimed that in twenty years all the European states except those that used to be part of the USSR would be members of the EU. That statement was used by anti-European forces in Ukraine to discredit President Yushchenko's European project. Travel restrictions imposed on Ukrainians wishing to go to Germany and other EU countries also served to derail the efforts of the pro-European lobby in Ukraine. "Actually," said Andrukhovych, "I am not asking for very much: I want Ukrainians to be able to travel in Europe without restrictions. If only because they, too, are Europeans."[12]

By the autumn of 2006, Andrukhovych was even more critical of the European Union's policy toward Ukraine. In his writings and public statements, he distinguished clearly between Europe and the EU—terms that had been used interchangeably in Ukrainian political discourse since 1991. According to Andrukhovych, they were not identical. Europe, in his mind, had no clear boundaries and extended as far eastward as European culture itself. From that perspective, Ukraine was and remains a European country. The European Union, on the other hand, is a conglomerate of West European powers that lost their colonies and created the EU in an effort to recover their past glory and influence by launching a joint eastward expansion. As the countries of the "new Europe" refused to take orders from the old ones, the latter lost interest in EU expansion.

Andrukhovych accused the European "neo-imperialists" of helping to bring about the de facto defeat of the pro-European forces in the Ukrainian parliamentary elections of 2006. The same elections that pushed Andrukhovych over the edge in his critique of the EU have been treated more positively by another prominent Ukrainian publicist and supporter of "European Ukraine," Mykola Riabchuk. Long and painful negotiations between political blocs in the Ukrainian parliament eventually resulted in the revenge of the forces backed by Russia in the presidential election of 2004 and the return to prime-ministerial office of Yushchenko's principal opponent in that election, Viktor Yanukovych. The new/old prime minister did not overtly reverse Ukraine's course toward integration into European institutions; instead, he made common cause with Ukraine-cautious Brussels bureaucrats and labeled Yushchenko and his supporters "Euro-romantics."

Some observers saw Yanukovych's return as the beginning of the end of Ukraine's pro-European policy, but Riabchuk remained more optimistic. He argued that the ideas of the Orange Revolution, as the embodiment of European values, were poised to gain ground in the future. Ukraine's civilizational matrix would lead it toward Europe one way or another. Riabchuk believed that, despite the setback of the 2006 elections, Ukraine has preserved an essentially European political culture embodied in the rising power of civil society and free mass media; Europe has retained its positive image and attractiveness in the eyes of Ukrainians; and the Ukrainian oligarchs were sure to be increasingly interested in stability and the rule of law.[13]

To many in Ukraine, Riabchuk's vision of the new European Ukraine seemed more like wishful thinking than a realistic assessment of the current situation. This applied particularly to the hopes that he pinned on the Ukrainian oligarchs. However, there were increasing signs that, if a consensus on any aspect of Ukrainian foreign policy was emerging between the Yush-chenko and Yanukovych camps, then it concerned Ukraine's integration into European institutions. In October 2006, Ya-nukovych stated in an article in the *Washington Post*: "President Yushchenko and I also agree that Ukraine has made a choice for Europe and will pursue closer relations with all European and Euro-Atlantic institutions. With the European Union, we are working on an action plan of reforms under the auspices of the European Neighborhood Policy, which we hope will lead to the beginning of negotiations on an E.U.-Ukraine free-trade agreement."[14] President Yushchenko, for his part, restrained his pro-European rhetoric, countering Yanukovych's accusations that he was a "Euro-romantic."

If that was the position of the elites, what did Ukraine's or-dinary citizens think about the country's European prospects? It would appear that, despite the failure of Ukraine's desperate attempts to secure from the EU a mere promise of future mem-bership in the aftermath of the Orange Revolution, the Ukrainian population at large remained quite sympathetic to Europe and believed that its new government had a chance of achieving its goal. Even before the Orange Revolution, 40 percent of the Ukrainian population was favorably disposed to the EU, accord-ing to a poll conducted by the National Institute of Strategic Studies of Ukraine in October 2004.

A poll conducted in May 2005 by the newspaper *Dzerkalo tyzhnia* (Weekly Mirror) indicated that more than 66 percent of Ukrainians believed that the new government was more trusted by the EU than the Kuchma regime, and more than 56 percent of those polled believed that the new government was making real steps toward Europe. The percentage of those who thought so was much higher in western than in eastern Ukraine. Even so, sympathy for a European orientation has been making spec-tacular progress in both western and eastern Ukraine since 1991.

The whole country had been undertaking what it calls a "Iev-roremont"—the renovation of apartments, offices, and entire buildings according to European standards. But the "Ievrore-mont" was not limited to physical reconstruction. Ukraine's new government and society at large put enormous effort into organizing the Eurovision song contest in Kyiv in the summer of 2005. According to an opinion poll conducted by the Ukrainian Oleksandr Razumkov Center in September 2005, 33.3 percent of the Ukrainian population considered itself European. Almost 85 percent of those polled considered Ukraine to be part of Europe in geographic terms and 61 percent in historical terms, but most respondents—54 and 51 percent respectively—did not believe that Ukraine was a European state in political and cultural terms, while 77 and 74 percent did not consider Ukraine to be on a par with European economic and social standards. Clearly, it was not geography, history, or even culture but the difference between the standard of living in Ukraine and the countries of the EU that presented the main obstacle to the Ukrainian population's adoption of a full European identity.

Kyiv looked to many in Ukraine like a "normal" European capital, and the provinces interpret its economic and cultural success as a sign of belonging to Europe. Interviewed by a Radio Liberty correspondent in September 2005, a visitor from the city of Mykolaïv in southern Ukraine ignored the question of whether she had participated in the Orange Revolution and attended rallies on the Maidan—Kyiv's Independence Square—and commented instead on the European appearance of Kyiv, which greatly impressed her. Kyivans, in her opinion, were already living in Europe, something that she defined by the level of services and wages, as well as smiles on people's faces. The provinces, she said, were lagging behind. Fifteen years earlier, a visitor from the provinces commenting on the same phenomenon of Kyiv's higher standard of living would probably have said that Kyivans were already living under communism, or compared Ukraine's capital to Moscow. Therefore, people in the Ukrainian provinces began using a different scale—a European one—to measure their capital's successes and failures, as well as their own. In this connection, one might note the successive renaming of the square at the northern end of Khreshchatyk in downtown Kyiv. Before 1917, it was known as the Tsar's Square; in the mid-twentieth century, it was Stalin Square; later still, it was the Square of the Leninist Young Communist League. Its current name is European Square.

Given the Mykolaïv visitor's refusal to answer the loaded question about the Maidan and her readiness to speak about Kyiv's European character, it remains tempting to think about the emergence of the European idea in Ukraine as a potential keystone in the formation of a new Ukrainian identity. That identity is oriented toward elements in Ukrainian history and culture that are consonant with the ideas of individual freedom and democracy; it includes all citizens of the state; and it is profoundly different from the post-1991 Russian identity, which is based not only on recognition of the Russian Federation's geostrategic position in Eurasian space but also on the tradition of Russian statism, authoritarianism, and great-power status. President Yushchenko once formulated the Ukrainian national idea as follows: "A European Ukraine with liberal values and human rights and liberties."

According to a Razumkov Center poll carried out in December 2006, 63 percent of Ukraine's opinion-makers agreed that European integration could indeed become a goal uniting Ukrainian society and providing the basis for a new type of Ukrainian identity, but only 27 percent of Ukraine's population shared that optimistic attitude. This represents a decrease of 10 percent since the spring of 2005, when Ukrainians believed that the Orange Revolution would bring them closer to the European Union, and the percentage of those who believed in the unifying force of the European idea and those who disagreed with them was almost equal. It would appear that Ukrainian proponents of European integration have their work cut out for them not only abroad but also at home. That work can hardly be accomplished without support from the European Union.

Ukraine is interested in Europe, but so should Europe be interested in an independent and democratic Ukraine. In theory it is, but in practice it is still checking the textbooks to find out where Europe ends and Asia begins. One hopes that it will not take too long to accomplish that task. Commenting on the Orange Revolution and Ukraine's relations with Russia and the EU, Alexander Motyl argued that the isolation of Ukraine in the strategic desert between democratic Europe and authoritarian Russia automatically turns any pro-democratic movement in Ukraine into a pro-European one and helps define Ukraine's European identity first and foremost in opposition to Russia.[15]

It is hard to disagree, especially in light of the subsequent events of 2013–14, when Viktor Yanukovych provoked mass protests and eventually lost power after caving in to Russian pressure and refusing to sign the association agreement with the EU, on which he himself had been insisting for almost a year. Surprisingly, little of substance has changed in Ukraine since the times of Mykhailo Drahomanov, when the "awakeners" of the Ukrainian nation oriented their young national movement toward Europe and away from Russia.

20.

The New Eastern Europe

More than thirty years after the fall of the Berlin Wall and the disintegration of the Soviet empire in Eastern Europe, the region is still grappling with the problem of its new identity and the choice of an appropriate name to reflect it. There has been considerable talk about a "return to Europe," as well as the emergence of a "new Europe" and, as a consequence of the latter, the birth of a "new Eastern Europe." Where is Eastern Europe today? And if it is not where it used to be, where did it go? If you google "Eastern Europe+Map," you will get about 11,600,000 results, a reassuring sign that the region is alive and well. But do not expect an easy answer to the question of where it is actually located.

The web will provide you with endless variants, starting with those that treat the region as everything between Prague in the west and the Ural Mountains in the east, and ending with more "modest" proposals, like that of the CIA *World Factbook*, which would limit the region to the former western borderlands of the Soviet Union, from Estonia in the north to Moldova in the south. The confusion is understandable on more than one level. After all, it is no easy matter to determine where Eastern Europe ends if you do not know where Europe per se ends. Europe is not a continent in its own right, and its imagined eastern frontier is constantly on the move. It would seem, however, that Europe and Eastern Europe are now moving in opposite directions. If "Europe" is becoming more and more coterminous with the European Union, and not with the geographic entity ending at the Urals, then "Eastern Europe," for its part, is moving not westward but eastward, encompassing the regions left outside the borders of the recently expanded European Union.

The world at large is understandably confused about the meaning of the term "Eastern Europe." So is the community of experts, whom the general public holds mainly responsible for the persistent confusion. Political scientists and specialists in security studies and international relations, who (unlike historians) have to deal with the region in "real time," are trying hard to come up with new definitions of the area. Their solution is to fragment the region, dividing it into ever-smaller entities. One result of this development is the eastward extension of Central Europe, which now includes a number of former East European countries whose historians insisted for decades on their East-Central European status. Another outcome is the reinvention of the term "Eastern Europe." As it went out of fashion among former East Europeans, they passed it on as a kind of intellectual hand-me-down to the East, which has now been reinvented by specialists in international studies as the "New Eastern Europe" (NEE).

The geographic scope of the term depends on the author and his or her location. For the publishers of the journal *Nowa Europa Wschodnia* in Wrocław, the NEE includes almost everything east of Poland. The authors of a position paper on the European Union's Eastern Partnership, produced in Stockholm, include Ukraine, Belarus, Moldova, and the three Transcaucasian states of Georgia, Azerbaijan, and Armenia in the NEE. A study produced in Austria limits the term to the first three countries, excluding the Transcaucasus. There is clearly a growing tendency to treat Ukraine, Belarus, and Moldova as the core of the "New Eastern Europe."

These countries have recently found themselves in a unique geopolitical position, sandwiched between the extended European Union in the west and Russia in the east. They had never been thought to constitute a distinct region and thus had no established group designation in the world of international relations. The concept of East-Central Europe, so popular in Poland since the 1950s, failed to fire the imagination of local elites in the NEE. But even outside the region, there is no consensus on whether the countries of the NEE belong to East-Central Europe. If Jerzy Kłoczowski, the most loyal supporter of the East-Central

European idea, insists on Ukraine's belonging to the region, Paul Robert Magocsi includes only west and central Ukraine in his *Historical Atlas of East-Central Europe.*

For better or for worse, "New Eastern Europe" emerges as the only term capable of linking Ukraine, Belarus, and Moldova together in their geopolitical no-man's-land. The Baltic states, which are included in the "Eastern Europe" of the CIA *World Factbook*, and the Transcaucasian states, which are included in the "New Eastern Europe" of the EU Eastern Partnership Program, have regional identities of their own. Not so Ukraine, Belarus, and Moldova. If you partition the old Eastern Europe between the new Central Europe, the Baltics, the Balkans, the Transcaucasus, and, finally, Russia and Central Asia, the residue turns out to be the three countries stuck in between: Ukraine, Belarus, and Moldova—the quintessential "New Eastern Europe."

Looking at the new political map of Eastern Europe, the question one wants to ask is whether there is anything more to this otherwise nameless region than pure geopolitical accident. Some scholars justifiably argue that the NEE identity has been invented outside the region and imposed on it by political developments beyond its control. Others say that talking about these countries as a separate region in historical terms means justifying the current division of Europe and making it all but permanent. There are also voices claiming that a definition of this region as a European rather than a Russian borderland is bound to encourage unwanted bids for EU membership on the part of local elites. I shall leave aside the question of political expediency. What I am interested in here is history and, in particular, the question of whether looking at the history of Ukraine, Belarus, and Moldova as that of one region can help us better understand its past and explain its current situation.

Let us begin by considering whether the immediate past of these three countries contains some common element that differentiates them from their neighbors on the other side of the EU's eastern border. Indeed it does: a mere thirty years ago they were western borderlands of the USSR. Countries that were not part of the Soviet Union, like Bulgaria and Romania, whose political and economic situation was little better than that of Ukraine or Moldova through most of the 1990s, made it into the European

Union, but those of the NEE did not, despite the frantic efforts of Ukrainian governments of the Orange Revolution era to crash the European party. It appears that the internal "iron curtain" between the USSR and the socialist countries of Eastern Europe was more formidable than the outer one that divided the capitalist West from the socialist East.

This explanation would probably suffice were it not for the Baltic states—former Soviet republics that managed to join the European Union. Because the Baltic states are former Soviet republics, the CIA *World Factbook* groups them together with Ukraine, Belarus, and Moldova as constituents of "Eastern Europe." There are, however, major geographic, cultural, and historical factors that link the NEE countries together while distinguishing them from the Baltic states. The most "primordial" of these is geography. The northern border of the NEE more or less coincides with the watershed between the Baltic and Black Sea basins.

Estonia, Latvia, and Lithuania belong to the Baltic basin, while most of Belarus and all of Ukraine and Moldova belong to the Black Sea basin, with the Dnieper, Dniester, and Prut as their largest rivers. If the Baltic countries have been oriented for centuries toward the Baltic Sea and Northern Europe, the NEE countries have been oriented toward the Black Sea. Throughout history they have occasionally participated in Mediterranean political and cultural developments, but more often than not they were cut off from the Mediterranean world by nomads. The Ottomans, who came to dominate the nomads in the fifteenth century, controlled not only the northern Black Sea steppes but the Black Sea Straits as well.

Thus, although the NEE countries belonged to the Black Sea region, they gained little benefit from the sea, early on becoming Europe's ultimate midlands—an arena of competition among foreign powers. Belarus, located on the Great European plain, found itself on the route of choice for Western armies marching toward Russia and Russian armies marching west. Ukraine became a bone of contention among Poland, Russia, Austria-Hungary, and the Ottomans, while Moldavia, long an Ottoman outpost, became Russia's gateway to the Balkans. The contrasting geographic orientations of the countries of the Baltic and Black

Sea basins mean that their societies bring different historical experiences to the present and conceptualize the borderlands of the European Union in various ways.

Culture and ethnicity are other important factors that set the countries of the NEE apart from their Baltic neighbors. It suffices to mention religion. If, in the case of the Baltics, we are dealing with Catholic and Protestant traditions, which set the region apart from Russia, the dominant religious tradition in Ukraine, Belarus, and Moldova is Orthodoxy, which links them intimately with Russia's old and new imperial ideology. In the cases of Ukraine and Belarus, there is also the phenomenon of East Slavic proximity, which allows Patriarch Kirill of Moscow to speak of Holy Rus´—an ethnoreligious entity that includes Russia, Ukraine, and Belarus. Where religion and East Slavic identity work together, as in Belarus and eastern Ukraine, the spell of the former imperial center is strongest. Where they do not reinforce each other, as in Moldova and the former Habsburg lands of Ukraine, attachment to Moscow is less prominent or completely nonexistent.

Thus, the NEE is not just a figment of current geopolitical imagination. There are geographic, cultural, ethnic, and historical factors that set it apart from its neighbors. But can history as a discipline and we as its practitioners benefit from this new conceptualization of the old Eastern Europe? I believe so, and I think that historians working in the region will be among the primary beneficiaries of this approach. Now that the Soviet narrative has been largely abandoned, EU prospects denied, and nationalist myths attacked, historians of the former Soviet republics of Ukraine, Belarus, and Moldova are experiencing confusion and uncertainty. Imagining the history of these three countries as that of a unit will help liberate their historiographies from the isolation imposed by the dominance of local/national, pan-Russian, and pan-Romanian paradigms and contribute to a better understanding of the histories of each individual country and the region as a whole. In countries like Ukraine, history has once again become a battleground between the old Soviet- or Russocentric narrative and national or overtly nationalist paradigms. Under these circumstances, a new framework for historical analysis can break the existing intellectual deadlock and lead historians and society at large to think about their history in broader and more inclusive terms.

If there is one overriding paradigm that can link the countries of the NEE together and help scholars of the region pose new questions and provide new answers, it is that of the borderland or the political and/or cultural frontier. Imagining the countries of Eastern Europe as a European frontier or even a bulwark of European civilization to enhance one's European credentials is of course an old device employed, not without success, by the intellectual elites of the "old" Eastern Europe, which now count themselves as part of its Central European core. Tony Judt wrote in this regard that "Poles, Lithuanians and Ukrainians have all represented themselves in their literature and political myths as guarding the edges of 'Europe' (or Christianity). But, as a brief glance at a map suggests, their claims are mutually exclusive: they can't all be right."[1] In fact they can if one looks at the map of early modern Eastern Europe, but that is not the point. The point is to move beyond the "defenders of European values" paradigm. The frontier approach, as developed in American and European historiography, allows one to speak about much more than one nation's role in the "defense" of European and Christian values.

It is much more productive to think of the NEE frontier as a meeting place of various states, cultures, and nationalities. Historically, there were at least three types of borders that came together in the NEE region: imperial (Russian, Ottoman, Habsburg, and Commonwealth); cultural/religious, which divided Orthodoxy, Catholicism, Islam, and Judaism; and ethnic/national. The list of the largest ethnic groups in the region would include, apart from Ukrainians, Belarusians, and Moldovans/Romanians, also Poles, Lithuanians, Jews, Crimean Tatars and, last but not least, Russians. These borders were associated with different cultures that met, confronted one another, and negotiated a *modus vivendi*, producing new kinds of meaning and understanding that shaped the region's long-term identity. Here is just one of many examples of such a hybrid identity in the region, which has to do with a religious encounter. In the Middle Ages, Catholicism and Orthodoxy met here, producing by the late sixteenth century a hybrid Uniate Church that combined Orthodox ritual with Catholic dogma. In the 1830s, that church was liquidated in Belarus by the tsarist authorities, but its successor, the five-million-strong Ukrainian Catholic Church, still exists in Ukraine.

Another cultural encounter in the region was that between Christianity and Islam, which took place as Moldova, the Crimea, and the northern Black Sea steppes all fell under Ottoman tutelage in the fifteenth century. The return of the Crimean Tatars to their ancestral homeland after the collapse of the Soviet Union reintroduced the Islamic factor into the region's politics, reminding us of the importance of the Christian-Islamic encounter in the past. Finally, in the sixteenth century the region became a destination of choice for Jews expelled from Western and Central Europe. It is the homeland of some of the best-known Jewish political and cultural figures, including Golda Meir, Leon Trotsky, and Isaac Babel.

As part of the Russian imperial Pale of Settlement, it also became the scene of some of the most horrendous crimes against the Jewish population, including pogroms and the Holocaust. Administered at various times by states dominated by Mongols, Lithuanians, Poles, Austrians, Romanians, Germans, and Russians, the NEE also became a meeting point for a variety of administrative systems and political cultures. This encouraged a unique popular adaptability to political change at the top. It is no accident that the region has seen no major upheaval between 1992 (the military conflict in the Transnistria region of Moldova) and 2014 (Russian aggression against Ukraine).

Did we not know all this before we began thinking about the NEE as a region with a common historical identity? Of course we did, but a new analytical framework makes it possible to see things not seen or neglected previously. Here are two examples of how looking at the region as a whole can help us better understand its individual parts and, indeed, East European history as a whole. The first example highlights the importance of the region as a major actor in the history of cultural transfers not only between Europe's West and East but also between its two Easts: one Slavic, the other Greek or Mediterranean.

Although the important role of Eastern Orthodox hierarchs in the region was long stressed by scholars such as Ihor Ševčenko and Edward Keenan, it all but escaped the attention of historians focused on cultural relations between Russia and the West. If the

NEE countries are considered as a region, one sees more clearly the role of the Greek East and the Mediterranean in the cultural transformation of the "old" Eastern Europe long after its adoption of Christianity. The figure of the seventeenth-century Kyivan metropolitan Petro Mohyla—a Moldavian prince, Polish noble, Ruthenian hierarch, and reformer of world Orthodoxy (he produced the first Orthodox Confession of Faith)—is emblematic of the historical importance of the region and its internal and external connections.

The other example comes from the modern era. A focus on national history prevents one from understanding what eventually caused the most profound change in the region, namely, the "closing" of its cultural frontier—in other words, the elimination of its traditional ethnic and cultural diversity. Blaming nationalism alone for this development will not do, given the profound differences in the maturation and aggressiveness of ethnic nationalism in that part of the world. The disappearance of many ethnic and religious minorities from the territory of Belarus can hardly be attributed to the strength of Belarusian nationalism.

When we look at the region as a whole, it becomes more apparent that the transformation of the borderland from a multiethnic and multicultural space into an ethnic and cultural monolith was accomplished largely by "outside" powers with strong imperial ambitions. They managed to marshal resources and mobilize the population on a scale unthinkable for the weak national movements of the region, which generally served as junior partners in the cleansing of the borderlands, occasionally undertaken with the tacit or even explicit approval of democratic world leaders. The existing borders of the NEE countries are the best examples of such outside influence. The Molotov-Ribbentrop Pact, the Holocaust, and the Yalta agreements shaped the new ethnocultural landscape of the region, and we have a better chance of understanding such changes if we think about the region as a unit.

Finally, I would like to address the question of the place that the history of the NEE can or should occupy in university curricula in North America. It is immediately obvious that the study of the borderlands makes sense only in the broader context of the study of the entities that possessed those borderlands. Thus defined, the study of these borderlands and frontiers illuminates not only their history but also that of the dominant powers, which arguably define themselves best on the margins, at points of encounter with their multiple others. The history of the NEE, then, is best studied within the framework of an Eastern Europe broadly understood—one that includes not only Poland but also Russia. There is probably no better way to understand the frontier than to remove the borders.

21.

Reimagining the Continent

The Ukraine Crisis, as the Russian annexation of the Crimea and the hybrid war in the Donbas became known in international media, began in late December 2013 with a group of young Kyivan urbanites, many of them students, camping on the Maidan (Independence Square in downtown Kyiv) to protest the refusal of the Ukrainian government to sign an Association Agreement with the European Union. The protests became known as the EuroRevolution or Revolution of Dignity. As government forces attacked the protesters, hundreds of thousands of Ukrainians showed up on the streets of their capital to voice their disapproval of the authorities' actions.

It was the largest political rally in history sparked by a foreign-policy decision, as well as a manifestation of belief in the transforming power of the European Union and its institutions at the very time when trust in those institutions inside the Union was at one of its lowest points. The protests led to a change of government in Kyiv and provoked Russian aggression against a West-leaning country. Thousands were killed and wounded, and millions of Ukrainian citizens were displaced as a result of the conflict. Despite the war and unprecedented pressure from Russia, the new Ukrainian government signed an Association Agreement with the EU and embarked on a series of reforms, viewing the country's future as linked to the family of European nations, either within the European Union or in close alliance with it.[1]

The vision of Ukraine as an integral part of Europe and a future member of the European Union took off in Ukraine in the aftermath of the Orange Revolution of 2004, one of whose main slogans was "joining Europe." The leader of the revolution, Viktor Yushchenko, declared in his inaugural address in January 2005: "Our path to the future is the one now being followed by United Europe. We belong to the same civilization as its peoples; we share the same values."[2] President Yushchenko and his numerous supporters were in for a disappointment. The leaders of the European Union, troubled by its internal problems and preoccupied with the difficulties accompanying the two waves of eastward expansion in 2004 and 2007, were not eager to consider any new members. Moreover, Ukraine was far behind its western neighbors who had joined the Union in bringing its legal and economic system up to EU standards.

The Yushchenko years became known as a period of "Euroromanticism," but they left some important marks on the identity of Yushchenko's countrymen. They also put Ukraine on the mental map of Europe. Western media coverage of the Orange Revolution familiarized the publics of English-speaking countries with the names "Kyiv" and "Ukraine." When the pro-European protests began in Kyiv in November 2013, Ukraine was no longer an unknown country in Eurasia. Whatever the Western public thought about Ukraine's pro-EU aspirations, few questioned its European credentials, and many sympathized with the protesters' demands for closer ties with the European Union. Ukrainian resistance to Russian aggression only enhanced these attitudes.

The Ukrainian protesters' belief in Europe as a model for reform in their own country and the ability of the member countries of the European Union to stand by Ukraine in its time of trouble surprised the Russian leadership and dramatically affected EU-Russian relations. That belief also launched a process that could lead to the political and cultural redefinition of Europe, which until recently has been delimited in the minds of most Europeans by the borders of the European Union. The role of Ukraine in this process is yet to be fully studied and explained.

The Lure of Central Europe

In February 2011, a Kyiv tourist firm called KievClub offered its clients a sweet Valentine's Day deal. Advertised as a "romantic weekend in the heart of Europe," it cost only £660 per couple and included round-trip airfare from Luton Airport near London, accommodations in a three-bedroom apartment in downtown Kyiv, and "meet and greet parking." Only twenty years earlier Kyiv, the city in the "heart of Europe" that British tourists were being invited to visit, had been regarded by many in the West as part of Russia, and thus not European at all.

KievClub is not the only firm luring Western clients to the capital of Ukraine by calling it the heart of Europe. The same advertising strategy is employed by Studio Kiev, which offers visa support, lodging, language courses, and medical insurance to visitors, and Kiev Apartments, which advertises on Facebook, as do many other tourist and real-estate firms in Kyiv. What do the authors of the Kyiv ads mean when they call their city the "heart" of Europe? Whether their British clients know it or not, they are referring to the geographic center of the continent (or, rather, subcontinent). Once the guests arrive, they can find tour guides who will be happy to bring them to a globe-crowned column on Kyiv's main street that they call the midpoint of Europe.[3]

There was nothing absolutely new or unexpected in the efforts of Ukrainian political and cultural elites to present their country to the world as a nation at the center of Europe. This tactic had been used for decades by East European intellectuals and politicians whose nations were left out of the prosperous, democratic West European core. As mentioned earlier, in 1950, Oskar Halecki, a Polish émigré historian living in the United States, offered a version of the European historical and cultural map that redrew the boundaries of Central Europe so as to include Poland in its eastern subdivision.

Importantly, the term "East-Central Europe"—the counterpart to "West-Central Europe," which included Germany—also gained currency in Western academic discourse. In the early 1980s Milan Kundera, a Czech writer living in Paris, published an essay that not only put his country, along with Poland and Hungary, in the center of Europe but also defined it as part of the European West. Kundera's assumptions were fully reflected in his title, "The Stolen West or the Tragedy of Central Europe." The essay, translated in 1984 from its French original into English and published in the *New York Review of Books*, became one of the most influential late Cold War texts shaping the views of educated Westerners about the Soviet-occupied lands of Europe on the eve of the collapse of Soviet power in the region.[4]

Both Halecki and Kundera sought to modify an established mental map of Europe that placed Germany and areas immediately south and east of it at the center of the continent. In the second half of the nineteenth century, Otto von Bismarck had turned a newly united Germany into the hub of European diplomacy; then, at the dawn of the new century, his countrymen declared Dresden the geographic center of Europe. It was the territories around that center to which German political thinkers such as Friedrich List and Friedrich Naumann gave the name *Mitteleuropa*, a German-dominated area between France in the west and Russia in the east. Writing in the midst of World War I, Neumann rejected the idea of German imperial rule and military occupation of the region but never clearly defined the form that German predominance was to take.

Despite strong misgivings about German plans in the region, the idea of a federal organization of *Mitteleuropa* soon took root among the leaders of peoples struggling against Austro-Hungarian rule. In October 1918, Thomas Masaryk created in the United States a Mid-European Democratic Union composed of representatives of twelve European nations that sought to promote regional economic cooperation as an initial step toward federalization. The Union did not last long, but its creation showed that *Mitteleuropa* was not only a German idea: its non-German inhabitants were also prepared to imagine themselves as part of a separate grouping between France and Russia.[5]

The defeat of the Kaiser's Germany in World War I, the disintegration of Austria-Hungary, and the diminution of the Russian Empire dramatically changed the situation in the region. The elites of the newly independent countries were in search of a common new identity but wanted nothing to do with the now discredited name of *Mitteleuropa*. The new states of the region settled for the name "Eastern Europe," despite its implication that this "other" Europe was less than fully civilized. An even worse alternative presented itself: Hitler's attempt to create a German *Lebensraum* in the lands earlier defined as *Mitteleuropa* led to a disastrous world war that completely discredited the older

German term. But the idea of mid-European unity did not disappear completely.

Masaryk's vision lived on as an ideal after Eastern Europe was overrun by the Red Army and subjected to rule from Moscow. East European intellectuals were now eager to distance themselves as much as possible from the communist East and associate themselves with the democratic West. As soon as the Berlin Wall fell and Moscow began the gradual withdrawal of its troops from the region, the leaders of Poland, Czechoslovakia, and Hungary met in the Hungarian castle of Visegrád and created a Central European alliance to promote integration with their western neighbors—the European Union and NATO. By 2004, their dream had come true: all of them (Czechoslovakia now divided into the Czech Republic and Slovakia) had joined Western institutions, shedding the legacy of Soviet occupation and the civilizational stigma of Eastern Europe.[6]

Is it fair to say, then, that the Ukrainians are simply following in the footsteps of their western neighbors, trying to sell themselves to the European West as a central and thus indispensable part of Europe that was forgotten, if not betrayed, by its rich western cousin? Yes and no. Yes, in the sense that this was exactly the argument employed by some Ukrainian political leaders and intellectuals in the years following the Orange Revolution. No, in the sense that the Ukrainians are using a different map to make their case. This is not the Germanocentric map of *Mitteleuropa*, even though both Naumann and Halecki regarded parts of Ukraine as components of Middle/East-Central Europe, and the practical realization of Naumann's vision led to the German occupation of Ukraine in 1918.

Ukrainian leaders, intellectuals, and business people have something else in mind when they claim a central position for their country on the map of Europe. Their mental map can be found in atlases used in schools from Tokyo in the east to San Francisco in the west—with Kyiv, of course, somewhere in the center. Their Europe does not end at the eastern borders of the European Union or even at the western borders of Russia but extends all the way to the Urals. Such a perspective greatly changes how one defines the center of the European subcontinent.[7]

The map of Europe used by Ukrainian proponents of European integration is a product of the Enlightenment, and it is as confusing and contradictory as the legacy of the Enlightenment itself. That era produced not only the fathers of the American Revolution but also a cohort of "enlightened despots." The latter included Catherine II, who proclaimed that the Russian Empire, with its vast Asian possessions going all the way to the Pacific, was a European state. Although this definition was unpalatable to Europeans, Russia eventually got its way. After the partitions of Poland—a development welcomed by Voltaire, who believed that, along with Russian troops, civilization and order had finally arrived in that forsaken part of the world—few European rulers or their cartographers dared to challenge the claim. They rejected the age-old tradition beginning with Strabo, who had placed the eastern boundaries of Europe on the river Tanais, or Don, and redrew the map of Europe by moving its boundaries eastward, all the way to the Ural Mountains.

According to the Russian promoters of the change, that was where Russia proper ended and its colonies began. But the Russian success was incomplete. While European geographers agreed to move their border eastward, the "map of Europe on the mind of Enlightenment," to use Larry Wolff's phrase, remained largely the same. Strabo's map of Europe fitted West European self-perceptions much better than that of Catherine's geographers, and it persisted in the minds of educated European elites for generations to come, no matter what map they had studied in school. This disjunction of the physical, political, and cultural geographies of Europe persisted for most of the twentieth century. It is only if one thinks in Strabo's terms that Dresden can be imagined as the geographic center of Europe, while Hungary, Poland, and Czechoslovakia are consigned to Eastern Europe.[8]

It would be fair to say that Ukrainians treat the Enlightenment-era map of Europe much more seriously than their West European counterparts. They were instructed by generations of teachers that their country was located at the geographic center of Europe. It was on the territory of today's Ukraine, near the town of Rakhiv (47°57'46"N, 24°11'14"E), that in 1887 Austrian geographers placed the first known landmark indicating the geographic center of Europe. In so doing, the Austrians were claiming

European centrality for themselves. The Soviets, who took control of the area in 1945, followed suit.

The Ukrainians are now doing likewise, but the field has become crowded in the meantime: the Czech Republic, Slovakia, Hungary, Lithuania, Estonia, and Belarus have all made similar calculations to boost their European credentials. Politics were part and parcel of all the "discoveries" of the center of Europe. The French did the calculation for Lithuania when that country was about to leave the Soviet Union, and the Russians confirmed the findings of the Belarusians at a time when Belarus had become an international outcast, counting only the Russian Federation and Venezuela as friendly nations.[9]

Politics are not solely to blame for present-day confusion with regard to establishing the center of Europe. The complex geography of Europe is also a factor. All recent attempts to "discover" its geographic center have been undertaken on the basis of a map that goes all the way to the Urals, but calculations differ depending on whether islands are counted and, if so, which ones. There seems to be general agreement among geographers, whatever their political and cultural biases, that the center of Europe is located somewhere along a line extending through Lithuania, Belarus, Ukraine, and Moldova and bisecting the continent. This line is located east of the countries that make up what is now known as Central Europe. However naïve and inaccurate the definition of Kyiv as the center or heart of Europe (it lies more than 500 km northeast of Rakhiv), it is not completely arbitrary and reflects certain geographic realities that Ukrainians are now trying to turn to their political, economic, and cultural advantage.

The Shadow of Mitteleuropa

In the early 1990s, the distinguished French geographer Michel Foucher, one of the world's leading experts on borders and frontiers, put forward his vision of the new Europe that had just emerged from the geopolitical turmoil caused by the fall of the Berlin Wall, the unification of Germany, and the disintegration of the Soviet empire. In the atlas of "Middle and Eastern Europe" that he produced in 1993, Foucher proposed a concept of Middle Europe (*Europe médiane*) that differed from the *Mitteleuropa* of

Friedrich Naumann or Thomas Masaryk. While reminiscent of Oskar Halecki's East-Central Europe, it also included the Balkans. Foucher's Middle Europe was characterized by "an intermediate geopolitical situation between the West and the USSR or Russia; a current state of historic transition between these two organizing centers: territorial and political legacies imposed by the East, but modernization henceforth impelled by the West."

The region was made up largely of countries that were under communist control before 1989. Its northern part consisted more or less of those states that now define themselves as belonging to Central Europe: Germany, Poland, the Czech Republic, Slovakia, Hungary, Slovenia, and Croatia. Its southern part included the Balkans, with the sole exception of Greece. According to Foucher, the region "overflowed toward Ukraine and Belarus." Foucher included in Middle Europe those parts of Ukraine and Belarus that belonged to Poland before 1939. Judging by some of the maps, he also included Moldova.

By 2007, fourteen years after the atlas appeared, the eastward expansion of the "West" as defined by its political, economic, and military institutions, such as the European Union and NATO, had largely swallowed up Foucher's "Middle Europe." It certainly continues to exist as a historical concept but makes less and less sense in terms of contemporary geopolitics. Still, the area between the "West," defined in political, institutional, and military terms, and Russia has not disappeared altogether. It has simply moved east toward the countries that Foucher considered to be on the margins of Middle Europe in 1993: Ukraine, Belarus, and Moldova.[10]

This eastward geopolitical shift of the last decade of the twentieth century and the first decade of the twenty-first has also brought Foucher's "Middle Europe" to the region where the continent's center has been located since the Enlightenment-era revision of Strabo. This is also the region through which Europe's cultural dividing line has run ever since the eleventh century, when the Christian world split into East and West. When the Roman legates excommunicated the patriarch of Constantinople, who responded in kind, the church was divided, leaving the princes of Kyiv on one side and the Polish, Hungarian, and German kings on the other. It soon became apparent that the differences between the two parts of the Christian world were not limited to questions of church jurisdiction, clerical celibacy, or the *filioque* controversy about the origins of the Holy Spirit.

The split reinforced already existing differences in relations between church and state: an autonomous if not fully independent church in the West, and a church subservient to the state in the East. These differences turned out to be crucial for the subsequent development of social and political structures. In the West, the existence of a Roman-dominated church often independent of state power helped build autonomous institutions. In the East, the Byzantine legacy of a state-controlled church left little scope for autonomous bodies of any kind. The limited impact of the Reformation on the Orthodox world further contributed to the growth of differences in religious and political culture between the Christian East and West.

The map of Eastern and Western Christendom in Samuel Huntington's bestselling *Clash of Civilizations* shows the boundary between them passing generally along the geographic axis of Europe, with Lithuania, Poland, Slovakia, and Hungary on one side of the divide and Ukraine, Belarus, and Moldova on the other. Indeed, Huntington's line runs through Ukraine, Belarus, and Romania, assigning the western parts of those countries to the sphere of Western civilization. The map allegedly indicates the eastward extent of Western Christianity ca. 1500. In reality, it more or less follows the Soviet-Polish border before 1939. But it was not the geopolitical border of interwar Europe that the cartographers had in mind as they struggled to recreate the realities of pre-Reformation Europe. Their main problem was that of turning the relatively broad Christian frontier, which is not easily mapped, into a clear line.

What any such line fails to reflect is the existence of structures and entire regions that were neither eastern nor western or, alternatively, both eastern and western. This pertains to the Uniate Church established on the Catholic-Orthodox border in the late sixteenth century, a product of the Catholic Counter-Reformation and the Orthodox need for reform. The Uniate Church was thus Orthodox or Eastern in ritual and tradition but Western in jurisdiction and dogmas. With strong Polish support, it became the dominant church in most of Ukraine and Belarus by the mid-eighteenth century. It was wiped out by the tsars once they took possession of those lands after the partitions of Poland.[11]

The tsars wanted to abolish a church controlled from Rome that had the potential to corrupt the Orthodox world with Western values, the most dangerous of which was independence of church structures from the imperial authorities. This was also the motive of Joseph Stalin: in 1946, soon after Roosevelt and Churchill agreed at Yalta to the Soviet incorporation of western Ukraine and western Belarus, Stalin oversaw the incorporation into the Russian Orthodox Church of the Uniate (Greek Catholic) Church, which had survived in the western Ukrainian lands ruled from Vienna and then Warsaw.

What Stalin tried to achieve, apart from pursuing the goal of the tsars, was to turn the chaotic religious and civilizational frontier into a clearly defined and easily policed cultural and political border. He shipped hundreds of thousands of Roman Catholic Poles to Poland and turned millions of Greek-Catholic Ukrainians and Catholic Belarusians into pro forma Orthodox. This was a dream come true for modern map makers. Finally there was a line that could be drawn not only between Eastern and Western Christianity but also between Eastern and Western civilization. Collapsing religious, national, political and other frontiers into borders turned out to be a favorite project of modernizing states and societies. Stalin was simply its most brutal and most successful practitioner.[12]

The borders imposed by Stalin have now been taken over and reinforced by the European Union. If in the past it was the Soviets who built walls like the one in Berlin, and Westerners who wanted to tear them down, we now see a reversed situation. It is the proponents of Western values who are surrounding their world with walls, from the US-Mexico border to the strictly policed boundaries of the European Union. Keeping out the "barbarians" (generally associated in the public mind with such negative phenomena as illegal immigration, terrorism, and the smuggling of drugs and weapons) while admitting the products of their labor has been a basic task of the European states for decades. During the Cold War they did not have to worry about their eastern borders and could indulge in rhetoric about the free flow of people and ideas. With the fall of the Berlin Wall and the eastward shift of the EU borders, the rhetoric has changed: it is no longer about walls but about frontiers and neighborhoods. But the frontiers of the EU are not regarded in Brussels as open contact zones; rather, they are seen as outer defensive lines, like those of the Roman Empire.

The EU is involved beyond its borders and present in its neighborhood, but one of its reasons for being there is to provide neighboring governments with incentives to help police the approaches to Fortress Europe. This was certainly an important aspect of EU policy in Ukraine, where, in return for the liberalization of the visa regime, the Ukrainian government was expected to take on the task of policing the perimeter of the European Union. With EU financial assistance and expertise, it has been reinforcing its border controls and promising to take back, process, house, and deport illegal aliens who have managed to cross its territory into the EU. The European Union provides funds to improve detention facilities and train Ukrainian policemen to respect the rights of migrants and asylum seekers, but it is the task of the Ukrainian government to deal with tens of thousands of refugees and illegal immigrants from all over the world who are trying to claim their share of the European dream. The EU purgatory has effectively been moved beyond the walls of the Union to its frontier.[13]

There is certainly a danger of overdramatizing the situation by comparing Stalin's frontier-building endeavors with those of the EU. After all, the current visa wall between Ukraine and Poland is minuscule in comparison to the one that divided them before 1991. It is enormous, however, as compared to the one that was there before 2004, the year in which the EU established itself on the borders of Ukraine. Since the fall of communism, many things have changed in the western borderlands of the former Soviet Union. Stalin's Iron Curtain was slowly giving way to the old political, cultural, and economic frontier that had previously existed.

The victory of Solidarity in the Polish elections of 1989 not only triggered the implosion of the Soviet outer empire in what was then known as Eastern Europe but also sent a powerful signal across the border that did not exist before 1939—to Vilnius, the capital of the Soviet republic of Lithuania. The start of Soviet disintegration is often correctly associated with the Baltics. It is important, however, to remember that of the three Baltic countries it was Lithuania, with its close traditional connections to Poland, Belarus, and Ukraine, that began the process. In December 1989, a few months after the victory of Solidarity in Poland and a few weeks after the success of the Velvet Revolution in Czechoslovakia and the fall of the Berlin Wall, the Lithuanian communists broke with Moscow, and in March 1990 Lithuania became the first Soviet republic to proclaim its independence.

Ukrainians in western Ukraine, which had been part of Austria-Hungary before 1918 and part of Poland before 1939, first voted for independence in March 1991. They confirmed their choice, together with Ukrainians from the center and east of the country in December 1991, effectively putting an end to the Soviet Union. By that time, the Greek Catholic Church—the most vivid institutional embodiment of the East-West frontier—had emerged from the catacombs and renewed its activity with the help of Pope John Paul II and the reluctant "blessing" of Mikhail Gorbachev. The Moscow-controlled church in Ukraine split in two, with one of the new churches proclaiming its independence of Moscow. The Stalin-imposed cultural border crumbled, and the frontier came back into the everyday life of Ukrainian citizens. They could now travel not only to Russia but also to Poland, Hungary, Czechoslovakia, and Romania. Then came the expansion of the European Union, which shifted Foucher's Middle Europe to the east and promptly built a visa fence to separate the old Middle Europe from the new one.

The fact that the European Union came so close to Ukraine but stopped at its borders not only caused severe dislocations in the post-Soviet economics of the region but also dealt a stunning blow to the self-identification of the Ukrainian elites. Ukraine was cut off not only from Poland but also from Lithuania, with which it had had long-standing cultural and religious ties. Since the second half of the nineteenth century, Europe had been a historical, cultural, and political mainstay of Ukrainian identity. As discussed earlier in this volume, the desire to join Ukraine's European neighbors by means of an association agreement with the EU, which was a driving force behind the Maidan protests of

2013–14, led to the Russian invasion of Ukraine and the annexation of the Crimea.

It comes as no surprise that Russian aggression has made many Ukrainians who used to look at the West with suspicion into proponents of closer ties with the European Union. If in February 2014 36 percent of Ukrainians supported their country's joining the Russian-led Eurasian Union, that number fell to 12 percent in June 2015. The proportion of those who wanted to join the EU grew from 41 percent in February 2014 to 67 percent in June 2015. These numbers, however, reflect not only the change in the attitudes of Ukrainians but also the Ukrainian state's loss of the Crimea and parts of the Donbas, where pro-Russian sentiment was traditionally stronger than in other parts of Ukraine.[14]

The Russo-Ukrainian war forced many to start rethinking the map of Europe as it has existed for generations in the minds of Western elites and the public at large. In June 2015, only 1 percent of those polled in the countries of the EU questioned Ukraine's right to join the Union; 31 percent believed that Ukraine had the right to do so as a European country, and another 30 percent believed that membership of the EU would help Ukraine to defend its sovereignty against Russian aggression. Ukraine has come a long way in redefining the map of Europe in the imagination of its own citizens, but the same process seems to be beginning to the west of its borders. Both processes are far from over. Neither are they irreversible.[15]

It is more important than ever to acknowledge not only that Ukraine belongs to Europe but also that it occupies a central geopolitical position on the continent. The region to which Ukraine belongs has functioned as Europe's geopolitical axis since the dawn of modernity and as its religious and cultural axis ever since the great schism between Rome and Constantinople. Ukraine and its neighborhood constitute the quintessential geographic, cultural, and now geopolitical midpoint of Europe. Arguably, placing that area closer to the center of today's geopolitical map of Europe can help the West construct a new arch of European security as much as it can help the newly emerged focal point of European geopolitics to find its place in the political, economic, and security structures of Europe.

Notes

Preface

1   Vladimir Putin, "On the Historical Unity of Russians and Ukrainians," The President of Russia, http://en.kremlin.ru/events/president/news/66181; idem., "Address by the President of the Russian Federation," The President of Russia, February 21, 2022, http://en.kremlin.ru/events/president/news/67828.

2   Serhii Plokhy and Mary Sarotte, "The Shoals of Ukraine: Where American Illusions and Great-Power Politics Collide," *Foreign Affairs* 99, no. 1 (January/February 2020): 85–91.

3   See Oxana Shevel, "Memory of the Past and Visions of the Future: Remembering the Soviet Era and Its End in Ukraine," in *Twenty Years after Communism*, ed. Michael Bernhard and Jan Kubik (Oxford, 2014), 146–69; Shevel, "The Politics of Memory in a Divided Society: A Comparison of Post-Franco Spain and Post-Soviet Ukraine," *Slavic Review* 70, no. 1 (Spring 2011): 137–64.

4   Patricia Herlihy, "What Vladimir Putin Chooses Not to Know about Russian History," *Los Angeles Times*, 1 May 2014; Tarik Cyril Amar, "Another Conflict in Ukraine: Differing Versions of History," *Time*, 25 February 2015; Andriy Portnov, "On Decommunization, Identity, and Legislating History, from a Slightly Different Angle," *Kyiv Post*, 12 May 2015. See also relevant articles on "The Ukrainian Crisis and History" in the special issue of *Kritika* 16, no. 1 (Winter 2015) and the discussion of the Ukrainian crisis in the journal *Ab Imperio* 2014, no. 3.

Quo Vadis Ukrainian History?

Adapted from "Quo Vadis Ukrainian History?" in *The Future of the Past: New Perspectives on Ukrainian History*, ed. Serhii Plokhy (Cambridge, Mass., 2016), 1–24.

1   Edward Brown, preface to Pierre Chevalier, *A Discourse of the Original, Country, Manners, Government and Religion of the Cossacks* (London, 1672), fasc. A2–A3.

2   Dmytro Doroshenko, *History of the Ukraine* (Edmonton, 1939); W. E.D. Allen, *The Ukraine: A History* (Cambridge, UK, 1940); Michael Hrushevsky, *A History of Ukraine* (New Haven, Conn., 1941).

3   Ivan L. Rudnytsky, "The Role of the Ukraine in Modern History," *Slavic Review* 22, no. 2 (June 1963): 199–216, and Rudnytsky, "Reply," ibid., 256–62; Arthur E. Adams, "The Awakening of the Ukraine," ibid., 217–23; Omeljan Pritsak and John S. Reshetar, Jr., "The Ukraine and the Dialectics of Nation-Building," ibid., 224–55.

4   Ivan L. Rudnytsky, "Introduction," in *Rethinking Ukrainian History*, ed. Ivan L. Rudnytsky, with the assistance of John-Paul Himka (Edmonton, 1981), viii–x.

5   Roman Szporluk, *Ukraine: A Brief History* (Detroit, 1982); Orest Subtelny, *Ukraine: A History* (Toronto, 1988); Paul Robert Magocsi, *A History of Ukraine* (Toronto, 1996).

6   Mark von Hagen, "Does Ukraine Have a History?" *Slavic Review* 54, no. 3 (1995): 658–73, here 670, 673.

7   Georgiy Kasianov and Philipp Ther, "Introduction," in *A Laboratory of Transnational History: Ukraine and Recent Ukrainian Historiography*, ed. Georgiy Kasianov and Philipp Ther (Budapest and New York, 2009), 1–4; Andreas Kappeler, "From an Ethno-national to a Multiethnic to a Transnational Ukrainian History," ibid., 51–80.

8   The papers given at the Munich conference were published in *Ukraïna na istoriohrafichnii karti mizhvoiennoï Ievropy* (Kyïv, 2014). For the papers of the Kyiv conference, see *Svitlo i tini ukraïns'koho radians'koho istoriopysannia*, ed. Hennadii Boriak et al. (Kyïv, 2015), http://www.history.org.ua/?libid=10376.

9   *The Future of the Past: New Perspectives on Ukrainian History* (Cambridge, Mass., 2016).

10   *Istoriia Ukraïns'koï RSR*, ed. Iurii Kondufor et al., 8 vols. (Kyïv, 1977–79); *Ukraïna kriz' viky*, ed. Valerii Smolii et al., 13 vols. (Kyïv, 1998–99). Most of the volumes in the latter publication constitute monographic contributions by individual authors.

11 Johann Christian von Engel, *Geschichte der Ukraine und der ukrainischen Cosaken, wie auch der Königreiche Halitsch und Wladimir* (Halle, 1796).

12 Larry Wolff, *The Idea of Galicia: History and Fantasy in Habsburg Political Culture* (Stanford, Calif., 2010).

13 For criticism of Russian interpretations of Ukrainian history by some of the authors of *The Future of the Past*, see Heorhii Kasianov, Valerii Smolii, and Oleksii Tolochko, *Ukraïna v rosiïs'komu istorychnomu dyskursi: problemy doslidzhennia ta interpretatsiï* (Kyïv, 2013).

Placing Ukraine on the Map of Europe

For background information on the history of Ukraine, this essay draws on the relevant chapters of my book *The Gates of Europe: A History of Ukraine* (New York, 2015), on which I worked concurrently with producing the original draft of this paper. First published as "Princes and Cossacks: Putting Ukraine on the Map of Europe," in *Seeing Muscovy Anew: Politics, Institutions, Culture: Essays in Honor of Nancy Shields Kollmann*, ed. Michael S. Flier, Valerie Kivelson, Erika Monahan, and Daniel Rowland (Bloomington, Ind., 2017), 323–38.

1 Guillaume Levasseur de Beauplan, *A Description of Ukraine*, trans. Andrew B. Pernal and Dennis F. Essar (Cambridge, Mass., 1993).

2 See a copy of the 1613 edition of the map in the Stanford University Libraries: *MAGNI DVCATVS LITHVANIAE, CAETERARVMQVE REGIONVM ILLI ADIACENTIVM EXACTA DESCRIPTIO. Ill[ustri]ss[i]mi ac Excell[enti]ss[i]mi Pri[n]cipis et D[omi]ni D[omini] Nicolai Christophori Radziwil, D[ei] G[ratia] Olicae ac in Nieswies Ducis, S[acri] Rom[ani] Imperii Principis in Szylowiec ac Mir Comitis et S[ancti] Sepulchri Hierosolimitani Militis etc. opera, cura et impensis facta ac in lucem edita*, https://searchworks.stanford.edu/view/10366631; for a 1633 edition of the map, which includes a map of the Dnieper River, see https://searchworks.stanford.edu/view/10366743.

3 On the history of the production of the map, see H. Bartoszewicz, "Geodeci i kartografowie radziwiłłowscy," *Geodeta* 2001, no. 2: 45–49; Stanisław Alexandrowicz, "Rola mecenatu magnackiego w rozwoju kartografii ziem Rzeczypospolitej Obojga Narodów w XVI–I połowie XVII wieku," in *Europa Orientalis: Studia z dziejów Europy Wschodniej i Państw Bałtyckich* (Toruń, 2010), 235–54; Stanisław Alexandrowicz and Anna Treiderowa, "Makowski Tomasz," in *Polski słownik biograficzny* 19 (Wrocław, 1974), 248–49; Jarosław Łuczyński. "Przestrzeń Wielkiego Księstwa Litewskiego na mapie

radziwiłłowskiej Tomasza Makowskiego z 1613 r. w świetle treści kartograficznej i opisowej," *Ukraina Lithuanica* 2 (2013): 121–52.

4 Stanisław Alexandrowicz, *Rozwój kartografii Wielkiego Księstwa Litewskiego od XV do połowy XVIII wieku* (Poznań, 1989); "The Radziwiłł Map of the Duchy of Lithuania," Cartographia Rappersviliana Polonorum. Muzeum Polski w Rapperswilu, http://mapy.muzeum-polskie.org/articles-about-the-collection/the-radziwi-map-of-lithuania.html (accessed 7 April 2017).

5 On the Union of Lublin, see Robert Frost, *The Oxford History of Poland-Lithuania*, vol. 1, *The Making of the Polish-Lithuanian Union, 1385–1569* (Oxford, 2015).

6 On Ostrozky and his cultural activities, see Vasyl´ Ul´ianovs´kyi, *Kniaz´ Vasyl´-Kostiantyn Ostroz´kyi: Istorychnyi portret u halereï predkiv i nashchadkiv* (Kyïv, 2012).

7 For a detailed biography of Radvila, see Tomasz Kempa, *Mikołaj Krzysztof Radziwiłł Sierotka* (Warszawa, 2000).

8 "Mikhalon Litvin o nravakh tatar, litovtsev i moskvitian," trans. Kateryna Mel´nyk, in *Memuary otnosiashchiesia k istorii Iuzhnoi Rusi*, 8: *XVI v.* (Kyïv, 1890), 19.

9 On the economic preconditions of steppe colonization in seventeenth-century Ukraine, see chap. 11, "Socio-Economic Developments," in Paul Robert Magocsi, *A History of Ukraine: The Land and Its People*, 2nd ed. (Toronto, 2010), 144–58.

10 "Kozacÿ est genus militum ex honore privatis expulsis laboremq[ue] evitantibus conflatum. Hi armis levibus antea utebantur, unde et Velites dicti sunt, arcubus videlicet frameis, bombardis levioribus: nunc autem tormenta muralia et omne genus, annorum antea illis inusitatum, usui est. Hi itaq[ue] vitam d Porohas sive Cataracta in insulis Borÿsthenis, sub casis quibusuis tempestatibus expositi, degunt, in obedientia atq[ue] suprema [supremo] exercituum Poloniae praefecti continentur. Ducum [Ducem] inter se eligunt, electum facile deponunt, infeliciter autem illi rebus succedentibus nonnunquam trucidant tum vero inopia annonae laborant, clam civitates vicinis invadere et illis depopulatis praeda onusti reverti Solent, ut Duce Podkowa Tehiniam Moldaviae kosinscio kozlonum. Turcarum Imperatoris civitates depraedati ac depopulati sunt. Si vero ad exteros eundi occasio sese illis non obtulerit ita paternis inhiant possessionibus ut non nunquam feroces eorum impetus cum detrimento reprimantur." Cf. Jarosław Łuczyński, "Przestrzeń Wielkiego Księstwa Litewskiego na mapie radziwiłłowskiej Tomasza Makowskiego z 1613 r. w świetle treści kartograficzneji opisowej," *Zapiski Historyczne: Kwartalnik poświęcony historii Pomorza* 78, no. 1 (2013): 141–42.

11 *Kronika Polska Marcina Bielskiego,* ed. Kazimierz J. Turowski (Sanok, 1856), 3: 1346–58, 1358–61, 1430–35.

12 Mikhalon Litvin, *O nravakh tatar, litovtsev i moskvitian* (Moskva, 1994), 52–53.

13 On the early history of the Ukrainian Cossacks, see Mykhailo Hrushevsky, *History of Ukraine-Rus´,* 7: *The Cossack Age to 1625,* trans. Bohdan Struminski, ed. Frank E. Sysyn and Serhii Plokhy (Edmonton, 1999); Serhii Plokhy, *The Cossacks and Religion in Early Modern Ukraine* (Oxford, 2001).

14 On Lassota and his diary, see *Habsburgs and Zaporozhian Cossacks: The Diary of Erich Lassota von Steblau, 1594,* trans. Orest Subtelny, ed. Lubomyr R. Wynar (Littleton, Colo., 1975). On Komulović and his encounters with Ostrozky and the Cossacks, see Lubomyr R. Wynar, *Ukrainian Kozaks and the Vatican in 1654* (New York, 1965). For an English translation of the papal letters to the Cossacks, see *Habsburgs and Zaporozhian Cossacks,* 120–23.

Russia and Ukraine: Did They Reunite in 1654?

This essay has not been previously published.

1 See Viacheslav Lypyns´kyi, *Ukraïna na perelomi, 1657–59: Zamitky do istoriï ukraïns´koho derzhavnoho budivnytstva v XVII-im stolitti* (Vienna, 1920), 28–29.

2 On the events of the period and the rise of the cult of Bohdan Khmelnytsky in the late 1720s, see Serhii Plokhy, *Tsars and Cossacks: A Study in Iconography* (Cambridge, Mass., 2002), 45–54.

3 See Orest Subtelny, *Ukraine: A History* (Toronto, 1988), 203.

4 On the interpretation of Russo-Ukrainian relations in Russian imperial historiography, see Stephen Velychenko, *National History as Cultural Process: A Survey of the Interpretations of Ukraine's Past in Polish, Russian, and Ukrainian Historical Writing from the Earliest Times to 1914* (Edmonton, 1992), 79–140.

5 On Hrushevsky's "deconstruction" of the Russian imperial narrative, see my *Unmaking Imperial Russia: Mykhailo Hrushevsky and the Writing of Ukrainian History* (Toronto, 2005).

6 On the interpretation of Russo-Ukrainian relations in Soviet historiography of the 1940s and 1950s, see Serhy Yekelchyk, *Stalin's Empire of Memory: Russian-Ukrainian Relations in the Soviet Historical Imagination* (Toronto, 2004).

7 On the treatment of the Pereiaslav Agreement in Soviet historiography in connection with the 1954 celebrations of the "reunification of Ukraine with

Russia," see John Basarab, *Pereiaslav 1654: A Historiographical Study* (Edmonton, 1982), 179–87, and the introduction to the book by Ivan L. Rudnytsky, "Pereiaslav: History and Myth," xi–xxiii. For an English translation of the "Theses," see ibid., 270–87.

8 See, for example, Henadz´ Sahanovich, *Neviadomaia vaina, 1654–67* (Minsk, 1995). On the treatment of the term "reunification" in contemporary Russian and Ukrainian historiography, see my article "The Ghosts of Pereiaslav: Russo-Ukrainian Historical Debates in the Post-Soviet Era," *Europe-Asia Studies* 53, no. 3 (2001): 489–505.

9 See *Akty, otnosiashchiesia k istorii Zapadnoi Rossii* (Sankt-Peterburg, 1854), 4: 47–49.

10 See P.N. Zhukovich, "Protestatsiia mitropolita Iova Boretskogo i drugikh zapadnorusskikh ierarkhov, sostavlennaia 28 aprelia 1621 goda," in *Stat´i po slavianovedeniiu*, ed. V.I. Lamanskii (Sankt-Peterburg, 1910), vyp. 3: 135–53, here 143. Cf. Plokhy, *The Cossacks and Religion*, 291.

11 See "Hustyns´kyi litopys," in *Ukrains´ka literatura XVII stolittia* (Kyiv, 1987), 146–66, here 147.

12 For the text of the letter, see *Vossoedinenie Ukrainy s Rossiei: Dokumenty i materialy v trekh tomakh* (Moskva, 1954), 1: 46–48. Cf. Plokhy, *The Cossacks and Religion*, 289–90.

13 See letters from Kopynsky to Filaret (December 1622) and Filaret's letter to Boretsky (April 1630) in *Vossoedinenie Ukrainy s Rossiei*, 1: 27–28, 81. On the negotiations of 1632, see Sergei Solov´ev, *Istoriia Rossii s drevneishikh vremen* (Moskva, 1961), 5: 176.

14 On the origins of the "Ukase" and its impact on Muscovite religious policy, see Tat´iana Oparina, "Ukrainskie kazaki v Rossii: edinovertsy ili inovertsy? (Mikita Markushevskii protiv Leontiia Pleshcheeva)," *Sotsium* 3 (2003): 21–44, here 32–33. Cf. Oparina, *Ivan Nasedka i polemicheskoe bogoslovie kievskoi mitropolii* (Novosibirsk, 1998), 60–65.

15 For a detailed discussion of the rebaptism of Ukrainian Cossacks in Muscovy, see Oparina, "Ukrainskie kazaki v Rossii," 34–44.

16 On the legal nature of the Pereiaslav Agreement, see the articles by Mykhailo Hrushevs´kyi, Andrii Iakovliv, and Oleksander Ohloblyn in *Pereiaslavs´ka Rada 1654 roku (istoriohrafiia ta doslidzhennia)* (Kyïv, 2003). For recent debates on the issue, see my article "The Ghosts of Pereiaslav: Russo-Ukrainian Historical Debates in the Post-Soviet Era," *Europe-Asia Studies* 53, no. 3 (May 2001): 489–505.

17 See *Vossoedinenie Ukrainy s Rossiei*, 3: 189.

18 See the ambassadorial report of Ivan Fomin, the Muscovite emissary to Khmelnytsky, on his discussions with the hetman in August 1653 (*Vossoedinenie Ukrainy s Rossiei*, 3: 357).

19 See the report on Ivan Iskra's embassy to Muscovy in the spring of 1653 in *Vossoedinenie Ukrainy s Rossiei*, 3: 209.

20 For a survey of developments in the Muscovite church in the mid-seventeenth century, see Paul Bushkovitch, *Religion and Society in Russia: The Sixteenth and Seventeenth Centuries* (New York and Oxford, 1992), 51–73, 128–49. On the publication of Kyivan books in Moscow, see Oparina, *Ivan Nasedka*, 245–86.

21 On the course of the negotiations of 1653, which took place in Lviv and involved a Muscovite embassy headed by Boris Repnin-Obolensky, see Hrushevs´kyi, *Istoriia Ukraïny-Rusy* (New York, 1958) 9, pt. 2: 619–41.

22 See the decisions of the Assembly of the Land in *Vossoedinenie Ukrainy s Rossiei*, 3: 414.

23 For the texts of the speeches, see the report of Buturlin's embassy in *Vossoedinenie Ukrainy s Rosiiei*, 3: 423–89. Cf. Plokhy, *The Cossacks and Religion*, 318–25.

24 See Khmelnytsky's letter dated 29 July (8 August) 1648 in *Dokumenty Bohdana Khmel´nyts´koho (1648–1657)*, comp. Ivan Kryp'iakevych (Kyïv, 1961), 65.

25 There was also no attempt to play on the theme of ethnic affinity in Khmelnytsky's letter of 29 September (9 October) 1649 to the voevoda Fedor Arseniev, in which the hetman complained about attacks on "the Orthodox Rus´ and our faith" (ibid., 143). Khmelnytsky's use of the formula "sovereign of all Rus´" in his letters to the tsar seems to have been fairly insignificant, given that in his letters to Muscovite correspondents (including the missive to Arseniev) the hetman also used the full title of John Casimir, which included a reference to the king as "Prince of Rus´."

26 See Khmelnytsky's letters in *Dokumenty Bohdana Khmel´nyts´koho*, 286, 298, 316.

27 On the tsar's new title, see Mykhailo Hrushevs´kyi, "Velyka, Mala i Bila Rus´," *Ukraïna* 1917, nos. 1–2: 7–19; A.V. Solov´ev, "Velikaia, Malaia i Belaia Rus´," *Voprosy istorii* 1947, no. 7: 24–38.

28 See Plokhy, *The Cossacks and Religion*, 326.

29 See Khmelnytsky's petition of 17 (27) February 1654 to the tsar in *Dokumenty Bohdana Khmel´nyts´koho*, 323.

30 See Khmelnytsky's letter of 19 (29) July 1654 to the tsar in *Dokumenty Bohdana Khmel´nyts´koho*, 373.

31 See the description of the disagreement over the oath in Buturlin's ambassadorial report (*Vossoedinenie Ukrainy s Rossiei*, 3: 464–66).

32 Andreas Kappeler, *The Russian Empire: A Multiethnic History* (Harlow, 2001), 52.

33 Quoted in Oparina, *Ivan Nasedka*, 342.

Hadiach 1658: The Origins of a Myth

This essay draws on two of my earlier articles: "Hadjac 1658: The Origins of a Myth," in *Nel mondo degli Slavi. Incontri e dialoghi tra culture: Studi in onore di Giovanna Brogi Bercoff*, ed. Maria Giovanna Di Salvo, Giovanna Moracci, and Giovanna Siedina (Florence, 2008), 449–58, and "Reconstructive Forgery: The Hadiach Agreement (1658) in the *History of the Rus'*," *Journal of Ukrainian Studies*, nos. 35–36 (2010–2011) [2013]: 37–49.

1 On the Union of Hadiach, see Vasyl´ Herasymchuk, "Vyhovshchyna i hadiats´kyi traktat," *Zapysky Naukovoho tovarystva im. Shevchenka* 87 (1909): 5–36; 88 (1909): 23–50; 89 (1909): 46–91; Mykola Stadnyk, "Hadiats´ka uniia," *Zapysky Ukraïns´koho naukovoho tovarystva u Kyievi* 7 (1910): 65–85; 8 (1911): 5–39; Wacław Lipiński (Viacheslav Lypyns´kyi), *Z dziejów Ukrainy* (Kyïv and Kraków, 1912), 588–617; Mykhailo Hrushevs´kyi, *Istoriia Ukraïny-Rusy* (New York, 1958), 10: 288–359; Władysław Tomkiewicz, "Ugoda hadziacka," *Sprawy narodowościowe* 11, nos. 1–2 (1937): 14–21; Stanisław Kot, *Jerzy Niemirycz, w 300-lecie Ugody Hadziackiej* (Paris, 1960); Andrzej Kamiński, "The Cossack Experiment in Szlachta Democracy in the Polish-Lithuanian Commonwealth: The Hadiach (Hadziacz) Union," *Harvard Ukrainian Studies* 1, no. 2 (June 1977): 178–97, here 195–97; Janusz Kaczmarczyk, "Hadziacz 1658: Kolejna ugoda czy nowa unia," *Warszawskie Zeszyty Ukrainistyczne* 2 (1994): 35–42; A. Mironowicz, *Prawosławie i unia za panowania Jana Kazimierza* (Białystok, 1997), 149–89; Tetiana Iakovleva, *Het´manshchyna v druhii polovyni 50-kh rokiv XVII stolittia: Prychyny ta pochatok Ruïny* (Kyïv, 1998), 305–23.

2 On the negative aspects of the Hadiach Agreement, see Stefania Ochmann-Staniszewska and Zdzisław Staniszewski, *Sejm Rzeczypospolitej za panowania Jana Kazimierza Wazy: prawo, doktryna, praktyka* (Wrocław, 2000), 1: 315–18. Cf. Serhii Plokhy, *The Cossacks and Religion in Early Modern Ukraine* (Oxford, 2001), 62–64.

3 See Lipiński, *Z dziejów Ukrainy*, 595–98; Hrushevs´kyi, *Istoriia Ukraïny-Rusy*, 10: 352–57.

4 Ivan Franko, "Poza mezhamy mozhlyvoho," http://franko.lviv.ua/faculty/Phil/Franko/Poza_mezhamy.pdf.

5   See Andrzej Kamiński, *Historia Rzeczypospolitej Wielu Narodów, 1505–1795* (Lublin, 2000), 134–35. For a survey of the ideas that informed traditional Polish historiography, see Hrushevs'kyi, *Istoriia Ukraïny-Rusy*, 10: 354–55. On the approaches dominant in modern Polish historiography, see A.B. Pernal, "The Union of Hadiach (1658) in the Light of Modern Polish Historiography," in *Millennium of Christianity in Ukraine, 988–1988* (Winnipeg, 1989), 177–92.

6   Nataliia Iakovenko, *Narys istoriï Ukraïny z naidavnishykh chasiv do kintsia XVIII stolittia* (Kyïv, 1997), 212. Cf. Iakovenko, *Narys istoriï seredn'ovichnoï ta rann'omodernoï Ukrainy* (Kyïv, 2005), 373–74.

7   Direct references to the Hadiach articles are to be found, for example, in the instructions of Hetman Petro Doroshenko to his representatives at the Ostrih Commission (1670), as well as in the instructions to Polish delegates to the commission. See *Tysiacha rokiv ukraïns'koï suspil'no-politychnoï dumky u dev'iaty tomakh*, vol. 3, bk. 2 (Kyïv, 2001), 56, 63, 67.

8   See *Litopys samovydtsia*, ed. Iaroslav Dzyra (Kyïv, 1971), 81. Cf. the two distinct versions of the Hadiach Agreement in Hrushevs'kyi, *Istoriia Ukraïny-Rusy*, 10: 334–43. Although the final text of the agreement contains no reference to the Diet, such a provision appears in Wespazjan Kochowski's account of it. See Iakovleva, *Het'manshchyna v druhii polovyni 50-kh rokiv XVII stolittia*, 433.

9   See *Litopys samovydtsia*, 76.

10   Samuel Twardowski, *Wojna Domowa z Kozaki i Tatary, Moskwą, potem Szwedami i z Węgry Przez lat Dwanaście* (Kalisz, 1681).

11   Ibid., 262–65.

12   See *Samiila Velychka Skazaniie o voini kozatskoi z poliakamy* (Kyïv, 1926), 166, 184–86.

13   On the time of writing of the chronicle, its author and his sources, see Yuri Lutsenko's introduction to *Hryhorij Hrabjanka's "The Great War of Bohdan Xmel'nyc'kyj"* (Cambridge, Mass., 1990), xv–xliv. Cf. Serhii Plokhy, *The Origins of the Slavic Nations: Premodern Identities in Russia, Ukraine and Belarus* (Cambridge, 2006), 343–45.

14   See *Hryhorij Hrabjanka's "The Great War of Bohdan Xmel'nyc'kyj,"* 378.

15   Ibid., 379–81.

16   See [Wespazjan Kochowski], *Annalium Poloniae ab obitu Vladislai IV: Climacter primus* (Kraków, 1683). For a nineteenth-century Polish translation of Kochowski's work, *see Historia panowania Jana Kazimierza z Klimakterów*, 3 vols. (Poznań, 1859), 1: 363–65.

17   See *Hryhorij Hrabjanka's "The Great War of Bohdan Xmel'nyc'kyj,"* 379–80.

18   See *Litopys samovydtsia*, 80–81; Twardowski, *Wojna Domowa*, 262–63.

19   See Serhii Plokhy, *Tsars and Cossacks: A Study in Iconography* (Cambridge, Mass., 2002), 45–54; cf. Plokhy, *The Origins of the Slavic Nations*, 348–50.

20   See *Hryhorij Hrabjanka's "The Great War of Bohdan Xmel'nyc'kyj,"* 378–81.

21   On the popularity of Hrabianka's chronicle and the *Brief Description of Little Russia*, see Elena Apanovich, *Rukopisnaia svetskaia kniga XVIII veka na Ukraine: istoricheskie sborniki* (Kyïv, 1983), 137–201; Andrii Bovhyria, "'Korotkyi opys Malorosiï' (1340–1734) u rukopysnykh spyskakh XVIII st.," *Istoriohrafichni doslidzhennia v Ukraïni*, vyp. 14 (Kyïv, 2004), 340–63.

The Return of Ivan Mazepa

This essay draws on two of my earlier articles, "Reconstructive Forgery: The Hadiach Agreement (1658) in the *History of the Rus'*," *Journal of Ukrainian Studies*, nos. 35–36 (2010–2011) [2013]: 37–49, and "Forbidden Love: Ivan Mazepa and the Author of the *History of the Rus'*," in *Poltava 1709: The Battle and the Myth*, ed. Serhii Plokhy (Cambridge, Mass., 2012), 553–68.

1   I refer here to the broad definition of myth employed by George Schöpflin in his article "The Functions of Myth and a Taxonomy of Myths," in *Myths and Nationhood*, ed. Geoffrey Hosking and George Schöpflin (London, 1997), 19–35.

2   On the anathematization of Mazepa, see Nadieszda Kizenko, "The Battle of Poltava in Imperial Liturgy," in *Poltava 1709: The Battle and the Myth*, 227–70.

3   A. I. Martos, "Zapiski inzhenernogo ofitsera Martosa o Turetskoi voine v tsarstvovanie Aleksandra Pavlovicha," *Russkii arkhiv*, no. 7 (1893): 345. On Oleksii Martos, see Volodymyr Kravchenko, *Narysy z istoriï ukraïns'koï istoriohrafiï epokhy natsional'noho Vidrodzhennia (druha polovyna XVIII–seredyna XIX st.)* (Kharkiv, 1996), 91–98. On Ivan Martos, see I. M. Gofman, *Ivan Petrovich Martos* (Leningrad, 1970).

4   Diary of Mikhail Pogodin, Russian State Library, Manuscript Division, fond 231, vol. 1, fols. 188v–189r. Cf. Nikolai Barsukov, *Zhizn' i trudy M. P. Pogodina*, vol. 1 (Sankt-Peterburg, 1888), 153.

5   Diary of Mikhail Pogodin, vol. 1, fols. 188v–189r. Cf. Barsukov, *Zhizn' i trudy*, 1: 153; Oleksander Ohloblyn, *Liudy staroï Ukraïny* (Munich, 1959), 155–57; "Pamiatnoe delo," *Osnova* (July 1861): 41–74, here 52–53.

6   *Istoriia Rusov ili Maloi Rossii: Sochinenie Georgiia Koniskogo, arkhiepiskopa Belorusskogo* (Moskva, 1846); Volodymyr Sverbyhuz, *Starosvits'ke panstvo* (Warsaw, 1999), 122–24; I. F. Pavlovskii, *Poltavtsy: ierarkhi, gosudarstvennye i obshchestvennye deiateli i blagotvoriteli* (Poltava, 1914), 38–45.

7 See Mykhailo Vozniak, *Pseudo-Konys´kyi i pseudo-Poletyka ("Istoriia Rusov" u literaturi i nautsi)* (L´viv; Kyïv, 1939), 5–7; O. P. Ohloblyn, *Do pytannia pro avtora "Istorii Rusiv"* (Kyïv, 1998); Kravchenko, *Narysy*, 87, 101–57; Serhii Plokhy, *Ukraine and Russia: Representations of the Past* (Toronto, 2008), 49–65.

8 *Istoriia Rusov*, 200.

9 Voltaire, *History of Charles the Twelfth, King of Sweden* (New York, 1858), 127–28; *Istoriia Rusov*, 200.

10 *Istoriia Rusov*, 209.

11 Ibid., 203–5.

12 *Persha konstytutsiia Ukraïny het´mana Pylypa Orlyka, 1710 rik* (Kyïv, 1994), iii–vii; see Orlyk's letter to Metropolitan Iavorsky in *Osnova*, no. 10 (October 1862): 1–28; Orest Subtelny, *The Mazepists: Ukrainian Separatism in the Early Eighteenth Century* (Boulder, Colo., 1981), 190.

13 "Kratkoe istoricheskoe opisanie o Maloi Rossii do 1765," *Chteniia v Obshchestve istorii i drevnostei rossiiskikh*, no. 6 (1848): 37.

14 *Istoriia Rusov*, 209–10.

15 Ibid., 210.

16 Kravchenko, *Narysy*, 151, 154.

17 *Istoriia Rusov*, 214.

18 Ibid., 206–7.

19 Semen Divovych, "Razgovor Velikorossii s Malorossieiu," in *Ukraïns´ka literatura XVIII stolittia* (Kyïv, 1983), 398.

20 *Istoriia Rusov*, 208–9.

21 Ibid., 212–13.

22 Ibid., 215.

23 Kravchenko, *Narysy*, 97.

24 *Istoriia Rusov*, 211–12.

How Russian Was the Russian Revolution?

This essay first appeared as a discussion piece in a forum entitled "The Geopolitical Legacy of the Russian Revolution," *Geopolitics* 22, no. 3 (2017): 665–92.

1 Nicholas P. Vakar, *Belorussia: The Making of a Nation. A Case Study* (Cambridge, Mass., 1956), 103.

2 V. I. Lenin, *Polnoe sobranie sochinenii* (Moskva, 1969), 39: 335.

3 V. I. Lenin, *Polnoe sobranie sochinenii* (Moskva, 1969), 45: 361.

Killing by Hunger

This is the original version of an article published with some revisions as "Killing by Hunger," a review of Anne Applebaum, *Red Famine: Stalin's War on Ukraine* (New York, 2017), in the *New York Review of Books* 65, no. 13 (16 August 2018), https://www.nybooks.com/articles/2018/08/16/stalin-ukraine-killing-by-hunger/. All quotations in this review are cited from the book.

Mapping the Great Famine

First published under the same title in *The Future of the Past: New Perspectives on Ukrainian History* (=*Harvard Ukrainian Studies* 43, nos. 1–4 (2015–2016): 385–430).

1 "Z shchodennyka vchytel´ky O. Radchenko," in *Holodomor 1932–1933 rokiv v Ukraïni: Dokumenty i materialy*, ed. Ruslan Pyrih (Kyïv, 2007), 1012–25.

2 For the variety of approaches to the study of the Holodomor, see S. Maksudov, "Losses Suffered by the Population of the USSR, 1918–1958," in *The Samizdat Register II*, ed. R. Medvedev (London and New York, 1981); Robert Conquest, *The Harvest of Sorrow: Soviet Collectivization and the Terror-Famine* (New York and Edmonton, 1986); Mark B. Tauger, "The 1932 Harvest and the Famine of 1933," *Slavic Review* 50, no. 1 (1991): 70–89; Andrea Graziosi, *The Great Soviet Peasant War: Bolsheviks and Peasants, 1918–1934* (Cambridge, Mass., 1996); Terry Martin, *The Affirmative Action Empire: Nations and Nationalism in the Soviet Union, 1923–1939* (Ithaca, N.Y., 2001); *Komandyry velykoho holodu: Poïzdky V. Molotova i L. Kahanovycha v Ukraïnu ta na Pivnichnyi Kavkaz, 1932–1933 rr.*, ed. Valerii Vasyl´iev and Iurii Shapoval (Kyïv, 2001); J. Vallin, F. Meslé, S. Adamets, and S. Pyrozhkov, "A New Estimate of Ukrainian Population Losses during the Crisis of the 1930s and 1940s," *Population Studies* 56, no. 3 (November 2002); Mark Tauger, *Natural Disasters and Human Actions in the Soviet Famine of 1931–1933*, The Carl Beck Papers in Russian & East European Studies (Pittsburgh, 2001); Stanislav Kul´chyts´kyi, *Demohrafichni naslidky Holodomoru 1933 r. v Ukraïni* (Kyïv, 2003); Stephen Wheatcroft, "Towards Explaining the Soviet Famine of 1931–3: Political and Natural Factors in Perspective," *Food and Foodways* 12, nos. 2–3 (2004): 107–36; R. W. Davies and Stephen G. Wheatcroft, *The Years of Hunger: Soviet Agriculture, 1931–33* (Basingstoke, 2004); Michael Ellman, "The Role of Leadership Perceptions and of Intent in the Soviet Famine of 1931–1934," *Europe-Asia Studies* 57, no. 6 (September 2005): 823–41; Roman Serbyn,

"The Ukrainian Famine of 1932–33 as Genocide in the Light of the UN Convention of 1948," *Ukrainian Quarterly* 62, no. 2 (2006): 181–94; *Hunger by Design: The Great Ukrainian Famine and Its Soviet Context*, ed. Halyna Hryn (Cambridge, Mass., 2008); Hiroaki Kuromiya, "The Soviet Famine of 1932–33 Reconsidered," *Europe-Asia Studies* 60, no. 4 (2008): 663–75; V.V. Kondrashin, *Golod 1932–33 godov: Tragediia rossiiskoi derevni* (Moskva, 2008); N.A. Ivnitskii, *Golod 1932–33 godov v SSSR: Ukraina, Kazakhstan, Povolzh'e, Tsentral'no-Chernozemnaia oblast', Zapadnaia Sibir', Ural* (Moskva, 2009); Timothy Snyder, *Bloodlands: Europe between Hitler and Stalin* (New York, 2010); Norman Naimark, *Stalin's Genocides* (Princeton, N.J., 2010); Stanislav Kul'chitskii [Stanyslav Kul'chyts'kyi], "Ukrainskii Golodomor kak genotsid," in *Sovremennaia rossiisko-ukrainskaia istoriografiia goloda 1932–33 gg. v SSSR*, ed. V.V. Kondrashin (Moskva, 2011), 217–316. For a historiographic overview of recent discussions on the Holodomor, see Liudmyla Grynevych [Hrynevych], "The Present State of Ukrainian Historiography on the Holodomor and Prospects for Its Development," *The Harriman Review* 16, no. 2 (2008): 10–20; Heorhii Kas'ianov, *Danse Macabre: Holod 1932–33 rokiv u politytsi, masovii svidomosti ta istoriohrafiï (1980-ti–pochatok 2000-kh)* (Kyïv, 2010).

3   On the Digital Atlas of the Holodomor as a collaborative project, see Hennadii Boriak and Rostyslav Sossa, "GIS-Atlas Holodomoru v Ukraïni 1932–33 rr.," in *Natsional'ne kartohrafuvannia: stan, problemy ta perspektyvy rozvytku*, vyp. 5 (Kyïv, 2012), 30–34. Joseph Livesey (University of New York) collected and systematized data on government policies; Heorhii Papakin (Institute of History, Kyiv) collected and systematized data on blacklisted communities; Hennadii Iefimenko (Institute of History, Kyiv) collected and systematized data on collectivization in Ukraine; and Tetiana Boriak (National Academy of Cadres in Culture and Arts, Kyiv) systematized data based on the testimonies of famine survivors. The map of the 1928 famine is based on data collected by Liudmyla Hrynevych (Institute of History, Kyiv). Hennadii Boriak (Institute of History, Kyiv) provided intellectual leadership for the research projects conducted in Ukraine in conjunction with the Digital Atlas of Ukraine project, and Alexander Babyonyshev (Sergei Maksudov), an associate of the Davis Center at Harvard, provided consultations for our project on more than one occasion. Research on the project has been supported by the Ukrainian Research Institute at Harvard University and the Ukrainian Studies Fund.

4   *Holodomor 1932–1933 rokiv v Ukraïni: Dokumenty i materialy*, ed. Ruslan Pyrih [Cited henceforth as *Holodomor*].

5 On the steppe areas of Ukraine, see V. Dokuchaev, *Nashi stepi prezhde i teper'* (Sankt-Peterburg, 1892); A. Izmail'skii, *Kak vysokhla nasha step'* (Poltava, 1893); V. Pashchenko, "Stepnaia zona," in *Priroda Ukrainskoi SSR: Landshafty* (Kyïv, 1985); *Priroda Ukrainskoi SSR: Landshafty i fizikogeograficheskoe raionirovanie*, ed. A.M. Marinich, V.M. Pashchenko, and P.G. Shishchenko (Kyïv, 1985).

6 The maps discussed here are available online at the HURI Mapa website: Map 1: Famines of the 1920s, Map 2, https://gis.huri.harvard.edu/media-gallery/detail/1382387/1085949.

Map 2: Famines of the 1920s, Map 3, https://gis.huri.harvard.edu/media-gallery/detail/1382387/1085950.

Map 3: Demography, Population Losses, Map 1, https://gis.huri.harvard.edu/media-gallery/detail/1381000/1082125.

Map 4: Demography, Population Losses, Map 2, https://gis.huri.harvard.edu/media-gallery/detail/1381000/1082128.

Map 5: Demography, Population Losses, Map 3, https://gis.huri.harvard.edu/media-gallery/detail/1381000/1082131.

Map 6: Demography, Population Losses, Map 4, https://gis.huri.harvard.edu/media-gallery/detail/1381000/1082132.

Map 7: Government Policy, Collectivization, Map 1, https://gis.huri.harvard.edu/media-gallery/detail/1383000/1084434.

Map 8: Ecology and Agriculture, Map 1, https://gis.huri.harvard.edu/media-gallery/detail/1381978/1083803. The source for the map is Volodymyr Kubiiovych, *Atlias Ukraïny i sumizhnykh kraïv* (Lviv, 1937), no. 4, xii.

Map 9: Ecology and Agriculture, Map 2, https://gis.huri.harvard.edu/media-gallery/detail/1381978/1083804.

Map 10: Ecology and Agriculture, Map 3, https://gis.huri.harvard.edu/media-gallery/detail/1381978/1083806.

Map 11: Government Policy, Blacklisted Localities, Map 1, https://gis.huri.harvard.edu/media-gallery/detail/1382384/1085780.

Map 12: Government Policy, Procurement and Grain Loans, Map 3, https://gis.huri.harvard.edu/media-gallery/detail/1382386/1088169.

7 On famines in Ukraine in the twentieth century, see O.M. Veselova et al., *Holodomory v Ukraïni 1921–23, 1932–33, 1946–47: Zlochyny proty narodu* (Kyïv and New York, 2002); Liudmyla Hrynevych, *Khronika kolektyvizatsiï ta Holodomoru v Ukraïni*, vol. 1, bk. 2: *Pochatok nadzvychainykh zakhodiv: Holod 1928–1929 rokiv* (Kyïv, 2012).

8 O. Rudnytsky, N. Levchuk, O. Wolowyna, and P. Shevchuk, "1932–33 Famine Losses in Ukraine within the Context of the Soviet Union,"

in *Famines in European Economic History: The Last Great European Famines Reconsidered*, ed. D. Curran, L. Luciuk, and A. Newby (Abingdon, 2015).

9 See Steven Uitkroft [Stephen G. Wheatcroft], "Pokazateli demograficheskogo krizisa v period goloda v SSSR," 89–90, online at http://rusarchives.ru/publication/wheatcroft-pokazateli-demografy-crizis-golod-sssr/; cf. FamineWeb—Comparative History of Famines, Map Gallery, http://www.famine.unimelb.edu.au/ussr33bd/ukraine33d.php.

10 "Iz informatsionnoi svodki no. 52 Kolkhoztsentra o khode kollektivizatsii v zernovykh raionakh v kontse sentiabria–nachale oktiabria 1930 g. 18 oktiabria 1930 g." in *Tragediia sovetskoi derevni: Kollektivizatsiia i raskulachivanie: Dokumenty i materialy*, vol. 2, *Noiabr´ 1929-dekabr´ 1930* (Moskva, 2000), 670–76; "Povidomlennia informatsiinoï hrupy Narkomzemu USRR pro khid sutsil´noï kolektyvizatsiï i stavlennia do riznykh verstv selianstva, 17 bereznia 1931 r.," in *Kolektyvizatsiia i holod na Ukraïni: 1929–1933: Zbirnyk dokumentiv i materialiv*, comp. H.M. Mykhailychenko and Ie.P. Shatalina (Kyïv, 1992), no. 139. Between 1925 and 1930 the division of Ukraine into zones was changed more than once, but steppe areas were always treated as a separate zone or set of zones.

11 "O tempe kollektivizatsii i merakh pomoshchi gosudarstva kolkhoznomu stroitel´stvu, Postanovlenie TsK VKP(b), 5 ianvaria 1930 g.," in *KPSS v rezoliutsiiakh i resheniiakh s˝ezdov, konferentsii i plenumov TsK 5* (Moskva, 1984), 72–75; "Direktivy Politbiuro TsK VKP(b) po kontrol´nym tsifram na 1930/31 g. o programme rekonstruktsii sel´skogo khoziaistva, 25 iiulia 1930 g.," in *Tragediia sovetskoi derevni*, 2: 548.

12 "Postanova TsK VKP(b) pro traktory dlia Ukraïny," in *Holodomor*, 95; "Lyst sekretaria TsK KP(b)U S. Kosiora do sekretaria TsK VKP(b) I. Stalina," 26 April 1932, in *Holodomor*, 127–30.

13 "Lyst sekretaria TsK KP(b)U S. Kosiora do sekretaria TsK VKP(b) I. Stalina," 26 April 1932, in *Holodomor*, 127–30.

14 "Lyst V. Chubaria do V. Molotova ta I. Stalina," 10 April 1932, in *Holodomor*, 201.

15 "Lyst sekretaria Kyïvs´koho obkomu partiï M. Demchenka do S. Kosiora," 6 April 1932, in *Holodomor*, 115; "Zi shchodennyka partiinoho slidchoho Kyïvs´koï kontrol´noï komisiï D. Zavoloky," in *Holodomor*, 1005.

16 "Lyst upovnovazhenoho TsK KP(b)U A. Richyts´koho do S. Kosiora," 20 May 1932, in *Holodomor*, 166–67; "Lyst V. Chubaria do V. Molotova ta I. Stalina," 10 June 1932, in *Holodomor*, 201.

17 "Postanova Politbiuro TsK KP(b)U," 17 May 1932, in *Holodomor*, 161; "Lyst H. Petrovs´koho do V. Molotova ta I. Stalina," 10 June 1932, in *Holodomor*, 198;

"Dopovidna zapyska Kharkivs´koho obkomu partiï TsK KP(b)U," June 1932, in *Holodomor*, 221–24.

18 "Postanova TsK KP(b)U pro dodatkovu prodovol´chu dopomohu," 21 June 1932, in *Holodomor*, 213–14.

19 "Vytiah iz lysta I. Stalina do L. Kahanovycha," 15 June 1932, in *Holodomor*, 206.

20 "Vytiah iz lysta L. Kahanovycha do I. Stalina," 16 June 1932, in *Holodomor*, 207–8. On the policies and politics of famine relief, which often came in the form of loans to be repaid with interest the following year, see Tetiana Boriak, "Prodovol´cha dopomoha Kremlia iak instrument Holodomoru v Ukraïni," in *Zlochyny totalitarnykh rezhymiv v Ukraïni: naukovyi ta osvitnii pohliad* (Kyïv, 2012), 1–33.

21 "Lyst sekretaria Kyïvs´koho obkomu partii M. Demchenka do S. Kosiora," 6 April 1932, in *Holodomor*, 115; "Zi shchodennyka partiinoho slidchoho Kyïvs´koï kontrol´noï komisiï D. Zavoloky," in *Holodomor*, 1005.

22 "Zi shchodennyka partiinoho slidchoho Kyïvs´koï kontrol´noï komisiï D. Zavoloky," in *Holodomor*, 1006–8.

23 "Postanova Politbiuro TsK KP(b)U," 5 May 1932, in *Holodomor*, 149; "Lyst V. Kuibysheva do V. Chubaria," 10 May 1932, in *Holodomor*, 154–55; "Telehrama sekretaria TsK VKP(b) I. Stalina do sekretaria TsK KP(b)U S. Kosiora i holovy RNK USRR V. Chubaria," 29 May 1932, in *Holodomor*, 191.

24 "Postanova RNK SRSR i TsK VKP(b) 'Pro plan khlibozahotivel´ z urozhaiu 1932 roku…,'" 6 May 1932, in *Holodomor*, 150.

25 "Lyst V. Molotova i L. Kahanovycha do I. Stalina," 6 July 1932, in *Holodomor*, 231; "Postanova TsK VKP(b) pro orhanizatsiiu khlibozahotivel´ u 1932 rotsi," in *Holodomor*, 236; "Lyst TsK KP(b)U i RNK USRR do TsK VKP(b) iz prokhanniam perehlianuty rozbyvku khlibozahotivel´ po sektorakh dlia Ukraïny," in *Holodomor*, 255–56.

26 "Postanova Politbiuro TsK VKP(b) pro plan khlibozahotivel´ v Ukraïni z urozhaiu 1932 roku," in *Holodomor*, 260.

27 "Lyst L. Kahanovycha ta V. Kuibysheva do I. Stalina ta V. Molotova," 24 August 1932, in *Holodomor*, 298; "Postanova Politbiuro TsK VKP(b) pro plan khlibozahotivel´ v USRR," 28 August 1932, in *Holodomor*, 303–4.

28 "Plan khlibozahotivel´ po USRR na 1932 rik," in *Holodomor*, 242; "Postanova Politbiuro TsK KP(b)U," 30 October 1932, in *Holodomor*, 356.

29 "Telehrama M. Khataievycha do S. Kosiora, V. Molotova, V. Chubaria," 4 November 1932, in *Holodomor*, 367.

30 "Dyrektyva TsK VKP(b) obkomam, kraikomam ta TsK kompartiï soiuznykh respublik," 2 January 1933, in *Holodomor*, 571–72.

31 "Postanova TsK KP(b)U pro zmenshennia obsiahiv khlibozdachi," in *Holodomor*, 601–2.

32 "Z shchodennyka vchytel´ky O. Radchenko," in *Holodomor*, 1018–19.

33 "Analiz tsyfrovykh danykh pro operatyvnu robotu orhaniv DPU USRR," 8 December 1932, in *Holodomor*, 465; "Vytiah iz zvitu DPU USRR pro borot´-bu z teroryzmom," January 1933, in *Holodomor*, 631.

34 "Z shchodennyka vchytel´ky O. Radchenko," in *Holodomor*, 1022, 1024–35.

35 "Postanova Politbiuro TsK VKP(b) pro vidpusk zerna Dnipropetrovs´kii oblasti," 7 February 1933, in *Holodomor*, 663; "Postanova Politbiuro TsK VKP(b) pro vidpusk zerna Odes´kii oblasti," 7 February 1933, in *Holodomor*, 663; "Postanova TsK KP(b)U pro stan khlibopostachannia Donbasu," 17 February 1933, in *Holodomor*, 689–90.

36 "Dovidka DPU USRR," 12 March 1933, in *Holodomor*, 756; "Vidomosti TsK KP(b)U pro vydilennia prodovol´choï dopomohy," on or after 27 March 1933, in *Holodomor*, 795.

37 "Zapyska Narkomzemu USRR TsK KP(b)U," 14 March 1933, in *Holodomor*, 765.

38 "Postanova Politbiuro TsK KP(b)U pro zakhody, spriamovani na podolannia holodu v Kyïvs´kii oblasti," 17 March 1933, in *Holodomor*, 775–78; Oleh Wolowyna, "Seasonal Distribution of 1932–34 Famine Losses in Ukraine" (paper presented at the international conference "Holod v Ukraïni u pershii polovyni XX stolittia: prychyny i naslidky," Kyïv, 20–21 November 2013).

39 In early 1933, the rural population of Ukraine was 23.9 million. Of that number, Kyiv Oblast accounted for 4.95 million; Kharkiv, 4.76; Vinnytsia, 4.10; Dnipropetrovsk, 2.82; Chernihiv, 2.54; Odesa, 2.29; Donetsk, 1.98; and the Moldavian Autonomous Republic, 0.52 million people.

40 "Lyst S. Kosiora i V. Chubaria do I. Stalina," 29 May 1933, in *Holodomor*, 852; "Postanova Politbiuro TsK VKP(b) pro prodovol´chu pozyku Ukraïni," 30 May 1933, in *Holodomor*, 857–58; Wolowyna, "Seasonal Distribution."

41 "Svodnaia vedomost´ ob otpravlenii éshelonov s pereselentsami na Ukrainu," 28 December 1933, in *Holodomor*, 993.

42 See Andrey Shlyakhter's chapter "Borderness and Famine: Why Did Fewer People Starve to Death in Soviet Ukraine's Western Border Districts during the Holodomor, 1932–33?" in his forthcoming University of Chicago dissertation, "Smugglers and Soviets: Contraband Trade, the Soviet Struggle against It, and the Making of the Soviet Border Strip, 1917–1939." On Ukrainian peasants fleeing across the border to Poland in 1930, see Timothy

Snyder, *Sketches from a Secret War: A Polish Artist's Mission to Liberate Soviet Ukraine* (New Haven and London, 2005), 92–95.

43 Wolowyna, "Seasonal Distribution."

44 Uitkroft, "Pokazateli demograficheskogo krizisa," 89–90.

45 "Vytiah iz dopovidnoï zapysky Vinnytsʹkoho obkomu partiï TsK KP(b) U," 18 March 1933, in *Holodomor*, 779–83.

46 "Dovidka Narkomzemu USRR," 2 December 1932, in *Holodomor*, 439.

The Call of Blood

First published as "The Call of Blood: Government Propaganda and Public Response to the Soviet Entry into World War II" in *L'Union soviétique et la Seconde Guerre mondiale / The Soviet Union and World War II*, ed. Alain Blum, Catherine Gousseff, and Andrea Graziosi (=*Cahiers du monde russe. Russie, Empire russe, URSS, États indépendants* 53, nos. 2–3 (2012)).

1   *Na prieme u Stalina. Tetradi (zhurnaly) zapisei lits priniatykh I. V. Stalinym (1924–1953 gg.)*, ed. A.A. Chernobaev (Moskva, 2008), 272–73; *Dokumenty vneshnei politiki SSSR*, vol. 22, bk. 2 (Moskva, 1992), 25–28; Mykola Lytvyn and Kim Naumenko, *Stalin i Zakhidna Ukraïna, 1939–41* (Kyïv, 2010), 10–12; *The Diary of Georgi Dimitrov*, ed. Ivo Banac (New Haven, Conn., 2003), 115–16.

2   Schulenburg to the German Foreign Office, 10 September 1939, in *Nazi-Soviet Relations, 1939–1941: Documents from the Archives of the German Foreign Office*, ed. Raymond James Sontag and James Stuart Beddie (Washington, D.C., 1948), 91.

3   Schulenburg to the German Foreign Office, 14 September 1939, in *Nazi-Soviet Relations*, 92–93; *Wrzesień 1939 na kresach w relacjach*, ed. Czesław Grzelak (Warszawa, 1999), 41–42; Natalija Liebediewa, "Wrzesień 1939 r.: Polska między Niemcami a Związkiem Sowieckim," in *Kryzys 1939 roku w interpretacjach polskich i rosyjskich historyków*, ed. Sławomir Dębski and Michaił Narinski (Warszawa, 2009), 437–75, here 447–48.

4   "O vnutrennikh prichinakh porazheniia Polʹshi," *Pravda*, 14 September 1939, 1; Ribbentrop to Schulenburg, 15 September 1939, in *Nazi-Soviet Relations*, 94.

5   Schulenburg to the German Foreign Office, 16 September 1939, in *Nazi-Soviet Relations*, 95.

6   "Rechʹ po radio predsedatelia Soveta narodnykh komissarov SSSR tov. V.M. Molotova 17 sentiabria 1939 g.," *Pravda*, 18 September 1939, 1; "Nota pravitelʹstva SSSR, vruchennaia polʹskomu poslu v Moskve utrom 17

sentiabria 1939 goda," ibid., 1; Schulenburg to the German Foreign Office, 17 September 1939, in *Nazi-Soviet Relations*, 96.

7 V. Kovaliuk, "Novi arkhivni dokumenty pro Narodni zbory Zakhidnoï Ukraïny (zhovten´ 1939 r.)," *Arkhivy Ukraïny*, 1991, no. 5–6: 88; *Radians´ki orhany derzhavnoï bezpeky u 1939-chervni 1941 r. Dokumenty HAD SBU Ukraïny*, comp. Vasyl´ Danylenko and Serhii Kokin (Kyïv, 2009), 46–49, here 48.

8 Schulenburg to the German Foreign Office, 20 September 1939, in *Nazi-Soviet Relations*, 101; Ribbentrop to Schulenburg, 23 September 1939, ibid., 102; Schulenburg to the German Foreign Office, 25 September 1939, ibid., 102–3.

9 On the German interest in Galicia, see Michael Jabara Carley, *1939: The Alliance That Never Was and the Coming of World War II* (Chicago, 1999), 192–93.

10 A *New York Times* correspondent reported from Paris on 17 September: "Some people here think that Russia intends to take that part of Poland that was offered to her in the plan for settlement of Marquess Curzon of Kedleston. This went to a considerable distance west of the Soviet's present legal border. Then, it is presumed, the Russians would declare that they had a logical basis to claim this territory on the ground that even so extreme an opponent of the Bolsheviki as Lord Curzon had been willing to concede the Soviet's right to it." See Harold Denny, "Paris Sees Stalin in Betrayer Role," *New York Times*, 18 September 1939, 6. The London *Times* published a map of Poland including the Curzon Line and the new Soviet-German boundary in its issue for 18 September 1939. On the origins of the Curzon Line, see Jerzy Borzecki, *The Soviet-Polish Peace of 1921 and the Creation of Interwar Europe* (New Haven, Conn., 2008), 79–104. On the significance of Stalin's speech at the Eighteenth Congress of the Communist Party, see Donald Cameron Watt, *How War Came: The Immediate Origins of the Second World War* (New York, 1989), 110–11.

11 See Ingeborg Fleischhauer, "The Molotov-Ribbentrop Pact: The German Version," *International Affairs* (Moscow) 37, no. 8 (August 1991): 114–29. For the texts of the documents signed by Ribbentrop and Molotov in the early hours of 29 September (but dated the previous day), see *Nazi-Soviet Relations*, 105–9.

12 For Stalin's remark to Ribbentrop, see Simon Sebag Montefiore, *Stalin: The Court of the Red Tsar* (New York, 2003), 311. On negative reaction to the pact among the Nazi anti-Bolshevik core, see Ian Kershaw, *Hitler, 1936–45: Nemesis* (London, 2000), 205–6.

13 *Khrushchev Remembers*, introduction, commentary and notes by Edward Crankshaw; trans. and ed. Strobe Talbott (New York, 1971), 133; Viacheslav

Molotov, *Soviet Peace Policy: Four Speeches* (London, 1941), 16. For NKVD reports on public reaction to the Molotov-Ribbentrop Pact and Molotov's speech at a session of the USSR Supreme Soviet explaining the reasons for signing, see *Radians'ki orhany derzhavnoï bezpeky,* 968–85.

14 "O vnutrennikh prichinakh porazheniia Pol'shi." Cf. E. Sosnin, "Germano-pol'skaia voina (Obzor voennykh deistvii)," *Pravda,* 11 September 1939, 4.

15 "O vnutrennikh prichinakh porazheniia Pol'shi."

16 "Russia: Dizziness from Success," *Time,* 25 September 1939.

17 "Rech' po radio predsedatelia Soveta narodnykh komissarov SSSR tov. V.M. Molotova."

18 See Terry Martin, *The Affirmative Action Empire: Nations and Nationalism in the Soviet Union, 1923–1939* (Ithaca and London, 2001), 8–9, 225–27, 292–93, 312–19, 351–52.

19 See Joseph Stalin to Lazar Kaganovich, 11 August 1932, in *Stalin i Kaganovich: Perepiska, 1931–1936,* comp. Oleg Khlevniuk et al. (Moskva, 2001), no. 248; "Iz otchetnogo doklada pervogo sekretaria TsK KP(b)U N.S. Khrushcheva XIV s'ezdu KP(b)U," in *Politicheskoe rukovodstvo Ukrainy 1938–1989,* comp. V. Iu. Vasil'ev, R. Iu. Podkur, Kh. Kuromiia, Iu. I. Shapoval, and A. Vainer (Moskva, 2006), 35–47.

20 "Akt vsemirno istoricheskogo znacheniia," *Pravda,* 18 September 1939, 2.

21 "Krasnaia armiia neset schast'e narodu," *Pravda,* 18 September 1939, 3.

22 "Red Army in Polish territory. Molotoff excuses Soviet action. Protection of 'blood-relations.' A stab in the back," *The Times,* 18 September 1939, 6; G. E.R. Gedye, "Soviet 'Neutrality' Stressed in Move. Moscow Assures Other States on Invasion—Molotoff Gives Talk to Bewildered People," *New York Times,* 18 September 1939, 1.

23 Carley, *1939: The Alliance That Never Was,* 216–26. On the relation between ideology and *realpolitik* in Stalin's foreign policy of the period, see Amir Weiner, "Saving Private Ivan: From What, Why, and How?" *Kritika* 1, no. 2 (Spring 2000): 305–36, here 309–13. For research on public opinion during World War II, see Sarah Davies, *Soviet Public Opinion in Stalin's Russia: Terror, Propaganda and Dissent* (Cambridge, 1997); Steven Casey, *Cautious Crusade: Franklin D. Roosevelt, American Public Opinion, and the War against Nazi Germany* (New York, 2001); Daniel Hucker, *Public Opinion and the End of Appeasement in Britain and France* (Farnham, UK, 2011).

24 On the peculiarities of Soviet secret-police reports as a historical source concerning the state of public opinion, see Davies, *Soviet Public Opinion in Stalin's Russia,* 9–14.

25 See Jochen Hellbeck's exchange with Sarah Davies in a reprint of the *Kritika* polemics: *The Resistance Debate in Russian and Soviet History*, ed. Michael David-Fox (Bloomington, Ind., 2003). For a continuation of the debate, see Hiroaki Kuromiya, "How Do We Know What the People Thought under Stalin?" in *Sovetskaia vlast'—narodnaia vlast'?* ed. Timo Vihavainen (Sankt-Peterburg, 2003), 1–16.

26 *Radians'ki orhany derzhavnoï bezpeky*, nos. 431–56, 998–1073.

27 *Radians'ki orhany derzhavnoï bezpeky*, 49.

28 *Radians'ki orhany derzhavnoï bezpeky*, 998, 1001.

29 *Radians'ki orhany derzhavnoï bezpeky*, 995, 1001, 1054.

30 *Radians'ki orhany derzhavnoï bezpeky*, 1009–11, 1015, 1049; Harvard University, Widener Library, The Harvard Project on the Soviet Social System, Schedule B, vol. 6, case 193, 4.

31 *Radians'ki orhany derzhavnoï bezpeky*, 999.

32 See Davies, *Soviet Public Opinion in Stalin's Russia*, 97–99.

33 *Radians'ki orhany derzhavnoï bezpeky*, 1055; Vladyslav Hrynevych and Oleksandr Lysenko, "Ukraïna na pochatkovomu etapi Druhoï Svitovoï viiny," in *Ukraïna: politychna istoriia, XX–pochatok XXI stolittia* (Kyïv, 2007), 675.

34 *Radians'ki orhany derzhavnoï bezpeky*, 1012, 1018, 1021, 1032.

35 Like many others interviewed by the Harvard Project, this particular interviewee did not trust the Soviet media. She stated in that regard: "I read the newspapers very rarely because I knew that in the newspapers there was only Soviet propaganda." See Harvard University, Widener Library, The Harvard Project on the Soviet Social System, Schedule A, vol. 34, case 148/(NY) 1398, 30.

36 *Radians'ki orhany derzhavnoï bezpeky*, 1001, 1011, 1047, 1060.

37 G. E. R. Gedye, "Moscow Outlines Polish Partition," *New York Times*, 19 September 1939, 1, 5; V.I. Vernadskii, *Dnevniki, 1935–1941*, ed. V.P. Volkov, 2 vols. (Moskva, 2006), 2: 56, 67. On the revival of Russian national themes on the official and popular levels in the years leading up to World War II, see David Brandenberger, *National Bolshevism: Stalinist Mass Culture and the Formation of Modern Russian National Identity, 1931–1956* (Cambridge, Mass., 2002), 43–114.

38 Vernadskii, *Dnevniki, 1935–1941*, 2: 68.

39 *Radians'ki orhany derzhavnoï bezpeky*, 1030.

40 *Radians'ki orhany derzhavnoï bezpeky*, 998–99, 1021–22.

41 Martin, *Affirmative Action Empire*, 9; Serhy Yekelchyk, *Stalin's Empire of Memory: Russian-Ukrainian Relations in the Soviet Historical Imagination*

(Toronto, 2004), 13–62; Vladyslav Hrynevych, "Viina z Hitlerivs´koiu Nimechchynoiu (1941–1945)," in *Ukraïna: politychna istoriia*, 736–56.

42 Jan Tomasz Gross, *Revolution from Abroad: The Soviet Conquest of Poland's Western Ukraine and Western Belorussia* (Princeton, N.J., 2002), 71–114, 125–43; Serhii Plokhy, *Yalta: The Price of Peace* (New York, 2010), 166–82; Viktor Koval´, "Borot´ba za mizhnarodne vyznannia ukraïns´koho vidtynku novoho Zakhidnoho kordonu SRSR (1941–45)," in *Ukraïna: politychna istoriia*, 814–48.

The Battle for Eastern Europe

First published as "Stalin and Roosevelt," *Diplomatic History* 42, no. 4 (September 2018): 525–27.

1   "Foundations of Leninism" in Joseph Stalin, *Works* (Moscow, 1953), 6: 196.

The American Dream

This essay has not been previously published.

1   "Postanovlenie Politbiuro TsK VKP(b) "O vospreshchenii brakov mezhdu grazhdanami SSSR i inostrantsami," 15 February 1947, Fond Aleksandra Iakovleva, http://www.alexanderyakovlev.org/fond/issues-doc/69332; "V SSSR zapreshcheny braki mezhdu sovetskimi grazhdanami i inostrantsami," *Calend.ru* http://www.calend.ru/event/6932/.

2   M.M. Wolff, "Some Aspects of Marriage and Divorce Laws in Soviet Russia," *Modern Law Review* 12, no. 3 (July 1949): 290–96; Mie Nakachi, "N.S. Khrushchev and the 1944 Soviet Family Law: Politics, Reproduction, and Language," *East European Politics and Societies* 20, no. 1 (2006): 40–68; Norman M. Naimark, *The Russians in Germany: A History of the Soviet Zone of Occupation, 1945–1949* (Cambridge, Mass., 1995); Rachel Applebaum, *Empire of Friends: Soviet Power and Socialist Internationalism in Cold War Czechoslovakia* (Ithaca, N.Y., 2019), 59–63.

3   Serhii Plokhy, *Forgotten Bastards of the Eastern Front: An Untold Story of World War II* (London, 2019), 104–21, 176–85, 261–69.

4   "John Bazan in the 1940 Census," http://www.archives.com/1940-census/john-bazan-ny-58629820; "Catherine Bazan in the 1940 Census," http://www.archives.com/1940-census/catherine-bazan-ny-58629819; "John J. Bazan—WWII Enlistment Record, Bronx County, New York," http://wwii-army.mooseroots.com/l/3148004/John-J-Bazan; Photos of John Bazan, Arkhiv Sluzhby bezpeky Ukraïny (henceforth SBU Archives), fond 13, no. 1200, after f. 288.

5 Head of Zhovkva MGB department, Major Kudriashov, to head, 2nd department, Lviv MGB, Colonel Fokin, "Dokladnaia zapiska po delu-fomuliar no. 7236 na Tkachenko Zinaidu Danilovnu, podozrevaemuiu v prinalezhnosti k agenture amerikanskoi razvedki," SBU Archives, fond 13, no. 1200, fols. 325–26; Lieutenant Colonel Reshetnikov (Poltava) to Colonel Fokin (Lviv), 25 March 1948, SBU Archives, fond 13, no. 1200, f. 321.

6 See correspondence between the Zhovkva district MGB office and MGB headquarters in Lviv and Kyiv between May 1947 and April 1948, SBU Archives, fond 13, no. 1200, fols. 308–24.

7 Major Kudriashov (Zhovkva) to Colonel Fokin (Lviv), "Dokladnaia zapiska," after 25 June 1948, SBU Archives, fond 13, no. 1200, fols. 325–26; Colonel Fokin and head of 1st section, 2nd department, Lviv MGB directorate, Senior Lieutenant Gorbunov, to deputy chief, 2nd department, Ministry of State Security of Ukraine, Lieutenant Colonel Kovalev, 24 November 1948, ibid., f. 335; idem to Kudriashov, 24 November 1948, ibid., f. 336.

8 "Spravka po delu-formuliar no. 897 na [Tkachenko] Zinaidu Danilovnu," December 1952, SBU Archives, fond 13, no. 1200, fols. 296–98.

9 "Spravka po delu-formuliar no. 897 na [Tkachenko] Zinaidu Danilovnu," December 1952; Senior operative plenipotentiary, 1st section, 2nd department, Poltava MGB directorate Lieutenant Panfilov; Chief, 1st section, 2nd department, Poltava MGB directorate Lieutenant Colonel Meshcheriakov; and Head, 2nd department, same directorate, Colonel Reshetnikov, "Spravka po delu-formuliar no. 897" to head, Poltava MGB directorate Colonel Alekseev, 3 March 1953, SBU Archives, fond 13, no. 1200, fols. 281–84.

10 "Spravka po delu-formuliar no. 897 na [Tkachenko] Zinaidu Danilovnu," 3 March 1953; "Spravka po delu-formuliar no. 897 na [Tkachenko] Zinaidu Danilovnu," December 1952; Senior operative plenipotentiary, 1st section, 1st department, Poltava MGB directorate Lieutenant Kal´nitskii; Chief, 1st section Lieutenant Colonel Meshecheriakov, and Head, 2nd department Colonel Reshetnikov, "Zadanie agentu 1-go upravleniia MVD USSR 'Kareninoi,'" July 1953, SBU Archives, fond 13, no. 1200, fols. 290–91.

11 "Spravka po delu-formuliar no. 897 na [Tkachenko] Zinaidu Danilovnu," 3 March 1953; "Spravka po delu-formuliar no. 897 na [Tkachenko] Zinaidu Danilovnu," December 1952; Lieutenant Colonel Meshcheriakov and Colonel Reshetnikov, approved by Colonel Alekseev, October 1952, "Plan vvoda v razrabotku Tkachenko Zinaidy Danilovny agenta 'Nikolaeva,'" SBU Archives, fond 13, no. 1200, fols. 302–3; Meshcheriakov, Reshetnikov and Alekseev, "Zadanie Nikolaevu," October 1952, ibid., f. 304; "Zadanie Nikolaevu," October 4, 1952, ibid., f. 306.

12 Joshua Rubenstein, *The Last Days of Stalin* (New Haven and London, 2016).
13 "Spravka po delu-formuliar no. 897 na [Tkachenko] Zinaidu Danilovnu," 3 March 1953, SBU Archives, fond 13, no. 1200, fols. 281–84.
14 Panfilov, Meshcheriakov, and Reshetnikov, "Plan verbovki Tkachenko Zinaidy Danilovny," approved by Colonel Akopov, head, Poltava MGB directorate, on 3 March 1953, SBU Archives, fond 13, no. 1200, f. 285; "Plan doprosa Tkachenko Zinaidy Danilovny," 3 March 1953, ibid., fols. 286–88.
15 Montefiore, *Stalin*, 651.
16 "Zadanie agentu 1-go upravleniia MVD USSR 'Kareninoi,'" July 1953, SBU Archives, fond 13, no. 1200, fols. 290–91.
17 Senior plenipotentiary, 1st section, 2nd department, Poltava KGB directorate Lieutenant Kal´nitskii; Head, 1st section, Lieutenant Colonel Lukinykh; Head, 2nd department, Colonel Kolikov, "Zakliuchenie o sdache dela-formuliara v arkhiv," 22 September 1954, approved on 23 September 1954 by Major Klochko, head, Poltava directorate, KGB of the Ukrainian Soviet Socialist Republic, SBU Archives, fond 13, no. 1200, fols. 342–44.
18 "Ukaz Prezidiuma VS SSSR ot 26.11.1953 'Ob otmene Ukaza Prezidiuma Verkhovnogo Soveta SSSR ot 15 fevralia 1947 goda 'O vospreshchenii brakov mezhdu grazhdanami SSSR i inostrantsami',," http://bestpravo.com/sssr/eh-dokumenty/j3n.htm; John Bazan †70 (1911–1981), https://www.sysoon.com/deceased/john-bazan-35.

The Soviet Collapse

First published as "The Soviet Union Is Still Collapsing," *Foreign Policy*, 22 December 2016, https://foreignpolicy.com/2016/12/22/the-unlearned-lessons-from-the-collapse-of-the-soviet-union/.

Chornobyl

Originally published in Spanish in the March/April 2016 issue of *Política Exterior*, under the title "La lápida del imperio temerario."

Truth in Our Times

This essay is based on the Baillie Gifford Prize lecture delivered at the Edinburgh International Book Festival on 14 August 2019. It first appeared as a pamphlet published by the Edinburgh Book Festival, *Chernobyl: Truth in Our Times* (Edinburgh, 2019).

1   Serhii Plokhy, *Chernobyl: The History of a Nuclear Catastrophe* (New York, 2018). The British edition appeared under the title *Chernobyl: History of a Tragedy* (London, 2018).

The Empire Strikes Back

First published as "The Return of the Empire: The Ukraine Crisis in Historical Perspective," *South Central Review* 35, no. 1 (2018): 111–26.

1   Vladimir Putin, "Obrashchenie Prezidenta Rossiiskoi Federatsii," 18 March 2014, http://kremlin.ru/news/20603; cf. "Transcript: Putin says Russia will protect the rights of Russians abroad," *Washington Post*, 18 March 2015.

2   Peter Baker, "Pressure Rising as Obama Works to Rein In Russia," *New York Times*, 2 March 2014; Douglas Ernst, "Bill Clinton: Putin Trying to "re-establish Russian greatness," *Washington Times*, 14 May 2014; "Iatseniuk: Putin mriie vidrodyty SRSR," *BBC Ukraine*, 20 April 2014, http://www.bbc.com/ukrainian/politics/2014/04/140420_yatsenyuk_putin_ok.

3   On the history of the disintegration of the Soviet Union, see Stephen Kotkin, *Armageddon Averted: The Soviet Collapse, 1970–2000* (New York, 2008), and my *The Last Empire: The Final Days of the Soviet Union* (New York, 2014).

4   On Ukraine in the 1990s, see Alexander J. Motyl, *Dilemmas of Independence: Ukraine after Totalitarianism* (Washington, D.C., 1993); Bohdan Harasymiw, *Post-Communist Ukraine* (Edmonton and Toronto, 2002).

5   On the Orange Revolution, see Andrew Wilson, *Ukraine's Orange Revolution* (New Haven and London, 2006); *Democratic Revolution in Ukraine: From Kuchmagate to Orange Revolution,* ed. Taras Kuzio (London and New York, 2013).

6   Oleksandr Zinchenko, "Shchodennyk Maidanu. Pro shcho my todi dumaly," *Istorychna pravda*, 17 February 2015, http://www.istpravda.com.ua/articles/2015/02/17/147354/. Unless otherwise indicated, all translations from the Russian and Ukrainian are mine.

7   For an overview of events on the Maidan, Kyiv's Independence Square, from November 2013 to February 2014, see Andrew Wilson, *Ukraine Crisis: What It Means for the West* (New Haven and London, 2014), chapters 4 and 5.

8   "Putin rasskazal, kak prinimalos´ reshenie o vozvrashchenii Kryma," *NTV,* http://www.ntv.ru/novosti/1356399/; Putin, "Obrashchenie Prezidenta Rossiiskoi Federatsii," 18 March 2014, http://kremlin.ru/news/20603. The Russian takeover of the Crimea is discussed in Wilson, *Ukraine Crisis,*

chapter 6. On the prehistory of the Russian annexation of the peninsula, see Taras Kuzio, *The Crimea: Europe's Next Flashpoint?* (Washington, D.C., 2011); Gwendolyn Sasse, *The Crimea Question: Identity, Transition, and Conflict* (Cambridge, Mass., 2014).

9   The Russian hybrid war in eastern Ukraine received extensive coverage in the rapidly growing literature on the Ukraine crisis. Apart from the book by Andrew Wilson cited above, monographic contributions to the field include Richard Sakwa, *Frontline Ukraine: Crisis in the Borderlands* (London, 2014), and Rajan Menon and Eugene B. Rumer, *Conflict in Ukraine: The Unwinding of the Post-Cold War Order* (Boston, 2015).

10   "Al´fred Kokh i Boris Nemtsov o realiiakh Rossii i Putina," *Krugozor*, October 2014, http://www.krugozormagazine.com/show/article.2370.html.

11   Philip Rucker, "Hillary Clinton says Putin's actions are like 'what Hitler did back in the '30s,'" *Washington Post*, 5 March 2014; Vera Mironova and Maria Snegovaya, "Putin is behaving in Ukraine like Milosevic did in Serbia. History repeats itself," *New Republic*, 19 June 2014, http://www.newrepublic.com/article/118260/putin-behaving-ukraine-milosevic-did-serbia.

When Stalin Lost His Head

First published as "When Stalin Lost His Head: World War II and Memory Wars in Contemporary Ukraine," in *War and Memory in Russia, Ukraine and Belarus*, ed. Julie Fedor, Markku Kangaspuro, Jussi Lassila, and Tatiana Zhurzhenko (Cham, Switzerland, 2017), 171–88.

1   "Komunisty khytristiu vstanovyly Stalina v Zaporizhzhi," *Ukraïns´ka pravda*, 5 May 2010, http://www.pravda.com.ua/news/2010/05/5/5010465/; "Obezholovlenyi skandal´nyi pam'iatnyk Stalinu?" *Ukraïns´ka pravda*, 28 December 2010, http://www.pravda.com.ua/news/2010/12/28/5727613/; "Vidpovidal´nist´ za holovu Stalina vziala na sebe mobil´na hrupa," *Ukraïns´ka pravda*, 29 December 2010, http://www.pravda.com.ua/news/2010/12/29/5728631/; "U Zaporizhzhi idol Stalina znyshcheno," http://www.youtube.com/watch?v=RlmbIZfffNg&feature=related.

2   On the formation and history of the Stalin cult, see Adam Hochschild, *The Unquiet Ghost: Was Stalinism Really Necessary?* (New York, 1994); Jan Plamper, *The Stalin Cult: A Study in the Alchemy of Power* (New Haven and London, 2012). On the polling data, see Iurii Levada, *Ot mnenii k ponimaniiu: sotsiologicheskie ocherki* (Moskva, 2000), 453–59; Sarah Mendelson and Theodore Gerber, "Failing the Stalin Test," *Foreign Affairs* 85, no. 1 (January–February 2006); Aleksei Levinson, "Zachem mertvyi Stalin nuzhen zhivym

rossiianam," *Polit.ru*, 25 March 2010, http://polit.ru/article/2010/03/25/stalin/; "Sotsiologi porassuzhdali nad zagadkoi Stalina v sviazi s godovshchinoi smerti—i 'krovavyi tiran' i 'mudryi vozhd'" *News RU*, 4 March 2013, http://www.newsru.com/russia/04mar2013/stalin.html.

3   "Petro I u reitynhu heroïv Ukraïny obiishov Banderu," *TSN*, 28 September 2010, http://tsn.ua/ukrayina/petro-i-stav-geroyem-ukrayini.html.

4   "U Zaporozhzhi pidirvaly pam'iatnyk Stalinu," *Ukraïns'ka pravda*, 1 January 2011, http://www.pravda.com.ua/news/2011/01/1/5740807/; "Stalin Monument Opens in Zaporizhzhia, Ukraine," http://www.youtube.com/watch?v=exKx46yyoNQ.

5   "Ivan Shekhovtsov. Advokat Stalina," *Vremia*, 29 November 2004, http://timeua.info/011204/shehovcov.html.

6   "Pamiatnik Stalina v Zaporozh'e. Rech' veterana VOV Shekhovtsova," YouTube, http://www.youtube.com/watch?v=_W9mfJQMOR8.

7   "Kniga otzyvov. Otkrytie pamiatnika I.V. Stalinu. Zaporozhskii obkom Kompartii Ukrainy," 2, 4, 5, 11.

8   "U Zaporozhzhi pidirvaly pam'iatnyk Stalinu," *Ukraïns'ka pravda*, 1 January 2011; "Pam'iatnyk Stalinu vidnovyly," *Ukraïns'ka pravda*, 29 December 2010, http://www.pravda.com.ua/news/2010/12/29/5731032/.

9   "U Zaporozhzhi pidirvaly pam'iatnyk Stalinu," *Ukraïns'ka pravda*, 1 January 2011.

10   "Vidpovidal'nist' za pidryv pam'iatnyka Stalinu vziala na sebe orhanizatsiia 'Rukh Pershoho sichnia.' Ofitsiina zaiava," *Politiko*, 1 January 2011, http://politiko.ua/blogpost50828.

11   "U poshukakh terorystiv," *Halyts'kyi korespondent*, http://www.gk-press.if.ua/node/4236.

12   "Petro I u reitynhu heroïv Ukraïny obiishov Banderu," *TSN*, 28 September 2010.

13   "Stepan Bandera—heroi Ukraïny," *Radio Svoboda*, 23 January 2010, http://www.radiosvoboda.org/content/article/1936818.html.

14   Iurii Lukanov, "Spasybi Banderi za pam'iatnyk Stalinu," *Livyi bereh, LB.ua*, 10 May 2010, http://society.lb.ua/life/2010/05/10/43269_spasibi_banderi_za_pamyatnik_sta.html.

15   "Cherez pidryv pam'iatnyka Stalinu KPU vymahaie zabraty heroia u Bandery," *Zaxid.net*, 1 January 2011, http://zaxid.net/home/showSingleNews.do?cherez_pidriv_pamrzquoyatnika_stalinu_kpu_vimagaye_zabrati_geroya_u_banderi&objectId=1119893.

16   Clifford J. Levy, "Hero of Ukraine Prize to Wartime Partisan Revoked," *New York Times*, 12 January 2011, A11; "EU to Ukraine's New President:

Please Reverse Honoring Nazi Collaborator," *RT*, 25 February 2010, http://rt.com/politics/eu-resolution-bandera/; "Kniga otzyvov. Otkrytie pamiatnika I.V. Stalinu. Zaporozhskii obkom Kompartii Ukrainy," 2.

17 See articles by Kost´ Bondarenko, Iaroslav Hrytsak, Mykola Riabchuk, Volodymyr Kulyk, and Andrii Portnov in *Strasti za Banderoiu*, comp. Tarik Syril Amar, Ihor Balyns´kyi, and Iaroslav Hrytsak (Kyïv, 2010), 321–40.

18 Iaroslav Hrytsak, "Shche raz pro Iushchenka, shche raz pro Banderu," in *Strasti za Banderoiu*, 340–45; Hrytsak, "Klopoty z pam'iattiu," ibid., 346–57.

19 See the articles by David Marples, Zenon Kohut, Timothy Snyder, Alexander Motyl, Per Anders Rudling, John-Paul Himka, and Moisei Fishbein in *Strasti za Banderoiu*, 129–309.

20 "V Zaporozh´e s drakami i skandalom otkryli novyi pamiatnik Stalinu," *MIG.news.com.ua*, 7 November 2011, http://mignews.com.ua/ru/articles/92033.html.

21 "V Zaporozh´e Gitler voproshaet gorozhan, chem on khuzhe Stalina, i trebuet sebe pamiatnik," *Bagnet*, 6 December 2011, http://www.bagnet.org/news/society/168114.

22 "V Zaporozh´e prodolzhaetsia bor´ba s pamiatnikom Stalinu," *Novosti*, 12 January 2012, http://abzac.org/?p=12383.

23 "'Nasha Ukraina' prizvala dobit´ stalinizm i spasti 'trizubovtsev,'" *Gazeta. ua*, 23 November 2011, http://gazeta.ua/ru/articles/politics/_nasha-ukraina-prizvala-ukraincev-dobit-stalinizm-i-spasti-trizubovcev/410984.

24 "Sprava Stalina zhyve, abo derzhavnyi teroryzm v Ukraïni 21 stolittia," *Pohliad*, 27 June 2012, http://poglyad.te.ua/podii/sprava-stalina-zhyve-abo-derzhavnyj-teroryzm-v-ukrajini-21-stolittya/.

Goodbye Lenin!

This essay was first published online under the title "Goodbye Lenin! A Memory Shift in Revolutionary Ukraine" as part of the MAPA: Digital Atlas of Ukraine project, https://gis.huri.harvard.edu/leninfall. It appears here for the first time in print.

1 Reuters Timeline: Political crisis in Ukraine and Russia's occupation of Crimea, http://www.reuters.com/article/us-ukraine-crisis-timeline-idUSBREA270PO20140308; BBC Ukraine Crisis: Timeline, http://www.bbc.com/news/world-middle-east-26248275; Andrew Wilson, *Ukraine Crisis: What It Means for the West* (New Haven and London, 2014), 66–85.

2 "Istoriia pam'iatnyka Leninu v Kyievi," *Istorychna pravda*, 9 December 2013, http://www.istpravda.com.ua/articles/2013/12/9/140323/.

3 "Na Lenini lytsia nemaie! Ukraïns'ka presa u seredu," *BBC Ukraine*, 1 July 2009, http://www.bbc.com/ukrainian/pressreview/story/2009/07/090701_ua_press_1_06.shtml; "Sud otlozhil na neopredelennoe vremia srok rassmotreniia dela o razrushenii pamiatnika Leninu v Kieve," *Korrespondent*, 9 April 2013.

4 "MVS povidomliaie pro 8 hospitalizovanykh militsioneriv pislia sutychky bilia pam'iatnyka Leninu," *Tyzhden.ua*, 1 December 2013, http://tyzhden.ua/News/95462.

5 Oleksandr Aronets', "Povalennia pam'iatnyka Leninu v Kyievi," YouTube, https://www.youtube.com/watch?v=HVgjjvoWcX8#t=516; "Svobodivtsi vzialy na sebe vidpovidal'nist' za povalennia Lenina," *IPress*, 8 December 2013, http://ipress.ua/news/svobodivtsi_vzialy_na_sebe_vidpovidalnist_za_povalenogo_lenina_35123.html; "Povalennia pam'iatnyka Leninu v Kyievi," Wikipedia, uk.wikipedia.org/wiki/Повалення пам'ятника Леніну в Києві.

6 "V Kieve vozveli barrikady i snesli pamiatnik Leninu," *BBC Russia*, 9 December 2013, http://www.bbc.com/russian/international/2013/12/131208_ukraine_kiev_lenin; Mariia Semenchenko, "Valentyn Syl'vestrov: chytaite Shevchenka poky ne pizno," *Den'*, 29 December 2013.

7 "Khronolohiia Leninopadu (2013–2014)," https://uk.wikipedia.org/wiki/Хронологія_Ленінопаду_(2013–2014); Oleksandra Haidai, *Kam'ianyi hist': Lenin u tsentral'nii Ukraïni* (Kyïv, 2016), 172–89.

8 "Khronolohiia Leninopadu (2013–2014)," https://uk.wikipedia.org/wiki/Хронологія_Ленінопаду_(2013–2014).

9 Vitalii Chervonenko, "Rada ukhvalyla 'dekomunizatsiinyi paket,'" *BBC Ukraine*, 9 April 2015, http://www.bbc.com/ukrainian/politics/2015/04/150409_communizm_upa_vc; "Poroshenko signs laws on denouncing Communist, Nazi regimes," *Interfax-Ukraine*, 16 May 2015, http://en.interfax.com.ua/news/general/265988.html; "Khronolohiia Leninopadu (2013–2014)," https://uk.wikipedia.org/wiki/Хронологія_Ленінопаду_(2013–2014); "Khronolohiia Leninopadu (2015)," https://uk.wikipedia.org/wiki/Хронологія_Ленінопаду_(2015); "Khronolohiia Leninopadu (2016)," https://uk.wikipedia.org/wiki/Хронологія_Ленінопаду_(2016); "Khronolohiia Leninopadu (2017)," https://uk.wikipedia.org/wiki/Хронологія_Ленінопаду_(2017).

10 "History and Identity," MAPA: Digital Atlas of Ukraine, http://harvard-cga.maps.arcgis.com/apps/webappviewer/index.html?id=5c2c743e132f4b048293d3e3adc075fc.

11 On Ukraine's memory wars, see Oxana Shevel, "Memory of the Past and Visions of the Future: Remembering the Soviet Era and Its End in Ukraine," in *Twenty Years After Communism*, ed. Michael Bernhard and Jan Kubik (Oxford, 2014), 146–69; Shevel, "The Politics of Memory in a Divided Society:

A Comparison of Post-Franco Spain and Post-Soviet Ukraine," *Slavic Review* 70, no. 1 (Spring 2011): 137–64.

12   Dominique Arel, "Language and the Politics of Ethnicity: The Case of Ukraine," University of Illinois at Urbana-Champaign, 1993, http://www.ideals.illinois.edu/handle/2142/23297; Lowell W. Barrington and Erik S. Herron, "One Ukraine or Many? Regionalism in Ukraine and Its Political Consequences," *Nationalities Papers* 32, no. 1 (2004): 53–86; Mykola Riabchuk, "Ukraine: One State, Two Countries," *Transit Online* 23 (2002), http://www.eurozine.com/pdf/2002–09–16-riabchuk-en.pdf.; Gwendolyn Sasse, "The 'New' Ukraine: A State of Regions," *Regional & Federal Studies* 11, no. 3 (2010): 69–100.

13   "Ikonohrafika. Padinnia vozhdia. Liutyi 2014," http://incognita.day.kiev.ua/infohraphics/padinnya-vozhdya.html.

14   Haidai, *Kam'ianyi hist´*, 102–32.

15   Pavlo Podobied, "Vid Leninizmu do Leninopadu," *Radio Svoboda*, 30 December 2014, https://www.radiosvoboda.org/a/26770232.html.

16   "Yanukovych: Famine of 1930s was not genocide against Ukrainians," *Kyiv Post,* 27 April 2014, https://web.archive.org/web/20140724173055/http://www.kyivpost.com/content/ukraine/yanukovych-famine-of-1930s-was-not-genocide-agains.html.

17   The decommunization laws provoked debate among Ukraine-watchers and produced a significant literature, including the following: Volodymyr Viatrovych, "Dekomunizatsiia i akademichna dyskusiia," *Krytyka*, May 2015, https://krytyka.com/ua/solutions/opinions/dekomunizatsiya-i-akademichna-dyskusiya; David Marples, "Decommunisation in Ukraine: Implementation, Pros and Cons," *New Eastern Europe*, 16 September 2016, http://neweasterneurope.eu/articles-and-commentary/2126-decommunisation-in-ukraine; Oxana Shevel, "Decommunization in Post-Euromaidan Ukraine: Law and Practice," PONARS Eurasia, January 2016, http://www.ponarseurasia.org/memo/decommunization-post-euromaidan-ukraine-law-and-practice.

18   For lists of deputies who voted for and against the Law of Ukraine on the Condemnation of the Communist and Nazi Regimes, see the records of the Ukrainian parliament at http://w1.c1.rada.gov.ua/pls/radan_gs09/ns_golos?g_id=1427.

19   "Prykarpattia uviishlo u knyhu rekordiv Ukraïny za kil´kistiu pam'iatnykiv Shevchenku," *Radio Svoboda*, 30 December 2014, https://www.radiosvoboda.org/a/26769910.html; "Pam'iatnyky Stepanovi Banderi," https://uk.wikipedia.org/wiki/Пам%27ятники_Степанові_Бандері; "P'iat´ pam'iatnykiv Stepanovi Banderi, shcho naibil´she nahaduit´ skul´ptury Lenina," *Gazeta*.

ua, 8 December 2009, https://gazeta.ua/articles/people-and-things-journal/_
pyat-pamyatnikiv-stepanovi-banderi-scho-najbilshe-nagaduyut-skulpturi-
lenina/318953.

20 "Stalo izvestno, skol ́ko pamiatnikov Bandere v Ukraine," *Apostrof*, 15 October 2016, https://apostrophe.ua/news/society/2016–10–15/stalo-izvestno-
skolko-pamyatnikov-bandere-v-ukraine-opublikovana-infografika/74209.

21 "Banderyzatsiï nemaie—Viatrovych krytykam dekomunizatsiï," *Gazeta.
ua*, 25 January 2017, https://gazeta.ua/articles/life/_banderizaciyi-nemaye-
vyatrovich-kritikam-dekomunizaciyi/748417; "Pro 'banderyzatsiiu' til ́ky fakty,"
Volodymyr Viatrovych, Facebook post, 16 January 2017, https://www.facebook.
com/volodymyr.viatrovych/posts/10208193515895091.

22 Interviews with Kyivans, 2 February 2014, University of St. Gallen
University Project "Region, Nation, and Beyond: An Interdisciplinary and
Transcultural Reconsideration of Ukraine."

23 Author's observations from his visit to the monument site on 16 September 2017.

24 Data on the use of pedestals was collected by Viktoriya Sereda.

The Russian Question

First published in *Cossacks in Jamaica, Ukraine at the Antipodes: Essays in Honor
of Marko Pavlyshyn*, ed. Alessandro Achilli, Serhy Yekelchyk, and Dmytro
Yesypenko (Brookline, Mass., 2020).

1 Aleksandr Solzhenitsyn, *Kak nam obustroit ́ Rossiiu?* (Paris, 1990); Solzhenitsyn, "Russkii vopros v kontse XX veka," *Novyi mir*, 1994, no. 7; Solzhenitsyn, *Rossiia v obvale* (Moskva, 1998).

2 Solzhenitsyn, *Rossiia v obvale*, 79.

3 "Putin Hints at Splitting Up Ukraine," *Moscow Times*, 8 April 2008,
www.themoscowtimes.com/news/article/putin-hints-at-splitting-up-
ukraine/361701.html.

4 For an in-depth treatment of these questions, see my *Lost Kingdom:
A History of Russian Nationalism from Ivan the Great to Vladimir Putin* (London, 2017).

5 On the appropriation of the Kyivan heritage in early modern Muscovy,
see "Novaia imperskaia istoriia Severnoi Evrazii," chapter 5, ed. I. Gerasi-
mov, S. Glebov, A. Kaplunovskii, M. Mogilner, and A. Semenov, *Ab Imperio*
2014, no. 3: 363–407; V.T. Pashuto, B.N. Floria, and A.L. Khoroshkevich,
Drevnerusskoe nasledie i istoricheskie sud ́by vostochnogo slavianstva (Moskva,
1982); Jaroslaw Pelenski, *The Contest for the Legacy of Kievan Rus ́* (Boulder,

Colo., 1998); Serhii Plokhy, *The Origins of the Slavic Nations: Premodern Identities in Russia, Ukraine and Belarus* (Cambridge, 2006).

6   On the "grand strategy" of the Russian Empire, see John P. LeDonne, *The Russian Empire and the World, 1700–1917: The Geopolitics of Expansion and Containment* (Oxford, 1997); John P. LeDonne, *The Grand Strategy of the Russian Empire, 1650–1831* (Oxford, 2003).

7   On the role of Orthodoxy in Russian political culture and East European history, see Donald Ostrowski, *Muscovy and the Mongols: Cross-Cultural Influences on the Steppe Frontier, 1304–1589* (Cambridge, 2002); Tatiana Tairova-Yakovleva, "The Role of the Religious Factor and Patriarch Nikon in the Unification of Ukraine and Muscovy," *Acta Poloniae Historica* 110 (2014): 5–22; Barbara Skinner, *The Western Front of the Eastern Church: Uniate and Orthodox Conflict in Eighteenth-Century Poland, Ukraine, Belarus, and Russia* (DeKalb, Ill., 2009); Mikhail Dolbilov, *Russkii krai, chuzhaia vera: Ètnokonfessional'naia politika imperii v Litve i Belorussii pri Aleksandre II* (Moskva, 2010); Nathaniel Davies, *A Long Road to Church: A Contemporary History of Russian Orthodoxy*, 2nd ed. (Boulder, Colo., 2003).

8   On the *Synopsis* and its place in Russian and Ukrainian historiography, see articles by Zenon Kohut in his *Making Ukraine: Studies on Political Culture, Historical Narrative, and Identity* (Edmonton and Toronto, 2011).

9   On the rise of state nationalism in imperial Russia, see Hans Rogger, *National Consciousness in Eighteenth-Century Russia* (Cambridge, Mass., 1960); Liah Greenfeld, *Nationalism: Five Roads to Modernity* (Cambridge, Mass., 1992); Vera Tolz, *Russia: Inventing the Nation* (London and New York, 2001).

10   On the ethnic "fragmentation" of Eastern Europe in the first half of the nineteenth century, see Serhiy Bilenky, *Romantic Nationalism in Eastern Europe: Russian, Polish, and Ukrainian Political Imaginations* (Stanford, Calif., 2012); Vytautas Petronis, *Constructing Lithuania: Ethnic Mapping in Tsarist Russia, ca. 1800–1914* (Stockholm, 2007); Steven Seegel, *Mapping Europe's Borderlands: Russian Cartography in the Age of Empire* (Chicago and London, 2012); Darius Staliunas, *Making Russians: Meaning and Practice of Russification in Lithuania and Belarus after 1863* (Amsterdam and New York, 2007); P. V. Tereshkovich, *Ètnicheskaia istoriia Belarusi XIX–nachala XX vv. v kontekste Tsentral'no-Vostochnoi Evropy* (Minsk, 2004).

11   On the rise of Ukrainian political activism, see Alexei Miller, *The Ukrainian Question: The Russian Empire and Nationalism in the Nineteenth Century* (Budapest and New York, 2003); Orest Pelech, "The History of the St. Cyril and Methodius Brotherhood Reexamined," in *Synopsis: A Collection of Essays in Honour of Zenon E. Kohut*, ed. Serhii Plokhy and Frank Sysyn

(Edmonton and Toronto, 2005), 335–44; Johannes Remy, "The Valuev Circular and Censorship of Ukrainian Publications in the Russian Empire (1863–1876): Intention and Practice," *Canadian Slavonic Papers* 49, nos. 1–2 (2007): 87–110; David Saunders, "Mikhail Katkov and Mykola Kostomarov: A Note on Petr A. Valuev's Anti-Ukrainian Edict of 1863," *Harvard Ukrainian Studies* 17, nos. 3–4 (1993): 365–83; Saunders, "Pan-Slavism in the Ukrainian National Movement from the 1840s to the 1870s," *Journal of Ukrainian Studies* 30, no. 2 (Winter 2005): 27–50; Saunders, "Russia and Ukraine under Alexander II: The Valuev Edict of 1863," *International History Review* 17, no. 1 (1995): 23–50.

12 On imperial policies and the rise of modern nationalism in the late nineteenth and early twentieth centuries, see Theodore R. Weeks, *Nation and State in Late Imperial Russia: Nationalism and Russification on the Western Frontier, 1863–1914* (DeKalb, Ill., 1996); Faith Hillis, *Children of Rus´: Right-Bank Ukraine and the Invention of a Russian Nation* (Ithaca and London, 2013); D.A. Kotsiubinskii, *Russkii natsionalizm v nachale XX stoletiia: Rozhdenie i gibel´ ideologii Vserossiiskogo natsional´nogo soiuza* (Moskva, 2001).

13 On the nationality question in the Russian Revolution and the formation of the Soviet Union, see Richard Pipes, *The Formation of the Soviet Union: Communism and Nationalism, 1917–1923*, rev. ed. (Cambridge, Mass., 1997); Anna Procyk, *Russian Nationalism and Ukraine: The Nationality Policy of the Volunteer Army during the Civil War* (Edmonton and Toronto, 1995); Stephen Velychenko, *Painting Imperialism and Nationalism Red: The Ukrainian Marxist Critique of Russian Communist Rule in Ukraine, 1918–1925* (Toronto, 2015).

14 On national communism, *korenizatsiia* and their impact on the development of Ukrainian and Belarusian culture, see Terry Martin, *The Affirmative Action Empire: Nations and Nationalism in the Soviet Union, 1923–1939* (Ithaca and London, 2001); Terry Martin, "An Affirmative Action Empire: The Soviet Union as the Highest Form of Imperialism," in *A State of Nations: Empire and Nation-Making in the Age of Lenin and Stalin,* ed. Ronald Grigor Sunny and Terry Martin (Oxford, 2001), 67–92; George Y. Shevelov, *The Ukrainian Language in the First Half of the Twentieth Century (1900–1941): Its State and Status* (Cambridge, Mass., 1989); Per Anders Rudling, *The Rise and Fall of Belarusian Nationalism, 1906–1931* (Pittsburgh, 2015).

15 On the "Russian Question" in the USSR, see Aleksandr Vdovin, *Russkie v XX veke: fakty, sobytiia, liudi* (Moskva, 2004); Francine Hirsch, *Empire of Nations: Ethnographic Knowledge and the Making of the Soviet Union* (Ithaca and London, 2005); Geoffrey A. Hosking, *Rulers and Victims: The Russians in the Soviet Union* (Cambridge, Mass., 2006).

16   Concerning the impact of World War II on Russian and Ukrainian nationalism, see David Brandenberger, *National Bolshevism: Stalinist Mass Culture and the Formation of Modern Russian National Identity, 1931–1956* (Cambridge, Mass., 2002); Serhy Yekelchyk, *Stalin's Empire of Memory: Russian-Ukrainian Relations in the Soviet Historical Imagination* (Toronto, 2014); Serhii Plokhy, "The Call of Blood: Government Propaganda and Public Response to the Soviet Entry into World War II," *Cahiers du monde russe* 52, nos. 2–3 (2011): 293–320.

17   On Russian nationalism after World War II, see Yitzhak M. Brudny, *Reinventing Russia: Russian Nationalism and the Soviet State, 1953–1991* (Cambridge, Mass., 2000); Simon Cosgrove, *Russian Nationalism and the Politics of Soviet Literature: The Case of Nash Sovremennik 1981–91* (New York, 2004); John Dunlop, *The Faces of Contemporary Russian Nationalism* (Princeton, N.J., 1983); Nikolai Mitrokhin, *Russkaia partiia: Dvizhenie russkikh natsionalistov v SSSR, 1953–1985* (Moskva, 2003); Roman Szporluk, *Russia, Ukraine, and the Breakup of the Soviet Union* (Stanford, Calif., 2001).

18   On nationalist mobilization and the fall of the USSR, see Mark R. Beissinger, *Nationalist Mobilization and the Collapse of the Soviet State* (Cambridge, UK, 2002); George W. Breslauer and Catherine Dale, "Boris Yeltsin and the Invention of a Russian Nation-State," *Post-Soviet Affairs* 13, no. 4 (1997): 303–32; Timothy Colton, *Yeltsin: A Life* (New York, 2008); David D. Laitin, *Identity in Formation: The Russian-Speaking Populations in the New Abroad* (Ithaca, N.Y., 1998); Serhii Plokhy, *The Last Empire: The Final Days of the Soviet Union* (New York, 2014).

19   On Russian nationalism and foreign policy after the Soviet collapse, see *Russian Nationalism and the National Reassertion of Russia*, ed. Marlene Laruelle (London and New York, 2009); Marlene Laruelle, *In the Name of the Nation: Nationalism and Politics in Contemporary Russia* (New York, 2009); Igor Torbakov, "Emulating Global Big Brother: The Ideology of American Empire and Its Influence on Russia's Framing of Its Policies in Post-Soviet Eurasia," *Turkish Review of Eurasian Studies* 2003, no. 3: 41–72; Igor Torbakov, "A Parting of Ways? The Kremlin Leadership and Russia's New-Generation National Thinkers," *Demokratizatsiya: The Journal of Post-Soviet Democratization* 23, no. 4 (Fall 2015): 427–57; Igor Torbakov, "Ukraine and Russia: Entangled Histories, Contested Identities, and a War of Narratives," in *Revolution and War in Contemporary Ukraine: The Challenge of Change*, ed. Olga Bertelsen (Stuttgart, 2016), 89–120; Andrei P. Tsygankov, *Russia's Foreign Policy: Change and Continuity in National Identity* (Lanham, Md., 2006); Andreas Umland, "Eurasian Union vs. Fascist Eurasia," *New Eastern Europe*, 19 November 2015;

Andrew Wilson, *Ukraine Crisis: What It Means for the West* (New Haven, Conn., 2014), 118–43.

20 On the Russo-Ukrainian War, see Andrew Wilson, *Ukraine Crisis: What It Means for the West* (New Haven, Conn., 2014); Serhy Yekelchyk, *The Conflict in Ukraine: What Everyone Needs to Know* (New York, 2015).

The Quest for Europe

The first version of this essay appeared as a brochure entitled *Ukraine's Quest for Europe: Borders, Cultures, Identities* (Saskatoon, 2007).

1 "Comment of Roman Shpek, Representative of Ukraine to the EU, regarding the statement of B. Ferrero-Waldner, EU Commissioner (Ukrainian Service "BBC")," http://ukraine-eu.mfa.gov.ua/eu/en/publication/content/2094.htm.

2 See Ahto Lobjakas, "EU: Updated 'Action Plan' for Ukraine Wards Off Talk of Membership," Brussels, 24 January 2005, *RFE/RL*, http://www.rferl.org/featuresarticle/2005/01/86C89707-1759-4DAE-8774-7FF75DAC0710.html.

3 George Parker, "Our Rotten, Defensive Attitude to Change," *Financial Times*, 15 November 2006.

4 "Stat´i o narodnoi poèzii" in Vissarion Belinskii, *Sobranie sochinenii*, 9 vols. (Moskva, 1976–82), 4: 163–64.

5 Mykhailo Drahomanov, "The Lost Epoch: Ukrainians under the Muscovite Tsardom, 1654–1876," in *Towards an Intellectual History of Ukraine: An Anthology of Ukrainian Thought from 1710 to 1995*, ed. Ralph Lindheim and George S.N. Luckyj (Toronto, 1996), 157.

6 Ibid., 160.

7 "Novi perspektyvy" (1918) in Mykhailo Hrushevs´kyi, *Na porozi novoï Ukraïny: Statti i dzherel'ni materialy*, ed. Lubomyr R. Wynar (Kyïv, 1992), 21–22.

8 See Mykola Khvylovy, "Pamphlets (Excerpts)," in *Towards an Intellectual History of Ukraine*, 276–77.

9 Quoted in Serhii Plokhy, *Unmaking Imperial Russia: Mykhailo Hrushevsky and the Writing of Ukrainian History* (Toronto, 2005), 244.

10 *Wall Street Journal*, 26 September 2005.

11 *The Action Ukraine Report* (Washington, D.C.), no. 575, article 13, 3 October 2005.

12 Iurii Andrukhovych, "Evropa, moï nevrozy," *Krytyka* 10, no. 5 (May 2006): 29–30.

13 See Mykola Riabchuk, "Zbii prohramy," *Krytyka* 11, nos. 1–2 (January–February 2007): 2–4.

14 Viktor Yanukovych, "Ukraine's Choice: Toward Europe," *Washington Post*, 5 October 2006, A33.

15 See Alexander J. Motyl, "Institutional Legacies and Systemic Transformation in Eastern Europe: Ukraine, Russia and the EU." Ukrainian version in *Krytyka* 9, nos. 7–8 (July–August 2005): 17.

The New Eastern Europe

First published as "The 'New Eastern Europe': What to Do with the Histories of Ukraine, Belarus, and Moldova?" *East European Politics and Societies* 25, no. 4 (November 2011): 763–69.

1 Tony Judt, *Postwar: A History of Europe since 1945* (New York, 2006), 752–53.

Reimagining the Continent

The first version of this essay appeared under the title "The EuroRevolution: Ukraine and the New Map of Europe," in *Ukraine and Europe: Cultural Encounters and Negotiations*, ed. Giovanna Brogi Bercoff, Marko Pavlyshyn, and Serhii Plokhy (Toronto, 2017), 433–48.

1 Andrew Wilson, *Ukraine Crisis: What It Means for the West* (New Haven, Conn., 2014).

2 "Romantic weekend in the heart of Europe!" http://www.klubkiev.com/index.php/romantic-weekend; "The Center of Europe," http://www.tripfilms.com/Travel_Video-v64305-Kiev-The_Center_of_Europe-Video-Embed.html; Kiev Studio, http://crytek.com/career/studios/overview/kiev; "Kiev Apartments," http://www.facebook.com/Kiev.Apartments.Rent.

3 "Romantic weekend in the heart of Europe!" http://www.klubkiev.com/index.php/romantic-weekend; "The Center of Europe," http://www.tripfilms.com/Travel_Video-v64305-Kiev-The_Center_of_Europe-Video-Embed.html; Kiev Studio, http://crytek.com/career/studios/overview/kiev; "Kiev Apartments," http://www.facebook.com/Kiev.Apartments.Rent.

4 Oscar Halecki, *The Limits and Divisions of European History* (New York, 1950); Milan Kundera, "The Tragedy of Central Europe," *New York Review of Books* 31, no. 7 (26 April 1984): 33–38.

5 Friedrich Naumann, *Mitteleuropa* (Berlin, 1915); Peter Bugge, "The Nation Supreme: The Idea of Europe, 1914–45" in Pim den Boer et al., *The History* *of the Idea of Europe* (London, 1993), 60–70; Bo Strath, "Mitteleuropa from List to Naumann," *European Journal of Social Theory* 11 (May 2008): 171–83.

6   See the official portal of the Visegrád group at http://www.visegradgroup. eu/main.php. On the origins of civilizational bias in Western treatment of Eastern Europe, see Larry Wolff, *Inventing Eastern Europe: The Map of Civilization on the Mind of the Enlightenment* (Stanford, Calif., 1994).

7   On the treaty of Brest-Litovsk, which brought German and Austro-Hungarian troops to Ukraine, see John Wheeler-Bennett, *Brest-Litovsk: The Forgotten Peace, March 1918* (London, 1938; repr. New York, 1971). On the German and Austro-Hungarian visions of Ukrainian statehood, see Mark von Hagen, *War in a European Borderland: Occupations and Occupation Plans in Galicia and Ukraine, 1914–1918* (Seattle, 2007); Timothy Snyder, *The Red Prince: The Secret Lives of a Habsburg Archduke* (New York, 2008), 99–120.

8   On the "Russian revolution" in European cartography, see Vera Tolz, *Russia: Inventing the Nation* (New York, 2001), 155–61.

9   N. Gardner, "Pivotal Points: Defining Europe's Centre," *Hidden Europe* 5 (November 2005): 20–21; "Dilove. The Center of Europe," http://www.castles. com.ua/dilove.html.

10   *Fragments d'Europe—Atlas de l'Europe médiane et orientale,* ed. Michel Foucher (Paris, 1998), 55, 60.

11   Samuel P. Huntington, *The Clash of Civilizations and the Remaking of World Order* (New York, 1996), 157. On the establishment of the Uniate (Greek Catholic) Church, see Borys Gudziak, *Crisis and Reform: The Kyivan Metropolitanate, the Patriarchate of Constantinople and the Genesis of the Union of Brest* (Cambridge, Mass., 2001).

12   On the liquidation of the Greek Catholic Church, see Bohdan R. Bociurkiw, *The Ukrainian Greek Catholic Church and the Soviet State, 1939–1950* (Edmonton, 1996).

13   See articles on the website of the EU-sponsored program "Rights of Refugees and Migrants in Ukraine," http://www.migration.org.ua/english/ index.html.

14   Cynthia Kroet, "EU approves visa-free travel for Ukrainians," *Politico,* 11 May 2017, http://www.politico.eu/article/eu-approves-visa-free-travel-for-ukrainians/; "V ES khotiat 53% ukraintsev, v Tamozhennyi Soiz—28%," *24kanal,* 5 April 2014, http://24tv.ua/news/showNews.do?v_es_hotyat_53_ ukraintsev_v_tamozhenniy_ soyuz__28&objectId=429597&lang=ru; Katie Simmons, Bruce Stokes, and Jacob Poushter, "Ukrainian Public Opinion: Dissatisfied with Current Conditions, Looking for an End to the Crisis," *Pew Research Center,* 10 June 2015, http://www.pewglobal.

org/2015/06/10/3-ukrainian-public-opinion-dissatisfied-with-current-conditionslooking- for-an-end-to-the-crisis/.

15   Anastasiia Zanuda, "Shcho dumaiut´ ievropeitsi pro Ukraïnu ta ïi vstup v IeS," *BBC Ukraine*, 24 June 2015, http://www.bbc.com/ukrainian/politics/2015/06/150624_europeans_ukraine_az.

Index